IRISH FOOD LAW

The production, marketing and exportation of foo   , ...u..uiarly important to the Irish economy. The sector continues to grow and has played a very significant role in Ireland's financial recovery. This important new book provides a much-needed overview of the field. It traces the history and development of the fledgling system of food law as it was in Ireland during colonial times and the Irish Free State, through to an examination of the current dynamic relationship between International, European Union and domestic laws on matters such as food safety, food labelling and advertising, protected food names, hygiene and food contamination. The book also contains detailed assessments of the ways in which the law is used to address current health concerns, such as those related to nutrition, obesity and alcohol abuse, as well as such issues as food fraud, animal welfare, organics and the use of technologies like genetic modification, cloning and nanotechnology in food production.

Irish Food Law

European, Domestic
and International Frameworks

Caoimhín MacMaoláin

·HART·
OXFORD · LONDON · NEW YORK · NEW DELHI · SYDNEY

HART PUBLISHING

Bloomsbury Publishing Plc

Kemp House, Chawley Park, Cumnor Hill, Oxford, OX2 9PH, UK

HART PUBLISHING, the Hart/Stag logo, BLOOMSBURY and the Diana logo are
trademarks of Bloomsbury Publishing Plc

First published in Great Britain 2019

Copyright © Caoimhín MacMaoláin, 2019

A catalogue record for this book is available from the British Library.

Library of Congress Cataloging-in-Publication data

Names: MacMaoláin, Caoimhín, author.

Title: Irish food law : European, domestic and international frameworks / Caoimhín MacMaoláin.

Description: Oxford, UK ; Portland, Oregon : Hart Publishing, 2019. |
Includes bibliographical references and index.

Identifiers: LCCN 2018049638 (print) | LCCN 2018051097 (ebook) |
ISBN 9781509907809 (Epub) | ISBN 9781509907793 (paperback)

Subjects: LCSH: Food law and legislation—Ireland. | BISAC: LAW / Health. | LAW / Consumer.

Classification: LCC KDK940 (ebook) | LCC KDK940 .M33 2019 (print) | DDC 344.41704/232—dc23

LC record available at https://lccn.loc.gov/2018049638

ISBN: PB: 978-1-50990-779-3
       ePDF: 978-1-50990-778-6
       ePub: 978-1-50990-780-9

Typeset by Compuscript Ltd, Shannon
Printed and bound in Great Britain by CPI Group (UK) Ltd, Croydon CR0 4YY

To find out more about our authors and books visit www.hartpublishing.co.uk.
Here you will find extracts, author information, details of forthcoming events
and the option to sign up for our newsletters.

Do Shíofra, le buíochas

CONTENTS

TABLE OF CASES

UNITED KINGDOM

TABLE OF LEGISLATION

UNITED KINGDOM

Acts of the Scottish Parliament

Acts of Parliament

Statutory Instruments

UNITED STATES OF AMERICA

ARGENTINA

ITALY

THAILAND

FRANCE

EUROPEAN UNION

Treaty On The Functioning of the European Union (TFEU)

Directives

Other International and European Agreements

European Convention on Human Rights

European Convention for the Protection of Farmed Animals

European Convention for the Protection of Animals for Slaughter

World Trade Organization

General Agreement on Tariffs and Trade

1

History and Development
of Irish Food Law

1.1. Introduction

Food law first emerged as an identifiable strand of academic legal inquiry across the European Union (EU) in the late 1990s. Prior to this, there had been some literature in this part of the world related to aspects of the subject.[1] Most of it tended to be based on articles on EU law on the free movement of goods.[2] Some books had been published. They tended to be guides for practitioners on EU rules, with no significant contextual analysis of the application of these laws at national level, the political environment, social considerations or judicial decision making. 'Mad cow disease' changed all of this.

While food laws have existed since ancient times and were well developed by the nineteenth century it was really accession to the EU that most significantly affected Irish law in this area. When Ireland joined the European Economic Community (EEC), as it then was, in 1973, many of the EEC food laws that were transposed into domestic law as part of the *acquis communautaire* tended to be very general in nature and poorly implemented. They dealt with a range of disparate, unrelated and often relatively unimportant issues. It was difficult to identify a coherent body of rules regulating the production and marketing of food at this time. Food law was not really a subject yet in its own right.

A series of well-publicised issues on the relationship between food regulation and human health led to a vastly increased impetus for the creation of a new, more reasoned way of controlling how the food sector operates. The first of these was the crisis involving BSE (bovine spongiform encephalopathy, or 'mad cow disease') in the mid to late 1990s. There were two issues here. The first was that a possible link between beef consumption and the human form of BSE (variant Creutzfeldt-Jakob disease (vCJD)) was suggested by scientists. The claim was that people could

---

[1] It should be noted that food law had already emerged as a subject for examination in the United States of America, where the *Food and Drug Law Journal* (formerly the *Food, Drug and Cosmetic Law Journal*) was first published in 1946.

[2] See, eg, O Brouwer, 'Free movement of foodstuffs and quality requirements: Has the Commission got it wrong?' (1988) 25 *Common Market Law Review* 237; and H von Heydebrand, 'Free movement of foodstuffs, consumer protection and food standards in the European Community: Has the Court of Justice got it wrong?' (1991) 16 *European Law Review* 391.

contract this deadly disease just by eating meat, or even beef products, such as gelatine. People now believed that the consumption of burgers, steaks, prepared puddings and children's sweets, such as jellies, could all kill them. The second issue was that existing laws were shown to be hopelessly inadequate in dealing with a crisis such as this. Because of EU membership, many of the decisions on how to control the spread of the disease were outside the control of Member States. It would be up to the EU institutions to reassure the public that all necessary steps were being taken to safeguard health. On this, they failed. While the disease was most prevalent in British herds, the legal and political response had a significant impact on the sector in Ireland as well. Most significantly, it completely changed the nature of EU and consequently Irish, food law.

The second 'headline-grabbing' issue that acted as a catalyst in the creation of increased interest in the study of food law was the initial regulation of genetically modified organisms (GMOs). Again, it was scientists who sparked public controversy here by making suggestions that the use of genetic modification techniques in food production could damage the intestines of rats and therefore presumably those of humans as well. Outrage ensued, fostered by the fact that the presence of a GMO in food did not have to be stated on the label. Consumer groups protested that the law was again failing to protect them from the potential, or unknown, harms of food consumption.

They were right. A series of loopholes in the legislation allowed genetically modified foods onto the market without adequate disclosure that the foods were in fact genetically modified. The resultant pressure on politicians led to a ban on the approval of new GMOs across the EU. This in turn created difficulties for the EU at the international level, when the World Trade Organization called into question the legality of this prohibition.

These two sagas and other incidents, really brought the way in which the law regulates the food sector into public and consequently increased academic, focus. A plethora of articles and a series of books were published, not just on general issues of food law, but also detailed works on more specific areas, such as genetic modification, food safety, labelling and the precautionary principle. Subject-specific journals such as the *European Food and Feed Law Review* have come into existence and are published several times per year. There have been special issues of the *European Law Journal* and the *European Journal of Consumer Law* dealing exclusively with food law. University students have organised successful postgraduate research conferences where all of the sessions over entire weekends had aspects of this newly discovered subject alone as their central focus. There are academies of food law run every summer across Europe, there are firms that specialise or deal exclusively with food law matters and there are now multiple annual food law conferences organised by a range of bodies across many EU Member States. Food law is taught at undergraduate and postgraduate levels in Ireland and across the EU. Food law has become an established, stand-alone subject, supported by a wealth of peer-reviewed articles, journals and books. Food laws have significant implications for human health, the environment, animal welfare, consumer satisfaction, sectoral employment and the wider economy. While 'mad cows' and 'Frankenstein foods' may have been responsible for bringing increased attention to the study of food law, its growth and further establishment as a topic of student, academic and practitioner inquiry is perhaps sustained by the fact that many of the issues assessed are not just interesting to those professionally engaged in the food industry, but also concern matters of fundamental personal importance.

1.2. History of Food Laws

Laws controlling the production and marketing of food have existed since ancient times. The Code of Hammurabi makes several references to grain and cattle stocks, the former often being used as the currency of fines. Ancient Egypt carried laws on the labelling of wines, similar to those in existence today. Details would have to be provided of the name and the location of the producer and the estate, the type of wine, its vintage and an assessment of its quality. Consumer protection laws were introduced in Ancient Rome to minimise fraud and the sale of poor-quality food.[3]

The Bible makes many references to which foods should and should not be eaten. Leviticus 11:3 permits the eating of 'clean' animals: 'Whatsoever parteth the hoof, and is clovenfooted, and cheweth the cud ... that shall ye eat.' Pigs, hares and camels are specifically excluded from this category. They are all deemed 'unclean'. Fish that have fins and scales may be eaten. Others, such as shellfish, may not. There follows a long list of birds which may not be eaten, including storks, owls, eagles and vultures. Similar references are made in Deuteronomy 14.

Most ancient laws on food dealt with requirements for specific, rather than for all, foodstuffs – also known as 'vertical' legislation.[4] They were general in nature and usually prescribed that a substance could, or could not, be eaten, or that it had to be labelled in a particular way. Another feature of early food law was that it sought to prevent the adulteration of products, which were often laced with cheap ingredients, many of which could be very harmful to human health.

1.2.1. Aspects of Early Irish Food Law

Ancient Irish laws did deal with some matters related to food. The *Bechbretha*, for example, stipulated how disputes over the ownership of fruit that fell onto a neighbour's land could be resolved. Food grown on A's land that falls onto B's land

---

[3] FAO and WHO, 'Origins of the codex alimentarius' in *Understanding the Codex Alimentarius* (1999), ISBN 92-5-104248-9.

[4] As opposed to 'horizontal' legislation, which deals with one aspect, or aspects, of food law but across all foodstuffs. An example of a 'horizontal' provision might be food labelling requirements, applicable to all foods. A 'vertical' provision, however, might set labelling requirements, but just for one type of food, such as beef or chocolate.

should be divided equally between A and B for three years. It should all belong to B in year four.[5]

The earliest English food laws to affect Ireland included the Assize of Bread and Ale, introduced during the reign of Henry III in 1266.[6] It, too, was specific in its content, regulating the quality, weight and price of bread and beer. The price of beer, for example, was to be set according to the price of the raw materials used in its production. Harsh penalties were set to deter bakers from short-changing their customers – often resulting in the inclusion of an extra portion of bread in the customer's order to ensure compliance with minimum weight requirements, hence the expression 'a baker's dozen' referring to the number 13. Acts of Parliament were later introduced to set specific requirements designed to maintain the quality and safety of certain foods and drinks. These included the Adulteration of Tea and Coffee Act 1724 and later the Adulteration of Tea Acts of 1730 and 1776. The latter prohibited the inclusion of sloe, liquorice or previously used leaves in retailed tea. More of this vertical legislation was introduced through the Bread Acts of 1822 and 1836, which stipulated that bread now had to be sold by the pound or a multiple thereof and the Corn, Peas, Beans or Parsnips and Cocoa Act 1822, which established a licensing system for the sale of these foodstuffs. Much of this early legislation continued along these vertical lines. The first significant statutes to set legal requirements for the manufacture and/or sale of food more generally, or 'horizontal' legislation, were the Adulteration of Food or Drink Act 1860 and, perhaps more importantly, the Sale of Food and Drugs Act 1875.

The 1860 Act made it an offence to knowingly sell any foodstuff which endangered health, or which had been adulterated in any way.[7] Adulteration, in this context, came to mean, quite simply, 'the mixing of other substances with food', but it was not defined in the 1860 Act – one of several reasons underlying its lack of effectiveness in achieving the stated aim. The term 'adulteration' was never specifically defined in any Irish Act of the Oireachtas or in any Statutory Instrument after 1922. However, the Sale of Food and Drugs Act 1875 did provide for the offence of rendering a product 'injurious to health', which could, upon conviction, lead to a sentence of up to six months' imprisonment with hard labour. Article 3 provided that:

> [n]o person shall mix, colour, stain, or powder, or order or permit any other person to mix, colour, stain, or powder, any article of food with any ingredient or material so as to render the article injurious to health, with intent that the same may be sold in that state.

The 1875 Act did not define what was meant by 'injurious to health', despite making several references to it in relation to the sale of both food and drugs.[8] The Act did

---

[5] For more on this see F Kelly, *A guide to early Irish Law* (Dublin, Dublin Institute for Advanced Studies, 1988).

[6] 51 Hen 3 Stat 1. This was later amended by the Bread Acts of 1822 and 1836, before being repealed by the Statute Law Revision Act 1863.

[7] Statute Law Revision Act 1863, s 1.

[8] The word 'injurious' obviously means 'to cause damage or harm'. However, in a legal context it can also be used to describe an act as being 'malicious', such as an 'injurious falsehood', which is also known

clear up some of the confusion that surrounded the application of the possible offence of causing 'adulteration' by merely mixing substances together. Article 6(1) provided that an offence was not committed:

> [w]here any matter or ingredient not injurious to health has been added to the food … because the same is required for the production or preparation thereof as an article of commerce, in a fit state for carriage or consumption, and not fraudulently to increase the bulk, weight, or measure of the food or drug, or conceal the inferior quality thereof.

More recently, the English Food Act 1984 had provided that jurisdiction with some guidance on what is meant by 'injurious to health' – guidance that did not exist in any equivalent Irish statute. Under this English Act it was made an offence to add any substance to food that would render it 'injurious to health',[9] stating that:

> [i]n determining for the purposes of this Act whether an article of food is injurious to health, regard shall be had not only to the probable effect of that article on the health of a person consuming it, but also to the probable cumulative effect of articles of substantially the same composition on the health of a person consuming such articles in ordinary quantities.[10]

In English law, therefore, the test of whether an offence has been committed has been based on both immediate and longer-term risks of consumption at ordinary levels. This has had the potential to include foods that are both 'dangerous' and 'harmful', if we define the former as being those foods which contain something that can make the person unwell in the short term, such as a non-fatal amount of contaminant or toxic substance and, if we define the latter as including those foods which are more likely to have an effect on health over the long term, such as foods of poor nutritional quality. It is not usual to query whether the lawfulness of manufacturing and/or selling the latter is contrary to the test of being 'injurious to health'. We will return to this important, yet insufficiently considered, distinction between 'dangerous' and 'harmful' foods later in this book. This distinction highlights how food law has developed in a way that deals with 'dangerous' foods, but which, it will be argued, has been negligent in its treatment of 'harmful' foods.

Although the term 'injurious to health' had not been properly codified in Irish law, there have been indications from the case law as to how it should be defined. A series of cases on immigration, deportation and use of the European Arrest Warrant have identified that consequences can be 'profoundly injurious' in

---

as a 'malicious falsehood'. There are several references to substances, acts or omissions being 'injurious to health' in Irish law, such as that contained in s 20 of the Local Government Act 1925, in relation to structures used for human habitation. Section 92(1) of the Factories Act 1955 refers to places of work being deemed 'injurious or dangerous to the health of the persons employed therein'. The term 'injurious to health' is also referred to in several pieces of Irish food legislation, such as the Health (Official Control of Food) Regulations 1991 (SI No 332/1991) and the European Communities (Hygiene of Foodstuffs) Regulations 1998 (SI No 86/1998) and usually in the context of being 'unfit for human consumption'. It is relatively clear as to what it is meant to mean, but it remains undefined in any of the relevant legislation.

[9] Food Act 1984, s 1(1).
[10] Ibid, s 1(4).

some circumstances. For example, in *Minister for Justice v Rostas* it was stated by the High Court that the respondent had not shown how surrendering her to the Romanian authorities would 'have profoundly injurious or extraordinary consequences for her, or her family'.[11] Similarly, in *Attorney General v NSS* it was found that there was no reason to believe that the extradition of the respondent would 'have profoundly injurious or extraordinary consequences for him, or his family [although it] would certainly be distressing and upsetting for them'.[12] This implies that for something to be 'injurious' in law it need not necessarily be 'profound'. The consequences of consuming a foodstuff may therefore be 'injurious' if doing so causes damage – either 'dangerous' or 'harmful'. This is further supported by case law taken from elsewhere. In *R v Bristol City Council, ex parte Everett*, the term 'injurious to health' was equated with being 'prejudicial to health'.[13] It was further stated that 'the object of concern was plainly the direct effect on people's health', in this case of habitation in filthy or unwholesome premises and that the outcome of this would be 'the risk of illness or disease'. It was also stated here that this did not include protection against accidental physical injury. In *Crowley v Cork Corporation* it was held in the Supreme Court that the conditions causing housing to be dangerous or injurious to health could only be remedied by the demolition of the offending buildings.[14] In *Ryan v Attorney General* it was found that the levels of fluoridation added to public drinking water were not at 'a concentration [that was] injurious to health'.[15] It is here suggested that the term 'injurious to health' had come to refer to anything that could make the recipient unwell. Properly defining this term and identifying the circumstances to which it should be applied, is crucial to determining liability for breaches of Irish food law. This has now happened by the direct application of the General Food Law Regulation in Irish law.[16] This is discussed in much more detail in Chapter 5.

The 1860 Act also contained provisions on the analysis of food for indications of adulteration,[17] as well as setting a legal definition for 'food and drink' for the first time. Section 14 provided that this included:

> not only all alimentary substances, whether solids or liquids, but also all eatables or drinkables whatsoever not being medical drugs or articles usually taken or sold as medicines.

---

[11] *Minister for Justice and Equality v Magdalena Rostas* [2015] 1 ILRM 1.
[12] *Attorney General v NSS* [2015] IEHC 349.
[13] *R v Bristol City Council, ex parte Everett* [1999] 2 All ER 193.
[14] *Crowley v Cork Corporation* [1941] 1 IR 92.
[15] *Ryan v Attorney General* [1965] 1 IR 294.
[16] Article 14(4) of Regulation 178/2002 of the European Parliament and of the Council of 28 January 2002 laying down the general principles and requirements of food law, establishing the European Food Safety Authority and laying down procedures in matters of food safety, [2002] OJ L 31/1, states that: '[i]n determining whether any food is injurious to health, regard shall be had: not only to the probable immediate and/or short-term and/or long-term effects of that food on the health of a person consuming it, but also on subsequent generations; to the probable cumulative toxic effects; to the particular health sensitivies of a specific category of consumers where the food is intended for that category of consumers'.
[17] Adulteration of Food or Drink Act 1860, ss 3–5.

As stated, the 1860 Act was largely ineffective and was supplemented by two further adulteration acts, in 1862 and 1872. These facilitated the appointment of inspectors who could take food samples for analysis. They also provided a more developed definition of 'adulteration', making it illegal to 'admix, with any article of food or drink any injurious or poisonous ingredient or material to adulterate the same for sale'. Problems persisted. In particular, some producers were prosecuted under the 1872 Act for merely changing foods from their original form by adding non-injurious ingredients. A government select committee, charged with reviewing the Adulteration Acts, heard that there had been cases of prosecution for selling mustard which contained not only mustard seed, but also turmeric and chillies. Over-zealous and often erroneous interpretations of the new legislation led to accusations that the mere addition of other ingredients to food was 'adulteration'. Difficulties were also reported with the sale of cocoa, when it was mixed with sugar and starches. The select committee reported that consumers were being 'cheated rather than poisoned' by adulteration and that most food manufacturing was perfectly safe. The focus of regulation should, therefore, it was stated, be on retailers who tampered with goods in an active attempt to mislead or deceive consumers.[18] The Licensing Act 1872, for example, prohibited the addition of salt to beer, which had been used to induce additional thirst in consumers.[19]

Since the eighteenth century, it has also been an indictable offence at common law to provide someone with food that is not fit for human consumption, regardless of whether this was done out of malice or profit-seeking.[20] Selling, or being in possession with intent to sell, diseased or unwholesome food is a common law nuisance.[21] A supplier can be indicted for manslaughter if someone dies from eating diseased meat or contaminated food that he has provided. There can be a conviction on these charges if the evidence shows that it was provided in the knowledge that it was unfit for consumption or if the supplier was guilty of gross negligence in this regard.[22]

The recognised need for a change in the Adulteration of Food Acts later materialised through the introduction of the Sale of Food and Drugs Act 1875, which consolidated the more progressive provisions introduced since 1860, along with clearer legal definitions and enforcement mechanisms for those given responsibility for ensuring compliance with the law.

---

[18] For further discussion on the proceedings before the select committee see J Phillips and M French, 'Adulteration and food law, 1899–1939' (1998) 9 *Twentieth Century British History* 350, esp pp 354–356.
[19] Schedule 1 to the Licensing Act 1872. Other substances which could no longer be added to beer under the Act included opium, hemp and tobacco.
[20] *R v Treeve* (1796) 2 East PC 821.
[21] *Shillito v Thompson* (1875) 1 QBD 12. Selling unwholesome food for human consumption was also an offence under Public Health (Ireland) Act 1878, ss 132–133. See also *Dunne v Uden* [1923] ILTR 25.
[22] *R v Kempson* (1893) 28 L Jo 477.

1.2.2. Sale of Food and Drugs Act 1875

The Sale of Food and Drugs Act 1875 repealed the Act of 1860,[23] simplifying many of the provisions that had been introduced in this area in the earlier Victorian period. 'Food' was defined simply as including 'every article used for food and drink by man, other than drugs or water'.[24] The Act also separated the provisions on adulteration, categorising them according to whether the addition of other substances to food was of a nature that was either (i) injurious to health or (ii) affected the quality of the food concerned. Section 3 provided that:

> [no] person shall mix, colour, stain, or powder, or order or permit any other person to mix, colour, stain, or powder, any article of food with any ingredient or material so as to render the article injurious to health, with intent that the same may be sold in that state, and no person shall sell any such article so mixed [etc.] under a penalty in each case.

Conviction under this provision of the Act was punishable by a fine or up to six months' imprisonment, with hard labour. Section 6 further provided that:

> [no] person shall sell to the prejudice of the purchaser any article of food ... which is not of the nature, substance, and quality of the article demanded by such purchaser.

This was qualified by the fact that ingredients that were not harmful to health and the inclusion of which was necessary to make the product, could be added. This would not now be considered 'adulteration' – provided that this was not done 'fraudulently to increase the bulk, weight, or measure of the food ... or conceal the inferior quality thereof'.[25] The inclusion of ingredients would now, under the 1875 Act, have to be stated on a label. This would have to be 'distinctly and legibly written or printed on [the packaging of the food]'.[26] Despite this, studies undertaken at the time indicated that there was plenty of evidence to show that these adulteration laws were not properly applied in Ireland. Milk was found

---

[23] Sale of Food and Drugs Act 1875, s 1.

[24] Ibid, s 2.

[25] In *Hotchin v Hindmarsh* [1891] 2 KB 181, the appellant, a foreman of a dairy company, was prosecuted and convicted under the Sale of Food and Drugs Act 1875, s 6 for supplying milk to which water had been added. It was a clear dilution of the 'quality of the article demanded by [the] purchaser'. The seemingly widespread adulteration of milk in Ireland at the turn of the twentieth century also led to the matter being discussed in Parliament, where the level of fines imposed at a petty sessions in County Cork, which were deemed to be merely 'nominal', was discussed. It was also deemed to be an offence under s 6 of the 1875 Act to sell '[...] a pure food and favourably comparable in nutritive value with genuine [in this case cornflour, where this] was not of the same nature, substance and quality as that for which the purchaser had asked'. See *Wicklow County Council and O'Dwyer v Clarke* [1946] 1 Ir Jur Rep 1. It was not, however, an offence to sell oatmeal which contained a number of husks and splinters as the product sold was deemed to be '[...] of the nature, substance and quality demanded'. See *O'Neill v Egan* [1942] 76 ILTR 26. Under s 6 it would have to be shown that the sale was 'to the prejudice of the purchaser', *Cavan County Council v Byrne* [1938] 72 ILTR 114.

[26] Sale of Food and Drugs Act 1875, s 8.

to have had fat removed and significant amounts of water added.[27] Butter and whiskey were also found to have been fraudulently diluted.

The Sale of Food and Drugs Act 1875 also set out a range of provisions on the role of analysts in certifying the safety and quality of food. These analysts, who were appointed at local authority level,[28] could, for a fee, be called upon by any purchaser of food to analyse and certify the safety or otherwise of a product.[29] Analysts were also obliged to report quarterly to their appointing authority on the number and outcome of their investigations.[30] The analyst's report was also deemed to be the most significant piece of evidence in any resulting prosecution under the Act, although the analyst himself could be cross-examined in court on this.[31] Those convicted of an offence under the Act could appeal, subject to the satisfaction of certain conditions.[32] The main defence available to those charged under the Act was a satisfactory demonstration that they could not have been aware that what they were selling was adulterated, in particular where it could be shown that the offending article had been purchased by them in the same condition as that in which it was subsequently sold.[33] Figures published in the Annual Reports of the Local Government Boards in England and Wales show that between 5 and 10 per cent of purchased food samples were usually found to have been adulterated. In 1899 the figure stood at around 9.4 per cent. The figures for adulteration levels tended to be higher in Scotland, reaching 14.4 per cent in 1899. Evidence from the *Lancet* report of 1903 and from the Annual Reports of the Local Government Board suggests that food adulteration, in particular that of dairy products, remained a significant problem in Ireland in the early part of the twentieth century.

Finally, the 1875 Act also included special provisions on tea. All imported tea was to be subjected to an examination by the customs authorities. This was to be done to ensure that the tea had not been mixed with other, usually cheaper, substances, or that the leaves had not already been used to make tea.[34] All products that were deemed after analysis to be unfit for sale as tea were to be forfeited and destroyed.

---

[27] Anon. 'Food adulteration in Ireland' (1903) 162 *Lancet* 1519. This article suggested that milk sold to consumers was '[…] deprived of one-half its fat and with 20 per cent. added water'.

[28] Sale of Food and Drugs Act 1875, s 10.

[29] Ibid, s 12. The *Lancet* article referred to in n 27 above also pointed out that the best way of remedying these widespread cases of adulteration would be to appoint properly qualified analysts and support for them in each county council district.

[30] Sale of Food and Drugs Act 1875, s 19.

[31] Ibid, s 21.

[32] Ibid, s 23.

[33] Ibid, s 25. A person who innocently sold food in the same condition as that in which he had bought it from another, not knowing it to be defective and who was subsequently prosecuted under the 1875 Act could recover, from the person from whom he had innocently made the purchase, both damages and costs incurred by him in defending the said prosecution. See *Duffy v Sutton* [1955] 1 IR 248.

[34] Ibid, s 30.

1.2.3. Acts of the Irish Free State 1922–1937

In the first half of the twentieth century it was widely believed, amongst those charged with regulating the food sector, that the law was not in need of further reform. It was felt that 'the processes and ingredients of production were essentially sound and in little need of regulation'.[35] There was little consideration for consumers' concerns. The use of chemicals and pesticides was becoming more common in food production, but these were mostly unregulated until the 1920s. Deliberate adulteration still occurred. It may have been more likely to be in a form that posed less of an immediate danger to human health, but, as the discussion above points out, there was clearly still deliberate deception of the purchasing public going on.

The first food act to be introduced after the establishment of the Irish Free State was a piece of vertical legislation, primarily designed to amend aspects of the Sale of Food and Drugs Act related to that most adulterated of foodstuffs – milk.[36] The Sale of Food and Drugs (Milk) Act 1935 set out a range of provisions aimed at eliminating instances of fraudulent milk and dairy product adulteration. Section 2 of the Act stated that it was an offence to sell whole milk or low-fat milk that had a lower fat content than that suggested. Cream would also have to have a fat content that was equal to or more than that set out. Similar requirements were set for buttermilk. Selling a product that did not meet these content requirements was contrary to Section 6 of the Sale of Food and Drugs Act 1875. As noted above, this provision of the 1875 Act stipulated that products must be 'of the nature, substance, and quality of the article demanded'. Further amendments were also made to procedures for sampling and analysis.[37]

Several statutory instruments related to the production and marketing of food were also introduced during this period. These included the Public Health (Saorstát Eireann)(Preservatives, Etc, in Food) Regulations 1928,[38] the First Schedule to which set out the limitations on and labelling requirements for, preservative use in foods for sale in Ireland. Sausages could contain sulphur dioxide up to a maximum level of 450 parts per million. This could rise to 600 parts per million for non-alcoholic drinks such as cordials and fruit juices. Part II of the First Schedule to the 1928 Regulations prohibited the use of arsenic, cadmium, copper, mercury and lead as food colouring. The Second Schedule set out the labelling requirements for certain foods containing preservatives, including sausages, coffee, pickles, sauces and, where preservative use was at a particularly high level, grape juice and wine. These products would have to include a clear indication on the labelling where they contained preservatives.

---

[35] J Phillips and M French, 'Adulteration and Food Law, 1899–1939' (1998) 9 *Twentieth Century British History* 350, which provides a comprehensive account of the history of food law during this period.

[36] See n 27 above.

[37] Sections 7–9 of the Sale of Food and Drugs (Milk) Act 1935. Further amendments on this were made by the Sale of Food and Drugs (Milk) Act 1936.

[38] SI No 54/1928.

Other food legislation introduced during this period included that which established the Sugar Confectionery and Food Preserving Trade Board,[39] and the Foot and Mouth Disease Order 1927,[40] which introduced a number of precautionary measures to be taken before imported meat, or any waste food which had been in contact with imported meat, could be fed to cattle, pigs, sheep or goats. Feeding these substances to animals where they had not been boiled for at least one hour was made an offence, contrary to the Diseases of Animals Act 1894. Finally, there were also efforts made at addressing the ongoing problem with the adulteration of some dairy products through the introduction of the Sale of Food and Drugs (Milk Sampling) Regulations 1936.[41]

1.2.4. Food Standards Act 1974

No significant Acts of the Oireachtas on food were introduced between 1937 and Ireland becoming a Member State of the European Economic Community in 1973. Some important secondary legislation was, however, introduced. This included new regulations on the use of colourings,[42] antioxidants[43] and preservatives in the production of food,[44] as well as those setting out more detail on tolerable levels of arsenic and lead in some food products, such as fish, edible seaweed and hops.[45]

There were signs in the type of legislation that was being introduced during this period that public health matters related to the consumption of food were being taken far more seriously. The Health (Sampling of Food) Regulations 1970 offer a good example of this.[46] These set out a range of powers for 'authorised officers' to take samples of foods that were suspected to be 'diseased, contaminated or otherwise unfit for human consumption'.[47] Regulation 6, in particular, provided that authorised officers could take a sample of any food, with or without payment, for analysis by an approved examiner. He could also prohibit the removal of all the suspected food for a period of up to two weeks, until the sample was properly analysed. Any food found to be unfit for consumption, for whatever reason, could then, of course, be dealt with. These Regulations built upon existing safety provisions, such as those that had been introduced by the Food Hygiene Regulations 1950.[48] Food labelling requirements were initially covered in Ireland by the Sale of

[39] SI No 50/1933.
[40] Foot and Mouth Disease (Boiling of Animal Food) Order 1927. SI No 50/1927.
[41] SI No 312/1936.
[42] Health (Colouring Mater in Food) Regulations 1972. SI No 41/1972.
[43] Health (Antioxidant in Food) Regulations 1972. SI No 42/1972.
[44] Health (Preservatives in Food) Regulations 1972. SI No 43/1972.
[45] Health (Arsenic and Lead in Food) Regulations 1972. SI No 44/1972.
[46] Health (Sampling of Food) Regulations 1970. SI No 50/1970.
[47] 'Authorised officers', for the purposes of the Regulations, were appointed by the Minister for Agriculture or, more commonly, officers of local health authorities – as set out in the Health Act 1947, s 91.
[48] SI No 205/1950.

Food and Drugs Acts of 1875 and 1899, although the Sale of Food and Drugs Acts Adaptation Order 1928 (introduced under the terms of the Adaptation of Enactments Act 1922) did enable the making of modifications to these British food law statutes by the Executive Council of Saorstát Éireann.[49] Food labelling requirements remained relatively unchanged until the introduction of the Food Standards Act 1974 – the first significant piece of food law legislation to be introduced in Ireland after taking up membership of the EEC the previous year – and, more specifically, the introduction of the European Communities (Labelling, Presentation and Advertising of Foodstuffs) Regulations 1982.[50]

1.3. European Integration

As has already been stated, it is membership of the EU which has led to the vast majority of food laws as they stand in Ireland to take their current format and content. This, of course, presupposes a complex relationship between the two systems. Some EU rules have direct applicability. Regulations automatically become part of Irish law on the date stated in the legislation. Significantly, the use of this format for introducing new EU food law has become more commonplace since the turn of the millennium, meaning there is little room for derogation at national level from the rules set out in the regulations – the revised labelling requirements which, for the most part, have been directly applicable in Ireland since December 2014, offers a good example of this.[51] Directives, which had previously been the traditional format for many of the EU rules on food, do require some further implementation by the Member States and will not always, therefore, have 'direct effect' – meaning that individuals may not always be able to rely on their provisions until after they have been formally and effectively transposed into Irish law. This is discussed in more detail below. Despite this, it can usually be accepted that secondary legislation adopted by the EU legislative institutions must also be adopted and applied in Ireland. As a result, it is European obligations and some international requirements arising out of this, which now account for the introduction of almost all the laws in Ireland which apply specifically to food. It could be stated, therefore, that the two biggest influences now on Irish food law are

---

[49] In this instance, in relation to provisions on margarine. SI No 16/1928.

[50] SI No 205/1982. These are discussed in more detail in Ch 7, below.

[51] As introduced by Regulation (EU) No 1169/2011 of the European Parliament and of the Council of 25 October 2011 on the provision of food information to consumers, amending Regulations (EC) No 1924/2006 and (EC) No 1925/2006 of the European Parliament and of the Council and repealing Commission Directive 1987/250/EEC, Council Directive 1990/496/EEC, Commission Directive 1999/10/EC, Directive 2000/13/EC of the European Parliament and of the Council, Commission Directives 2002/67/EC and 2008/5/EC and Commission Regulation (EC) No 608/2004, [2011] OJ L 304/18. Regulation 1169/2011 is incorporated into domestic Irish law by the European Union (Provision of Food Information to Consumers) Regulations 2014, SI No 556/2014. This is discussed in much more detail in Ch 7 below.

(i) the supremacy of European Union law in Ireland and (ii) EU rules on the free movement of food. Both are introduced below.

1.3.1. Supremacy of European Union Food Law

The European Communities Act 1972, which gives internal legal effect to EU law in Ireland, provides that:

> the treaties governing the European [Union] and the existing and future acts adopted by the institutions of [the Union] shall be binding on the State and shall be part of the domestic law thereof under the conditions laid down in those treaties.[52]

This effectively means that any EU legislation which is designed to become part of the domestic law of the Member States must be applied at national level. Directly effective provisions of EU law are thus, under the terms of the European Communities Act 1972, incorporated into Irish law. This includes all Treaty on the Functioning of the European Union (TFEU) provisions, regulations and directives that together form the body of EU food law. The Act further states that:

> [a] Minister of State may make regulations for enabling [EU law] to have full effect, regulations under this section may contain such incidental, supplementary and consequential provisions as appear to the Minister making the regulations to be necessary for the purposes of the regulations (including provisions repealing, amending or applying, with or without modification, other law, exclusive of the Act).[53]

Secondary legislation, such as statutory instruments, can thus be used to give effect to the many EU food directives and to provide the necessary detail and administrative requirements for the practical application of EU regulations.[54]

Although having no formal basis in the original Treaty of Rome, it has long been established that EU law takes precedence over the national laws and national constitutions of EU Member States. This issue is, of course, discussed in much more detail in other books dealing with European Union law and Irish Constitutional law.[55] However, it is important to make a few brief points about this here.

---

[52] European Communities Act 1972, s 2.

[53] Ibid, s 3.

[54] Although EU Regulations have direct applicability in Ireland, some domestic provision is often required to ensure the proper incorporation and functioning of the Regulation in the domestic legal system. A good example of this is the need to adopt the European Union (Provision of Food Information to Consumers) Regulations 2014, n 51 above, to tailor the application of the EU Food Information Regulation, also n 51 above, to Ireland. The Irish Regulations 2014 therefore set out, amongst other things, who has responsibility for the enforcement and application of the provisions of the EU Regulation in Ireland, how sampling takes place and how prosecutions are brought against offenders before the domestic courts.

[55] See, eg, the forthcoming text by O Doyle, *The constitution of Ireland: A contextual analysis*, (Hart, Bloomsbury, 2018) on the Irish Constitutional law issues. For an EU law perspective see, ch 9 of P Craig and G de Búrca, *EU law: Text, cases and materials*, 6th edn (OUP, Oxford, 2015).

In addition to the European Communities Act 1972, outlined above, Article 29.4.6 of the Constitution of Ireland, Bunreacht na hÉireann, provides that:

> [n]o provision of this Constitution invalidates laws enacted, acts done or measures adopted by the State, before, on or after the entry into force of the Treaty of Lisbon, that are necessitated by the obligations of membership of the European Union.

It is clear from both the European Communities Act 1972, Article 29 of the Constitution, as well as related case law, that that supremacy of European Union law has been accepted in Ireland.[56] The vast majority of Irish food laws come directly from the European Union and those which do not are subject to interpretation in a manner that is in harmony with the requirements of EU law. Making it very clear, it has been stated that:

> [t]he wording [of Article 29 of the Constitution] is overarching and conclusive, establishing constitutional immunity to European Union laws, measures and acts. Lawmaking powers which had previously vested in the Irish Parliament were now transferred to the Community. The judicial power of the State, which had been sovereign and subject to no appeal, was now, in terms of the interpretation of European instruments, subject to the ultimate ruling in legal disputes before the Court of Justice. Thus, *Costa v ENEL* was given written recognition in the Irish Constitution.[57]

In *Costa v ENEL*,[58] the Court of Justice had made it clear that EU law should have supremacy over national law. According to the Court, in its deliberations in *Costa*, Member States had, by signing up to the then-named EEC, 'limited their sovereign rights' and had 'thus created a body of law which binds both their nationals and themselves'. This was followed-up by decisions such as that in *Simmenthal*,[59] where the Court pointed out that this doctrine of the supremacy of EU law would apply to all national laws – regardless of whether they had been in existence prior to the introduction of the relevant European Union measure. The Irish Supreme Court further clarified the position (that is insofar as it was still necessary to do so) in *Pringle*,[60] where it was found that the domestic courts could not interfere with foreign policy decisions taken by the Government, including entering into binding international legal obligations such as the Treaty on the Functioning of the European Union or, as in this particular case, the European Stability Mechanism.

All of this makes decisions of the Court of Justice on matters related to food law applicable in Irish law and binding on the Irish courts. We can also normally presume that EU directives and regulations addressed to the food sector will also

---

[56] See, eg, *Pigs and Bacon Commission v McCarren* [1978] JISEL 87; *Minister for Fisheries v Schonenberg* [1979] JISEL 35; *Campus Oil Ltd v Minister for Industry and Energy* [1983] IR 82; and *Crotty v An Taoiseach* [1987] IR 713.

[57] P Charleton and A Cox, 'Accepting the judgments of the Court of Justice of the EU as authoritative' (2016) 23 *Maastricht Journal of European and Comparative Law* 204 at 206.

[58] Case 6/1964, *Flaminio Costa v ENEL* [1964] ECR 585.

[59] Case 106/1977, *Amministrazione delle Finanze dello Stato v Simmenthal SpA* [1978] ECR 629.

[60] *Pringle v Ireland* [2013] 3 IR 1.

be applied, in one way or another, at national level. Sometimes, however, it can be more complicated than this.[61] Where such complications arise, they will be addressed throughout this book.

1.3.2. Free Movement and Food Law

It is difficult to understate the impact that EU rules on the free movement of goods have on Irish food law. They are significant in three main ways. First, the creation of an internal market in goods means that almost all standards related to the production and marketing of food are set at EU level, through the adoption of harmonised rules that are then applied in the Member States, including Ireland. Free movement is facilitated by the application of the same or similar rules in all EU Member States. This is usually done by the introduction of regulations and directives. Second, Treaty provisions prohibiting the application of charges equivalent to customs duties on imported food, as well as those on ensuring that domestic systems of taxation do not directly or indirectly discriminate against non-national food producers, ensure that imported products from other EU Member States can compete more fairly with domestic produce. This is discussed in much more detail in Chapter 4. Finally and perhaps most significantly, the Treaty prohibition on the application of measures equivalent to quantitative restrictions on traded goods ensures that no Member State can maintain any national law which has the effect, whether direct or indirect, of inhibiting to any degree the importation of food from elsewhere in the EU. This has hugely significant consequences for Irish law. It has dictated that certain laws, such as those on the composition of foodstuffs, will not be introduced and that others cannot be introduced, such as those designed to deal with rising rates of obesity or alcohol abuse.

1.4. Conclusion

The food sector is vital to the Irish economy and people. The agriculture and food sectors in Ireland account for almost one-eighth of all exports, while also providing around one in every 11 jobs.[62] The way in which this sector is managed and regulated is crucial to the maintenance, or possible improvement, of the important position that food and agriculture have in Irish life. This book is designed to provide a broad conspectus of Irish food law. This involves a lot of references to EU law because, as has been made clear already, it is from this source that almost

---

[61] For discussion on the difficulties that EU supremacy can create for the preservation of food culture and tradition more generally see D Chalmers, 'Food for thought: Reconciling European risks and traditional ways of life' (2003) 66 *Modern Law Review* 532.
[62] According to the Department of Agriculture, Food and the Marine. Details available at: agriculture.gov.ie.

all domestic legal requirements are now created. As this chapter has identified, this relatively new influence has created a whole series of requirements for the State, for producers and for retailers, as well as introducing additional ways of protecting consumers. However, it should be stressed that in some areas the EU's laws provide insufficient protection, yet the system prevents Member States from initiating local laws to protect their population – most notably in the areas of food standards, obesity and the misuse of alcohol, or as was most evident in the way in which the BSE crisis was mishandled – a mishandling that is discussed in some detail in Chapter 5. EU law prescribes that free movement requirements usually take precedence over domestic initiatives designed to improve or maintain the value, integrity or quality of food.

In its assessment of food law, this book deals with the relevant legislation in a variety of ways. Where EU regulations or directives have been introduced, their key provisions are identified and analysed. In addition to this, the book also indicates the national implementation of these EU legislative requirements, identifying any shortcomings in the domestic transposition. This usually takes place by using statutory instruments. Directives will always require national application through the introduction of a national legislative measure such as this. Regulations, which are directly applicable in Irish law, do not require any implementing measures but usually carry some corresponding national legislation to give full and proper meaning to these, identifying national competent authorities or domestic remedies for example, as they are required to do by the terms of the EU legislation. Interpretation of these measures, both the original EU versions and the domestic implementations, is usually done by the Court of Justice. Relevant domestic cases are also identified where they show some additional point of interpretation on the provisions under review. To summarise, the book identifies the relevant EU legislation, Court of Justice case law on this, national implementing measures and domestic case law where appropriate. It also discusses related policy documents, legislative proposals, codes of conduct, national standards and international conventions where these identify a policy direction or a method of interpretation for existing measures.

The book chapters deal with four key aspects of, or influences on, Irish food law. The first of these, including Chapters 2, 3 and 4, outline and discuss the main sources of food law and the role of those charged with developing and applying legal requirements in this area. This involves an examination of the relationship between national, EU and international law, with specific focus on how this relates to regulation of the food sector. It includes an assessment of the roles of the institutions of the EU in this regard, as well as that of international organisations such as the World Trade Organization, the Codex Alimentarius Commission and the United Nations. At national level, the roles of the main actors in the devising and implementation of food law and policy are all addressed, including the relevant government departments, national competent authorities and local authorities and important statutory bodies, such as the Food Safety Authority of Ireland and the Health Service Executive, as well as others. This first part of the book concludes with a discussion on the significant influence that EU rules on the free movement of goods exercise on the content and application of both national and EU legal requirements and responsibilities and the restrictions that this can then place on national policy. This is the single biggest influence on national food law.

The next part of the book looks at the important issue of food safety. It was concerns over the spread of disease through the consumption of contaminated beef that really set much of the agenda for EU food law makers over the past couple of decades. It is contended in this book that there has been an overemphasis on safety since the BSE crisis, possibly at the expense of other, often more problematic considerations, such as nutrition and quality. Chapter 5 includes a comprehensive assessment of the key provisions of the Food Standards Act 1974, the Food Safety Authority of Ireland Act 1998 and the directly applicable EU General Food Law Regulation, which together provide the template for all national controls in this area. It also includes an examination of the role of the European Food Safety Authority in preventing the spread of contamination and disease through the production and consumption of food, as well as looking at its other functions and responsibilities. This part concludes with a chapter on the chemical and biological safety of food, which mostly involves an identification of the main provisions related to hygienic production, as well as the controls which have been placed over the use of hormones, pesticides and radiation in the preparation of food.

Food labelling is the main line of communication between producer and consumer. It can be used to clarify details about the content, quality, value and origin of food. It is a key marketing tool, enabling differentiation between products and the palatability, or otherwise, of their characteristics or quality. It can also be manipulated to deceive consumers into believing that a product is better, more wholesome, more local, more environmentally-friendly or more welfare-friendly than is really the case. Chapter 7 identifies existing laws in this area, with a strong emphasis on the changes that have been made by EU regulation from 2014 onwards. It addresses the increasingly important and somewhat controversial issues surrounding the use of nutrition labelling and the making of nutrition and health claims. It assesses the quality requirements that have been introduced for specific foodstuffs. The next chapter focuses on the protection of food names for quality products or for those possessing identifiable characteristics and the extent to which Irish producers are using the newest versions of the geographical indications scheme.

The book concludes with two chapters on the most pressing concerns for many food lawyers. The first of these provides an examination of how the legal regulation of food affects the health and well-being of those that consume it. This involves an assessment of the interplay between national policy on obesity prevention and health protection on the one hand and the requirements of harmonising with EU legislation and free movement of food obligations on the other. It shows how efforts made at national level to deal with a national health crisis are mostly in vain due to the application of the TFEU – including ongoing efforts being made by the Department of Health to minimise the over-consumption of alcohol. It argues that this will continue to be the case until there is a reassessment of some of the most established rules in this area. Some of the ethical and environmental aspects of food production and marketing are considered, including an assessment of existing rules on organic production, genetic modification and animal welfare, as well as a discussion on the relationship, both existing and potential, between food law and climate change.

2

Domestic, European Union and International Food Law

2.1. Introduction

Irish food law is tied up in a complex relationship with EU rules and international laws, policies and recommendations. There are a vast range of influences on the content and application of food law at national level. These are introduced in this chapter and are discussed in more detail, in the domestic context, in Chapter 3. If we take as a starting point the fact that almost all Irish food law now comes directly from EU initiatives, then we can say that the very first place to look for a source of this is the Treaty on the Functioning of the European Union (TFEU). This includes a range of provisions, such as those on the free movement of goods, the protection of consumers and the protection of human health, which constitute the basis for the development of new EU laws in a range of areas. Many of the Irish statutory instruments that give effect to the EU legislation started life as proposals from the European Commission, based on one or more of these TFEU provisions. Following the exhaustion of the relevant legislative process, either a directive or a regulation is published, instructing Member States as to how they are to go about making this part of their national law.

Many of the directives and regulations that become part of Irish law will be designed to 'harmonise' or 'approximate' the laws of all Member States. The ideas behind EU legislative initiatives often arise because similar provisions exist within some of the Member States already. The EU legislation is designed to ensure that the same or similar rules exist in all Member States. In some cases, therefore, food laws that were already operating in Ireland may not be significantly altered by the introduction of new EU legislation because of their similarity to those provisions that already existed at national level.

International codes and guidelines for food, such as those of the Codex Alimentarius, can also have a cross-influence on the provisions of EU and national laws. While international standards are often developed from laws that already exist amongst many Codex members, a Codex standard can be used as a template in the drafting of new EU requirements, ultimately becoming part of the national laws of EU Member States. Codex standards can also be of persuasive authority in cases before the European Court of Justice. The World Trade Organization (WTO) Agreements set parameters within which new EU and consequently national, legislation must be created. Any measures operating outside these limits are open to challenge before the WTO's Dispute Settlement Body and, if found to contravene these Agreements, may either need to be amended accordingly or result in the imposition of fines or the suspension of international trade concessions. International policy recommendations and guidelines can also be used as the basis for the development of codes at national level. Advice on best practice from bodies such as the World Health Organization (WHO) often underlie the publication of non-binding standards for both the corporate sector and for individuals, such as was the case in the issue of guidance by the Scientific Advisory Committee on Nutrition (SACN) on sugar intake in June 2014 or the data presented in the periodic Global Status Reports on Alcohol and Health.

2.2. TFEU Obligations

The TFEU permits the EU institutions to create legislation in many areas that affect the food sector. Several key provisions transfer power away from the Member States and towards the Commission.

Article 30 TFEU prohibits Member States from imposing customs duties or any charges of equivalent effect on the importation or exportation of food. Articles 34 and 35 TFEU also require that no quantitative restrictions, or measures of equivalent effect, are placed on food traded within the Union. The limits placed on both customs duties and quantitative restrictions and measures deemed equivalent to them, are discussed in much more detail in Chapter 4.

Article 43 TFEU stipulates that secondary legislation may be introduced, via the consultation procedure, to support the Common Agricultural Policy (CAP). Article 114 TFEU facilitates the introduction of legislation designed to support free movement objectives. It states that the ordinary legislative procedure, involving full parliamentary participation, is to be used to harmonise national laws in a manner that enhances the internal market. There should be consultation with the EU's Economic and Social Committee during this process. Paragraph 3 makes specific reference to health and consumer protection forming the basis for legislative initiatives. The Commission is to 'take as a base a high level of protection, taking account in particular of any new development based on scientific facts' when drafting proposals for new legislation.[1] Where legislation is adopted under Article 114 TFEU, Member States may make a plea to the Commission that national laws contrary to these new EU laws should be allowed to continue in force to fulfil some specific health or intellectual property protection policy objective.[2] The Commission then has six months to decide whether, on the basis of the supporting evidence submitted, it approves of the Member State's action.[3]

---

[1] TFEU, Art 114(3).
[2] Ibid, para 4.
[3] Ibid, para 6.

The Commission's failure to make a decision constitutes approval.[4] Authorisation of the Member State's request can be used to trigger a re-examination of the content of the legislation.[5] All harmonising measures introduced under Article 114 TFEU are to include, where appropriate, a safeguard clause authorising Member States to take provisional measures, such as a ban on the importation of certain goods from other Member States, when this is deemed necessary for health protection reasons.[6]

Article 4 TFEU provides that the EU and its Member States share competence to act in a range of areas, including consumer protection and common safety concerns in public health matters. Article 168 TFEU, originally introduced by the Maastricht Treaty in 1993, provides that '[a] high level of human health protection shall be ensured in the definition and implementation of all Community policies and activities'. EU strategy is to complement, rather than replace, national policy in this area. The ordinary legislative procedure is to be used for the introduction of veterinary and phytosanitary measures which are designed to protect human health, even where the scope of the legislation might suggest that the subject matter is directly related to the Common Agricultural Policy.[7]

The protection of consumers is first mentioned in the Treaty in Article 12 TFEU. Here it is listed as one of the 'provisions having general application', alongside other important areas such as the promotion of equality, protecting employment and combating discrimination on a range of grounds. It states that:

[c]onsumer protection requirements shall be taken into account in defining and implementing other Union policies and activities.

A more specific Treaty provision on the protection of consumers, again first introduced by Maastricht, is set out in Article 169 TFEU. It states that:

[i]n order to promote the interests of consumers and to ensure a high level of consumer protection, the Union shall contribute to protecting the health, safety and economic interests of consumers, as well as to promoting their right to information, education and to organise themselves in order to safeguard their interests.

This is to be achieved by using harmonising legislation designed to support the internal market, introduced under Article 114 TFEU, as well as other measures which 'support, supplement and monitor the policy pursued by the Member States'. Again, the ordinary legislative procedure is to be used.[8] According to Article 169(4) TFEU, Member States may maintain or introduce more stringent

---

[4] Ibid.

[5] Ibid, para 7.

[6] TFEU Art 114(10). The use of these 'safeguard clauses' is now widespread in food law. For further discussion on this see G Berends and I Carreño, 'Safeguards in food: Ensuring food scares are scarce' (2005) 30 *EL Rev* 386.

[7] TFEU Art 168(4).

[8] Ibid, Art 169(3). The ordinary legislative procedure, by which most new EU food laws are now introduced, is discussed in more detail later in this chapter.

protective measures, provided these are compatible with other Treaty provisions, primarily the free movement of goods. The Commission must be notified where a Member State introduces any such domestic measure.

Finally, most of the EU legislation referred to throughout this book is either in the form of a regulation or a directive. To summarise the previous discussion, the key difference between the two is that regulations are 'directly applicable', meaning that they automatically become part of the national laws of the EU Member States on the date(s) set out in the terms of the legislation. Directives, on the other hand, usually require some implementing or transposing action at national level. Article 288 TFEU provides that:

> [a] regulation shall have general application ... be binding in its entirety and directly applicable in all Member States [but] a directive shall be binding, as to the result to be achieved, upon each Member State to which it is addressed, but shall leave to the national authorities the choice of form and methods.

Directives can have 'direct effect' in some circumstances, meaning that they create rights for individuals enforceable before national courts. This is a complicated area and a full discussion of it is beyond the scope of this book. However, it can be pointed out at this stage that most EU legislation, be it regulations or directives, is enforceable at national level after the date has passed for implementation, as set out in that legislation. Most EU food legislation becomes part of Irish law after the introduction of a statutory instrument, where this is necessary. Regulations, of course, will be part of national law regardless, but they are often accompanied by statutory instruments designed to give them proper meaning and clarification as to the implementation of their provisions at national level.

2.2.1. Role of the Commission

As mentioned already, most new food laws enter into the Irish legal system either as a transposition or direct application of EU directives and regulations or as a consequence of judgments delivered by the European Court of Justice. The EU is responsible for the introduction of legislative initiatives on a whole range of issues related to the production and marketing of food, many of which are explored in this book. Initially, much of this EU legislation was designed to harmonise the laws of the Member States on, for example, preservative use[9] and antioxidant authorisation.[10] They also served to harmonise standards designed to minimise

---

[9] Council Directive 1964/54/EEC of 5 November 1963 on the approximation of the laws of the Member States concerning the preservatives authorised for use in foodstuffs intended for human consumption [1964] OJ L 12/161. English Special Edition Series I, Chapter 1963–1964, p 99.

[10] Council Directive 1970/357/EEC of 13 July 1970 on the approximation of the laws of the Member States concerning the antioxidants authorised for use in foodstuffs intended for human consumption [1970] OJ L 157/31. English Special Edition Series I, Chapter 1970 (II), p 429.

the potential impact of disease on trade in animals and meat,[11] as well as facilitating the free movement of food by setting standardised compositional requirements for a range of specified products, such as honey,[12] coffee[13] and chocolate.[14]

The Commission plays a central role in the development and application of food laws. There are three aspects to this. First, the Commission, in particular through the Directorate-General for Health and Consumers (DG SANCO), proposes new or amending legislation in a range of areas, such as labelling, nutrition and safety. Second, following the 1987 Council Decision to delegate to committees the power to make legislation,[15] the Commission has the most significant role to play in the introduction of regulations through what is known as 'comitology'. Third, under the terms of Article 258 TFEU, the Commission brings proceedings against Member States where it considers that there has been a failure to fulfil Treaty obligations. Much of the jurisprudence of the Court of Justice on many areas of food law has developed out of these 'enforcement actions'.

Directorate-General for Health and Food Safety

The bureaucracy of the Commission is made up of Directorates-General (DGs). Each DG has responsibility for an area of Commission competence, such as agriculture, competition, employment and regional policy. DG SANTE (formerly DG SANCO, *Santé et Consommateurs*) deals with health and food safety. DG SANCO was originally founded in October 1999 and rebranded and restructured as DG SANTE in 2015. The primary change brought about by this was a shift in focus from the broader remit of protecting consumers to the more specific aim of protecting health – in particular through food safety regulation.

The primary role of DG SANTE is to draft and propose EU laws on food and product safety, consumer rights and health protection – and then to oversee the application of these and other measures at national and local level. It also organises consultation with stakeholders, both before and after the introduction of legislation, or other, initiatives. The outcomes and conclusions of these consultation processes have tended to be very influential over the final content and direction of the related Commission proposals. DG SANTE reports, on this and other matters, to the EU Commissioner for Health and Food Safety, an office which was

---

[11] Council Directive 1964/432/EEC of 26 June 1964 on animal health problems affecting intra-Community trade in bovine animals and swine [1964] OJ L 121/1977. English Special Edition Series I, Chapter 1963–1964, p 164.
[12] Council Directive 1974/409/EEC of 22 July 1974 on the harmonisation of the laws of the Member States relating to honey [1974] OJ L 221/10.
[13] Council Directive 1977/436/EEC of 27 June 1977 on the approximation of the laws of the Member States relating to coffee extracts and chicory extracts [1977] OJ L 172/20.
[14] Council Directive 1973/241/EEC of 24 July 1973 on the approximation of the laws of the Member States relating to cocoa and chocolate products intended for human consumption [1973] OJ L 228/23.
[15] Council Decision 1987/373/EEC of 13 July 1987 laying down the procedures for the exercise of implementing powers conferred on the Commission [1987] OJ L 197/33.

also rebranded, in 2014. Having said that, duty is owed to the Commission as an institution, rather than to the individual commissioner.

The Directorate-General for Health and Food Safety is headed at bureaucratic level by the Director-General, assisted by two deputies, one of which is responsible more specifically for health and the other for food safety. Beneath this, DG SANTE is split into seven areas: resource management and better regulation (linked directly to the Director-General); health systems, medical products and innovation; public health, country knowledge and crisis management; food chain: stakeholder and international relations; food and feed safety; health and food audits and analysis; and crisis management in food, animals and plants. These areas of responsibility have been shaped this way following a significant reorganisation in more recent years. The Director-General is also assisted by the Consumer, Health, Agriculture and Food Executive Agency (Chafea). Staff are based in Brussels, Luxembourg and Ireland. The Directorate-General is assisted in the development of legislative proposals by the Standing Committee on Plants, Animals, Food and Feed (PAFF), formerly that on the Food Chain and Animal Health, as originally established by the General Food Law Regulation.[16] This committee is composed of representatives of the Member States. It is chaired by a representative of the Commission.[17] The Committee is now organised into 14 different sections (formerly eight), dealing with general food law; biological safety of the food chain, toxicological safety of the food chain; controls and import conditions; animal nutrition; genetically modified food and feed and environment risk; animal health and animal welfare; phytopharmaceuticals; plant health; propagating material of ornamental plants; propagating material and plants of fruit genera and species; seeds and propagating material for agriculture and horticulture; forest reproductive material; and vine. The Standing Committee on Plants, Animals, Food and Feed plays a key role in the EU decision-making process on food matters, especially through the comitology procedure. This is discussed in more detail in the next section. The European Commission has also established the Advisory Group on the Food Chain and Animal and Plant Health, another key contributor to policy and legislation development and application, also discussed below.

Creating Ordinary Legislation

Since the introduction of the TFEU, the vast majority of new EU rules are to be introduced under what is now called the 'ordinary legislative procedure'. This was previously known as 'co-decision' and the method to be used was set out in Article 251 EC. Article 294(2) TFEU now states that '[t]he Commission shall

---

[16] Art 58 of Regulation (EC) No 178/2002 of the European Parliament and of the Council of 28 January 2002 laying down the general principles and requirements of food law, establishing the European Food Safety Authority and laying down procedures in matters of food safety [2002] OJ L 31/1.

[17] Ibid.

submit a proposal to the European Parliament and the Council'. There then follows the procedure that is to be employed to bring this proposal to fruition as legislation. There are first and second readings for the Parliament and for the Council, where amendments can be proposed and accepted or rejected. When agreement cannot be reached between these two institutions, a Conciliation Committee can be formed, comprising representatives of both. This Committee is then charged with producing a compromise text, which can then be sent back to the Parliament and the Council for a third reading.

The Commission plays a very prominent role in the ordinary legislative procedure. Despite the level of participation of the other two institutions in this, it is clearly the Commission which exerts the most influence over the content of new EU food legislation. First, it produces the proposal on which the parliamentary and Council readings are based. Second, it is very difficult for amendments to be carried during the first two readings without the Commission's acceptance of this. Finally, while the Commission is not directly involved in the conciliatory stage, other than as a conciliator between the Council and Parliament positions, most texts are adopted prior to this and therefore never require a third reading. Most legislation related to the food sector has traditionally been introduced by this ordinary legislative procedure. Agriculture and fisheries were previously outside those areas where new legislation was introduced following co-decision. However, the amendments made by the Lisbon Treaty have changed this. Measures designed to implement or alter aspects of both the Common Agricultural Policy and the Common Fisheries Policy are now subject to the ordinary procedure.[18] Having said that, some significant aspects of fisheries policy, such as the setting of annual catch limits and quotas, are to be decided by the Council, acting on a Commission proposal.[19] Legislation on animal and plant health, zootechnics and animal welfare are now also to be introduced by way of the ordinary legislative procedure, having previously required mere consultation with the Parliament.

To summarise, legislation is usually introduced using the ordinary procedure outlined above or, in some circumstances, by a special legislative procedure – set out on a provision-by-provision basis in the Treaty. Special procedures used include the consultation procedure. This is also initiated by the submission of a proposal from the Commission to the Council. The Council then consults on its content with the Parliament, before deciding on the adoption of the measure. There is a duty to consult with the Parliament,[20] but it is not required to take account of the Parliament's views.

The other main special procedure used is assent. This procedure differs from the others in that the Commission is not the only institution that can introduce the initial proposal. Depending on the issue; subject to what is stated in the Treaty, proposals can also be made by either the Parliament, the Member States or by the

---

[18] TFEU Art 43(2).
[19] Ibid, Art 43(3).
[20] Case 138/1979, *Roquette Frères v Council* [1980] ECR 3333.

European Council. Key to the assent procedure is that no matter who initiates the legislation, the Parliament must consent to what is proposed before it can become law. In addition, depending on the circumstances, the Council or the European Council may also have to consent to the measure. While the Parliament may use its powers of veto under the ordinary legislative procedure (although it rarely does) it must actively consent to legislation under the assent procedure. There are no time limits placed on the Parliament in this regard. It can delay the introduction of such proposals for as long as it likes. It can also prevent them from ever reaching the statute book.

Little detail is provided on how the special legislative procedures are to operate, which is why we must look to individual provisions of the TFEU to see which course is to be followed and which institutions are to be involved. Special procedures have less relevance for food law than the ordinary procedure, in any case. They are mainly used to introduce legislative initiatives in other areas of Union competence, such as anti-discrimination measures (Article 19 TFEU), aspects of citizenship (Article 21 TFEU), capital movement (Article 64 TFEU), taxation harmonisation (Article 113 TFEU), the tasks of the European Central Bank (Article 127 TFEU), the management of natural resources, including water (Article 192 TFEU)and the EU's own resources (Article 311 TFEU).

Comitology

Law making in the EU can be in either the 'ordinary' format, discussed above, where institutions draft, propose, consult and consent to legislation, in the form of directives and regulations, or it can be introduced by the Commission, using powers delegated to it by the 'ordinary' type – the enabling act. The use of delegation powers has become relatively commonplace since the introduction of the comitology procedure in 1987, being contained in around one in every four or five pieces of legislation. Measures introduced using comitology are known as 'delegated acts'.[21] The TFEU describes ordinary legislation, introduced by either the ordinary legislative procedure or a special legislative procedure, as 'legislative acts',[22] whereas the delegated and implementing legislation are deemed to be 'non-legislative acts'.[23]

The comitology procedure works on the basis that committees should provide the Commission with expert advice during the development of policy and legislation. These committees are made up of national representatives of the Member States and are chaired by the Commission. They provide advice during the policy development phase, identifying emerging issues in need of attention and contributing to proposal drafting; the legislation implementation phase; and on policy

---

[21] TFEU Art 290.
[22] Ibid, Art 289.
[23] Ibid, Arts 290 and 291.

monitoring and evaluation, assessing the enforcement of legislative measures by national authorities and the efficacy of the legislation introduced.

The nature of the comitological relationship between the committees and the Commission is now set out in the 2011 Comitology Regulation.[24] Most of the delegated acts referred to in this book were introduced under the old system, established by the original Comitology Decision.[25] The 2011 Regulation establishes a more streamlined set of procedures than that which previously existed under the old Decision. There are now only two ways in which comitology can be used – either the 'examination procedure' or the 'advisory procedure' should be employed. Article 2 of the Regulation states that the basic legislation may provide for the application of the advisory procedure or the examination procedure, taking into account the nature or the impact of the implementing act required. The examination procedure applies, in particular, for the adoption of implementing legislation relating to the common agricultural and fisheries policies; the environment, security and safety, or protection of the health or safety of humans, animals or plants; the common commercial policy; and taxation.[26]

The advisory procedure is to be used for the adoption of other legislation which does not come within the scope of those types listed above. It may, however, be used in some of those areas which are usually subject to the examination procedure, where deemed appropriate.[27] Whichever of the two procedures applies, the Commission is assisted in its decision making by a committee, composed in the usual manner – representatives of the Member States and chaired by a representative of the Commission.[28] The Commission submits a draft proposal to the committee, which then delivers its opinion on the document to the Commission, subject to whichever procedure is to be used. The opinion of the committee carries a different authority, depending on the procedure. If the advisory procedure is being used, the Commission is only obliged to take 'the utmost account of the conclusions drawn from the discussions within the committee and of the opinion delivered'.[29] If, however, it is the examination procedure that has been used to introduce the implementing legislation, the committee delivers either a 'positive', 'negative' or no opinion, based on qualified majority voting, weighted according to the size of the Member State represented.[30] A positive opinion should lead to

---

[24] Regulation (EU) No 182/2011 of the European Parliament and of the Council of 16 February 2011 laying down the rules and general principles concerning mechanisms for control by Member States of the Commission's exercise of implementing powers [2011] OJ L 55/13.

[25] The original Comitology Decision was introduced in 1987, Decision 1987/373/EEC of 13 July 1987 laying down the procedures for the exercise of implementing powers conferred on the Commission [1987] OJ L 197/33. This was later replaced by Decision 1999/468/EC [1999] OJ L 184/23, which was itself amended by Council Decision 2006/512/EC [2006] OJ L 200/11. All have since been repealed by Reg 182/2011, n 24 above.

[26] Reg 182/2011, Art 2(2), n 24 above.

[27] Ibid, Art 2(3).

[28] Ibid, Art 3(2).

[29] Ibid, Art 4(2).

[30] Ibid, Art 5(1).

the adoption of the legislation.[31] The legislation should not, however, be adopted in its proposed form if the committee has issued a negative opinion. An amended version may be returned to the committee for reconsideration,[32] or its introduction may be referred to an appeal committee.[33] The Commission may usually go ahead and adopt its proposal where no opinion has been delivered[34] and must ensure that there is transparency in the procedures and committee proceedings.[35] Both the European Parliament and the Council must be properly and continuously informed of committee proceedings through the Comitology Register. The Commission must also publish an annual report on the work of the committees.[36] This report noted in 2015 that 287 comitology committees existed, issuing nearly 2,000 separate opinions and adopting 1,563 implementing acts.[37] Eighteen of these dealt with agriculture and rural development. A further 21 committees were dealing with health and food safety – adopting an incredible 695 implementing acts! Almost half of all implementing acts introduced by comitology during 2014 directly related to either agriculture and rural affairs or health and food safety, despite the fact that 28 distinct comitological areas exist, including those on climate action, education and culture, justice and consumers, mobility and transport, fraud, trade and taxation – all directly linked to a specific EU Commissioner and Directorate-General.

Advisory Group on the Food Chain

Distinction should be drawn between the committees that are involved in the comitology procedure and the expert groups, created by the Commission and used to provide expertise in the preparation and implementation of law and policy. One such expert group is the Advisory Group on the Food Chain and Animal and Plant Health, which was established in 2004.[38] In their 2001 White Paper on European Governance,[39] the Commission committed itself to opening up the policy-making process in the EU, involving more people and organisations in the development and implementation of policies. The General Food Law Regulation also provides for 'open and transparent public consultation, directly or through representative bodies, during the preparation, evaluation and revision of food law'.[40] It was felt that this consultation system requires the support of structured meetings in the

---

[31] Ibid, Art 5(2).

[32] Ibid, Art 5(3).

[33] The appeal procedure is set out in Art 6 of the Regulation.

[34] Reg 182/2011, Art 5(4), n 24 above.

[35] Ibid, Art 10(1).

[36] Ibid, Art 10(2).

[37] Report from the Commission on the Working of the Committees During 2014, COM (2015) 165.

[38] By Commission Decision 2004/613/EC of 6 August 2004 concerning the creation of an advisory group on the food chain and animal and plant health [2004] OJ L 275/17.

[39] COM (2001) 428 final.

[40] Reg 178/2002, Art 9.

context of an advisory group, facilitating direct dialogue between the Commission and interested parties, such as consumer associations.[41] The Advisory Group on the Food Chain was thus established.[42]

Under the terms of the Decision, the Commission consults with the Advisory Group on matters related to safety, labelling, nutrition, animal welfare and crop protection.[43] The group itself is made up of no more than 45 representatives of relevant interest groups, who are required to express an interest in participation in the Advisory Group.[44] The Commission then chooses from these applicants on the basis of their suitability. The Group should meet at least twice yearly in plenary sessions and working groups may be established to examine more specific matters.[45] Experts or observers may also be invited to participate in the work of the Group.[46] It should be noted that consultation with the Advisory Group may not always be possible, nor is it always required, in emergency situations.[47]

Enforcement Actions

The Commission is entitled to bring an action before the Court of Justice where it considers that a Member State has breached its Treaty obligations. Article 258 TFEU states that:

> [i]f the Commission considers that a Member State has failed to fulfil an obligation under the Treaties, it shall deliver a reasoned opinion on the matter after giving the State concerned the opportunity to submit its observations.

It further states that:

> [i]f the State concerned does not comply with the opinion within the period laid down by the Commission, the latter may bring the matter before the Court of Justice of the European Union.

It is clear that two things must happen before the alleged failure to observe Treaty obligations ends up in the Court. First, an issue related to non-compliance has to be identified. This can occur when a complaint is made to the Commission that a Member State is acting inappropriately, usually either by the application of domestic measures that are incompatible with EU Treaty requirements, or

---

[41] Preamble to Decision 2004/613.

[42] Commission Decision 1980/1073/EEC establishing a new statute of the Advisory Committee on Foodstuffs [1980] OJ L 318/28 was repealed. Decision 2004/613, Art 6.

[43] Decision 2004/613, Art 2(1).

[44] Ibid, Art 3. These interest groups have included, amongst others, the Animal Welfare Association, the European Crop Protection Association, the European Cold Storage and Logistics Association, the European Dairy Association the European Federation of Food, Agriculture and Tourism Trade Unions, the European Modern Restaurant Association, the European Community of Consumer Cooperatives, Slow Food Associazione Internazionale and Friends of the Earth Europe.

[45] Ibid, Art 4.

[46] Ibid, Art 4(3).

[47] Reg 178/2002, Art 9.

by the non-implementation, late transposition or improper application of EU regulations or directives. Many enforcement actions are commenced following a private complaint.[48] These can come from a variety of sources, including private citizens or petitions made to the European Parliament by individuals, businesses or other interested parties. The number of complaints being brought by private actors has increased since 2011, rising to the registration of nearly 4,000 grievances during 2014.[49] The Commission must first attempt to get the matter resolved through bilateral discussions with the Member State concerned via what is known as the EU Pilot Procedure. Actual infringement proceedings can then be brought when the initial procedure does not lead to a satisfactory resolution of the matter. Proceedings may also be brought on the initiative of the Commission itself, in the absence of a private complaint. It would appear that the entire mechanism and the volume of complaints brought to the attention of the Commission, has been affected by the introduction of a standardised complaint form, which can be used to report grievances or issues relating to a Member State's failure to adhere to its obligations,[50] and also by the development of a user-friendly complaints mechanism which is accessible via the Europa portal 'Your Rights'. An ordinary letter may also still be used. Whichever mode is employed, it can be submitted to the Commission headquarters in Brussels, or to any of the Commission's offices in any of the Member States. It must relate to an infringement of EU law by a Member State.[51] Any applicant who is dissatisfied with the Commission's handling of their complaint may bring the matter to the European Ombudsman.[52]

The second thing that must happen before the matter reaches the Court, is that the specified procedure must be followed. When the Commission is alerted to or becomes aware of a possible breach of Treaty obligations, it should, as mentioned above, negotiate with the Member State concerned, affording it the opportunity to explain its position and to remedy the situation. If the matter is not resolved at this initial stage, the Member State must be formally notified of the alleged infringement in a letter from the Commission. The State then usually has two months

---

[48] The Commission has reported in the past that complaints account for the initiation of 54% of all enforcement proceedings, or 64% of all cases on issues other than the late transposition of directives: 26th Annual Report on Monitoring the Application of Community Law (2008), COM (2009) 675. As noted above, the amount of complaints being brought in this way has been steadily increasing since 2011.

[49] 'Monitoring the application of Union law', 2014 Annual Report of the European Commission. Available at: www.ec.europa.eu.

[50] Failure by a Member State to comply with Community law: Standard form for complaints to be submitted to the European Commission [1999] OJ C 119/5. Available at: http://ec.europa.eu/community_law/docs/docs_your_rights/complaint_form_en.rtf.

[51] There were 134 infringement cases opened in 2014 that related directly to health and consumer protection. A further 112 dealt with the operation of the internal market. See 'Monitoring the application of Union law', n 49 above.

[52] The operations of which are set out in Arts 24 and 228 TFEU.

to reply, at which stage the Commission can decide whether to proceed with its investigation of the complaint. Should the matter remain unresolved at this stage, the Commission can then issue a reasoned opinion, setting out the grounds on which the alleged infringement rests. The matter is then referred to the Court, if the Member State still refuses to comply. The hope is that most initial notifications of non-compliance with Treaty obligations will never make it as far as court referral. The total number of infringement proceedings making it as far as full court determination has been falling.[53] However, the percentage of judgments delivered by the Court of Justice that find in favour of the Commission in enforcement actions remains very high, at around 92 per cent.[54]

Many of the most significant decisions made by the Court of Justice on principles of EU food law have come about because of infringement proceedings. Examples include key cases related to the taxation of imported food and drink,[55] the free movement of food[56] and labelling and health claims.[57] Roles may also be reversed; cases can be brought against the Commission by the Member States. However, these are usually applications for the annulment of legislative measures.[58] This most famously happened, for example, when the UK took action in objection to the measures that were adopted at EU level to avoid the further spread of BSE amongst cattle[59] and also where several other EU Member States objected to the registration of 'feta' cheese as a protected geographical food name.[60] All of these cases and many others, are discussed in more detail in the relevant sections of this book.[61]

---

[53] See 'Monitoring the application of Union law', n 49 above.

[54] Of the 38 judgments delivered under Art 258 TFEU in 2014, 35 were in favour of the Commission. While Member States do, by and large, comply with decisions against them, 61 infringement procedures remained open at the end of 2014 as the Commission was of the opinion that the necessary measures had not yet been adopted, modified or withdrawn to their satisfaction. Data also taken from 'Monitoring the application of Union law', n 49 above.

[55] Such as Case 55/1979, *Commission v Ireland* [1980] ECR 481; Case 168/1978 *Commission v France* (spirit tax) [1980] ECR 347; Case 170/1978 *Commission v UK* (wine and beer tax) [1983] ECR 2265; and Case 184/1985 *Commission v Italy* (banana consumption tax) [1987] ECR 2013.

[56] See, eg, Case 178/1984 *Commission v Germany* (beer) [1987] ECR 1227; Case 216/1984 *Commission v France* (milk substitutes) [1988] ECR 793; Case 274/1987 *Commission v Germany* (meat products) [1989] ECR 229; and Case C-24/2000 *Commission v France* (fortified foods) [2004] ECR I-1277.

[57] Case C-221/2000 *Commission v Austria* (health claims) [2003] ECR I-1007.

[58] Annulment actions are dealt with in more detail in section 2.2.2. below.

[59] Case C-180/1996 *United Kingdom v Commission* (BSE) [1998] ECR I-2265.

[60] Joined Cases C-465/2002 and 466/2002 *Germany and Denmark v Commission* [2005] ECR I-9115.

[61] Ireland has been the responding Member State in approximately 102 enforcement actions brought by the Commission that reached full Court of Justice determination, such as Case 55/1979, *Commission v Ireland* [1980] ECR 481, where the State was found to have contravened what is now Art 110 TFEU by allowing Irish producers only to defer their payment of duty on alcohol. It has also brought at least 8 cases against the Commission, either on its own or in conjunction with another Member State, as was the case in Joined Cases C-296/1993 and C-307/1993, *France and Ireland v Commission* [1996] ECR I-795, seeking the annulment of a regulation on the use of intervention measures in the beef and veal sector. The case is discussed in more detail below.

2.2.2. European Union Courts and Irish Food Law

The Treaty on European Union (TEU) sets out that the EU is to have its own court structure, charged with ensuring that the law is observed in the interpretation and application of the Treaties. Article 19(1) TEU provides that:

> [t]he Court of Justice of the European Union shall include the Court of Justice, the General Court and specialised courts. It shall ensure that in the interpretation and application of the Treaties the law is observed. Member States shall provide remedies sufficient to ensure effective legal protection in the fields covered by Union law.

Article 19(3) further provides that the Court of Justice is to:

> rule on actions brought by a Member State, an institution or a natural or legal person; give preliminary rulings, at the request of courts or tribunals of the Member States, on the interpretation of Union law or the validity of acts adopted by the institutions; rule in other cases provided for in the Treaties.

The first two categories stated above are of particular significance to the development of food law and its application in Ireland. The former, actions brought by a Member State or an institution, relate to food law in that this includes the enforcement actions taken by the Commission where it considers that a Member State has breached its Treaty obligations, discussed above, as well as reviews of the legality of EU acts. The second of these categories set out in Article 19(3) TEU, preliminary rulings, is looked at in more detail below. Most cases concerning aspects of food law have come before the Court of Justice in one of these ways – they usually involve action taken by the Commission against Member States; applications for the annulment of EU legislation; or referrals from national courts or tribunals for clarification on points of EU law.

As Article 19 TEU also states, the Court of Justice of the European Union is made up of three layers – the Court of Justice, the General Court and specialised courts. The Court of Justice consists of judges from each of the Member States, assisted by eight Advocates General.[62] The Advocate General is required to issue an opinion on a case where the Statute of the Court of Justice requires this. These opinions, which set out the facts, reasoning and findings of the Advocate General, are adopted prior to the Court's judgment on a case. They are not binding on the Court, but they are usually a good indication of what it is likely to decide. The Court of Justice has a broad jurisdiction. The only exceptions to this are cases concerning matters related to the Common Foreign and Security Policy,[63] aspects of judicial co-operation in criminal and policing matters,[64] and the grounds for expelling a Member State from the Union.[65]

---

[62] TFEU Art 252.
[63] Ibid, Art 275.
[64] Ibid, Art 276.
[65] Ibid, Art 269 in conjunction with TEU, Art 7.

The General Court, formerly known as the Court of First Instance, also comprises at least one judge from each of the Member States.[66] The jurisdiction of the General Court is more limited than that of the Court of Justice, although it has expanded over the course of time. It can review the legality of EU activities, such as the introduction of new food laws and its decisions may be subject to an appeal to the Court of Justice on points of law.[67] It can also deal with actions initiated by Member States against the Commission.[68] Perhaps most significantly, it can also 'hear and determine questions referred for a preliminary ruling under Article 267, in specific areas laid down by the statute'.[69] However, '[w]here the General Court considers that the case requires a decision of principle likely to affect the unity or consistency of Union law, it may refer the case to the Court of Justice for a ruling'.[70] The Parliament and the Council can also establish specialised courts, which are attached to the general court, to hear and determine proceedings brought in specific areas.[71]

Preliminary References

The Irish courts can refer questions on points of EU law to the EU courts under what is known as the preliminary reference procedure. Article 267 TFEU states that:

> [t]he Court of Justice of the European Union shall have jurisdiction to give preliminary rulings concerning the interpretation of the Treaties [and] the validity and interpretation of acts of the institutions, bodies, offices or agencies of the Union.

It further states that:

> [w]here such a question is raised before any court or tribunal of a Member State, that court or tribunal may, if it considers that a decision on the question is necessary to enable it to give judgment, request the Court to give a ruling thereon.

The domestic court must first establish the facts and then identify whether any issues related to the interpretation of EU law arise. Where it is deemed that they do, the domestic, usually higher, court can then make a reference to the European Court of Justice – asking it to determine how EU law should be applied in the case. It is up to the national court to decide what gets referred. Private parties do not get any direct access to the European courts. Nor can they appeal national decisions to the courts of the EU. Representations by private parties before the Court of Justice are also limited. Essentially, it is the national court which makes the necessary submissions. It outlines the subject matter of the dispute, any applicable national

---

[66] TEU Art 19(2).
[67] TFEU Art 256.
[68] Ibid, Art 263(2).
[69] Ibid, Art 256(3).
[70] Ibid.
[71] Ibid, Art 257.

provisions and case law, relevant EU law provisions, the reasons that prompted the referral and summaries of the main arguments of the parties to the case. It is this submission upon which the Court of Justice's determination will be based.

The preliminary reference procedure has been and continues to be, vital to the development of food law. Many of the key principles that now underpin aspects of food law stem directly from decisions taken by the Court of Justice after a referral by a national court or tribunal. The Annual Reports of the Court of Justice show that usually over half of cases heard are preliminary references. They are discussed throughout this book.

Reviewing the Legality of EU Acts

The Treaty provides that the legality of EU legislation or acts can be challenged before the Court. Many pieces of food legislation have been subject to this sort of review. Article 263 TFEU states that:

> [t]he Court of Justice of the European Union shall review the legality of legislative acts, of acts of the Council, of the Commission and of … the European Parliament and of the European Council intended to produce legal effects vis-à-vis third parties.

While this provision clearly facilitates the challenging of EU food legislation, the legal standing to bring such an appeal is rather limited. Article 263(2) TFEU states that the Court has jurisdiction:

> in actions brought by a Member State, the European Parliament, the Council or the Commission on grounds of lack of competence, infringement of an essential procedural requirement, infringement of the Treaties or of any rule of law relating to their application, or misuse of powers.

This grants these named institutions the status of 'privileged applicant', meaning that they all have the legal standing to bring an application for the review of Union legislation before the Court. In many cases, however, those affected by the legislation at issue are likely to be private individuals, who have also had no formal role to play in the introduction of these contentious new rules in the first place. This category of applicant has 'non-privileged' status. This is set out in Article 263(4) TFEU, which states that:

> [a]ny natural or legal person may … institute proceedings against an act addressed to that person or which is of direct and individual concern to them and against a regulatory act which is of direct concern to them and does not entail implementing measures.

This is problematic. An applicant must demonstrate that they are directly and individually concerned by an act which is not specifically addressed to them. Establishing direct and individual concern is very difficult to do.[72] A regulation,

---

[72] For further discussion on this see A Arnull, 'Private applicants and the action for annulment since *Codorniu*' (2001) 38 *Common Market Law Review* 7.

for example, may prohibit commercial fishing for mackerel in a defined area off the south east coast of Ireland. At the time of the introduction of this (fictional) legislation there may be only one trawler actively engaged in fishing for mackerel in this area. However, the regulation is not addressed to the skipper of that trawler; it deals more generally with fishing for a certain species in a designated body of water. It is clear in our example that it could be that only one trawler is really affected by the regulation. Owing to previous court determinations on the matter, this potential applicant, who may seek to challenge the legality of the regulation, cannot do so as the regulation is not addressed to him. He cannot even demonstrate that the regulation is of 'direct and individual concern' to him.

This difficult situation arises out of the decision of the Court in *Plaumann*.[73] Here, the applicant sought the partial suspension of duty payable on the importation of mandarins and clementines imported from third countries. A Commission decision, addressed to the German Government, declined this request.[74] An application was brought to have this decision annulled. This application could only proceed, under the terms of the Treaty, if it could be shown that Plaumann was 'individually concerned' by the decision. It was made clear that this could only be deemed to be so where the decision affects the applicant 'by reason of certain attributes which are peculiar to them or by reasons of circumstances in which they are differentiated from all other persons'. Whether or not there was only one importer of clementines into Germany was not relevant. The fact that the applicant was involved in 'a commercial activity which may at any time be practised by any person' meant that they were not distinguishable. They were not, therefore, 'individually concerned'.

As stated, it is difficult for a private individual, or non-privileged applicant, to demonstrate that they have the legal standing required to challenge EU acts. Almost all commercial activities can be entered into by new operators at any time. Being the only, or the major, player in a particular market affected by new EU legislation does not indicate that one is individually concerned – and the test for standing cannot therefore be satisfied. It is only where those who are, or who in the future may be, affected by the legislation are a 'closed' group, identifiable and distinguishable from all other current or potential operators, that the required 'individual concern' may be established. In *Codorniu*,[75] for example, the fact that the applicant had held a trademark for use of the sales name Crémant in Spain since 1924 was held to distinguish that operator from all others, as no new wine producer could potentially be affected by a regulation limiting the use of this name.[76] There could only be one trademark holder. No other operator could have their intellectual property rights affected by the regulation in the same way.

---

[73] Case 25/1962 *Plaumann & Co v Commission* [1963] ECR 95.
[74] Decision No SIII 03079; 22/05/1962.
[75] Case C-309/1989 *Codorniu v Council* [1994] ECR I-1853.
[76] Council Regulation (EEC) No 2045/1989 of 19 June 1989 amending Regulation (EEC) No 3309/1985 laying down general rules for the description and presentation of sparkling wines and aerated sparkling wines [1989] OJ L 202/12.

If legal standing is established, the grounds upon which the challenge is based can be reviewed. For an EU act to be deemed illegal, it must be shown that it was entered into when the institutions responsible did not have the competence to do so; that there had been an infringement of an essential procedural requirement; that there had been an infringement of the Treaty; or that there had been a misuse of power.[77]

It is generally very difficult for non-privileged applicants to establish that they have the standing required to proceed with a challenge to the legality of a Union act. Hence most of the examples of food-related cases that have tested whether one of these four grounds listed has been breached involve privileged applicants – usually either inter-institutional contentions or applications brought by Member States. For example, one of the more significant food-related challenges brought under the Article 263 TFEU procedure centred on the inclusion of genetically modified organisms in the list of non-organic components that could be present in products lawfully labelled as 'organic'.

In *Parliament v Commission*,[78] the applicant sought the annulment of aspects of the Commission Regulation that facilitated this.[79] The Parliament pleaded that its prerogatives had been infringed and contested the validity of that inclusion of genetically modified micro-organisms as a substance permitted for inclusion in organic foodstuffs. Its action was based on three pleas: that the Commission had exceeded its powers; that the Commission had misused its powers; and that the statement of reasons for introducing the contested provision was insufficient. The action was dismissed, the Court finding that the relevant legislative procedures had been complied with. EU law was, however, later amended to remove genetically modified organisms from the list of permitted ingredients in organic foods, the Council stating that:

> [g]enetically modified organisms and products derived therefrom are not compatible with the organic production method; in order to maintain consumer confidence in organic production, genetically modified organisms, parts thereof and products derived therefrom should not be used in products labelled as from organic production.[80]

GMOs can no longer be used in organic products.

Examples of Ireland bringing an action for the annulment of EU legislation are few and far between; the State has rarely challenged the legality of any

---

[77] TFEU, Art 263(2).

[78] Case C-156/1993 *Parliament v Commission* [1995] ECR I-2019.

[79] Commission Regulation (EEC) No 207/1993 of 29 January 1993 defining the content of Annex VI to Regulation (EEC) No 2092/1991 on organic production of agricultural products and indications referring thereto on agricultural products and foodstuffs and laying down detailed rules for implementing the provisions of Art 5 (4) thereto [1993] OJ L 25/5.

[80] Preamble to Council Regulation (EC) No 1804/1999 of 19 July 1999 supplementing Regulation (EEC) No 2092/1991 on organic production of agricultural products and indications referring thereto on agricultural products and foodstuffs to include livestock production [1999] OJ L 222/1.

measure related to the food sector.[81] It did bring one joined claim,[82] alongside France, seeking the annulment of Regulation 685/1993 on special intervention measures designed to mitigate for any substantial fall in prices for beef and veal.[83] The Member States had concerns over the fact that the Regulation limited the weight of carcasses which would be eligible for financial intervention, claiming that by setting these limits that Commission had gone beyond what the relevant provisions of the framework legislation (in particular Article 6(7) of Regulation 805/1968, [1968] OJ L 148/24) allowed. The Court dismissed the application, finding that the 1968 Regulation had, in fact, delegated the power to the Commission to adopt measures which were deemed necessary to attain the specified objective of 'prevent[ing] market prices spiraling downward'.

As mentioned earlier, the Article 263 TFEU procedure was, perhaps, most famously used in relation to food when the UK sought to annul the Commission's ban on the export of cattle during the BSE crisis.[84] The focus of this particular challenge to EU law arose out of the Commission's adoption of a Decision banning the export of cattle, beef and beef derivatives from the UK to all EU Member States and to third countries.[85] The UK sought the annulment of the Decision on several grounds, including that the Commission had acted beyond its powers, that there had been a misuse of powers and that there was a failure to comply with the principle of the free movement of goods. According to the Court, EU law at the time did facilitate the taking of safeguard measures, such as this ban, where there was an outbreak of a disease that was likely to pose a serious risk to animal or human health.[86] The UK's Spongiform Encephalopathy Advisory Committee (SEAC) had stated in March 1996 that BSE was 'the most likely explanation' for the outbreak of the human variant, Creutzfeldt-Jakob disease. This, it was argued, could be used to justify the adoption of safeguard measures. One of the objectives of EU law, to enable the Commission to take swift action where necessary to prevent the spread of disease, would be stifled if it were to be prevented from taking the sort of action that it had, in circumstances such as these. The Court was of the opinion that the

---

[81] Most recently, for example, Ireland did bring an unsuccessful Art 263 TFEU case seeking the annulment of Directive 2006/24 on data retention on the ground that it was not adopted on an appropriate legal basis. See Case C-301/2006, *Ireland v Parliament and Council* [2009] ECR I-593.

[82] Joined Cases C-296/1993 and C-307/1993, *France and Ireland v Commission*, n 61 above.

[83] Commission Regulation (EEC) No 685/1993 of 24 March 1993 amending Regulation (EEC) No 859/1989 laying down detailed rules for the application of general and special intervention measures in the beef and veal sector. [1993] OJ L 73/9.

[84] The crisis itself and the new direction in which it has subsequently led the development of food law, is discussed in much more detail in Ch 5.

[85] Commission Decision 1996/239 of 27 March 1996 on emergency measures to protect against bovine spongiform encephalopathy [1996] OJ L 78/47.

[86] Art 10(1) of Council Directive 1990/425/EEC of 26 June 1990 concerning veterinary and zootechnical checks applicable in intra-Community trade in certain live animals and products with a view to the completion of the internal market [1990] OJ L 224/29 and Art 9(1) of Council Directive 1989/662/ EEC of 11 December 1989 concerning veterinary checks in intra-Community trade with a view to the completion of the internal market [1989] OJ L 395/13.

SEAC statement contained new information which significantly altered the existing perception of the risk posed.[87] The immobilisation of animals was deemed a proportionate and lawful response to this.[88] Although the Commission Decision clearly affected the free movement of goods, it was found that this did not automatically render it contrary to EU law as it was adopted in accordance with the terms of free movement promoting directives, such as those on compulsory veterinary inspections.[89] Finally, it was held that the Commission had not misused its powers. The Court noted that this would only be the case where an EU institution adopted a measure designed to achieve a result contrary to that stated in the Preamble.[90] Looking at the recitals in the Preamble to the Decision, the Court found that the Commission had introduced the contested measure in order to protect human health from the potential risk of BSE transmission and not, as was contested, for any economic reason, such as protecting the beef industry or maintaining consumer confidence in beef production. The action was dismissed.

2.3. International Obligations

2.3.1. World Trade Organization Agreements

International trade agreements have had more of an impact on domestic food law since the establishment of the World Trade Organization (WTO) in 1995. As we have earlier explained, practically all new and existing food law comes from EU legislation. It will now be demonstrated that it is also the influence that international trade law has on EU law that in turn impacts on the scope of national legislation and measures.

WTO agreements can affect the nature and content of EU rules in a number of ways. The most significant of these is where EU legislation or action is found to be contrary to one, or several, of the individual WTO agreements. These include the Agreement on the Application of Sanitary and Phytosanitary Measures (SPS Agreement), the Agreement on Technical Barriers to Trade (TBT Agreement), the Agreement on Trade-Related Aspects of Intellectual Property Rights (TRIPs Agreement) and the Agreement on Agriculture, as well as the General Agreement on Tariffs and Trade (GATT). Each of these and their impact on EU food law and consequently domestic food law, is examined below. These agreements also carry

---

[87] Case C-180/1996, n 59 above, para 52.

[88] Ibid, para 57.

[89] Ibid, para 63. The directives concerned are 1990/425 and 1989/662, n 86 above. The principle of Directive conformity being espoused by the Court here was first proclaimed in Case 37/1983 *Rewe-Zentrale v Landwirtschaftskammer Rheinland* [1984] ECR 1229, para 19.

[90] See Case C-84/1994 *United Kingdom v Council* [1996] ECR I-5755, para 69; Case C-156/1993 *Parliament v Commission* [1995] ECR I-2019, para 31; and Case C-248/1989 *Cargill v Commission* [1991] ECR I-2987, para 26.

the general principles of international trade law that oblige Members to act on the basis of: (i) most favoured nation; and (ii) national treatment. 'Most favoured nation' works on the basis that Members should, where possible, treat their trade relations and conditions with all other Members in the same way that they treat the most favourable of these. This can be problematic when a Member enters into a bilateral agreement because, by definition, the States involved should then extend the concessions of this agreement to all other WTO Members.[91] The principle of 'national treatment' provides that Members should provide the same advantages for traders from other States as they provide to their own. In both cases, there is a general exemption for regional trading blocs such as the EU. This means that the same treatment and advantages that are provided between EU Member States do not have to be extended to all WTO Members. They should, however, provide the same treatment and advantages in their dealings with all other WTO Members.

Individual WTO agreements and WTO rules or principles more generally, can also be used to challenge the legality of EU law, in a similar manner to that examined above in relation to Article 263 TFEU. Applications can be brought to annul Union legislation based on a claim that it does not adhere to international trade law requirements. While such applications are possible, it should be noted at this stage that this is a very difficult claim to make successfully. The Court of Justice has consistently held that the nature of the international trade law system dictates that the criteria for establishing the legal effect of WTO rules cannot be met – nullifying the possibility of using these rules to challenge EU law. Essentially, the Court states that the WTO does not oblige its Member States to adhere directly to the Agreements, therefore the ECJ will not tie the EU institutions to them either. This is explained below.

Effect of World Trade Organization Rules on Irish Law

According to the Court of Justice, neither the provisions of GATT nor WTO rules create rights for individuals. Their existence cannot be used to challenge the validity of EU law. EU legislation that is contrary to WTO obligations therefore remains valid and applicable. It cannot be deemed unlawful on the ground that it runs contrary to international legal obligations. This reduces the significance of GATT and the WTO Agreements on the development of EU and consequently domestic food law.

The principle that GATT would not have legal effect in EU law was first established in *International Fruit Company*.[92] Here, the applicant queried the validity of three EU regulations that placed restrictions on the importation of apples from

---

[91] For further discussion on the complications that can be created when such agreements are entered into, see P Benyon, 'Community mutual recognition agreements, technical barriers to trade and the WTO's most favoured nation principle' (2003) 28 *European Law Review* 231.

[92] Cases 21-24/1972 *International Fruit Company NV and others v Produktschap voor Groenten en Fruit* [1972] ECR 1219.

third countries on the grounds that they were contrary to Article XI of GATT. Article XI states that:

> [n]o prohibitions or restrictions other than duties, taxes or other charges, whether made effective through quotas, import or export licences or other measures, shall be instituted or maintained by any contracting party on the importation of any product of the territory of any other contracting party or on the exportation or sale for export of any product destined for the territory of any other contracting party.

In other words, quantitative restrictions on trade between GATT contracting parties should be abolished. The three regulations at issue placed a quantitative restriction on such trade in apples.

The Court found that international law must be binding on the EU before it can be used to test the validity of EU law. International law must also confer rights on individuals before it can be relied upon before a national court. Therefore, if GATT did not create rights for individuals it could not be used by those same individuals to demonstrate that some provision of EU law was invalid. Looking at the wording of GATT and in particular the references in the preamble to 'the principle of negotiations undertaken on the basis of reciprocal and mutually advantageous arrangements', the Court found that it was a document 'characterised by the great flexibility of its provisions, in particular those conferring the possibility of derogation, the measures to be taken when confronted with exceptional difficulties and the settlement of conflicts between the contracting parties'.[93] It was further noted that the settlement of disputes involved consultation and the issuing of recommendations, with the possibility of suspending concessions granted under GATT in some circumstances. States could withdraw from GATT if dissatisfied with any recommendations made or concessions suspended.[94] These factors combined demonstrated to the Court that Article XI of GATT could not confer rights on individuals, nor could it be used to test the validity of the three 'apple regulations'.[95]

Agriculture

The WTO Agreement on Agriculture is designed to facilitate market access for agricultural products amongst Member States. It is hoped that, through a

---

[93] Ibid, para 21.

[94] It should be noted that at the time of the decision in *International Fruit Company* no procedure existed for a Member State to withdraw from its membership of the EU. This has now changed with the introduction of Art 50 TEU by the Treaty of Lisbon. It states that '[a]ny Member State may decide to withdraw from the Union in accordance with its own constitutional requirements', suggesting that the validity of this line of reasoning by the Court here is no longer effective.

[95] The same principles, on the effect of international trade agreements in the legal systems of members, that were devised by the Court in Cases 21-24/1972 *International Fruit Company*, n 92 above, continue to apply since the establishment of the WTO, even in circumstances where the WTO's Dispute Settlement Body has specifically found that the EU legislation under examination is contrary to WTO obligations. See Case C-377/2002 *Van Parys* [2005] ECR I-1465. For more on the relationship between international agreements and food law see L Vaqué and I Roda, 'The impact of international agreements on European Union food law' (2016) 11 *European Food and Feed Law Review* 130.

combination of this and the provision of supports for domestic production, as well as enabling further competition between products, the Agreement will improve the prospects of achieving international food security. There is also provision for giving special and preferential treatment to producers in developing countries, to further their prospects of achieving access to markets elsewhere and to limiting competition from imports.[96] This is to be done by, amongst other things, liberalising trade in tropical agricultural products and for those who diversify their activities away from the illicit production of narcotics.

Agriculture has really only achieved significant coverage in international trade law and regulation since the GATT Uruguay Round Negotiations of 1986–1992. Articles 3–10 of the Agreement call for Members to limit the use of export subsidies for certain agricultural products to reduce protectionism and improve competition. These provisions also call for Members to commit to reducing tariffs on international trade in food, as well as providing for more access to their markets for goods produced elsewhere. Article 9 of the Agreement specifically calls for reducing the use of direct subsidies provided to and through firms, producers, co-operative societies and national marketing boards. Indirect subsidies can also sometimes be provided through reducing transportation costs, for example, for exporters. This should be minimised. Article 12, in accordance with Article XI of GATT, permits the placing of prohibitions or restrictions on the exportation of food, but only where there has been due consideration taken for the food security of the importing state. One of main reasons as to why agriculture received relatively little coverage during the GATT years 1947–1994 was that the Contracting Parties could not agree on many aspects of international trade regulation for this sector, such as the use of tariffs, quotas and subsidies. To reach a compromise on this, the WTO Agreement on Agriculture contains a 'peace clause' in Article 13, which provides that States should refrain from raising disputes on subsidies and similar issues for an initial period of nine years. They should also exercise 'due restraint' on actions relating to such support measures indefinitely. One of the key criticisms of the Agreement on Agriculture is that it is incomprehensible in places and is difficult to implement properly.[97]

Technical Barriers to Trade

The WTO Agreement on Technical Barriers to Trade (TBT) covers all products, including agricultural products.[98] Article 2 of the Agreement provides that WTO Members must take a series of considerations into account when drafting national technical standards, designed to minimise the impact that these requirements

---

[96] Through the use of Art 15 of the Agreement on Agriculture in particular.

[97] For further discussion on this point and for more analysis on the Agreement on Agriculture more generally, see B O'Connor, 'A note on the need for more clarity in the World Trade Organization Agreement on Agriculture' (2003) 37 *Journal of World Trade* 839.

[98] TBT Agreement, Art 1(3).

can have on the free flow of international trade in goods. Members are obliged to refrain from creating unnecessary obstacles to trade, except where this may be required to protect national security, prevent deception or protect health or the environment. Technical standards should only be introduced by Members where these are shown to be necessary and they should be withdrawn when no longer required. Members must be able to justify the existence of a national standard when requested by another Member. When standards are introduced, they should be based on the performance of the product and not, where it can be avoided, on its appearance or description. Members are also obliged to recognise that similar standards of other Members are equivalent to their own, where both sets achieve the same objective. Most significantly for the liberalisation of international trade in food, the TBT Agreement makes it clear that internationally set standards should be deemed to be the norm where these exist or where their completion is imminent. If a national standard is equivalent to a set international standard, it is to be presumed that it is in compliance with TBT obligations. The codes and guidelines for food which are set by the Codex Alimentarius Commission, which are discussed in more detail below, are recognised as a relevant international standard for this purpose.[99]

WTO Members are obliged to adhere to a notification procedure when introducing a new national technical standard that both differs from the international norm and is likely to affect international trade in some way. The new technical standard should be publicised or published in an appropriate place, preferably prior to introduction. The Member State should also provide others with copies of the new technical standard when requested, as well as clearly identifying those parts of the standard which differ from international guidelines. Other Members should also be facilitated in making comments on the proposed new national standard.

Article 4 of the TBT Agreement requires Members to comply with the Code of Good Practice when preparing, adopting and applying national standards. The Code itself is set out in Annex 3 to the Agreement. The Code mostly reiterates the points made in Article 2 of the Agreement on technical regulations, such as those referring to the use of internationally set requirements as the basis for national standards. It also sets out further stipulations on the notification procedure and acceptance of comments from other Members on proposed new standards. As with other WTO Agreements, there is special provision for the position of developing and least-developed WTO Members, such as allowing these States to deviate from international norms when necessary for the protection of their own domestic production.[100]

---

[99] This was certified to be the case by the Dispute Panel and Appellate Body in DS 231, *European Communities – Trade Description of Sardines*.

[100] TBT Agreement, Art 12.

Sanitary and Phytosanitary Measures

The WTO Agreement on the Application of Sanitary and Phytosanitary Measures enables Members to adopt and implement provisions for the protection of the health of humans, animals and plants. It has become an increasingly significant agreement for EU Member States, such as Ireland, since the White Paper on Food Safety brought about significant change in policy direction after its publication in 2000. The increased use of the precautionary principle and the impact of scientific developments have added to this significance. The terms of the SPS Agreement must be considered before science-based or precautionary measures are introduced in the interests of food safety.

SPS measures are an impediment to international trade. They should not, therefore, be introduced by WTO Members in an arbitrary way, nor should they be used as a disguised restriction on trade that offers little or no obvious benefit for health or environmental protection. As a result, the Agreement is set out in a way that permits these trade-restricting measures to be introduced, but within tight parameters that oblige those introducing them to do so exclusively based on supporting scientific evaluation of probable risk to human, animal or plant health. As with other WTO Agreements, such as that on Technical Barriers to Trade, there is a general acceptance within the terms of the SPS Agreement that existing international standards on safety or risk minimisation should be deemed the norm. Compliance, therefore, with the standards of bodies such as the Codex Alimentarius Commission, the World Organisation for Animal Health (formerly the International Office of Epizootics) or the Food and Agriculture Organization (FAO) run International Plant Protection Convention is usually deemed to be compliance with SPS obligations as well. The primary obligation set out in the SPS Agreement is that Members should base their own food safety measures on appropriate risk assessments.

As stated, WTO Members have the right to adopt SPS measures. However, this is limited to those measures which are consistent with the other parts of the Agreement and only to the extent that is absolutely necessary to protect health.[101] These other provisions that must be complied with include basing domestic requirements on international standards and guidelines where appropriate,[102] accepting the standards of other States as being equivalent to domestic requirements where an appropriate level of protection has been demonstrated,[103] basing measures on an appropriate risk assessment that minimises the negative effects of this on trade,[104] and providing prompt notification of any new measures

---

[101] Ibid, Art 2.

[102] Ibid, Art 3.

[103] Art 4. However, the European Court of Justice held in Case C-432/1992 *R v Minister of Agriculture, Fisheries and Food, ex parte Anastasiou* [1994] ECR I-3087 that this demonstration must be made by the presentation of certificates issued exclusively by national competent authorities. For further discussion on this, see M Cremona, 'Case C-432/92 *R v Minister of Agriculture*' (1996) 33 *Common Market Law Review* 125.

[104] SPS Agreement, Art 5.

introduced to all other Members through the appropriate channels.[105] The Agreement also permits the introduction of precautionary measures where the scientific evidence concerning a potential risk is inconclusive, but sufficient.

The SPS Agreement can impact upon Irish and European Union food law in several ways. The most obvious is the general obligation that new measures introduced should be based on international guidelines. Individual Members, such as Ireland, or free trade areas, such as the EU, must provide reasons for the taking of any action or the introduction of any measures that are not based on such international standards.[106] Where national or EU SPS measures are introduced or applied they are also, of course, subject to the scrutiny of the Dispute Settlement Body of the WTO where another Member raises a complaint. This has most famously happened in both the *Hormones Dispute*,[107] and later in the *GMO Dispute*.[108] In the former, the United States and Canada claimed that the EU had failed to comply with its SPS obligations, amongst other complaints, by the introduction of a directive which banned the use of hormones in meat production.[109] In particular, it was argued that the introduction of this legislation was contrary to Articles 3 and 5 of the Agreement in that the content of the directive was not in accordance with existing international guidelines, nor was its introduction supported by an appropriate scientific risk assessment. Both the Panel and the Appellate Body of the WTO's Dispute Settlement Body found that the risk assessment was inadequate and that the measures adopted deviated from internationally accepted standards. The introduction of this directive by the EU was thus deemed to be action that was contrary to SPS Agreement obligations. Compensation was offered by the EU as a resolution to the dispute as it did not believe that it would be in the interests of its Member States to repeal the ban on hormone use. Ultimately, however, concessions were suspended to the tune of nearly $130 million. The EU responded by introducing a new directive on the matter in 2003,[110] which it claimed was based on a full and appropriate risk assessment.[111] The *GMOs Dispute*, which also deals

[105] Ibid, Art 7.

[106] Ibid, Art 5(8).

[107] DS 26 and DS 48, *European Communities – Measures Concerning Meat and Meat Products*. For an early critique on the *Hormones Dispute* see R Quick and A Blüthner, 'Has the Appellate Body erred? An appraisal and criticism of the ruling in the WTO *Hormones Case*' (1999) 2 *Journal of International Economic Law* 603.

[108] DS 291, 292 and 293, *Measures Affecting the Approval and Marketing of Biotech Products*.

[109] Directive 1996/22/EC concerning the prohibition on the use in stockfarming of certain substances having a hormonal or thyrostatic action [1996] OJ L 125/3, transposed into Irish law by the Control of Animal Remedies and their Residues Regulations 1998, SI No 507/1998. Originally prohibited by the introduction of Council Directive 1981/602/EEC of 31 July 1981 concerning the prohibition of certain substances having a hormonal action and of any substances having a thyrostatic action [1981] OJ L 222/32. This ban is discussed in more detail in Ch 6.

[110] Directive 2003/74/EC of the European Parliament and of the Council of 22 September 2003 amending Council Directive 1996/22/EC concerning the prohibition on the use in stockfarming of certain substances having a hormonal or thyrostatic action and of beta-agonists [2003] OJ L 262/17.

[111] The complainants disagreed with this, however, resulting in another dispute process being initiated, DS 320 and DS 321, *Continued Suspension of Obligations in the EC – Hormones Dispute*. This was ultimately resolved in November 2008.

with the application of the SPS Agreement at EU and national level, is discussed in more detail in chapter ten. In both cases, action taken at EU and consequently Member State level had to be reversed or modified to bring it into compliance with SPS obligations. There has traditionally been widespread objection at EU Member State level, including in Ireland, to the use of both hormones and genetic modification in food production. However, international obligations, such as those arising out of the application of the WTO SPS Agreement, means that individual States and regional blocs are limited in the action that they can take to satisfy the objectors in such circumstances. Public or political objection to the use of certain practices in agriculture is not enough to warrant the implementation of any trade-restricting national measures designed to appease this. Any such measures must be based on scientific evidence indicating that there is a real or potential risk to health.[112]

Intellectual Property Protection

The WTO Agreement on Trade-Related Aspects of Intellectual Property Rights (TRIPs) has also been used to call into question the validity of EU and national law, ultimately compelling the EU to modify its existing legislation to bring it into line with the obligations set out in TRIPs. Articles 22–24 of the TRIPs Agreement are of particular relevance for food law. Article 22(2) provides that:

> [i]n respect of geographical indications, members shall provide the legal means for interested parties to prevent ... the use of any means in the designation or presentation of a good that indicates or suggests that the good in question originates in a geographical area other than the true place of origin in a manner which misleads the public as to the geographical origin of the good.

'Geographical indications' are defined in the TRIPs Agreement as being those which 'identify a good as originating in the territory of a Member ... where a given quality, reputation or other characteristic of the good is essentially attributable to its geographical origin'.[113] WTO Members are obliged, under the terms of Article 22(3) of the TRIPs Agreement, to refuse or invalidate the registration of a trademark which uses a geographical indication for goods that have not originated in the place suggested by this. Article 23 provides additional protection for geographical indications used for wines or spirits. Members should provide legal protection for interested parties who seek to prevent the use of a geographical indication for wines that do not originate in the place that their name suggests. The application of these provisions has been problematic. WTO Members have proved reluctant to de-register trademarks containing geographical indications for those goods which have traditionally used them, despite their lack of association with

---

[112] For more detailed discussion on the relationship between the SPS Agreement and regulation of the food sector see A Alemanno, *Trade in Food: Regulatory and Judicial Approaches in the EC and the WTO* (London, Cameron May, 2007) 239–290.

[113] TRIPs Agreement, Art 22(1).

the place used in their name. Article 24 is significant in this regard. It provides the possibility for further negotiations in this area, on both a bilateral and a multilateral basis, with a view to establishing lists of protected names that could be applied internationally.

As is discussed in more detail in Chapter 8, the EU originally developed a system for the registration of protected geographical indications and protected designations of origin in 1992.[114] Both the USA and Australia took issue with the fact that the EU Regulation did not offer protection for non-EU registered geographical indications and trademarks.[115] It was also very difficult, under the terms of the Regulation, for non-EU applicants to access the protection process established. Complaints were brought under Articles 22 and 24 of the TRIPs Agreement. It was also claimed that the perceived shortcomings with the EU Regulation contravened the general principles set out in Articles I–III of GATT, designed to ensure 'most favoured nation' and 'national treatment' status for producers or their representatives from third countries. These two important principles of international trade law are explained further in this chapter.

It was accepted by the parties to the *Geographical Indications Dispute* that the 1992 Regulation and the procedures that it established, were designed to fulfil a legitimate objective of the EU. It was felt, however, that the failure to facilitate applicants from third countries made the Regulation more restrictive on international trade than that which was necessary to achieve the stated aim. The Dispute Settlement Body Panel found that the EU had failed to provide for national treatment in that it had provided a privileged status for applicants from within its own Member States. It identified two problems with the original geographical indications regulation. The first was that geographical indications originating in a third country could only be registered for protected status in the EU, if the law of the third country provided equivalent protection for its own products there and also gave reciprocal protection for EU foodstuffs traded in that State. This was very limiting. It essentially meant that there would only be protection available for products in the EU where the State in which the food was produced had a system for registering food names that was as well developed as that established by the 1992 Regulation.[116] The second problem identified by the Panel was that even where access was provided to applicants from third countries, it was further restricted by another requirement set out in the Regulation. This provided that

---

[114] Regulation 2081/1992 of 14 July 1992 on the protection of geographical indications and designations of origin for agricultural products and foodstuffs [1992] OJ L 208/1. This established a mechanism for the registration of food products that possess characteristics or qualities that are related to their original area and/or method of production. Once registered, the protected food name could only be used by producers who were based within a defined geographical area and who were making the product using defined ingredients and/or production methods. Generic food names are not eligible for protection under this scheme. As stated, this is all discussed in much more detail in Ch 8.

[115] DS 174 and DS 290, *EC Protection of Trademarks and Geographical Indications for Agricultural Products and Foodstuffs*. For further discussion on the Dispute see M Handler, 'The WTO Geographical Indications Dispute' (2006) 69 *Modern Law Review* 70.

[116] See Reg 2081/1992, n 114 above.

the State must have inspection systems in place that were at least equivalent to those operating in the EU Member States, before any applications for protection, or objections to the registration of EU names, would even be considered. It was agreed that the EU would modify its legislation to reflect these findings.[117] It did this through the introduction of two new regulations in 2006.[118] The Preamble to the revised Protected Food Names Regulation recognised the significance of the TRIPs Agreement for the content and application of EU food laws. It was accepted that the obligations set out in this Agreement would require that EU law would facilitate the protection of geographical indications from third countries where they were also protected in their country of origin. It also meant that the EU registration process would have to operate in a manner that would enable those with legitimate interests from third countries to object to the registration of a name in the EU. These recognitions were reflected in the introduction of a new Article 5 (registration open to applicants from third countries) and a new Article 7 (objections to registrations possible for interested parties from third countries who lodge a duly substantiated claim with the Commission) into the Protected Food Names Regulation. The PDO/PGI registration system was thus properly opened up to applicants and objectors from third countries for the first time. This was as a direct result of the proper application of the TRIPs Agreement to the provisions of EU law.

General Agreement on Tariffs and Trade

There are several provisions of the General Agreement on Tariffs and Trade (GATT) that should be mentioned at this point. The two most obvious are the general principles of most favoured nation and national treatment, set out in Articles I and II and III respectively and which have been outlined above. These form the basis for all the WTO Agreements discussed above. Article 2 of the TBT Agreement, for example, provides that:

> [m]embers shall ensure that in respect of technical regulations, products imported from the territory of any Member shall be accorded treatment no less favourable than that accorded to like products of national origin and to like products originating in any other country.

---

[117] Under the terms of Art 21(3)(b) of the WTO Dispute Settlement Understanding, which provides that the parties to a dispute must find a resolution within 45 days of the adoption of recommendations by the DSB, it was agreed that the EU would have 11½ months to amend the 1992 Regulations to avoid the need for concessions to be suspended or compensation to be paid.

[118] Council Regulation 509/2006 of 20 March 2006 on agricultural products and foodstuffs as traditional specialities guaranteed [2006] OJ L 93/1 and Council Regulation (EC) No 510/2006 of 20 March 2006 on the protection of geographical indications and designations of origin for agricultural products and foodstuffs [2006] OJ L 93/12. These Regulations have since been replaced by Regulation (EU) No 1151/2012 of the European Parliament and of the Council of 21 November 2012 on quality schemes for agricultural products and foodstuffs [2012] OJ L 343/1.

Other specific provisions of GATT which are potentially significant for international traders in food include Article XI on quantitative restrictions. This provides that:

> [n]o prohibitions or restrictions other than duties, taxes or other charges, whether made effective through quotas, import or export licences or other measures, shall be instituted or maintained by any contracting party on the importation of any product of the territory of any other contracting party or the exportation or sale for export of any product destined for the territory of any other contracting party.

There are some exceptions to this general obligation to eliminate quantitative restrictions on international trade, such as where this is necessary for the temporary prevention or relief of shortages of foodstuffs, or where used to deal with a surplus of domestically produced agricultural or fisheries products. However, where any contracting party to GATT uses one of these, or any other permitted exemptions, it must first provide public notice of the details of any quantitative restriction imposed. Other States will then, of course, have an opportunity to object to such action being taken.

Article IX of GATT also provides for the application of the principle of most favoured nation in the setting of national requirements on origin markings. It states that where domestic regulation on the use of origin marks is applied, this should only be done with full consideration of 'the difficulties and inconveniences which such measures may cause to the commerce and industry of exporting countries'. The provision accepts that while labelling disclosures on the origin of products may be required in some circumstances to protect consumers against fraudulent or misleading indications, the inconvenience that this may cause to importers should be kept to a minimum. There is also a call in Article XI of GATT for the Contracting Parties to co-operate with each other with a view to preventing the use of trade names that may misrepresent the true origin of a product to the detriment of distinctive regional or geographical names. This has obvious implications for international trade in food, where a producer uses a name for his product which suggests or implies that it has an association with another, already well-known product, that is internationally recognised for its quality or distinguishing characteristics, as has been the case, for example, with American 'Champagne' and Canadian 'Parma' ham.[119]

---

[119] Use of the designation 'Champagne' for American sparkling wines, in particular those produced in California, or those produced in other parts of France or Europe outside the Champagne region has been problematic for some time. Efforts were made to resolve this and other issues by the introduction of the Madrid Agreement Concerning the International Registration of Marks in 1891, which made it possible to protect registered marks across all contracting states. However, while many states signed up to the Madrid Agreement, the United States did not do so until 2003. In addition to this, the Treaty of Versailles, settling the terms at the end of the First World War, provided in Art 275 thereof that states must respect recognised regional regulations for wines or spirits. Again, this provision did not apply in the United States as the Senate there never formally ratified the Treaty. While the matter relating specifically to Californian Champagne was finally settled in 2005, this settlement does not apply to those producers who were already marketing their products using this designation at this time. There is further interesting discussion on this at vinepair.com.

Other provisions of GATT which have the potential to impact upon international trade in food include Article V. This provides for freedom of transit for importers, with access to the most convenient transportation routes to be provided. Article VI of GATT is designed to limit the use of 'dumping', or the sale of imported goods at less than their normal value, in international trade. It sets out how goods are to be valued for customs purposes when traded internationally, which can, of course, have an impact on the level of import duties payable and the consequent effect that this can then have on the ability of imports to compete with domestic foodstuffs. Finally, Article XXIV deals with the application of GATT to free trade areas, such as the EU. It states that nothing in GATT should prevent the formation of customs unions and free trade areas.

2.3.2. Codex Alimentarius Commission

The United Nations Food and Agriculture Organization and the World Health Organization have combined to run the Codex Alimentarius Commission. This organisation, which was formed in 1963, exists to devise international standards and guidelines for food. These can be both horizontal, applying to all foods across a set theme (eg nutrition labelling) or they can be vertical, applying to a specific food or food type, such as canned fruits, desiccated coconut, frog legs or cheese.[120] Codex Standards are international and they can influence both national and EU food laws where they are used as the basis for legally binding compositional or safety requirements, or where they are considered to be the recognised benchmark in international trade regulation. As was noted above, Codex standards are directly referred to in the WTO Agreement on Sanitary and Phytosanitary Measures as setting the basis by which the validity of all national food safety stipulations will be judged. Compliance with Codex usually infers compliance with SPS obligations. Membership of the Codex Alimentarius Commission now covers 99 per cent of the world's population. Each Member appoints a contact point for dealing with Codex matters. The designated Codex contact point for Ireland is the Department of Agriculture, Food and the Marine. The rules of procedure for the Codex Alimentarius Commission are set out in the Procedural Manual, the most recent of which (edition 25) was published in 2016.[121] It sets out, amongst other things, the Codex Statutes, General Principles (primarily protecting consumers' health and ensuring fair practices in the food trade), definitions (such as those for 'food', 'additives', 'pesticides', 'traceability', etc.), details on risk analysis, subsidiary bodies of the Commission, membership and relations with other organisations, such as standardisation bodies and non-governmental organisations.

---

[120] For more on Codex standards see C Downes, 'Only a footnote? The curious Codex battle for control of additive regulations' (2012) 7 *European Food and Feed Law Review* 232.

[121] Codex Alimentarius Commission, Procedural manual, 25th edition, Rome, 2016. ISBN: 9789251093627.

Codex Standards have had a direct bearing in several important free movement of food cases that have come before the European Court of Justice.[122] They have been used to gauge whether EU Member States could potentially continue to apply national compositional requirements by making a demonstration that they were in accordance with those set by Codex. They have also formed the basis for new EU legislation, directly applicable at national level. A good example of this can be seen in the introduction of the EU Nutrition and Health Claims Regulation in 2006.[123] This is discussed in more detail in Chapter 7. Codex Standards, more generally, are referred to where relevant throughout this book.

2.3.3. Other International Organisations

There are really two different categories of international organisation that can have a bearing on national food law. The first of these deals specifically and almost exclusively with food, such as the Codex Alimentarius Commission. This type of organisation drafts codes and guidelines which may be used as a template for EU and subsequently national law. This is a two-way relationship. Existing EU and national requirements can also have an influence on the content of international standards, as many of these are drawn from what is already common practice amongst Members. The second category contains generic international organisations. They do not deal specifically or exclusively with food but this does come within their remit, either directly or indirectly (eg inter-state organisations such as the World Health Organization and the World Intellectual Property Organization). They issue generic guidelines and advice, which may relate to food on occasions. They can have an influence on national law and particularly on national policy. This is discussed in more detail below.

United Nations Agencies: World Health Organization and Food and Agriculture Organization

The World Health Organization co-ordinates and directs health policy within the United Nations. It does this by setting guidelines, standards and policies in a range of areas, including those aspects of health protection that relate to food. This can include preventing the emergence or spread of disease, as well as the formulation of guidance on good dietary practice. By 2018 there were 195 WHO members. Many WHO reports on the latter are subsequently used, at least in a persuasive

---

[122] Such as Case 298/1987 *Proceedings for Compulsory Reconstruction against Smanor SA* [1988] ECR 4489 and Case 286/1986, *Ministère Public v Gérard Deserbais* [1988] ECR 4907.

[123] Regulation (EC) No 1924/2006 of the European Parliament and of the Council of 20 December 2006 on nutrition and health claims made on foods [2007] OJ L 12/3, as applied in Irish law by the European Union (Nutrition and Health Claims made on Foods) Regulations 2014, SI No 11/2014.

way, in the adoption of national policies and guidance. This has been the case, for example, in relation to WHO advice on the prevention of being overweight and/or obese. The WHO has issued a series of guidelines in this area, including those on sugar intake for adults and children in 2014. This document and the related consultation process has suggested that people are consuming too much sugar in their diet and that this should usually be halved, reducing it to 5 per cent of daily total calorie intake, or roughly 25 g per day for an adult.

Since 2007 all members of the WHO have been bound by the revised International Health Regulations. These are designed to assist the international community, including Ireland, to prevent and respond to public health risks that could potentially cross borders, such as the outbreak of food-borne illness and disease. The Regulations oblige the WHO Members to report and respond to such disease outbreaks and public health events. The Agreement is legally binding and was to be implemented by June 2012, although most States agreed a two-year extension to this deadline. Some, albeit limited, further extensions may also be granted. While the Regulations do apply to public health emergencies in general, there is specific reference to food-related issues in their terms. They also designate the Food and Agriculture Organization as the competent inter-governmental organisation with which the WHO must co-operate and co-ordinate its activities where appropriate.

The Food and Agriculture Organization (FAO) is also a United Nations body, established between 1943 and 1945 towards the end and in the immediate aftermath of the Second World War. It was designed initially to deal with ongoing food shortages which had become a feature of the preceding war years. The achievement of food security is still the key objective of the FAO. 'Food security' was defined at the World Food Summit 1996 as existing 'when all people at all times have access to sufficient, safe, nutritious food to maintain a healthy and active life'. The FAO now has a broader remit. This includes the sustainable management and utilisation of natural resources, including land, water, air and climate. The FAO is driven by five stated strategic objectives. These are: helping to eliminate hunger, food insecurity and malnutrition; making agriculture, forestry and fisheries more productive and sustainable; reducing rural poverty; enabling inclusive and efficient agricultural and food systems; and increasing the resilience of food and agricultural systems to natural disasters. These objectives are to be achieved through the implementation of action plans, involving the devising of agreements, codes and standards with States, the collection, analysing and sharing of agricultural data and facilitating policy dialogue at global, regional and State levels. The FAO regularly publishes the results of its expertise and findings on a range of issues, such as the use of additives in food production, approaches to sustainable fishing and making adaptations to agriculture in response to climate change.

As discussed above, the WHO and the FAO share responsibility for the operation of the Codex Alimentarius Commission. They also jointly operate the International Food Safety Authorities Network (INFOSAN) designed to link national food safety authorities across UN Member States to bring about the best possible responses to food safety emergencies. This alert and emergency response system has been used, for example, in the recall of products, such as milk whey protein concentrate, which were found to be contaminated with potentially dangerous bacteria. It was also engaged in the aftermath of the Great East Japan earthquake and tsunami in 2011. It provided an assessment of the potential for this natural disaster and related nuclear fallout to present risks to human health, were the food supply to be contaminated. The network, which originated out of the Codex Alimentarius *Principles and Guidelines for the Exchange of Information in Food Control Emergency Situations* and which has been in existence since 2004, has 186 member states. Each has a designated contact point for communication between the national food safety authorities and the INFOSAN secretariat in cases of emergency. The contact point depends on the nature of the emergency. Each Member can nominate several. INFOSAN is alerted to potential emergencies in a number of ways (eg by reference from either the national contact points of the Member States, its own monitoring in conjunction with the WHO Alert and Response Operations Programme, or by working with the Global Outbreak Alert and Response Network and the Global Early Warning System for Major Animal Diseases, including zoonotic diseases).

World Intellectual Property Organization

The World Intellectual Property Organization (WIPO) provides a global forum for dealing with the international protection of rights attached to copyright, trademarks, patents and, most importantly from a food law perspective, geographical names. WIPO, which was established in 1967, has 189 member states, with a headquarters in Geneva and external offices in New York, Tokyo, Singapore and Rio de Janeiro. Around 250 non-governmental organisations and inter-governmental organisations also have official observer status at WIPO meetings. The work of WIPO is shaped by nine strategic goals, developed by the members in 2009. These include the co-ordination and development of global intellectual property infrastructure, providing a world reference source for intellectual property information and analysis, building respect for intellectual property protection and the operation of a responsive communications interface between WIPO, its member states and all stakeholders.

The protection of geographical food names takes place at both EU level, through the application of the relevant regulations[124] and at international level, through the application of the WTO TRIPs Agreement, as discussed above. WIPO does not have any direct control over the protection of these protected indications and designations of origin. It does, however, have a direct role to play in the protection of geographical names in other ways.

---

[124] See Reg 1151/2012, n 118 above.

First, WIPO operates the Standing Committee on the Law of Trademarks, Industrial Designs and Geographical Indications. This provides a forum for WIPO member states to discuss policy and legal issues relating to the development of the law in this area, at both regional and global levels.

Second, WIPO organises a biennial international symposium on geographical indications, bringing together governments, producer representatives and legal specialists for discussion on the development of national and international law in this area.

The third way in which WIPO has a direct role to play in the protection of geographical names is through the administration of the Lisbon Agreement for the Protection of Appellations of Origin and their International Registration. This was devised in 1958, revised and amended in 1967 and again in 1979. These establish the International Register of Appellations of Origin. Any country which is party to the Paris Convention for the Protection of Industrial Property can accede to the Lisbon Agreement. Those countries which adhere to the provisions of the Lisbon Agreement are also members of the Lisbon Union Assembly. There are, however, only 28 contracting parties to the Lisbon Agreement. These include France, Italy, Greece and Portugal. Other states which are party to the Agreement include Bulgaria, Burkina Faso, Costa Rica, South Korea and Macedonia.

The Lisbon Agreement provides that all parties to it must undertake to protect the appellations of origin of the other Assembly countries which have been registered at the International Bureau of Intellectual Property.[125] An 'appellation of origin' is defined in the Agreement as:

> the geographical denomination of a country, region or locality, which serves to designate a product originating therein, the quality or characteristics of which are due exclusively or essentially to the geographical environment, including natural or human factors.[126]

Protection of these appellations of origin is to be ensured 'against any usurpation or imitation, even if the true origin of the product is indicated [or is] accompanied by terms such as kind, type, make [or] imitation'.[127]

One of the major difficulties with the operation of the Lisbon Agreement system is that States can make a declaration that they are unable to protect an appellation of origin, a so-called 'declaration of refusal'.[128] Another problem with the system is that the name must first have been formally registered for protection in the country of origin. This means that the system is, in reality, only open to applicants from those States where such a formalised legal procedure is in place.

The main difficulty with the system, however, is how few States have signed up to its commitments. Neither the USA, China, Canada, Australia or Japan

---

[125] Lisbon Agreement, Art 1(2). The International Bureau is listed in the Convention establishing the World Intellectual Property Organization.
[126] Ibid, Art 2(1).
[127] Ibid, Art 3.
[128] Ibid, Art 5(3).

are members. Ireland is not a member. Nor is the UK. However, as noted above, some other EU Member States are. Protected appellations of origin cannot become legally generic in the country of origin.[129] They can also only remain protected internationally, amongst Lisbon signatories, for as long as they are similarly protected in the country of origin. Examples of appellations of origin registered under the Lisbon system include tequila, limiting the area of production for this to the territory of Jalisco in Mexico, Costa Rican bananas, Parmigiano-Reggiano and certain types of regionally produced olive oil. Around 900 products, many of which are foodstuffs, have been registered under the Lisbon Agreement. It has not, however, been as influential at international level as was intended. As will be discussed later in this book, this is due to the fact the different systems for protection now operate at EU and national levels. This has significantly reduced the need for an international protection system like the WIPO-operated Lisbon Agreement.

National Non-Governmental Organisations

There are several non-governmental organisations and umbrella bodies operating in Ireland which can influence the application of food law and the development of policy. These include the organisation 'Love Irish Food', established in 2009. Importantly, from a legal perspective, this body is member-funded. Given that its remit is the promotion of Irish food and drink brands to, primarily Irish, consumers, the body could not be State-funded. If it were, then its model of promotion would likely be deemed contrary to European Union rules on the free movement of goods. The previous 'Buy Irish' campaign, which was State-funded and mostly State-controlled, was found by the European Court of Justice to be a measure equivalent to a quantitative restriction on imports, as prohibited by Article 34 TFEU – primarily because it used State resources to promote Irish goods to the detriment of imports from other EU Member States.[130] This case and measures equivalent to quantitative restrictions on trade more generally, are dealt with in more detail in Chapter 4 below.

Food and Drink Industry Ireland (FDII) is the primary trade association for the sector. It was established to represent the interests of food and drink manufacturers and suppliers in three areas: consumer foods and beverages; dairy; and meat. FDII has an important role to play in the development and application of food laws at both Irish and EU levels. It exercises this role in several ways. Primarily, it organises a regulatory affairs service, which provides members with assistance on new legislative developments. In many cases it would be difficult for producers and suppliers to keep abreast of all these developments given the sheer volume of initiatives that are introduced, mainly by EU legislators, on an annual basis.

---

[129] Ibid, Art 6.
[130] Case 249/1981, *Commission v Ireland* [1982] ECR 4005.

The provision of such a service assists is avoiding accidental non-compliance with these ever-changing legal requirements. In addition to this, FDII also represents the interests of the sector to the Irish Government, playing a key role in consultation and implementation processes. Finally, FDII also plays a role in the EU legislative process by its contributions to and membership of FoodDrinkEurope, the latter being the primary consultative body representing the industry at European and international levels. FDII has a similar position in Ireland, where it liaises with the Food Safety Authority of Ireland, the Department of Agriculture and Food and the Department of Health and Children on policy matters affecting the food and drinks sector.

Consumers in Ireland are represented by several non-governmental organisations, in a variety of ways. Efficient Consumer Response (ECR Ireland) was established in 1998 to promote effective and efficient relations between industry providers and recipients. It is also a member of ECR Europe – now called 'ECR Community'. The Consumers' Association of Ireland was formed in 1966 to promote consumers' interests, including by making representations to government, State agencies and industry. It also interacts with the work of European consumer bodies, such as the European Consumers' Organisation (BEUC) and the European Consumer Voice in Standardisation (ANEC).

There are plenty of other organisations in operation in Ireland, representing different parts of the food and drinks industry. These include, for example, the Association of Irish Farmhouse Cheesemakers (Cáis), whose stated aims include to 'act as representatives of the industry with the various government departments and agencies'. There is also the Irish Breakfast Cereal Association (IBCA), which was established in 1992 'to represent the interests of the Irish breakfast cereal and oat milling industry at both national and European level'. The aims and objectives of these non-governmental interest groups often come into conflict with each other as they seek different outcomes from the same regulatory processes.

Several organisations are linked specifically to the alcoholic drinks industry. This includes the Irish Brewers Association (IBA) and the more recently established Irish Cider Association (ICA) – both of which also come under the umbrella of the Alcohol Beverage Federation of Ireland.

Organisations may also be established to campaign on a single issue, as is the case for Drinkaware. While funded directly by the alcohol industry, the stated vision of the campaign is to create '[a]n Ireland where alcohol is not misused'. Whether it assists in achieving this is open to debate. This is discussed in more detail in Chapter 9. A vast range of interests must usually be accommodated in the creation and application of new food laws at both European Union and national levels.

3

Key Actors in Irish Food Law

3.1. Introduction

Several government departments have a role to play in the devising, implementation and enforcement of food law and policy. The most significant of these is the Department of Agriculture, Food and the Marine. As will be seen throughout this book, this government department has a crucial role to play in most areas of food law and is the responsible national authority for overseeing the majority of the EU legislative initiatives that must be applied at national level. The Department of Health and the Department of Communications, Climate Action and the Environment also have key roles to play.

Most of the significant enforcement of food law comes at the local level, through the operations of the designated competent authorities. It is the individual units and officers of these authorities that interact directly with the food business operators, ensuring compliance with the regulatory requirements and acting where these standards have not been met. State agencies, most notably the Food Safety Authority of Ireland (FSAI), also have a crucial practical role to play in protecting the public from risks to their health which may arise from the consumption of unsafe food. They carry out this function through the provision of advice and recommendations and the taking of action, based on the findings of others or arising out of their own risk assessments or investigations. The Food Safety Authority also has an increasing role to play in the development of national policy, including through its representation of the government on food safety and standards issues in the EU and its working relationship with the European Food Safety Authority (EFSA).

3.2. Government Departments

3.2.1. Department of Agriculture, Food and the Marine

As mentioned, the Department of Agriculture, Food and the Marine has most of the responsibility for the oversight of law and policy on primary food production and many related environmental and rural issues. This includes ensuring the proper implementation of national and EU food-related legislation on sustainable development, the rural environment, farming, fisheries and animal health. It also usually represents the State in EU and international negotiations on food matters. It administers assistance through the operation of schemes such as the EU's Common Agricultural Policy (CAP).[1] The Head Office of the Department is on Kildare Street in Dublin. It also has several regional and local offices based in Cavan, Cork, Donegal, Galway, Naas, Leitrim, Navan, Roscommon and Portlaoise.

The key roles of the Department of Agriculture are discussed in more detail, as and when appropriate, throughout this book. In more general terms, its main functions that are directly related to food law include being the primary determinant of policy development, coupled with its stated role in EU and international negotiations. Most significantly, it also oversees, in a variety of ways, controls over food safety – especially at the primary production stage, animal welfare verification and plant health protection. It also directs State bodies related to the sector. There are twelve State bodies which come under the control of the Department of Agriculture. These include the Aquaculture Licences Appeals Board, Bord Bia, Bord Iascaigh Mhara, the Marine Institute, the National Milk Agency, the Sea-fisheries Protection Authority, Teagasc and the Veterinary Council of Ireland.

3.2.2. Department of Health

Other government departments have a less obvious, but still significant role to play in the formulation and application of food policy and law. The Department of Health, for example, is active in promoting good public health, through the development of strategies on countering obesity, alcohol abuse, food safety and nutrition-related disease. While the Department of Agriculture, Food and the Marine is charged with exercising control over primary production on farms or agricultural holdings, the Department of Health deals with other important food safety and consumer protection matters such as those related to labelling and claims, fortification, genetic modification, hygiene, official controls, novel foods and contaminants. National legislative initiatives, such as those introduced under the Public Health (Alcohol) Bill 2015, were devised by this Department. This Bill is discussed in much more detail in Chapter 9.

Apart from introducing new national legislation, the opportunities for which are already limited by the well-documented constraints of EU membership, the Department of Health plays a vital role in the enforcement of food laws in Ireland. This is normally carried out on behalf of the department by agencies and authorities, most notably the Health Service Executive (HSE) and the Food Safety Authority of Ireland. Although it is an independent body, the FSAI comes under

---

[1] All beneficiaries of CAP funding in Ireland must be published on an annual basis following the introduction of Article 111 of Regulation (EU) No 1306/2013 of the European Parliament and of the Council of 17 December 2013 on the financing, management and monitoring of the common agricultural policy and repealing Council Regulations (EEC) No 352/1978, (EC) No 165/1994, (EC) No 2799/1998, (EC) No 814/2000, (EC) No 1290/2005 and (EC) No 485/2008, [2013] OJ L 347/549.

the aegis of the Minister for Health. The department also oversees the development of policy in food-related areas of health protection, such as the new Obesity Policy and Action Plan, the consultation for which was launched in April 2015, resulting in the publication of a series of action points and recommendations in late 2016.[2] The plan is discussed in more detail in Chapter 9 below.

3.2.3. Department of Communications, Climate Action and the Environment

Formerly the Department of Communications, Energy and Natural Resources, the rebranded Department of Communications, Climate Action and the Environment took on a range of new functions from July 2016. This included broadening its remit to include policies and activities related to European Union and international measures designed to combat climate change and to promote protection of the environment. The department is assisted in this regard by the bodies such as the Environmental Protection Agency (EPA). More detail on the role of the EPA in the application of food law is provided in the State Agencies section below. However, it should be noted at this stage that the agency is the designated competent authority for dealing with aspects of the use of genetically modified organisms (GMOs) in Ireland.

To explain this further, EU legislation provides that initial applications for the deliberate release (eg commercial growth or use in foodstuffs) and contained use (primarily for research purposes) must be made to designated competent authorities where the GMO is to be used or released for the first time. Where this use may have an impact on the environment, perhaps by the establishment of a farm-scale trial or the commercial growth of GM crops, then these licensing applications must first be made in Ireland to the Environmental Protection Agency. Applications for other, non-environmental uses, such as the inclusion of GM ingredients in foodstuffs, may have to be made elsewhere, such as to the Food Safety Authority of Ireland (who also deal with GMO labelling) or to the Department of Agriculture (eg for GM seed controls, in conjunction with the EPA). Genetic modification policy matters are primarily determined by the Department of Health. This is all discussed in more detail in Chapter 10.

It must also be remembered that agriculture and the production of food are significant contributors to carbon emission levels. As will be discussed in Chapter 10, the growing, treatment, manufacture, transportation and consumption of food all have energy costs. In its new role, the Department of Communications, Climate Action and the Environment has a direct influence over the production and transportation of food. The Department (when operating under an earlier guise as the Department of the Environment, Heritage and Local Government) has

---

[2] Department of Health, 'A Healthy Weight for Ireland: Obesity Policy and Action Plan 2016–2025', ISBN 9781406429268.

identified several policies that have an impact on the regulation and control over the food sector in Ireland. In the National Climate Change Strategy 2007–2012 it was identified that reforming agriculture would have '[…] a key role to play in addressing climate change, through emission reductions […] emissions from the sector [being] closely linked to livestock numbers and the use of fertilisers'.[3] It was noted that Common Agricultural Policy reform, for example and the decoupling of direct payments from production, could be used to reduce the very significant impact that agriculture and food production was having on carbon emission levels.[4] The strategy also identified how the proper implementation of the EU Nitrates Directive could also help in this regard.[5] The relationship between food law and climate change is discussed in more detail in Chapter 10.

3.3. Enforcing Food Law

Each legislative act determines which authority has specific responsibility for the enforcement and oversight of the matters dealt with. However, primary responsibility for the enforcement of most food laws in Ireland now rests with the Food Safety Authority of Ireland (FSAI). This has been the case since the introduction of the Food Safety Authority of Ireland Act 1998. Prior to this, most enforcement was through local authorities and/or health boards, as set out in section 4(1) of the Food Standards Act 1974. Environmental health officers of the Health Service Executive (HSE) are still involved in food controls under a service contract with the FSAI.

Section 45 of the Food Safety Authority of Ireland Act 1998 provides that:

> […] in any food legislation, passed or made before the establishment [of the FSAI] any functions of an official agency in relation to the enforcement of the legislation shall be deemed to be a function of the Authority.

Section 46 then cements this function for the FSAI for all future relevant legislation as well by providing that:

> […] the Authority shall carry out or arrange to have carried out on its behalf […] the inspection, approval, licensing or registration of premises and equipment, including premises or equipment used in connection with the manufacture, processing, disposal, transport or storage of food; the inspection, sampling and analysis of food, including food ingredients; and the inspection and analysis of food labeling, to determine compliance with food legislation.

---

[3] Department of the Environment, 'National Climate Change Strategy 2007–2012'. Available at: www.housing.gov.ie.

[4] Although now out of date, the National Climate Change Strategy noted that by 2005 the agriculture sector in Ireland already accounted for 28% of national carbon emissions.

[5] Council Directive 1991/676/EEC of 12 December 1991 concerning the protection of waters against pollution caused by nitrates from agricultural sources. [1991] OJ L 375/1.

This provision of the 1998 Act provides far-reaching powers and a very significant role for the Food Safety Authority of Ireland in relation to food control. It is
the primary body in Ireland charged with ensuring that all relevant legal requirements are met from primary production through to marketing, preparation and
consumption.

The 1998 Act makes it clear that the FSAI is to be an independent[6] corporate
body[7] having 'all such powers as are necessary for or incidental to the performance
of its functions'.[8] Its main function is stated as being:

> to take all reasonable steps to ensure that food produced ... or marketed in the State
> meets the highest standards of food safety and hygiene reasonably available and ... in
> particular ... to ensure that such food complies with food legislation in respect of food
> safety and hygiene standards, or where appropriate, with the provisions of generally
> recognised standards or codes of good practice aimed at ensuring the achievement of
> high standards of food hygiene and food safety.[9]

As with other areas of food law in the post-BSE era, the Authority is to adopt
a 'farm to fork' approach in exercising this key function, applied in a manner
designed to 'promote, encourage and foster at all stages of food production, from
primary production through to final use by the consumer, the establishment and
maintenance of high standards of food hygiene and safety'.[10] This is to be carried
out through a combination of food inspections,[11] the adoption and application
of acceptable standards by food business operators,[12] and consultation processes
involving the Authority, consumers, producers, retailers, distributors, caterers,
manufacturers and official agencies.[13] In other words, appropriate standards will
be set, which then must be met and procedures will be adopted to ensure that this
happens – mostly consisting of inspections, sampling and analysis.[14]

3.3.1. Enforcement of Food Standards by the FSAI

The Food Safety Authority of Ireland Act 1998 provides that food safety,
hygiene and labelling standards are primarily to be maintained by the carrying out of inspections, approvals, sampling, analysis and licensing systems.[15]
It is the Authority's responsibility to ensure that this happens, by either fulfilling

---

[6] Food Safety Authority of Ireland Act 1998, s 10.
[7] Ibid, s 9(2).
[8] Ibid, s 9(3).
[9] Ibid, s 11.
[10] Ibid, s 12(1).
[11] Ibid, s 12(2).
[12] Ibid, s 12(3).
[13] Ibid, s 12(4).
[14] Ibid, ss 46–51.
[15] Ibid, s 46.

these functions itself or by arranging for these to be carried out on its behalf.[16] Its primary role, therefore, is to ensure that there is compliance with food legislation – and to take action when there is not. It is afforded a wide range of powers to enable it to carry out this function. Authorised officers may enter, search and inspect premises and records, remove records or take copies or extracts from them and oblige food business operators and their employees to provide them with relevant information.[17] Warrants can be issued by the District Court authorising entry to private dwellings. Members of the Garda Síochána can be called in by authorised officers to assist them with this or where necessary.[18] Failure to comply with the requests of FSAI authorised officers is a criminal offence, subject on conviction to fines and/or imprisonment.[19]

3.3.2. Improvement Notices, Improvement Orders and Closure Orders

Investigations by authorised officers of the FSAI may, of course, indicate that the premises or products inspected pose a likely or potential risk to public health. There are a range of options available to the FSAI where this is the case. In less serious instances, the proprietor of the offending establishment can be served with an improvement notice, which should identify the defect that has given rise to the risk, indicate what remedial action should be taken to address the risk, specify a time limit by which this action should be taken, as well as including any other requirements that are considered necessary by the authorised officer in the circumstances.[20] Notices served are normally effective immediately.[21] Non-compliance by the proprietor with the terms of the improvement notice, to the satisfaction of the authorised officer, the FSAI or its agent, can lead to the making of an improvement order.[22] This is an order of the District Court, directing proper compliance with the improvement notice. The improvement order should specify exactly what remedial work needs to be undertaken and when it needs to be satisfactorily completed by, as well as any other requirements that may be deemed appropriate by the Court.

---

[16] Under s 48 of the 1998 Act, the FSAI can enter into service contracts with official agencies for the purposes of carrying out its key functions. This section also provides that when such contracts are entered into, it is the responsibility of the FSAI to ensure that these functions are being carried out properly by the agency. These official agencies include the County Councils, the HSE, the Marine Institute, the National Standards Authority of Ireland and the Sea Fisheries Protection Authority and the Department of Agriculture, Food and the Marine.

[17] FSAI Act 1998, s 50(1). Under s 49, authorised officers of the FSAI are appointed by the Board or the Chief Executive and are issued with a warrant of appointment – which must be produced upon request.

[18] Ibid, s 50(2)–(4).

[19] Ibid, s 50(5).

[20] Ibid, s 52(1).

[21] Ibid, s 52(2).

[22] Ibid, s 52(4).

Finally, in the most serious of breaches of food safety or hygiene laws, a closure order may be served on the operator.[23] There are two ways in which a closure order can be served. The first is where the improvement order is not complied with. The improvement order made by the District Court should include provision for the FSAI or its agent to serve a closure order where the terms of the improvement order have not been complied with, or not complied with in time, or where a matter arises which warrants the serving of a closure order.[24] The second is where an authorised officer concludes that there is, or that there is likely to be, 'a grave and immediate danger to public health' posed by the establishment under inspection.[25] This category of closure order can be served directly after due consideration by the FSAI or its agent. It should state that the premises, or a specified part of them, should be closed, indicating why they should be closed, what the risk is and which aspects of the relevant food legislation have or are in danger of being breached. Closure orders are also effective once served, subject to appeal, which can include an application to have the order suspended.[26] Anyone aggrieved by the serving of a closure order can bring a full appeal to the District Court within seven days.[27] The Order can then either be confirmed, confirmed with modification, or cancelled. The FSAI can publicise details about any closure orders made, where this is in the interests of public health and consumer protection.[28]

3.3.3. Product Withdrawals

The Food Safety Authority of Ireland has the power to issue prohibition orders, preventing the sale of specified consignments, batches or items of food where there is a potentially serious risk posed to human health.[29] Again, reasons underlying this decision must be set out, clearly indicating the risk posed and/or the food legislation which has been breached. The public should be informed about the nature of the prohibition order, as should the relevant competent authorities in those States where the withdrawn food is also being sold.[30] Appeals against prohibition orders are made to the District Court, within seven days of the order being served. Again, the Court may order that the enforced withdrawal of the product is either confirmed, modified or cancelled.[31] Orders may be suspended while an

---

[23] Including, for example, '[...] failing to keep the ceilings of the premises in a proper state of repair, failure to provide a proper system of ventilation, [...] allowing clothes to be stored in a food room and failing to keep ice used in connection with the food business clean'. See *Eastern Health Board v Cumann Luithchleas Gaedheal Teoranta* [1999] 7 JIC 701.
[24] FSAI 1998, s 52(5).
[25] Ibid, s 53(1).
[26] Ibid, s 53(3) and (4).
[27] Ibid, s 53(5).
[28] Ibid, s 53(9).
[29] Ibid, s 54(1).
[30] Ibid, s 54(3).
[31] Ibid, s 54(6).

appeal is being brought, but only where the Court specifically thinks that it would be appropriate to do so.[32] The Food Safety Authority of Ireland can also revoke or modify a prohibition order that it has imposed at any time, provided that clear reasons can be given for this.[33]

While various bodies have responsibility for enforcing food law at local level, where there is a potential risk posed to human health or to consumers, it then becomes primarily the responsibility of the Food Safety Authority of Ireland to ensure that appropriate action is taken to minimise this risk.[34] However, it should also be noted that much of the EU legislation which brings national food laws into existence will require the designation of a national or local competent authority to oversee proper implementation. This is not always the FSAI.

3.3.4. EU Official Controls Regulation

The way in which there must be oversight of the domestic application of EU food regulations is set out in the Official Controls Regulation.[35] This Regulation, which will be replaced at the end of 2019,[36] provides that these official controls are necessary to ensure that EU Member States enforce feed and food law and monitor and verify that the relevant requirements are fulfilled by business operators at all stages of production, processing and distribution.[37] To properly achieve this, controls should be exerted regularly and proportionately to the potential risk involved in the activities of the operator concerned. There should also be ad hoc checks where there is any suspicion of non-compliance.[38] Overall, official controls that are implemented at national level must be designed to prevent, eliminate or reduce risks to human health to acceptably low levels.[39]

It must be understood at this stage that where EU rules are introduced, either by way of regulation or directive, they will, of course, be virtually meaningless if

---

[32] Ibid, s 54(5).

[33] Ibid, s 54(8).

[34] This differs somewhat from the role of the Food Standards Agency in the UK. This also has some responsibility for monitoring compliance and the enforcement of food law, but in the UK, the practical application of this rests primarily with the relevant local authorities who are then answerable to and monitored by the Food Standards Agency there, as set out in the Food Standards Act 1999.

[35] Regulation (EC) No 882/2004 of the European Parliament and of the Council of 29 April 2004 on official controls performed to ensure the verification of compliance with feed and food law, animal health and animal welfare rules [2004] OJ L 191/1.

[36] By Regulation (EU) 2017/625 of the European Parliament and of the Council of 15 March 2017 on official controls and other official activities performed to ensure the application of food and feed law, rules on animal health and welfare, plant health and plant protection products [2017] OJ L 95/1. The proposal to introduce this new regulation is discussed in more detail by L Vaqué, 'The European Commission proposal to simplify, rationalise and standardise food controls' (2013a) 8 *European Food and Feed Law Review* 308.

[37] Reg 882/2004, n 35 above, Preamble recital 6.

[38] Ibid, Preamble recital 13.

[39] Ibid, Art 1(1).

there is inadequate enforcement at both local and national levels. While the EU Commission does take some responsibility for overseeing the uniform application of legislation in the Member States, it is the domestic transposition of the EU rules that is so vital to ensuring their efficacy in achieving the aim pursued. This is particularly so in the case of EU regulations. They do not require any further implementing measures to be adopted at national level before they are applicable within the Irish legal system. However, they will usually require some form of domestic legislation to provide for their practical application, which is why we usually see statutory instruments introduced to provide for the proper functioning of EU regulations. One of the key roles of these statutory instruments is to set out who will have responsibility at local level for ensuring that the terms of the EU regulation are met by food business operators and how they are to go about ensuring that this happens. The Official Controls Regulation sets out the general obligations for Member States to ensure that this is done in the appropriate manner.

Regulation 882/2004 provides that Member States must ensure that official controls are carried out with some degree of regularity, the frequency of this being directly associated with the level of risk involved with the activity concerned.[40] So, for example, we are likely to see higher levels of monitoring of those businesses which are involved in the production of food from animals than for those involving non-animal-based raw materials. The frequency of monitoring the compliance of an individual food business operator is then to be determined based on the nature of any risk identified, the past record of compliance by the business with relevant food laws, any information that indicates non-compliance and the reliability of any previous checks carried out by the business itself. It is usual for official controls to be carried out without prior warning.[41] They can, of course, be carried out at any stage of production, processing or distribution of food.[42]

The EU Official Controls Regulation provides that it is for the individual Member States to designate who is to be the competent authority in each case.[43] Such designated authorities are then required to ensure that the controls they employ over the operation of food law are effective and appropriate; that staff carrying out their tasks are free from any conflict of interests; that they have access to adequate laboratory facilities for testing food samples; that they have the appropriate facilities and equipment for carrying out their tasks; that they have the legal powers to carry out their tasks; and that they have contingency plans in place in the event of an emergency.[44] Member States must ensure that they place a binding obligation on the food business operators to undergo inspections and assist the designated authority's staff in the carrying out of their functions.[45]

---

[40] Ibid, Art 3(1).
[41] Ibid, Art 3(2).
[42] Ibid, Art 3(3).
[43] Ibid, Art 4(1).
[44] Ibid, Art 4(2).
[45] Ibid, Art 4(2)(g).

As discussed above, the Food Safety Authority of Ireland, or any other designated national or local authority, can, in some circumstances, delegate specific controls to other bodies.[46] The comitology procedure is used at EU level to determine when this can happen.[47] Tasks can only be delegated where certain conditions are met, such as ensuring that the control body has the staffing levels, expertise, equipment and infrastructure required to carry out the activities assigned to it.[48] These organisations must also be accredited according to set EU standards.[49] They should also be audited and inspected as necessary by the designated national competent authority,[50] and their appointment should always be notified to the European Commission.[51]

National authorities charged with overseeing the implementation and enforcement of EU legislation must do so in accordance with documented procedures, which indicate instructions for their staff on what needs to be done.[52] As will be seen throughout this book, each individual regulation and directive clearly sets out what the designated competent authorities and those bodies to which their tasks have been delegated, must do, to ensure that the provisions of the EU legislation are properly applied at national level. Member States must support this work by ensuring that they have legal procedures in place that secure access for the competent authorities to the premises and documentation of food business operators within their jurisdiction.[53]

The methods that can be used by designated authorities to monitor compliance with food law include inspections, audits, sampling and analysis. The techniques to be employed vary, according to the area of food law that is being surveyed. This will usually be specified in the relevant EU and/or domestic legislation. Examples of this can be seen throughout this book. Laboratories used for sampling and analysis must, however, always be designated by the national authorities in accordance with specific EU standards, such as the 'General requirements for the competence of testing and calibration laboratories' or the 'General criteria for the assessment of testing laboratories'.[54] EU Commission experts can also carry out audits in the Member States on a regular basis.[55] Reports issued on the basis of these audits can then be used to make recommendations to the national authorities on how to go about improving compliance with food law.[56] The national authorities must then take appropriate follow-up action on this.[57]

---

[46] Ibid, Art 5(1).
[47] Ibid, Art 5(1) in conjunction with Art 62(3).
[48] Ibid, Art 5(2)(b).
[49] Ibid, Art 5(2)(c).
[50] Ibid, Art 5(3).
[51] Ibid, Art 5(4).
[52] Ibid, Art 8(1).
[53] Ibid, Art 8(2).
[54] Ibid, Art 12.
[55] Ibid, Art 45(1).
[56] Ibid, Art 45(3).
[57] Ibid, Art 45(5).

In a measure designed to standardise the implementation of EU legislation at national level across all of the Member States, the Official Controls Regulation provides that the Commission can organise training courses for competent authority staff on food law, systems of control and production methods.[58] The Regulation also provides that designated national authorities are obliged to take action where they identify instances of non-compliance with food law.[59] This action can include the imposition of sanitation procedures, marketing restrictions, product recalls and/or business closures.[60] The imposition of sanctions on operators for breaches of food law is left up to the Member States;[61] however, any sanction that is imposed must be 'effective, proportionate and dissuasive'.[62] The State must also inform the Commission about the nature and level of sanctions it intends to impose, as well as details of any subsequent amendments thereto.[63]

3.3.5. Official Control of Foodstuffs Regulations

As discussed above, the 2004 EU Official Controls Regulation stipulates that all Member States must designate national competent authorities to oversee the implementation of food law.[64] This designation is set at national level by the EC (Official Control of Foodstuffs) Regulations 2010.[65] These Regulations provide that this competence is divided between the Food Safety Authority of Ireland and the Health Service Executive, along with a number of designated official laboratories.[66]

The 2010 Regulations are only one part of the official controls framework. Different legislative obligations set specific roles for each of these competent authorities, depending on the area of food law in which the obligation arises. The 2010 Regulations do, however, specifically stipulate a number of general roles for the FSAI, the HSE and the laboratories in terms of obligations arising directly from the 2004 EU Regulation. For example, Regulation 4 of the EC (Official Control of Foodstuffs) Regulations 2010 provides that these national bodies must co-operate

---

[58] Ibid, Art 51. The Regulation provides that there must be adequate training for all designated authority staff charged with performing official controls, at both national and EU level. Annex II to Reg 882/2004 sets out the areas in which these staff must be trained, including control techniques and procedures, food law, production methods, health risks, HACCP, contingency arrangements during emergencies and examining records and documentation.
[59] Reg 882/2004, n 35 above, Art 54(1).
[60] Ibid, Art 54(2).
[61] This is a common principle in EU law known as 'national procedural autonomy'. For further discussion see, amongst others, P Craig and G de Búrca, *EU law: Text, cases and materials*, 6th edn (Oxford, OUP, 2015), ch 8; and D Chalmers, G Davies and G Monti, *European Union law*, 3rd edn (Cambridge, CUP, 2014), ch 7.
[62] Reg 882/2004, n 35 above, Art 55(1).
[63] Ibid, Art 55(2).
[64] Reg 882/2004, n 35 above.
[65] SI No 117/2010.
[66] Ibid, Reg 3.

with European Commission audits and inspections that are designed to verify the proper implementation of a range of EU food law obligations in Ireland.[67] They must also immediately and without request, inform the designated competent authorities in other EU Member States where they become aware of any breach of EU food legislation that may have an impact in or on those other States.[68] This information must also be communicated to the European Commission where the issue that has given cause for concern initially arose in a third country.[69]

In some circumstances specific tasks may be delegated to what are known as 'control bodies'.[70] These must be verified as having the expertise, equipment and infrastructure required to carry out assigned tasks, as well as having sufficient staff and being free from any potential conflicts of interest.[71] They must be accredited in accordance with European standards. There must be regular and clear communication between the control body and the national authorities. They are also subject to audit and inspections and their appointment must be notified to the EU Commission.[72] While control bodies can be used in the formulation of official controls over food, feed and animal welfare, they cannot be used in the actual enforcement of these standards, nor can they be charged with bringing proceedings against those who are identified as being non-compliant with food law.[73] Any action taken must be brought by the competent authority, that is either the FSAI or the HSE itself. This can include the imposition of sanitation procedures, restrictions or prohibitions on marketing – including product recalls and possible destruction of food or feed, forced closures of all or part of a business, the suspension or withdrawal of a previously granted approval, or any other measure that the authorities deem appropriate.[74] The types of control measures that can be delegated to control bodies include examination and inspections of primary producers' installations, feed and food businesses; their raw materials, ingredients and processing aids; semi-finished products; materials and articles intended to come into contact with food; cleaning and maintenance products and pesticides; and labelling, presentation and advertising of products.[75] They can also be delegated the responsibility of checking on hygiene standards, including the application of HACCP practices, in food and feed businesses.[76] The 2010 Regulations also provide more detail on the use of closure orders in circumstances other than those outlined in section 3.3 above. They also set out those circumstances in which a prohibition order may

---

[67] As set out in Reg 882/2004, n 35 above, Arts 41–45.
[68] EC (Official Control of Foodstuffs) Regulations 2010, n 65 above, Reg 5.
[69] Ibid, Reg 5(4), in conjunction with Reg 882/2004, n 35 above, Art 39.
[70] Ibid, Reg 6(1), in conjunction with Reg 882/2004, n 35 above, Art 5.
[71] Regulation 882/2004, n 35 above, Art 5(2).
[72] Ibid, Arts 5(3) and (4).
[73] Ibid, Arts 5 and 54.
[74] Ibid, Art 54(2).
[75] Reg 7(1) of the EC (Official Control of Foodstuffs) Regulations 2010, n 65 above in conjunction with Art 10 of Regulation 882/2004, n 35 above.
[76] For more detailed discussion on what HACCP involves see Ch 6.

be made, in particular where a food business operator has failed to comply with food legislation in such a way that constitutes a potential threat to human health or the protection of consumers.[77] This can ultimately lead to a full product recall or, where possible, remedying the defect in the food or feed to render it safe for human or animal consumption.

Sanctions that can be imposed for breach of either the Irish Regulations or the EU Regulation are relatively severe, with fines of up to €500,000 payable on conviction on indictment along with prison sentences of up to three years and the possible payment of all costs incurred in the related investigation and prosecution.[78]

3.4. State Agencies

The use of state agencies, advisory forums and corporate bodies, instead of the direct use of government departments to oversee the proper implementation of food law has become much more commonplace since the 1990s. Bodies such as the Food Safety Authority of Ireland, the Environmental Protection Agency, the Health Service Executive and Safefood all have a significant role to play in the development of policy and the application of the relevant legal requirements, throughout the State. In addition to this, other more specific groups, in particular advisory committees, can be established to debate and deal, in a variety of ways, with more targeted concerns. For example, the Healthy Ireland Council is a national forum of stakeholders designed to promote health and wellbeing across the State. The Council is charged with providing advice to government on the priorities for the promotion of the health of children. It has a potentially important role to play in the overall development and implementation of key policy within the Healthy Ireland Framework, which is a national framework of action that should be taken to assist in reducing health inequalities and promoting good health in the population across Ireland.[79] The administrative structures and procedures of the most significant of these designated agencies and bodies that assist the government in the formulation and application of food law are set out below.

3.4.1. Food Safety Authority of Ireland

The Food Safety Authority of Ireland (FSAI), which was of the first of its kind in Europe, is responsible for overseeing a wide range of food safety and related issues in Ireland. The FSAI rarely has sole responsibility for many of the matters

---

[77] EC (Official Control of Foodstuffs) Regulations 2010, n 65 above, Reg 20.
[78] Reg 24 of the 2010 Irish Regulations.
[79] Department of Health, 'Healthy Ireland: A framework for improved health and wellbeing 2013–2025'. ISBN: 9780957579903.

that are within its remit. It shares many of these with the HSE, as discussed above. As will be seen throughout this book, the FSAI has a role to play in many aspects of the regulation of the food sector, but it is usually just one part of the process, albeit a very important one. The main idea behind the establishment of the FSAI is to have a body in place which can connect the producing, scientific and regulating sectors with the public. The hope has always been that much of the public confidence in the safety of food which was lost both during the BSE crisis and the controversy surrounding the use of GMOs would be restored by having a public, yet independent, body in place which can direct industry, advise consumers and interject where necessary to prevent future concerns arising, or at least minimise the potential risks to health. This can be done by that body taking immediate and decisive action. While the FSAI may lack the power to make laws, it does possess a significant degree of persuasive power, both in relation to its dealings with government and with the general public.

The FSAI was established as an independent,[80] and corporate body, with the required powers to carry out its functions, by the Food Safety Authority of Ireland Act 1998.[81]

Functions of the Food Safety Authority of Ireland

The principal function of the FSAI is to ensure, as far as is possible, that all food produced and marketed in the State accords with the highest safety and hygiene standards. In particular it must ensure that products comply with relevant legislation and codes of good practice.[82] This is, as expected, to be based on a 'farm to fork' approach, designed to maintain the highest possible standards at all stages of food production through to final consumption.[83] The 1998 Act makes it clear that primary responsibility for ensuring that food is safe to eat rests with the food business operators.[84] Standards, however, should be developed and applied in a way that involves stakeholders, following consultation with consumer groups, retailers, distributors, caterers, manufacturers and relevant agencies.[85] One way in which this can be achieved is through the development of FSAI-promoted food safety assurance schemes.[86] This can include FSAI-endorsed schemes that have been

---

[80] FSAI Act 1998, s 10.

[81] Ibid, s 9.

[82] Ibid, s 11.

[83] Ibid, s 12(1).

[84] Ibid, s 12(3).

[85] Ibid, s 12(4).

[86] Ibid, s 13. Quality assurance schemes have been found to be effective in addressing food safety issues. Although a bit dated now, a survey conducted by the FSAI showed that over two-thirds of food industry representatives believed that these schemes have an important role to play in addressing food safety issues. Only one in ten stated that these schemes were not of any value in this regard. FSAI (2003) 'Industry Attitudes to Food Safety in Ireland'. Available at: www.fsai.ie. The Bord Bia Quality Assurance Mark is probably the best example of such a scheme in operation. For further details on this see www.bordbia.ie.

approved by the FSAI's Scientific Committee.[87] The FSAI does not actually operate the schemes, rather it sets guidelines, monitors and reports on the work of others, such as An Bord Bia, in this area.

The FSAI also has a key advisory role to play. The government can request its advice on a range of matters, including those related to food-borne diseases, nutrition and diet, statutory developments on food safety or food hygiene, the use of technology in food production, licensing and inspections, agricultural and aquacultural production, labelling, packaging, contact materials, communication with the public and any other relevant food safety or hygiene matter.[88] Any such advice can be published.

It is, of course, important that the FSAI is in possession of the information necessary to make properly informed decisions and to provide the most useful advice possible. To this end, the 1998 Act provides that it can collect all food legislation, codes of conduct and other relevant materials, such as statistical data on official controls or the prevalence of food-borne disease, that will assist them in the performance of these functions.[89] The FSAI can also commission, collaborate in or undertake its own research projects on these matters.[90] They must regularly review food inspection services and report on these to the Minister for Health on an, at least, annual basis.[91]

The FSAI represents Ireland in deliberations on food safety matters with the European Union. This can involve negotiations with and representations to the European Commission, the European Parliament and the European Food Safety Authority, in particular through its Advisory Forum, which is discussed in more detail in Chapter 5.

Administration of the FSAI

The FSAI is led at government level by the Minister for Health, assisted in an advisory capacity by the Scientific Committee, mentioned above, as well as the Food Safety Consultative Council and by the Board. The Consultative Council is made up of a broad range of up to 24 members, a maximum of half of which can be appointed by the Minister.[92] The FSAI is not obliged to consult with the Council; it should have regard to, but is not bound by, its opinions.[93]

The Board of the FSAI has a series of important legislative functions to play in the operation of food laws in Ireland. There are ten members, including a chair and the chair of the Scientific Committee.[94] The Scientific Committee is then charged

[87] FSAI Act 1998, s 13(7).
[88] Ibid, s 15.
[89] Ibid, s 16.
[90] Ibid, s 18.
[91] Ibid, s 17.
[92] Ibid, s 14(1)–(3).
[93] Ibid, s 14(6).
[94] Ibid, s 31.

with advising the Board on relevant scientific matters, including those related to food hygiene, inspections and nutrition.[95] The Board cannot act on any matter that it has referred to the Scientific Committee until it has received the advice requested. Both the Board and the Scientific Committee can be further divided into subcommittees on more specific matters.[96]

The Board of the FSAI is responsible for appointing the Chief Executive of the Authority.[97] This is a highly influential role – again having a whole range of responsibilities assigned to the post by various legislative requirements.[98] The Chief Executive may attend Board, Scientific Committee and subcommittee meetings, but cannot be a member of any of these. The administration of the FSAI is then further subdivided into five key areas of responsibility – corporate affairs; enforcement policy; risk management and regulatory affairs; audit and investigations; and food science and standards.

The role and responsibilities of the FSAI in the administration of Irish food law are discussed, where relevant, throughout this book. The creation of this specialist body has had a significant effect on the way in which the food sector is regulated in Ireland. Moving oversight of enforcement and controls to a focused, expert organisation brings a whole range of benefits to regulation in this area. There is more clarity on the designation of the roles of the various national and local authorities. Expert advice is readily available for the Government when required. Independent guidance on food safety is made available to the public and it is well-publicised. Food business operators are kept under closer scrutiny. Changes to the law are clearly communicated by the FSAI, through its website and in other ways. There are, perhaps, changes that could be made to further strengthen the role of the FSAI, in particular by unifying more, if not all, areas of enforcement under their aegis instead of the more disparate range of roles being shared by several authorities and agencies. There could also be a more significant part for the FSAI to play in tackling the prevalence in Ireland of the availability and consumption of low-quality and nutritionally unsound foods. There needs to be a clearer recognition that safety is about much more than contamination – although this is an issue across European Union food law and certainly not just in Ireland.

The positive change brought about by the establishment of the FSAI is echoed in its strategic plans, which offer further evidence of the type of important role the Authority can and continues to play in the organisation and functioning of Irish society. The Strategy 2016–2018 sets five strategic goals and a number of objectives.[99] These include leading a regulatory culture aimed at achieving the highest standards for food; using the best scientific knowledge and expertise available to underpin policy and risk analysis; creating an environment where

---

[95] Ibid, s 34.
[96] Ibid, s 35.
[97] Ibid, s 37.
[98] Including those set out in FSAI Act 1998, s 26 on the accounts and audits, s 49 on the appointment of authorised officers, s 52 on improvement notices and orders and s 53 on closure orders.
[99] Available at: www.fsai.ie.

Ireland is seen as being a trusted leader in food safety and integrity; and the development of digital information systems that maximise accessibility and effective communication.

3.4.2. Health Service Executive

The Health Service Executive, which was established by the Health Act 2004, came into existence in January 2005. It was set up as a replacement for the regional health boards, health authorities and agencies which administered the provision of public health and related social services in Ireland prior to this. Its primary objective, as set out in the 2004 Act, is '... to use the resources available to it in the most beneficial, effective and efficient manner to improve, promote and protect the health and welfare of the public'.[100] It is led by the Minister for Health, but administered by a relatively complex organisational structure of boards, directors, officers, heads, groups and community organisations. It has a key role to play in regulating the food sector in Ireland, primarily related to inspections, enforcement and controls. This was outlined above.

Environmental Health Officers are appointed by the HSE to monitor activities in the food sector in several areas. All officers appointed must be qualified in environmental health, usually to degree level.[101] Environmental health officers are a crucial part of the food controls mechanism, charged with inspecting establishments which provide food for public consumption, as well as having responsibility for examining food imports. As would be expected in the post General Food Law Regulation era, this function extends to all stages of food production and processing, through to distribution and marketing. As outlined above, officers are afforded a range of powers of entry and inspection, potentially leading to the serving of notices and orders and possibly prosecutions. They are also responsible for checking public and private supplies of drinking water, including monitoring fluoridation levels in the former.[102] Members of the public can bring complaints directly to the Environmental Health Service of the HSE for further investigation, either by contacting their local Environmental Health Officer or by bringing it to the HSE via the FSAI.

The HSE Environmental Health Service is responsible for the food sampling programme. Food samples are taken and analysed for composition verification

---

[100] Health Act 2004, s 7(1).

[101] As set by powers conferred by the Health Act 2004, s 22 in conjunction with the Public Service Management (Recruitment and Appointments) Act 2004. Requirements related to appointment to such posts were originally set by the Health (Officers) Regulations 1953, SI No 158/1953 and the Local Government (Officers) Regulations 1943, SI No 161/1943. The setting of minimum qualifications for the holders of such, or similar, posts was initially established by the Local Authorities (Officers and Employees) Act 1926.

[102] The role of the HSE in the ensuring the safety of public water supplies is outlined in section 3.4.3. below.

purposes, primarily to ascertain whether products contain unsafe quantities of certain chemicals or allergens or to check for possible contamination or putrification that could lead to poisoning.

3.4.3. Environmental Protection Agency

The Environmental Protection Agency is an independent body, established by the Environmental Protection Agency Act 1992. Its primary functions include '... the licensing, regulation and control of activities for the purposes of environmental protection'.[103] This includes being designated as the national competent body for the authorisation of the deliberate release into the environment of genetically modified organisms.[104] It is also the designated licensing agency for any activities related to agriculture[105] or to food production more generally,[106] which are deemed to have a significant potential to pollute.[107]

Under the terms of the European Union (Drinking Water) Regulations 2014,[108] the EPA is designated as the supervisory authority for the supply of drinking water by Irish Water.[109] This includes verifying that Irish Water has complied with the microbiological and chemical parametric values, such as those on the presence of E. coli, arsenic, mercury or pesticides, as set out in Part 1 of the Schedule to the Regulations.[110] The Agency also has overall supervision of Irish Water and

---

[103] Environmental Protection Agency Act 1992, s 52(1).

[104] As established by the Reg 4 of the Genetically Modified Organisms (Deliberate Release) Regulations 2003, SI No 500/2003. The deliberate release of genetically modified organisms is dealt with in more detail in Ch 10.

[105] Including the rearing of poultry in installations where the capacity exceeds 100,000 units (a broiler chicken being 1 unit and a turkey being 2 units per head) and the rearing of pigs in installations where the capacity exceeds either 1,000 (gley soils) or 3,000 (other soils) and where a pig is considered to be 1 unit and a sow 10 units.

[106] Environmental Protection Agency Act 1992, ss 82 *et seq*. The First Schedule to this Act provides a list of activities for which licences are required. This includes the manufacture of vegetable and animal oils and fats where the capacity for processing raw materials exceeds 40 tonnes per day; the manufacture of dairy products where the processing capacity exceeds 50 million gallons of milk per year; commercial brewing and distilling in installations where the production capacity exceeds 100,000 tonnes per year; the slaughter of animals in installations where the daily capacity exceeds 1,500 units and where a sheep is 1 unit, a pig 2 units and cattle 5 units per head; the manufacture of fish-meal and fish-oil; and the manufacture of sugar.

[107] Other food production related activities which may require a licence from the EPA include the manufacture of artificial fertilisers, the manufacture or formulation of pesticides and the manufacture of vitamins involving the use of heavy metals.

[108] SI No 122/2014. These Regulations now give effect in Ireland to Council Directive 1998/83/EC on the quality of water intended for human consumption, [1998] OJ L 330/32 and Directive 2000/60/EC of the European Parliament and of the Council establishing a framework for Community action in the field of water policy, [2000] OJ L 327/1.

[109] The EPA was originally established as the body responsible for monitoring the quality of water intended for human consumption by EPA Act 1992, s 58.

[110] European Union (Drinking Water) Regulations 2014, n 108 above, reg 7. These parametric values can be departed from in some circumstances. Any decision to grant such a departure and any conditions attached to this, rests primarily with the EPA. This is all set out in Reg 11 of the 2014 Regulations.

local authorities' monitoring and other obligations established by these Regulations. It can direct and guide these bodies in a variety of ways, designed to ensure that water supplied is safe and fit for human consumption.[111] Where Irish Water or a local authority, in consultation with the Health Service Executive, considers that a public or private water supply may pose a danger to human health then the EPA must be immediately informed about this threat, so that it can provide these other bodies with guidance on how this can be countered.[112] Finally, the EPA also publishes annual reports on the quality of drinking water. More recent reports have shown that private supplies tend to be much more contaminated than public supplies, with potentially very serious consequences for human health.[113]

While the EPA is an independent body, it does have strong ties to government and to the minister with responsibility for the environment, which has become part of the Department of Communications, Climate Action and the Environment. The Minister may, for example, assign additional functions for the EPA or may modify existing functions.[114] The Minister may also transfer functions from other public bodies to the EPA where it is felt that it is better placed to deal with the environmental protection matter at issue.[115] The Agency is also bound by the Act to provide a significant advisory role for government and for local authorities on the adoption or implementation of European Union rules, proposals, guidelines, standards or issues of concern.[116] The Agency must also report annually to the Minister on the quality and safety of drinking water supplies.[117] These reports are to be disseminated to each house of the Oireachtas.[118] They must also be made public.[119]

The Environmental Protection Agency also includes amongst its priorities the protection and improvement of water and land quality through tackling pollution, as well as acting to reduce climate change and its consequences. As is discussed in Chapter 10 of this book, the regulation of the food sector has the potential to play a very meaningful role in reducing carbon emissions and this presents real possibilities for assisting in the mitigation of climate change and pollution.

---

[111] Regs 7(11)–(15) of the 2014 Regulations, n 108 above.

[112] Reg 9 of the 2014 Regulations, n 108 above.

[113] See, for example, the EPA Report on Private Water Supplies, published in March 2017, which showed that water quality in private supplies was consistently poorer than public sources, with much higher incidence of the presence of the potentially deadly bacteria E. coli found in private schemes and supplies. ISBN: 9781840957082. Around 17% of the population of Ireland (or 170,000 households) are supplied by private sources, with 10% of the total getting their water directly from household wells, which also have the very highest incidence of non-compliance with set E. coli standards. This 2017 report also noted that Ireland has the highest incidence of VTEC (a pathogenic form of E. coli) in Europe, estimating that up to 30% of household wells in Ireland could be contaminated by E. coli from animal or human waste.

[114] EPA Act 1992, s 53.

[115] Ibid, s 54.

[116] Ibid, ss 55–57.

[117] Ibid, s 58(2).

[118] Ibid, s 58(3) thereof.

[119] Ibid.

3.4.4. Food Safety Promotion Board

Safefood is an all-Ireland body which was established to promote awareness about food safety and nutrition issues. It was set up by Part III of the British–Irish Agreement Act 1999, where it was officially named the Food Safety Promotion Board. It is a corporate body.[120] Its functions are set out in the Agreement between the Irish and UK Governments Establishing the Implementation Bodies.[121] These are the promotion of food safety, research into food safety, communication of food alerts, surveillance of food-borne diseases, the promotion of scientific co-operation and linkages between laboratories and the development of cost-effective facilities for specialised laboratory testing.

The Chief Executive of Safefood reports directly to the North/South Ministerial Council, which was itself established under the British–Irish, or Belfast, Agreement 1998.[122] An advisory board of 12 members, which should meet approximately once every six weeks, provides strategic advice to the Chief Executive and senior managers. Members of this board are drawn from a broad range of areas, including private food business operators, producers, environmental health officers, farmers, retailers and scientists. Safefood is also assisted by a voluntary advisory committee whose members are experts in food science, health science, nutrition, business interests and consumer interests. The remit of the organisation is subdivided into four areas or directorates – corporate operations; human health and nutrition; marketing and communications; and food science.

Safefood is a highly active organisation, with a strong public profile. It runs advertising and promotional campaigns across a range of areas, designed to inform consumers about food safety and nutrition. While it does not have any formal legislative role, it can propose new initiatives that can impact upon the way in which food products are produced, prepared or labelled. Its primary role, however, is to keep the public informed about the consumption of safe and wholesome food.

3.4.5. Patents Office

The Patents Office, despite its name, deals with several areas of intellectual property protection in Ireland, including aspects of copyright and trademark registration. It also has a key role to play in the application of the WTO Agreement on Trade Related Aspects of Intellectual Property Rights (TRIPs) in the State. However, it is the Trade Policy Unit of the Department of Business, Enterprise and Innovation

---

[120] British–Irish Agreement Act 1999, s 15.
[121] Ibid, Annex 1, Part 2. Other implementation bodies were also established at this time, including Waterways Ireland, the Trade and Business Development Body, the Special EU Programmes Body, the North/South Language Body (An Foras Teanga/The Boord o Leid) and the Foyle, Carlingford and Irish Lights Commission.
[122] British–Irish Agreement Act 1999, Art 2.

that is responsible for the formulation and development of Ireland's international trade policies. This role includes promoting Ireland's interests at European Union level, as well as participating in the work of the World Trade Organization. More significantly for the purposes of this book, it is the Department of Agriculture, Food and the Marine which has responsibility for protected geographical indications and designations of origin. While this type of intellectual property protection is discussed in more detail in Chapter 8, it should be noted at this stage that the WTO TRIPs Agreement provides a degree of international protection for qualifying designations of origin and geographical indications. The TRIPs Agreement also provides that WTO members should provide the legal means for parties to prevent the use of geographical names that indicate or suggest that a good originates in a geographical area other than its true place of origin in a manner that misleads consumers or which constitutes unfair competition. It also provides for an enhanced level of protection for the geographical names of wines and spirits, subject to the exception set out in Article 24 of TRIPs, which facilitates the continued use of previously registered trademarks. It is the Department of Agriculture and the Health Service Executive that oversee the implementation of all this,[123] which is the case for most aspects of Irish food law, as set out earlier in this chapter. National strategy on the use of PDOs and PGIS is set out in a 2012 Food Industry Development Division of the Department of Agriculture document entitled 'Linked to the Land: Developing Ireland's Local and Regional food and drinks', which clearly recognised the need to develop greater awareness of the potential of geographical name registration, as well as encouraging future applications from Irish producers.

3.5. Conclusion

There are many national bodies with responsibility for different aspects of the implementation of food law. Much of the time, however, their roles are limited to (i) the enforcement of EU-derived legislative requirements; and (ii) the setting of policies and guidelines. The latter, however, is often further limited to the creation of non-binding measures and advice. As is discussed in Chapter 4, EU rules on the free movement of food prevent Member States from either maintaining or creating national rules that create any sort of barrier to importation, no matter whether small or significant. Such rules may be deemed contrary to the TFEU prohibitions on measures equivalent to quantitative restrictions on trade or to that on charges of equivalent effect to customs duties. In some circumstances, national fiscal measures may be deemed unlawful where they discriminate, directly or

---

[123] European Union (Quality Schemes for Agricultural Products and Foodstuffs) Regulations 2015, SI No 296/2015.

indirectly, against non-national produce. Almost all 'national' food law is now therefore about the enforcement and implementation of EU requirements. There is very little scope left for national legislative initiative designed to regulate the food sector. This is also discussed in more detail in Chapter 4, where it is shown that EU rules on the free movement of food preclude Member States from adopting their own binding measures that are designed to protect their people in some way. Member States can be the subject of a Commission enforcement action before the European Court of Justice where they introduce a law to protect human health or consumers.

4

EU Rules on the Free Movement of Food

4.1. Introduction

There are four ways in which EU rules on the free movement of goods impact on Irish food law. The first of these is the prohibition on measures equivalent to quantitative restrictions on trade. This has come to mean that any national measure that has the potential to restrict the movement of food either into or out of a Member State must be discontinued. There are some circumstances where the Member State can justify the maintenance of such a national measure. The point is usually made that a compositional requirement or an outright prohibition on the sale of a food may be necessary to protect consumers from deception or to protect human health. The case law of the Court of Justice shows us that this is usually a difficult argument for a Member State to successfully make.

The second way in which EU rules impact upon Irish food law relates to the prohibition on charges of equivalent effect to customs duties. These charges must be set at 0 per cent on all goods traded between Member States. However, the Treaty extends this to any national measure that imposes an additional financial burden on the importer or exporter that the national producer operating in the national market does not have to face. Charges for inspections of imported animal produce offer an example of the type prohibited by this provision. Again, there are some exceptions to the rule, but these are hard for Member States to establish successfully and it is usually only where EU law has prescribed a particular activity that they will be permitted to pass on the costs of this to the food business operator.

Third, while the majority of taxation decisions remain at the discretion of the Member States themselves, the Treaty on the Functioning of the European Union does not allow national taxes to discriminate against non-national produce. Ad valorem taxes, in particular, can be shown to contravene this provision if they place a higher rate of tax on produce that is mostly made in other EU Member States. Any such tax must be modified where it is found to be contrary to these equality requirements, to reduce or eliminate the discriminatory element.

Finally, the harmonisation of food laws can have a very significant impact on national measures by obliging Member States to alter their rules so that they become the same, or at least very close to the same, as other rules operating across the EU. Most of the rest of this book deals with these harmonised requirements.

4.2. Measures Equivalent to Quantitative Restrictions on Trade in Food

The prohibition set out in Article 34 TFEU is the single most important and far-reaching element of EU law and policy on the free movement of goods. It states that '[q]uantitative restrictions on imports and all measures having equivalent effect shall be prohibited between Member States'. This provision of the Treaty has significant implications. It is designed to ensure that there are no unnecessary impediments set or applied in the domestic laws of EU Member States which restrict intra-Union trade in any way. The European Court of Justice defined these 'measures equivalent to quantitative restrictions' on trade in the broadest sense possible in *Dassonville*.[1] There it stated that '[a]ll trading rules enacted by Member States which are capable of hindering, directly or indirectly, actually or potentially, intra-Community trade are to be considered as measures having an effect equivalent to quantitative restrictions'.[2] Any national law setting a compositional or labelling requirement for food would thus be deemed to be within the scope of this provision, requiring an Article 34 TFEU compatibility examination. Unless this national law could be justified (and it has become clear that this is a difficult justification to make) then it would be contrary to Article 34 TFEU and consequently to the Treaty obligations of the imposing Member State. National law would have to be repealed or significantly modified to bring it back into line with EU requirements on the free movement of goods. It also prevents Member States from introducing new measures where these have the potential to 'directly or indirectly' affect trade, even where this is considered necessary to protect consumers or human health.

4.2.1. Restricting the Free Movement of Food

EU Member States may have national laws in place that stipulate the inclusion or exclusion of certain ingredients from a particular type of food. Only products that are manufactured in accordance with these rules are permitted to use a specified name, set out in the same legislation. To take a fictional example, Irish law prescribes that digestive biscuits can only be called 'digestive biscuits' where they contain wheat flour (at least 70 per cent), sugar (no more than 15 per cent), malt extract, vegetable oil and raising agents. A French producer who markets his 'digestive biscuits' in Ireland could not, because of EU rules on the free movement of food, be required to comply with this (fictional) Irish law.

---

[1] Case 8/1974 *Procureur du Roi v Benoît and Gustave Dassonville* [1974] ECR 837.
[2] Ibid, para 5.

He would have to be allowed to market his product as 'digestive biscuits' in Ireland even if they were made with only, say, 60 per cent flour and over 20 per cent sugar because of a principle developed by the European Court of Justice known as 'mutual recognition'. It means that once a product is lawfully marketed in one EU Member State, it must be lawfully marketable not only in Ireland but in all other EU Member States. There are some exceptions to this rule, but it remains difficult for Member States, such as Ireland, to argue that any national law that operates contrary to the principle of mutual recognition is necessary and should be able to persist.

Suppose, however, our fictional French producer of 'digestive biscuits' adds hazelnuts to his ingredients. The flour content remains at 60 per cent, the sugar 20 per cent, but in addition, 10 per cent is made up of nuts. There is now the potential for the Irish authorities to make the case that this biscuit is not lawfully marketable as a 'digestive biscuit'. The reason for this is that the Court of Justice of the EU has found that where there is a 'substantial difference' between a product entering the market (the French digestive biscuit) and the product normally known by that name (the existing Irish digestive biscuit) then it may be necessary to allow some form of restriction to be placed on the sales name that is used when marketing the former. It may be accepted that the need to protect consumers facilitates the imposition of national laws that impede free movement in such circumstances. However, it should be noted that this is also a difficult position for a Member State to argue successfully as the Court of Justice of the EU often holds that a prohibition on the use of a particular name, even when describing what is essentially a different product, may go beyond what is necessary in the circumstances. It is usually decided that a more proportionate response in these situations would be to oblige the producer of the different product to give a clear indication of this difference on the labelling. This 'principle of proportionality' is one of the general principles of EU law. As will be seen in the discussion below, there can, however, also be difficulties when determining what may constitute a 'substantial' difference between products.

Finally, if the French biscuit producer does not include hazelnuts, but does add a quantity of some other substance such as inverted sugar syrup or high levels of salt to the ingredients, then an argument can be put forward by the Member State of sale that the product should not be marketed in their territory, as it poses some sort of risk to human health. If studies show that the consumption of either of these constituents in high amounts can have a negative impact on health, then it may be deemed acceptable for the Member State to prohibit the sale of that foodstuff in that form. However, it should be noted that there must be evidence of the potential risk to health presented in support of any such action. The risk must be real and usually immediate. It is often also a requirement that the Member State imposing any such restriction does not permit similar quantities of these potentially harmful substances to be present in other foods which are not subjected to similar prohibitions. The case law and legislation that has created each of these positions is discussed in more detail below.

4.2.2. Compositional Requirements and the Principle of Mutual Recognition

If *Dassonville* is to be considered the seminal case in determining what a 'measure equivalent to a quantitative restriction on trade' is to be, then we must also consider that the decision of the Court of Justice in *Cassis* is of similar significance when assessing the impact of what is now Article 34 of the TFEU.[3] There, the Court determined, most significantly, that once a product is lawfully marketable in one EU Member State it must be marketable in all. This is known as the principle of 'mutual recognition', briefly mentioned earlier in this chapter. Each Member State must recognise the application of the laws of the other Member States as being adequate for the protection of consumers and health. In some, albeit relatively limited, circumstances there will be permissible exceptions to this rule. It has become the cornerstone of the application of Article 34 of the TFEU. In summary, it usually means two things. First, food produced anywhere in the EU can be sold anywhere in the EU, without restriction. Second, Member States cannot set or apply compositional, or similar, requirements for food which inhibit, in any way, the sale of products from other EU Member States. This is particularly significant when we come to consider the limitations placed on States wishing to take measures to counter public health concerns, such as rising rates of obesity or the over-consumption of alcohol.

This section aims to provide an overview of the key issues and principles involved in the application of Article 34 of the TFEU at national level, as well as their effects on Irish law and policy. Much more comprehensive assessments of the general prohibition on quantitative restrictions on trade and measures of equivalent effect are provided elsewhere.[4] In *Cassis*, a case was brought against federal German authorities for refusing to allow the marketing of imported French-produced blackcurrant liqueur, Cassis de Dijon. German law at the time prescribed that liqueurs like this one had to have a minimum alcohol content of 25 per cent to be lawfully sold there. The French product tended to be marketed with an alcohol content in the range of 15 to 20 per cent. It was argued that the German law was a measure equivalent to a quantitative restriction on imports. The law did not prohibit the sale of French liqueurs, but it did restrict the ability of French producers to sell products in Germany that were not in compliance with the minimum alcohol requirements set there. This is what is meant by a 'compositional requirement'. It is a domestic rule that stipulates compositional considerations essential to lawful marketability – in this case a minimum alcohol

---

[3] Case 120/1978 *Rewe-Zentral AG v Bundesmonopolverwaltung für Branntwein* (Cassis) [1979] ECR 649.

[4] See, eg, in C Barnard, *The substantive law of the EU*, 5th edn (Oxford, OUP, 2016), chs 4–6; P Oliver, *Free movement of goods in the European Union*, 5th edn (Oxford, Hart, 2010); P Craig and G de Búrca, *EU law*, 6th edn (Oxford, OUP, 2015), ch 19.

level requirement. Other obvious examples of these 'compositional requirements' would include stipulations about the inclusion or exclusion of certain ingredients, or the setting of minimum or maximum quantities for these ingredients, before a particular sales name can be used.

Using the formula developed in *Dassonville*, the European Court of Justice found that the German law on minimum alcohol level was a measure equivalent to a quantitative restriction on imports, examinable under Article 34 of the TFEU (Article 30 EEC at the time). It stated that:

> [a]ccording to the settled case law of the Court any measure of such a kind as to hinder, directly or indirectly, actually or potentially, trade between Member States falls under the prohibition contained in [Article 34 TFEU]. To prohibit the marketing of a prod-uct from one Member State in another Member State hinders the importation of that product in a direct and immediate manner; it is therefore a measure having an effect equivalent to a quantitative restriction on imports prohibited by [Article 34 TFEU], subject to the exceptions laid down by [Union] law.

These possible exceptions to the rule on limiting trade were listed as the effec-tiveness of fiscal supervision, the protection of public health, the fairness of commercial transactions and the defence of the consumer.[5] Together, these are known as the 'mandatory requirements'. Perhaps unnecessarily, the protection of health was listed here as a possible basis upon which a Member State could maintain a law that was, prima facie, contrary to the application of Article 34 of the TFEU. It was unnecessary because the protection of health is already listed in Article 36 as providing such an exception. This is discussed further below. However, the protection of consumers is not included in the Article 36 exceptions, but the Court here added it to the list of possible justifications for the maintenance of national trade-restricting rules.

Having decided that the rule was caught within the scope of Article 34 of the TFEU, it then had to be determined whether its existence could be justified on any of the grounds set out. Two arguments were put forward here. The first was that the application of the rule was necessary to protect public health. This was rejected. The German Government had claimed that the rule was necessary as it was designed to prevent the proliferation of low-alcohol products on the market. The Court noted that there was a wide range of other low-alcohol beverages freely available in Germany and that no similar restrictions had been placed on these. The second argument put forward was that the measure was necessary to protect consumer interests. This was also rejected. Here, the case made was that the alco-hol level in a product was usually reflected in the price, so lower-alcohol products would therefore have a competitive advantage over their higher-priced rivals. This turned out to be a weak point, as it failed to recognise that there are also advantages to the consumer of having both cheaper alternatives and a wider range of products on the market, facilitating better choice. A better argument that was made related

---

[5] Case 120/1978, n 3 above, para 8 of the judgment.

to the fact that allowing products into lawful free circulation where they comply with the rules laid down in another Member State would lead to standardisation at the lowest level. In other words, if a Member State had no minimum alcohol content requirement, then no other Member State could impose their minimum permitted levels. This could lead to a 'race to the bottom', where there could be no standards at all where even a single Member State had no compositional requirements in a particular area. This would '[render] any requirements in this field inoperative since a lower limit of this nature is foreign to the rules of several Member States'.[6]

The solution presented by the Court continues to be hugely significant in this area. It was presented as 'a simple matter'. Member States could not impose rules like these on imports. The more proportionate response would be 'to ensure that suitable information is conveyed to the purchaser by requiring the display of an indication of origin and of the alcohol content on the packaging of products'.[7] Labelling could be used to relay the details about the nature and composition of a product to consumers. Anything more inhibiting to trade than this would be deemed an unlawful obstacle to trade, prohibited by Article 34 TFEU. Consumers could be sufficiently protected by the more proportionate response of requiring adequate labelling disclosures.

Finally, the Court encapsulated all of this in the principle of mutual recognition, which is central to understanding EU rules on the free movement of food and the impact that they have on national laws. It stated that:

> [t]here is ... no valid reason why, provided that they have been lawfully produced and marketed in one of the Member States, alcoholic beverages should not be introduced into any other Member State; the sale of such products may not be subject to a legal prohibition on the marketing of beverages with an alcohol content lower than the limits set by the national rules.[8]

Therefore and most significantly, once a foodstuff is lawfully produced and marketed in one EU Member State, it must be lawfully marketable in all EU Member States.

The decision in *Cassis* applied to a set of circumstances where the use of labelling presented an easy remedy to satisfy the test of proportionality. The Court insisted that it was always, where possible, more trade-promoting to insist upon clear indications on the label than it would be to have an outright prohibition in place. However, sometimes, the labelling itself can be the issue. There may be no prohibition on the sale of a particular product, but instead there may be a restriction in place on the use of a particular sales name. Suppose, for example, domestic law was to prescribe that rye bread must contain at least 50 per cent rye flour. If it is produced and marketed as rye bread in another Member State but it is made with only 40 per cent rye flour, then it could still be sold in Ireland, but it could

[6] Ibid, para 12.
[7] Ibid, para 13.
[8] Ibid, para 14.

not be marketed as 'rye bread' under Irish law. It could still be sold as 'bread'. Irish law has not prohibited the sale of the product. It has just prohibited the use of a particular sales name, one that it wishes to preserve for products that meet a minimum standard in relation to the main ingredient of the product concerned. Article 34 TFEU would prevent this. On the application of the principle of mutual recognition developed by the Court of Justice in *Cassis*, it would require that Irish law be modified to allow the sale of imported rye bread as rye bread in Ireland, even where the 50 per cent rye flour standard was not met. Other labelling disclosures could be used instead to indicate this difference. A reference in the list of ingredients could be used to indicate that there was only 40 per cent rye flour and not the usual minimum 50 per cent. Here we see the far-reaching consequences of the decision in *Cassis*. There it applied to an outright prohibition. The liqueur could not be sold in its imported format under any name. The alcohol content was too low to allow this. In our hypothetical rye bread situation, it applies merely to a labelling indication – one where it would be considered a more proportionate response to indicate the difference between the products concerned by using another labelling disclosure to bring this to the attention of the consumer. The imported product could still be marketed as 'rye bread', with the ingredients list clearly indicating the quantity of rye flour used in production.

The principle of mutual recognition has been applied by the Court of Justice in a number of free movement of food-related cases since its original inception in *Cassis*. Liqueurs were also the subject of the Court's deliberations in *Fietje*, where proceedings had been brought at national level against a trader who was selling alcoholic drinks which did not carry the word 'likeur' on the labelling, as they were obliged to do for this type of drink under Dutch law.[9] It was recognised by the Court of Justice that the national law at issue did not prohibit the importation of the products in question into the State, but it did make their marketing there more difficult. It was thus capable of impeding, directly or indirectly, actually or potentially, interstate trade. As the rule was within the scope of that which was prohibited by the application of Article 34 TFEU, it would have to be justifiable on the grounds of health or consumer protection if it were to be maintained and if the action against the respondent in this case could proceed. The Court recognised, as it does in these Article 34 TFEU cases, that national rules like this may be deemed necessary where they provide consumers with protection by seeking to minimise confusion. This can be the case even where the rules oblige the importer to alter the labelling of their product in some way, such as with the addition of the word 'likeur'. While the Court regularly states this as being its position, it almost always finds that the other disclosures already made on the label are sufficient to prevent such confusion amongst consumers. In *Fietje*, for example, it was stated that:

> there is no longer any need for such protection if the details given on the original label
> of the imported product have as their content information on the nature of the product

---

[9] Case 27/1980 *Criminal proceedings against Anton Adriaan Fietje* [1980] ECR 3839.

and that content includes at least the same information and is just as capable of being understood by consumers in the importing State, as the description prescribed by the rules of that State.[10]

The Dutch rule on the labelling of these liqueurs was thus found to be in contravention of Article 34 TFEU where sufficient or similar information was still provided to consumers elsewhere on the labels used on the imported products, including those that did not directly comply with the 'likeur' requirement. The fact that the application of the rule made it necessary for some imported products to have their labels altered made the law a measure equivalent to a quantitative restriction on imports. This could not be justified unless it could be shown that its non-application would be likely to cause confusion amongst consumers. This would be a difficult thing to prove where the labelling disclosures of imported products provided information on the nature of the product. The Court of Justice decided in *Cassis* that additional labelling disclosures are preferable and more proportionate than prohibitions. The same court determined in *Fietje* that national obligations to provide additional labelling disclosures on food or drink may also, depending on the circumstances, be contrary to EU rules on free movement.

In similar circumstances to those examined by the Court of Justice in *Cassis*, Dutch rules setting a minimum alcohol requirement for 'jenever' came under scrutiny in *Miro*.[11] An off-licence operator had been prosecuted for selling Belgian jenever, a gin-style drink, in the Netherlands which failed to meet the stipulation on alcohol level. The product had been lawfully manufactured and marketed in Belgium for many years. The national court had already found that consumers were adequately protected and informed by the label of the Belgian drink, as it clearly indicated the origin of the product and its alcohol content.

The Dutch authorities argued before the European Court of Justice that this was not sufficient to indicate a significant difference between the varieties as (i) many consumers would not know that jenever 'traditionally' had an alcohol content of 35 per cent and not 30 per cent as was the case in Belgium; and (ii) the labelling would be completely ineffective where the drink was sold in hotels and restaurants. The Court rejected the Dutch claims, instead accepting that the information provided on the label of the Belgian variety was sufficient to inform consumers and needed no further examination. The Dutch rules were thus deemed contrary to Article 34 TFEU, being unjustifiable on consumer protection grounds.

In *van der Laan* proceedings had been brought in Germany against a meat distributor for selling products that were not in compliance with provisions of German food law.[12] Under this law, the producers of cured meats and meat products were obliged to be quite categorical with their labelling disclosures. For example, a product that the respondent had called 'Bristol' should, under the

---

[10] Ibid, para 12.
[11] Case 182/1984 *Criminal Proceedings against Miro BV* [1985] ECR 3731.
[12] Case C-383/1997 *Criminal Proceedings against Arnoldus van der Laan* [1999] ECR I-731.

terms of the Code, have been labelled as 'formed shoulder ham composed of ham pieces'. In addition to this, the German Code prohibited the addition of water to meat products and it required that cured pork products should actually contain 100 per cent pork meat, at least 90 per cent of which should be muscle meat protein. The disputed products did not meet any of these standards, so could not therefore be lawfully marketed in Germany. The Court of Justice was asked whether rules like these were allowable under any of the permitted exceptions to the terms of Article 34 TFEU.

It is clear that German food law, as it applied to these meat products, was a measure equivalent to a quantitative restriction on imports. It was argued that this was justifiable on the ground of consumer protection. In response to this, the Court of Justice stated that consumer protection:

> can be guaranteed by means which do not hinder the importation of products which have been lawfully manufactured and marketed in other Member States, in particular by suitable labelling giving the nature of the product sold.[13]

At the time of the decision, the original framework food labelling directive had come into effect.[14] If the labelling of 'Bristol' complied with this, it would have to be lawfully marketable in Germany, regardless of how diluted the meat product had become in its manufacture. The Court found that if the products concerned carried details about both the meat and water content levels, they would be deemed in compliance with EU law. A list of ingredients that included water and whichever other substances had been added to the product could not be restricted in any other way. It was stated that:

> a Member State cannot claim that a list of ingredients which complies with [the framework food labelling] directive none the less constitutes fraud ... justifying the application of non-harmonised rules.[15]

This is a very significant and unsurprising, statement. Effectively, this is a licence to include any non-dangerous substance in the production of a foodstuff and allow it to be in free competition with purer versions of the same product. All the manufacturer is required to do to avail of this advantage is to include those additional constituents in the ingredients' list. Rather than protecting consumers, the obligation to present a list of ingredients on all pre-packaged foodstuffs, set out in both EU law and national law, actually provides a means of lawfully reducing the quality of products, ensuring that they must be allowed to freely circulate between Member States. The existence of these harmonised labelling requirements thereby facilitates the marketability of inferior quality products. This presents a problem for the consumer, the producer and for the State. The consumer is presented with

---

[13] Ibid, para 24.

[14] See Council Directive 1979/112/EEC of 18 December 1978 on the approximation of the laws of the Member States relating to the labelling, presentation and advertising of foodstuffs for sale to the ultimate consumer [1979] OJ L 33/1Dir 1979/112.

[15] Para 37 of Case C-383/1997, n 12 above.

a lower-quality product as if it is equivalent to the higher-quality variety. The only way of determining this difference is to compare the lists of ingredients. The quantity of water or other substances used may not even be properly disclosed. Their presence should be indicated in the ingredients list, but there will not necessarily be any indication of how much of these have been added. There is no obligation to include the quantity of water, for example, used in production – unless, as is unlikely, water has been specifically referenced on the packaging as being a characteristic feature of the product.[16] The producer of the higher-quality product, who does not add water or other substances to his foods, must now compete in this environment with the cheaper substitute.

The quality and the nutritional value of food often deteriorates as other, cheaper, substances are added to foods. It was noted in Chapter 1 that these additions to food were prohibited by domestic law, as this was deemed to be 'adulteration'. This practice, depending on what is added to the food, can result in poorer health, higher rates of obesity and related disease. The cost of this to both the Health Service Executive and to economic output is substantial.[17] EU rules on the free movement of food are contributing to the proliferation of lower-quality and nutritionally inferior foods. Food law, which has done so much to improve the safety and quality of products in the past, is now being destabilised in the interests of free movement. As is clearly demonstrated by the findings of the Court of Justice in cases such as *van der Laan*, national laws designed to maintain quality standards are being undermined and their application deemed unlawful, by the process of harmonisation at EU level. The State may suffer also.

The case of *Gilli and Andres* concerned a more outright prohibition on the sale of certain foods.[18] Here, criminal proceedings had been brought at national level against both respondents for selling apple vinegar in Italy. Italian law prescribed that only products made through the fermentation of wine could be marketed as vinegar. It was contended that such a rule was in contravention of Article 34 TFEU, the apple vinegar in question being lawfully manufactured and marketed in Germany before importation into Italy. The Court agreed. It found that there were no grounds available for justifying the ban on apple vinegar. It contained no substances that could be harmful to human health. Nor was there the potential for there to be confusion amongst consumers, as the receptacles containing the apple vinegar were clearly labelled as such. The national law at issue served no purpose in the general interest that could take precedence over Union requirements on the free movement of goods.

---

[16] Art 22 of the Food Information Regulation 1169/2011, [2011] OJ L 304/18, provides that 'the indication of the quantity of an ingredient … used in the manufacture or preparation of a food shall be required where the ingredient … appears in the name of the food … is emphasised on the labelling in words, pictures or graphics or is essential to characterise a food'. Otherwise, ingredients need only be listed, albeit in descending order of weight or volume used in production – but actual quantities need not be disclosed. This is discussed in more detail in ch 7.

[17] For more detailed discussion on this, see ch 9.

[18] Case 788/1979 *Criminal Proceedings against Gilli and Andres* [1980] ECR 2071.

The Commission later took infringement proceedings against Italy for persisting with these restrictions on use of the name 'vinegar'.[19] Italy had already been issued with two reasoned opinions by the Commission indicating that the rules at issue contravened EU free movement requirements. Italy responded by claiming that Italian consumers considered all vinegar to be made from the fermentation of wine. Consequently, the use of this sales name by vinegars produced in a different manner or with alternative ingredients was therefore, in their opinion, liable to confuse Italian consumers. This was again rejected. The Court held that 'vinegar' was a generic term and that:

> it would not be compatible with the objectives of the common market and in particular with the fundamental principle of the free movement of goods for national legislation to be able to restrict a generic term to one national variety alone to the detriment of other varieties produced, in particular, in other Member States.[20]

However, the Court did not completely discard the possibility that there could be confusion amongst consumers in a State where they had become accustomed to the reservation of a particular generic name for a specific product, such as vinegar produced from wine. While the Member State could be permitted to intervene in support of its consumers, it would have to do so in a manner which was more proportionate to the aim being pursued. Labelling disclosures alerting them to the difference would suffice. This would only be acceptable practice, however, where the affixing of labels indicating details about the nature of the product applied to all types of the product concerned. According to the Court of Justice, this would place the importer at no more of a disadvantage than the domestic producer. All would have to comply with the same labelling obligations. However, this is not necessarily the case. The imported product could have to comply with two sets of national labelling requirements – those applicable in the importing State as well as those with which it must comply to be lawfully marketable in the State of production. The Court is therefore clearly differentiating between foods where a failure to provide detailed labelling disclosures could cause confusion, presumably for some factor like the degree to which national consumers associate a particular name with a product possessing specific characteristics.

While the Court demonstrates a degree of flexibility here with the way in which it applies EU rules on the free movement of goods, it is also at odds with its clear statement in *Commission v UK*, albeit in the context of discriminatory domestic taxation on wine and beer, that 'Member State [policies] must not therefore crystallise given consumer habits so as to consolidate an advantage acquired by national industries concerned to comply with them'.[21] Member States should not be able to use their failure to comply with EU free movement requirements to

---

[19] Case 193/1980 *Commission v Italy* [1981] ECR 3019.
[20] Ibid, para 26.
[21] Case 170/1978 *Commission v UK* [1980] ECR 417, para 14. For more on this see S Weatherill, *EU consumer law and policy* (Cheltenham, Edward Elgar, 2005) ch 2.

justify their continued flouting of the rules. If the Court were to compel all vinegars to carry clear labelling disclosures, beyond those set by their own national laws, thereby placing an additional burden on imports which could have to carry two sets of labels, one for their own market and one for the importing State, it would, in effect, be supporting something that was contrary to free movement rules. It would be allowing the fact that Italian consumers, for example, had been under-exposed to other types of vinegar, primarily due to the restrictive Italian laws, to justify the need for additional labelling presentations for imported vinegars, which were placing an additional burden on their producers.

One of the most significant cases on national compositional requirements came about when the Commission queried the lawfulness of Germany's centuries-old rules on beer production.[22] At issue was the application of the 'Biersteuergesetz', which set manufacturing requirements for breweries established in Germany, as well as conditions attached to the use of the sales name 'Bier' (beer) for all such products sold in Germany, regardless of where they had been manufactured. Under these rules, German Bier had to be made from a combination of malts (usually barley), hops, yeast and water – and nothing else. Imported beers not meeting this compositional requirement could be sold in Germany, but only under a different name. They could not be marketed as 'Bier'. They would also have to be additive-free. German law prescribed that additives could only be used in food production if they had been authorised for this purpose. Beer was, however, subject to special rules, which prescribed that only the specified ingredients listed above could be used in its manufacture. The use of any additional ingredients, including additives, was not allowed.

Germany maintained that the rules were necessary to protect consumers. In their view, there was an inseparable link in the German consumer's mind between the product 'Bier' and the application of the strict compositional requirements. In similar language to that mentioned above on the 'crystallisation' of consumer habits, the Court stated here that:

> consumers' conceptions which vary from one Member State to the other are also likely to evolve in the course of time within a Member State. The establishment of the common market is, it should be added, one of the factors that may play a major contributory role in that development. Whereas rules protecting consumers against misleading practices enable such a development to be taken into account, legislation of the kind [at issue here] prevents it from taking place.[23]

The EU's policy in support of the free movement of food is well encapsulated in this statement. It recognises that there are differences between consumer expecta-tions in different Member States; however, the proper promotion of free movement should diminish this. Consumer expectations will evolve, becoming more harmo-nised. Protecting consumers through trade prohibitions would prevent this from

---

[22] Case 178/1984 *Commission v Germany* [1987] ECR 1227.
[23] Ibid, para 32.

happening. Free movement itself will therefore reduce the need for compositional requirements like those at issue here.

There is a second argument that could be made here. The case law of the Court of Justice makes it clear that labelling disclosures are usually sufficient to inform consumers about the nature or characteristics of a product, even where these differ from what they may be expecting. As a result of the development of this line of reasoning in *Cassis*, the Commission later decided that this removed the need for the introduction of harmonised compositional requirements for most foodstuffs at EU level.[24] There would only be a need for food laws in the future where this was necessary for some obvious health, consumer or environmental protection purpose. It essentially decided that there would be no need for many more 'recipe laws', which set minimum standards for certain foodstuffs. These usually take the form of vertical legislation, applying to one type of food. They are discussed in more detail in Chapter 7. At this point, however, it must be remembered from *Cassis* that the German authorities argued that the principle of mutual recognition would lead to a 'race to the bottom', where no Member State could apply its minimum compositional rules if there were no similar rules in any other Member State. That threat remains. 'Recipe laws' offer a potential solution to this problem. Setting broad harmonised compositional requirements at EU level for certain foodstuffs, which would apply no matter where in the Union the products were made, would at least guarantee that some sort of minimum standards were being met. What has developed post-*Cassis* is a major drawback in the way in which maximising the potential for the free movement of food is pursued. There is little regard for consumer expectations in different Member States. There is almost no concern about the fact that foods must be allowed to trade freely even where they fail to meet basic compositional requirements. A return to the development of a body of 'recipe laws' could really assist in this regard. This is also discussed in more detail in Chapter 7.

The Court of Justice in *Commission v Germany* found that use of the German designation 'Bier' and its equivalents in other languages could not be restricted to products manufactured according to the purity law requirements.[25] Avoiding confusion and failing to meet consumer expectations could, it was stated, be ensured by other, more proportionate means, in particular labelling. According to the Court, a list of ingredients would achieve this.

Cases on the application of EU rules on measures equivalent to quantitative restrictions on trade often arise when laws are designed to protect, in some way, products that are an important part of national food culture. In *Zoni*, for example, proceedings had been brought before the Italian courts against a wholesaler who had imported pasta from Germany.[26] Italian law at the time provided that dry

---

[24] Commission Communication on the free movement of foodstuffs within the Community [1989] OJ C 271/3.

[25] See Case 178/1984, *Commission v Germany*, n 22 above.

[26] Case 90/1986 *Criminal Proceedings against Zoni* [1988] ECR 4285.

pasta had to be made from durum wheat only and that it could not be sold in Italy where it had been mixed with other wheats. Fresh pasta and that which was made for export could be made with a mixture of durum and non-durum wheats. The Italian Government claimed that the law was necessary to protect the quality of pasta available to consumers in Italy and to promote the durum wheat industry. The respondent claimed that this was contrary to EU rules on the free movement of food. The Court of Justice agreed. Noting its earlier decision in *Cassis*, the Court accepted that protecting consumers was a legitimate function of national law, but also that where this happens these laws must be based on the most proportionate response available in the circumstances.[27] Following its earlier decisions in *Commission v Italy*,[28] and the *Beer Purity* case,[29] the Court held that the most proportionate response available in circumstances like these was to require that appropriate disclosures should be made on the product's label. This would already happen here because the Italian law at issue and the relevant EU legislation,[30] required the listing of ingredients. This list would disclose the presence of other types of wheat used in the production of the pasta to the consumer. The Court also found that the option of restricting use of the wording 'pasta made from durum wheatmeal' to products which contained no other type of wheat was available to the Italian authorities, thus providing even more clarity for consumers.

While many free movement of food issues have been examined over the years by the European Court of Justice, one issue that has not been satisfactorily resolved is what is to happen in the case of foods served in restaurants and other catering establishments. They are not pre-packaged and are not subject to the same labelling requirements. The argument was made in *Zoni* that use of the word 'pasta' on a menu, for example, would suggest a product made exclusively from durum wheat. As noted earlier, however, Italian law did permit the use of other types of wheat for other types of pasta, such as that which was to be served fresh or which was manufactured for the export market. Pasta was, therefore, in the opinion of the Court, a generic term. The Italian authorities could not restrict its use, either for pre-packaged dry pasta, or for that which was to be served fresh or exported.

4.2.3. Packaging as an Impediment to the Free Movement of Food

The cases outlined up to this point have mostly related in one way or another to national laws designed to regulate the internal compositional requirements of

---

[27] Ibid, para 10.
[28] See Case 193/1980 *Commission v Italy*, n 19 above.
[29] See n 22.
[30] The relevant EU legislation in operation at the time was Council Directive 1979/112/EEC of 18 December 1978 on the approximation of the laws of the Member States relating to the labelling, presentation and advertising of foodstuffs for sale to the ultimate consumer [1979] OJ L 33/1. It is discussed in much more detail in ch 7.

foodstuffs. Those which limit, or compel, the use of specified external features, such as packaging, have also faced Court of Justice scrutiny. The shape of margarine tubs, for example, was examined in *Rau*.[31] Here, Belgian law only permitted the sale of margarine if it was packaged in cube-shaped containers. A German seller brought proceedings against a Belgian buyer who refused a consignment of margarine that had been packaged in cone-shaped tubs. It was questioned as to whether this packaging requirement was a measure equivalent to a quantitative restriction on imports of the type prohibited by Article 34 TFEU.

The Court found that there was clearly a restriction on trade, further evidenced by the fact that there was very little foreign margarine available for sale in Belgium, despite the product commanding appreciably higher prices there than in many other EU Member States. The only justification for this requirement was that it was necessary to prevent consumers from confusing margarine with butter by obliging that it be sold in different-shaped containers. It was accepted that this was a legitimate concern, but also that an outright prohibition on the use of a packaging type that was lawfully used elsewhere in the Union was completely disproportionate. Consumers could, in the opinion of the Court, be protected 'just as effectively by other measures, for example by rules on labelling, which hinder the free movement of goods less'.[32]

In *Prantl*, criminal proceedings had been brought against an Italian drinks dealer for persistently importing wine into Germany which was to be sold in bulbous-shaped bottles, or 'Bocksbeutel'. This type of bottle had been used by a range of quality German wines for centuries. It had also, however, been used by wine producers in parts of Italy for more than 100 years. There were some slight differences between the two varieties of bulbous-shaped bottles used, but they were very similar. National law prescribed that only specified German wines could be marketed in this type of bottle there.

It was queried whether the application of this rule was an unlawful and unjustifiable impediment to the free movement of goods. The German Government argued that the measure at issue was not contrary to EU law as it did not have an appreciable effect on trade between Member States; that it applied to national and imported products alike; that it only made the non-authorised use of the 'Bocksbeutel' an offence and did not therefore usually apply to imported products which were marketed in slightly different bottles; and, finally, that this was justified on grounds of consumer protection. The first point was dismissed on the basis of *Dassonville*.[33] The measure at issue would only have to 'directly or indirectly, actually or potentially' affect inter-State trade to be caught within the scope of Article 34 TFEU. It was not a requirement that any impact on trade would have to be 'appreciable'. The second argument was also dismissed, the Court pointing out that national measures would still be examinable under Article 34 if they, in

---

[31] Case 261/1981 *Walter Rau Lebensmittelwerke v De Smedt PVBA* [1982] ECR 3961.
[32] Ibid, para 17.
[33] See Case 8/1974, *Procureur du Roi v Benoît and Gustave Dassonville* above n 1.

practice, gave national products any trading advantage, even where there was detriment to other domestic production. A producer using a bulbous bottle in their own State would be met with an additional cost and burden if required to change the packaging or container shape to meet the marketing conditions of another Member State.

It was not accepted by the Court in *Prantl* that the application of law on bottle shape was necessary to protect consumers. Other legislation existed at Union level to ensure that such confusion would not arise. For example, provision was made in the 1979 Wines Regulation,[34] which set a range of labelling requirements for quality wines which, it was stated, were 'particularly comprehensive and enable the feared confusion to be avoided'.[35] The rules on bulbous bottle use were therefore deemed to be a measure equivalent to a quantitative restriction on imports, deemed to be unnecessary and unjustifiable on grounds of consumer protection.

EU Member States have also used the health protection exception to the prohibition on measures equivalent to quantitative restrictions, contained in Article 36 TFEU, to justify food packaging requirements which could potentially inhibit trade. In *Schwarz*, for example, the Court of Justice examined whether it was permissible for Austria to have a ban in place on the sale of unwrapped chewing-gum from vending machines.[36] Normally, questions such as this would be examinable for compatibility with EU hygiene regulations, but these did not apply to machine-vended confectionery at the time in question.[37] They therefore needed to be tested for compliance with free movement requirements only. The Court found that the rule at issue was an impediment to trade. Importers who wished to sell their confectionery through vending machines in Austria would have to ensure that it was pre-packaged, making importation into that State more expensive and cumbersome. They might even have been required to change the type of machine that they use for this purpose as those designed for non-packaged goods could not usually be used to vend packaged goods also. However, the Court did find that the rule was justifiable on health protection grounds. The Austrian Health and Food Safety Agency demonstrated to the Court how non-pre-packaged goods sold from vending machines were often contaminated with insects. Unwashed hands were used to retrieve chewing-gum from the machines, also leading to the spread of contamination between consumers. For these reasons, the prohibition on selling unwrapped goods was deemed both adequate and, most importantly, proportionate to the aim pursued, namely the protection of health.

---

[34] Council Regulation (EEC) No 355/1979 of 5 February 1979 laying down general rules for the description and presentation of wines and grape musts [1979] OJ L 54/99. Arts 12–18 of the Regulation, in particular Art 12, sets out a series of labelling and identification requirements for quality wines produced in specified regions within the Member States.

[35] Case 16/1983 *Prantl* [1984] ECR 1299, para 29.

[36] Case C-366/2004 *Georg Schwarz v Bürgermeister der Landeshauptstadt Salzburg* [2005] ECR I-10139.

[37] At the time, the EU legislation on hygiene standards in the food sector was Council Directive 1993/43/EC [1993] OJ L 175/1. The hygiene regulations and their application in Irish law are dealt with in more detail in ch 6.

4.2.4. Determining 'Substantial Difference' when Considering Consumer Protection

It is possible for national laws on a whole range of issues related to the manufacture and marketing of food to be subject to assessment for compatibility with EU rules on the free movement of goods. However, it is those rules which prescribe a minimum or maximum quantity for one of the food's constituents that most often leads to these rules facing Court examination, just as it originally was in *Cassis*. The Court made it clear in that case that imported products that were at variance with these national compositional requirements must still be lawfully marketable in the host State, without trade impediment. Despite this, there are some circumstances where Member States may be allowed to stipulate a compositional requirement, but this is effectively limited, as far as consumer protection is concerned, to those circumstances where there is a 'substantial difference' between the imported product and those which are normally marketed using the same name.

The possibility of allowing 'substantial difference' to be used as a basis for deviating from the usual interpretation of EU rules on the free movement of food was first established by the Court of Justice in *Deserbais*.[38] Here, French rules prohibited the marketing of cheese, in this case a consignment of German Edam, where the fat content was below 40 per cent. The German cheese in this case had a fat content of around 34 per cent. Proceedings were brought before the French courts against the respondent for a failing to comply with this requirement. As a defence, it was claimed that the French law at issue was in contravention of Article 34 TFEU, in that it was a measure equivalent to a quantitative restriction on imports. The cheese was lawfully produced and marketed in another Member State. Under the principle of mutual recognition, developed by the Court in *Cassis*, it would, therefore, have to be lawfully marketable in France, regardless of the French law on the matter. The Court of Justice agreed. Information on the packaging disclosing the actual fat content of the cheese would be a more proportionate response in the circumstances than would be a prohibition on the sale of the product. It did, however, also determine that in some circumstances consumers may not be adequately protected by such labelling disclosures. This could be the case where there was such a 'substantial difference' between the imported product and foods normally marketed using the same sales name that there was the probability of confusing consumers. This is potentially a key exception to the principle of mutual recognition – the test of 'substantial difference' – and it has come before the Court of Justice on a number of occasions.

Having followed the usual post-*Cassis* jurisprudence on the proportionality of labelling requirements, the Court turned its attention to those circumstances where there is a measure equivalent to a quantitative restriction on imports, but where there may also be a potential justification for the maintenance of such a

---

[38] Case 286/1986 *Ministère Public v Gérard Deserbais* [1988] ECR 4907.

measure due to the level of difference between the imported variety of a product and that with which it could be confused were the national law at issue not applied. It queried whether the principle of mutual recognition:

> must be applied where a product presented under a particular name is so different, as regards its composition or production, from the products generally known by that name in the [Union] that it cannot be regarded as falling within the same category.[39]

The Court went on to find that 'no situation of that kind arises ... in this case'. It reached this conclusion by looking at the defining characteristics of the 'product generally known by that name' to test whether there was substantial difference between this and those of the lower-fat cheese at issue. Here, the Court looked to the international standards for Edam cheese, noting that both the United Nations Codex Alimentarius Commission and the 1951 Stresa Convention on Cheese state that the minimum fat content should be 40 per cent. This level was not deemed to be sufficient to illustrate a substantial difference between the products at issue here. The difference between 34 per cent fat and 40 per cent fat was not 'substantial'. The Court also clearly stated that it would not be bound by such international instruments, noting that the Stresa Convention predated the existence of EU obligations on the free movement of food and should not apply to trade between Member States. International Conventions like this could continue to place obligations on Member States, but only in relation to their dealings with third countries who were not members of the EU.[40] If there was no substantial difference between the cheeses at issue, then there could be no grounds for maintaining a prohibition on the use of a food name for a product imported from another EU Member State on the basis that this might be necessary for consumer protection. This would be a disproportionate. Labelling disclosures on fat content would suffice.

Substantial difference and the consequent confusion or deception that this might cause, is really the only basis upon which the protection of consumers can be readily used by EU Member States as a justification for the maintenance of national trade-impeding compositional requirements, although, again, rarely with success. Any test for substantial difference will require an identification of the key characteristics of the foodstuff normally known by the name at issue in the importing State. If the imported alternative does not possess these characteristics or does not possess them to a similar or significant level, then there may be substantial difference and the prohibition or restriction on the import will stand. The issue came before the Court of Justice again in *Smanor*.[41] Here, the product at issue was frozen yoghurt. The French authorities had sought to ban the sale of the respondent's product as 'yoghurt', preferring instead that it should be marketable only as 'deep-frozen fermented milk'. The argument was that the term 'yoghurt' should

---

[39] Ibid, para 13.
[40] As held in Case 812/1979 *Attorney General v Burgoa* [1980] ECR 2787.
[41] Case 298/1987 *Proceedings for Compulsory Reconstruction against Smanor SA* [1988] ECR 4489.

only be used for fresh fermented milk products which contained live bacteria at the rate of 100 million per gram.[42]

The first issue of note in this case related to the fact that the Court was being asked to address a set of circumstances related to a wholly French situation. All the relevant prior decided cases dealt with some inter-State element. They examined national measures which placed restrictions on the sale of imported foodstuffs. Here, the measure at issue was a French ban on a French product being sold in France. The free movement of food between Member States was not really a concern here. It was therefore queried as to whether Article 34 TFEU could still apply in the circumstances. The French Government argued that it should not, as there was no restriction being placed on imports or exports. However, the wording of the *Dassonville* formula clearly stipulates that a national measure must only affect trade 'actually or potentially', meaning that the French decree on yoghurt products could apply to frozen products made and lawfully marketed in other Member States, should they be imported into France at some stage in the future. There was the 'potential' for French law to impede interstate trade. Such rules could therefore be examined for compatibility with EU rules on measures equivalent to quantitative restrictions on trade, even where the facts of the case related to a wholly internal situation at that time.

On the issue of 'substantial difference', the Court of Justice found that consumers could be provided with adequate information on the nature of the product without placing any prohibition on the use of the name 'yoghurt' if the description 'deep-frozen' preceded it on the labelling. This would clearly show the treatment that the product had undergone in production. It was recognised, however, that the consumer may not be properly protected where the deep-frozen version of the product did not possess or retain the same essential characteristics as regular yoghurt. As in *Deserbais*, the Court looked at international standards to help it determine what the key characteristics of yoghurt are. Both the Codex Alimentarius standards and the regulations of other EU Member States indicated that the main distinguishing feature of yoghurt was the presence of live bacteria in abundant amounts. Therefore, substantial difference could be shown if these levels were significantly less for the product after it had undergone a process of deep-freezing. It would be for the national court to ultimately determine whether the bacteria levels dropped to a level that meant that the product could no longer carry the term 'yoghurt' in its sales name. This level would have to be so substantial as to justify the obligation to use a different name. If not, the consumer would, in the opinion of the Court of Justice, be adequately and appropriately protected where the deep-frozen variety was properly labelled.

---

[42] Art 2 of French Decree No 63-695 on the prevention of fraud with regard to fermented milk products and yoghurt (Official Journal of the French Republic of 16 July 1963, p 6512) as amended by Decree No 82-184 of 22 February 1982 (Official Journal of the French Republic of 25 February 1982, p 676).

The test of 'substantial difference' is, of course, very subjective. In *Deserbais*, the Court ruled that a reduced fat content was insufficient to show this difference. In *Smanor*, it left this to the national court to decide based on the facts before it. In both cases it was made clear that the difference would have to be at a level that rendered the product very different in some way. Minor difference is clearly not enough. The difference must be sufficient to alter or remove the defining characteristic or characteristics of the food in question. The Court of Justice has clearly articulated this point in *Foie Gras*,[43] where it stated that while:

> it is legitimate to enable consumers, who attribute specific qualities to products which are manufactured from particular raw materials or which have a given content of a characteristic ingredient, to make their choice in the light of such criteria [this] objective may be attained by means, other than the reservation of certain trade descriptions to products possessing particular qualities, which would be less restrictive on the marketing of products coming from a Member State which satisfy the rules laid down by that State, such as affixing suitable labels concerning the nature and characteristics of the product for sale.

However, this does:

> not exclude the possibility that Member States could require those concerned to alter the denomination of a foodstuff where a product presented under a particular denomination is so different, as regards its composition or production, from the products generally known under that denomination in the [Union] that it cannot be regarded as being in the same category.[44]

This was mostly a restatement of what was delivered in *Deserbais*, but it provides a good summary of the position on 'substantial difference'. The Court did also provide further guidance here on what can be examined to establish whether the level of difference is at the level necessary to be deemed 'substantial'. It stated, first of all, that the mere fact that a product does not wholly conform to national composition requirements is not enough to warrant a prohibition. However, it also found that national authorities are entitled to monitor the way in which suspected products are made to establish whether the raw materials and production methods used match up with the information that is provided on the label. This could then entitle the authorities to bring proceedings against those responsible for selling foodstuffs which are described as being identical to those which are covered by the national requirements, but which in reality 'are so different in content as to give rise to suspicion of deceit'. For this level of difference to be reached the imported foodstuff must 'depart markedly from the requirements imposed by the legislation of the State concerned'.[45] There must be evidence of this level of difference before a prohibition on imports can be justified. Mere suspicion of incomplete compliance with national compositional requirements is not enough. There must still be full

---

[43] Case C-184/1996 *Commission v France* [1998] ECR I-6197.
[44] Ibid, para 23.
[45] Ibid, para 25.

mutual recognition of products which are lawfully made and marketed in other Member States, unless substantial difference can be proved.

The Court in *Deserbais* provided the only real ground upon which a Member State may successfully justify the existence of national compositional requirements as being necessary for the protection of consumers. The Court has restated its position from *Cassis* on many occasions – the protection of consumers is a legitimate basis for derogating from the law on the free movement of goods as set out in Article 34 TFEU. Despite this, it is rare that the Court will accept that a prohibition on the marketing of a food under a particular sales name is proportionate for this purpose. It will, on some occasions, leave this to the national court to decide, as it did in *Smanor*. However, it is clear that it is only where there is a considerable, or substantial, difference between the imported product and the foodstuff normally known by that name that it will allow the State to act to prevent confusion amongst consumers. It can only be looked at on a case-by-case basis; it remains relatively unclear as to just what constitutes 'substantial' in the level of difference between the products concerned.

The European Commission has attempted to give some guidance in this regard in a Communication to the Member States, which was designed to provide some clarity in the aftermath of *Smanor* and *Deserbais*.[46] It stated that any test of substantial difference should be carried out on the subjective basis of consumer expectations and the objective basis of already existing rules and standards, including those of the Codex Alimentarius Commission and the other EU Member States. It should also involve some scrutiny of the ingredients and manufacturing methods used in the production of the foods that are being compared for equivalence. The Commission sets out that a substantial difference in any one of these tests may be sufficient to facilitate the Member State prohibiting the use of a particular generic sales name for products not meeting the requirements set. However, there is no further clarity provided on the degree of difference that there must be before it can be rendered 'substantial'. It is difficult to quantify.

The Court of Justice will not always look to the test of 'substantial difference' in its examinations of national measures that have an effect equivalent to a quantitative restriction on trade, even where the circumstances are almost identical to those which were scrutinised in cases such as *Deserbais*. In *Nespoli and Crippa*, for example, the Court examined whether Italian legislation which set minimum fat content for cheese was compatible with EU rules on the free movement of food.[47] It was found that these requirements, which were effectively a prohibition on those products which failed to meet the standard set, were a measure equivalent to a quantitative restriction on trade and that they were disproportionate to the aim pursued. They were an obstacle to trade that could not be justified on consumer

---

[46] Commission interpretative communication on the names under which food products are sold [1991] OJ C 270/2.

[47] Case C-196/1989 *Criminal Proceedings against Enzo Nespoli and Giuseppe Crippa* [1990] ECR I-3647.

protection grounds. While the usual solution of using labelling to disclose actual fat content was offered by the Court, it made no assessment of whether there was a level of difference between the varieties of cheese at issue to warrant an investigation into the existence, or otherwise, of a 'substantial difference' between them.

4.2.5. Protecting Human Health

It is quite common for two, or even three or more justifications to be put forward by Member States in support of their own trade-impeding measures. It is very common for both consumer protection and human health protection arguments to be made together. Other potential lines that can be taken include the promotion of a fair trading environment, where it is claimed that facilitating those who use cheaper substitute ingredients, for example, puts the more traditional producer at a competitive disadvantage. This often arises in those circumstances where the protection of consumers has been used as a justification for a national measure that is, on the face of it, at odds with the objectives of Article 34 TFEU. They are often two sides of the same argument – the consumer is protected by an assurance that certain ingredients have been used in the production of a particular foodstuff and the producer has been consequently protected as only he will be able to use the disputed food name by meeting the compositional requirement that has been set. It has also been argued that promoting the same aims as those of the Union should be a valid justification for the application of national standards. In the *Milk Substitutes* cases, for example, it was put forward by the respondent Member States that a prohibition on the marketing of substitute milk favoured the consumption of regular milk and dairy products, which was, it was pointed out, also one of the aims of the Common Agricultural Policy.[48] This has been rejected on a number of occasions, on the basis that national measures cannot exist contrary to a fundamental principle of Union law, such as the free movement of goods, unless clearly justified by a reason recognised in EU law.[49] The strongest argument that can be put forward by a Member State in such circumstances is that the measure at issue is necessary to protect human health.

While Article 34 TFEU provides that quantitative restrictions on trade and all measures of equivalent effect are prohibited, Article 36 TFEU states that:

> [this] shall not preclude prohibitions or restrictions on imports, exports or goods in transit justified on grounds of … the protection of health and life of humans, animals or plants [provided that] such prohibitions or restrictions shall not, however, constitute a means of arbitrary discrimination or a disguised restriction on trade between Member States.

---

[48] Case 216/1984 *Commission v France* [1988] ECR 793 and Case 76/1986 *Commission v Germany* [1989] ECR 1021.

[49] The argument was similarly rejected by the Court of Justice in Case 274/1987 *Commission v Germany* [1989] ECR 229 in relation to the promotion of meat consumption.

While the Court of Justice developed the consumer protection exception to the prohibition on measures of equivalent effect to quantitative restrictions on trade, the Treaty has always clearly provided for an exception based on the need to protect human health. A more practical distinction between these two exceptions is that a ban on the sale of a foodstuff on health grounds more readily satisfies the proportionality test than one based on consumer protection. The case law already discussed in this chapter clearly shows just how difficult it is for Member States to ever demonstrate that a prohibition based on consumer protection is the most proportionate response available in the circumstances. Labelling will, in the opinion of the Court, be less restrictive on trade but just as effective in protecting the interests of the consumer. If, however, a foodstuff includes ingredients that may pose a threat to human health, a prohibition on the sale of that product may be the only reasonable option available in the circumstances.

Both consumer protection and health protection arguments were put forward by Member States to justify their trade-impeding measures in many of the early cases on the free movement of food. In *Cassis*, for example, as was pointed out earlier, a weak argument was made that the maintenance of minimum alcohol level requirements for fruit liqueurs was necessary to prevent the over-exposure of consumers to cheaper, low-alcohol varieties.[50] Failure to do this, it was claimed, could lead to a greater tolerance for alcohol amongst German consumers. Unsurprisingly, this was rejected by the Court, who found that many moderately alcoholic products were already widely available on the German market. It also noted that many of those products with a higher alcohol content were often consumed in diluted form. A stronger health protection argument was put forward by Germany in the *Beer Purity* case.[51] While the consumer protection justification was based on reserving the name 'Bier' for those beverages which were made entirely from a limited list of ingredients, it was stated that the rules were also necessary for health protection purposes in that they banned the inclusion of additives.

The German authorities sought to minimise the quantity of additives being ingested by their populace. They considered that the long-term dangers of consuming additives were not fully known and, in particular, that there was uncertainty about how health could be affected by the interaction of additives with alcohol in the body. As beer was consumed in large quantities in Germany, it would be desirable to prohibit the use of additives in production and, as was pointed out, their use was technologically unnecessary if the purity requirements were followed in the first place.

Noting its seminal decision in *Sandoz*,[52] which is discussed in more detail below, the Court accepted that uncertainty about the use of particular ingredients could be used by Member States to justify national measures designed to protect human health. This would, however, be limited to that which was absolutely

---

[50] See Case 120/1978 *Rewe-Zentral AG v Bundesmonopolverwaltung für Branntwein*, n 3 above.
[51] See n 22 above.
[52] Case 174/1982 *Criminal Proceedings against Sandoz BV* [1983] ECR 2445.

necessary to protect health, in particular where the measure at issue was a prohibition. The German rules prohibited all additive use in beer production. There was no assessment, therefore, of individual additives to test for their safety. Some expert reports were submitted by Germany in support of their claim that the ingestion of additives in general could be harmful to health. However, many of the additives used in the manufacture of beer in other Member States were permitted for use in the manufacture of food in Germany. It would be difficult, therefore, to stand over a claim that the purity requirements for beer were premised on a desire to protect health.

The extent to which Member States can legitimately limit the use of additives in food production is a controversial one. In the *Beer Purity* case, the German authorities pointed out that there was no technological need for the use of additives if only the prescribed natural ingredients were used in production. The Court, however, countered this by finding that a lack of necessity does not equate to a lack of technological function. This is discussed in more detail below in the context of additive use in food production more generally, but it does demonstrate a fundamental point about the jurisprudence of the Court of Justice when it comes to the health protection justification. It is usually, if not always, upheld that only where there is a clear and identifiable danger to human health, attached to the use of a specific ingredient or production process, that the Article 36 TFEU exception can be successfully invoked by Member States to justify their related national measures. This point is also made more clearly in other cases, in particular those which deal with the nutritional value of food.

Having said that, some more recent developments in the case law of the Court of Justice now suggest that there is an increasing recognition that, in some circumstances at least, decisions about the measures that should be adopted to address dangers posed to public health might be best determined by the organs of the State and not those of the EU.[53] This constitutes a new judicial approach.

The Court of Justice has found, in a number of cases, that national measures designed to promote or maintain the nutritional quality or value of food is not an acceptable use of the health protection exception set out in Article 36 TFEU. This was established in the *Meat Purity* case, where national requirements on the use of additional ingredients in meat products were assessed for compatibility with EU rules on the free movement of food.[54] German regulations prohibited the marketing of meat products which contained ingredients other than meat, subject to some exceptions. The national law on foodstuffs banned the importation of products that were not in compliance with this requirement. The German Government maintained that the contested prohibition was justified on grounds of health protection because it was necessary to ensure a sufficient intake of essential nutrients from meat, especially protein. Two reports, produced by the

---

[53] Case C-333/2014 *Scotch Whisky Association and Others v The Lord Advocate and the Advocate General for Scotland* ECLI:EU:C:2015:845. The decision in *Scotch Whisky* is also discussed in ch 9.
[54] Case 274/1987 *Commission v Germany* [1989] ECR 229.

German Government, showed that protein intake levels were, in general, more than adequate. Even where consumption was at a level below that which was recommended, especially amongst younger sections of the population, this was at a level that was found to pose no threat to health. The reports also showed that some meat ingredients could contain harmful substances, such as purine, cholesterol and saturated fatty acids and that therefore there should be concern about increased consumption.

What is most significant in the *Meat Purity* judgment, however, is what the Court had to say on national measures designed to maintain nutrient levels and the health benefits that could be derived therefrom. The German Government argued that vegetable proteins, present in the ingredients typically added to meat in these products, have a lower nutritional value than animal proteins. Referring to its earlier decision in the *Milk Substitutes* case,[55] the Court restated the position that:

> a Member State may not invoke public health grounds in order to prohibit the importation of a product by arguing that its nutritional value is lower than another product already available on the market in question, since it is plain that the choice of foodstuffs available to consumers in the [Union] is such that the mere fact that an imported product has a lower nutritional value does not pose a real threat to human health.[56]

This is crucial to understanding the limits that are now placed on the legislative activities of the Member States by EU rules on the free movement of food. It effectively prohibits and at the very least restricts the adoption of some measures at national level which are designed to promote good health through improved diet. National law cannot normally be used to ensure that the nutritional benefits to be derived from foods must be maintained or improved. The reason for this is clear. The absence of nutritional value poses no 'threat' to human health. The Court, in its case law on the use of the health protection exception set out in Article 36 TFEU, effectively distinguishes between 'danger' and 'harm'. The former is deemed by EU law makers to be something that needs regulating, the latter is not. This is discussed more in Chapter 9, but it should be noted at this stage that this position, combined with the other jurisprudence of the Court on measures equivalent to quantitative restrictions on trade, often bars Member States from taking meaningful interventionist action to deal with a public health crisis like obesity or the abuse of alcohol. It limits the government options to certain campaigns, promotions and enticements, rather than direct action, such as prescribing clearer labelling or messages on food. Needless to say, the German Government's argument in the *Meat Purity* case was ultimately rejected. A national measure designed to maintain the nutritional value of food was not deemed to be justifiable on the basis of being necessary to protect human health.

---

[55] Case 216/1984, n 48 above.
[56] Para 10 of Case 274/1987, n 49 above.

This issue of promoting nutritional content had previously been dealt with by the Court in the *Milk Substitutes* cases.[57] In the first of these enforcement actions, taken against France, the Commission had brought the proceedings based on the contention that national rules which prohibited the sale of substitute milk were contrary to Article 34 TFEU. The French Government sought to justify the ban on a number of grounds, such as the protection of consumers and the promotion of the aims of the Common Agricultural Policy which was discussed earlier in this chapter. It also argued that it was necessary to restrict the sale of substitute milk to protect human health.

It was claimed that there were two reasons as to why a prohibition such as this was necessary for health protection. The first related to nutritional value. A similar argument was made to that which was put forward by the German Government in *Meat Purity*. The Court immediately rejected this on the basis that public health grounds could not be used by a Member State to justify a prohibition by arguing that a product's nutritional value is lower or its fat content higher than another similar product already available on the market in question. It also agreed with the Commission's contention that a ban could not persist where other products were available in the Member State which were also of lower nutritional value or which had similar fat content to substitute milk. This line of reasoning indicates a flawed understanding of human diet and nutrition. While it is, of course, perfectly correct to find that there are products of similar nutritional inferiority available on the market, the judgment and the precedent that it sets fails to take into consideration the type of product at issue, or its importance to meeting personal dietary requirements.

The foods at issue in both *Meat Purity* and the *Milk Substitutes* cases are staples of the European diet. Their consumption contributes significantly to meeting recommended daily intakes for the key nutrients, such as proteins, carbohydrates, fats, vitamins and minerals. Comparing their replacements to 'other', dissimilar, products available on the market fails to take this into consideration. These 'other' foods should be consumed in addition to the staples, not as a substitute for them. It is as if the Court is saying that you cannot restrict the marketing of substitute milk when you do not place similar restrictions on the sale of sweets or crisps. This is not to say that, on balance, the Court has not come to the correct conclusion in the circumstances, namely that a prohibition was disproportionate to the aim pursued. The way in which it has reached this decision is, however, questionable. It is not comparing like with like to underpin its position or that of the Commission. The Court did not accept that any measure was necessary to protect health in the circumstances, so the fact that we happen to be dealing with a prohibition is not necessarily the crucial factor. The way in which the Court has refused to accept that there is any health protection purpose underlying the national law indicates that there is no proportionate measure that it would be deemed permissible to

[57] Case 216/1984 *Commission v France* and Case 76/1986 *Commission v Germany*, both n 48 above.

adopt either. It simply refuses to accept that placing restrictions on the marketing of nutritionally inferior substitutes is ever justifiable on health protection grounds.

The second argument put forward by France in the first of the *Milk Substitutes* cases was that these products could have harmful effects on certain groups of people. The Court rejected this contention on the ground that the consumption of milk itself is also potentially risky for people who suffer from certain diseases. This was backed up with a claim that there was disagreement between specialists as to the actual or potential dangers posed by the consumption of animal and vegetable fats. This, however, fails to recognise the key basis upon which national measures designed to protect health can be taken by Member States. Originally in *Sandoz*,[58] and later followed up through the development of the precautionary principle, it is precisely when there is uncertainty, or disagreement between the experts, as to the level or nature of risk involved that national measures can be adopted until the reality of those risks becomes realised. According to the Court, proper labelling of the list of ingredients and an identification of the characteristics of the milk substitutes being offered would enable those with an intolerance to these products to make their own decision on consumption. Had the Court followed its earlier decision in *Sandoz*, the Member State could have been facilitated in the adoption of interim measures to deal with any potential threat posed.

The respondent in *Sandoz* had been charged with selling unauthorised fortified foods in the Netherlands. The company was marketing sports bars and drinks with added vitamins. All the products in question were lawfully marketed in Germany or Belgium. It had applied for authorisation of the products, as was required under Dutch law. This was rejected on the basis that the addition of these vitamins, mostly A and D, to the products in question posed a danger to public health. On querying whether the authorisation process was compatible with EU Treaty rules on the free movement of food, the Court held that it was perfectly acceptable to have such a procedure in place, provided permission was granted to market products which are both safe and necessary. The company and the Commission had been of the view that these products would only ever be harmful if consumed to excess. Expert reports showed that the over-consumption of vitamins over a prolonged period could have detrimental effects on health. However, the scientific research available at the time was not conclusive on the quantities that could be consumed at a safe level, nor was it clear as to what the harmful effects could be. Most significantly, for the development of EU jurisprudence on the degree to which Member States can act in such circumstances, the Court of Justice stated that:

> [where] there are uncertainties at the present state of scientific research it is for the Member States, in the absence of harmonisation, to decide what degree of protection of the health and life of humans they intend to assure, having regard however for the requirements of the free movement of goods within the [Union].[59]

---

[58] See Case 174/1982 *Criminal Proceedings against Sandoz BV*, n 52. The Court had previously come to a similar conclusion in Case 272/1980 *Frans-Nederlandse Maatschappij voor Biologische Producten* [1981] ECR 3277.

[59] Ibid, *Sandoz*, para 16.

This principle was found by the Court to apply to substances such as vitamins which were not really harmful, but which could become so if taken to excess. National rules restricting the fortification of foods, requiring, for example, that prior authorisation is granted before these products can be sold to consumers, could therefore be justified, in principle at least, under the terms of Article 36 TFEU. They could be deemed necessary for the protection of human health.

By this stage in the judgment in *Sandoz*, the Court had accepted two things. The first was that scientific uncertainty surrounding a practice in food production could warrant the adoption of national measures by Member States. Second, these measures could, in principle, be justified under the Article 36 TFEU exceptions to the general prohibition on measures equivalent to quantitative restrictions on trade. However, the Court also held that all of this is subject to the principle of proportionality. Trade can be restricted on food safety grounds, but only if this happens where the proposed restriction has the most minimal impact on trade that is available in the circumstances. These restrictions were therefore justifiable, provided that authorisations were granted wherever possible. This would make them proportionate. The Court recognised, however, that it was difficult to assess such authorisations. It would be hard, for example, to monitor consumption levels that could be deemed excessive. This would be further complicated by the fact that vitamins are also present in most everyday foods. Consuming fortified foods in addition to a recommended diet could itself lead to excessive consumption, as could eating large amounts of a particular food which was also high in the same vitamins which were being used for fortification. There would therefore have to be a wide level of discretion afforded to the Member States on this issue, provided any response taken was proportionate in the circumstances. This would have to involve the granting of authorisations by national authorities to foodstuffs lawfully marketed elsewhere in the Union, especially where the fortification was designed to meet a real need, especially a technical or nutritional one.

National laws restricting the fortification of foods, such as those at issue in *Sandoz*, have been a persistent problem for producers looking to access new markets. They have also led to the Court of Justice being called upon to adjudicate on a number of occasions, in particular where prior authorisation is required for marketing a new nutrient or product. In *Greenham and Abel*, criminal proceedings were brought against the joint directors of a food company on two grounds, one of which was selling products fortified with the nutrient coenzyme Q10.[60] This substance was not authorised for human consumption at the time, as required under French law. The respondents claimed that this was contrary to EU rules on free movement, as the products were lawfully marketed in other Member States and no serious risk to health had been shown. It was submitted that the mere fact that a food supplement is freely marketed in other Member States is not enough

---

[60] Case C-95/2001 *Criminal Proceedings against Greenham and Abel* [2004] ECR I-1333. Coenzyme Q10 functions as an antioxidant and it is also needed for basic cell function. Its level in the body usually decreases with age.

for its marketing to be permitted automatically in all Member States. It should have to undergo the authorisation procedure first. The Commission disagreed. It was of the view that if a nutrient could be used in fortification in one Member State, then products which were fortified with this nutrient must be granted access to the importer's market, provided that international scientific research and the nutritional habits of the populace showed that this did not pose a risk for public health. This would not necessarily require the use of a full authorisation procedure. According to the Commission, national courts could decide whether the competent authorities of the Member State concerned had properly evaluated the risks related to the nutrient in question. No information was submitted to the Court showing that coenzyme Q10 was dangerous. However, the Court did find that the use of national authorisation procedures, such as that at issue here, could be justified despite their trade-restricting impact. Several conditions, however, had to be met.

First, any national rule requiring that prior authorisation is granted before marketing must involve a procedure that facilitates ready access for applicants to have their products included on the approved list. The procedure must be completed within a reasonable time. Any refusal to authorise must be open to appeal, including to a court of law. Second, applications for authorisation may only be refused where the substance is shown to pose a genuine risk to public health.[61] Provided they meet these conditions, Member States are entitled to have authorisation procedures in place if this is necessary to protect health. Following *Sandoz* they should also have a wide discretion in this regard where there is uncertainty about the risk type and/or level, although the *Milk Substitutes* cases might suggest otherwise. This discretion will always be subject to the principle of proportionality and a simple disguised restriction on trade is unjustifiable. Where alternative, less trade-restricting measures are available, which will still be effective to the level required in the circumstances, these must be chosen instead of a cumbersome authorisation procedure or refusal to authorise. Any such refusal must therefore be based on an assessment that establishes a definite or probable risk to human health.[62]

In *Greenham and Abel* the Court found that a decision to prohibit the marketing of a foodstuff could only, therefore, be adopted 'if the alleged risk for public health appears to be sufficiently established on the basis of the latest scientific data available at the date of the adoption of such decision'.[63] A Member State can take action based on the precautionary principle where this assessment indicates that there is still uncertainty as to the nature of the risk involved. The precautionary principle is discussed in more detail in the next chapter, in the context of food safety. However, it can be said at this stage that it permits the taking of interim measures on health protection grounds until the science is more certain

---

[61] As first established by the Court in Case C-192/2001 *Commission v Denmark* [2003] ECR I-9693.
[62] Ibid, para 47.
[63] Ibid, para 42.

about the existence and/or nature of a risk. Here, it was argued that the products at issue possessed no nutritional benefit. The Court found that 'nutritional need' was a legitimate consideration in the assessment of risk, but also that the absence of such a need was not enough to justify a total prohibition. There would have to be an identifiable risk, or at the very least 'the likelihood of real harm to public health … should the risk materialise'. It would ultimately be for the national court to decide if evidence provided warranted use of this precautionary approach in the circumstances. Member States can, therefore, subject to these conditions, have authorisation procedures for fortified foods in place. This is an important exception to the wide-scale application of the EU Treaty prohibition on measures equivalent to quantitative restrictions on trade. It allows Member States to ban the sale of foodstuffs lawfully manufactured and marketed elsewhere in the Union, provided that this decision follows a process that is readily accessible, timely and subject to appeal where required. Any refusal to authorise must also be based on a detailed risk assessment, which is based on the most reliable scientific data available and the most recent results of international research.

The significance of the position that developed out of *Commission v Denmark* and *Greenham and Abel* on the legitimacy of prohibitions based on valid authorisation procedures was further highlighted by the decision of the Court in *Red Bull*.[64] Multiple complaints had been made by operators based in several Member States to the European Commission. Their claims related to the difficulties they were encountering when attempting to market their fortified foods in France. The Commission brought proceedings on the basis that the applicable French law on the sale of fortified foods did not facilitate the mutual recognition of products lawfully marketed elsewhere in the Union. The French Government accepted that its national legislation was capable of hindering trade but that this was justified by its objectives of protecting public health and consumers and that it was proportionate. All fortified foods had to be approved by the authorities before they could be sold on the French market.

The Court accepted that the authorisation procedure at issue was not, in principle, contrary to EU law. However, it reiterated the conditions that must be satisfied before any refusal to authorise a fortified food would be deemed compatible with EU law. As held previously, the national authorisation procedure would have to be readily accessible by operators from other Member States. It would have to be completed within a reasonable time. It would also have to be open to challenge, including before the courts. Finally, the addition of the nutrient concerned would have to pose a genuine risk to human health.[65]

The Court has provided significant elaboration on how these conditions can be satisfied in its deliberations in *Red Bull*. It first stated that accessibility to the procedure should be assessed based on its transparency and openness. This should

[64] Case C-24/2000 *Commission v France* [2004] ECR I-1277.
[65] Case C-192/2001 *Commission v Denmark* [2003] ECR I-9693.

include the provision of clear information on what the process involves and what the applicant is required to do. Any refusal must also provide clear reasons underlying the decision, in particular to provide the applicant with potential grounds for an appeal. Decisions should be made as quickly as possible in each individual case.

For a national authorisation procedure to be deemed accessible it must be 'expressly provided for in a measure of general application which is binding on the national authorities'.[66] The procedure at issue in *Red Bull* was not one which was established in national legislation. A notice was provided to operators setting out the rules on marketing fortified foods, but this was not enough to meet the requirements stipulated. Applications were not routinely considered in a timely manner. The application for the authorisation of the energy drink Red Bull, for example, was not even formally acknowledged until seven months after its receipt by the assessing authorities. The decision to refuse authorisation was not communicated to the applicant for more than two years. The complaint against the French authorities about their failure to have an authorisation procedure in place that was compatible with EU law was therefore clearly well founded on the first two grounds.

On the third contention, that the refusal to authorise the marketing of Red Bull in France was not justifiable for health protection purposes, the Court found, as it had in *Sandoz*, that Member States have wide discretion in this regard where there is scientific uncertainty about the risk attached to the use of a substance. However, it also recognised that any exercise of this discretion must remain proportionate to the aim pursued. Whichever means they choose to achieve this should therefore be limited to that which is necessary to safeguard public health. Any exception to a fundamental principle of EU law, such as the free movement of goods should, of course, be interpreted strictly. A prohibition, which is the most trade-restricting of all measures that can be adopted, would therefore have to be based on a proper risk assessment, which clearly showed that a ban was necessary in the circumstances.[67] After dismissing the evidence offered by the French authorities in support of their action on a range of fortified foods, the Court did find that the existence of a Scientific Committee on Human Nutrition (SCHN) report, which gave an adverse opinion on the presence of certain nutrients, such as taurine and glucuronolactone, in caffeinated drinks could be sufficient to support a French ban. It also held that if the right sort of evidence showing potential risks can be produced, this switches the burden of proof from the Member State to the Commission in these enforcement actions. It stated that in such circumstances:

> the Commission [would have] to state explicitly why the [Member State's] argument based on that [evidence] cannot suffice to justify the refusal to authorise the marketing of [fortified products].[68]

---

[66] Case 176/1984 *Commission v Greece* [1987] ECR 1193, para 41.
[67] See Case C-24/2000, *Commission v France*, n 64 above, paras 53–56.
[68] Ibid, para 72.

The Commission's contention that the refusal to authorise the energy drink Red Bull was unjustifiable, was thus rejected. The Court found that it had not shown why the SCHN report failed to substantiate the ban. The Member State was required to have a more accessible authorisation procedure in place. It was also obliged to identify clear risks to health where it refused to authorise products lawfully available elsewhere in the EU. However, it was perfectly acceptable to prohibit the marketing of fortified foods and drinks where there was enough scientific evidence to support this, even where the reports and opinions were not entirely conclusive on the nature or level of the risks involved in consumption.

If we consider the SCHN report presented in *Commission v France* to be the type of scientific study which can be used as a legitimate basis for refusing the authorisation of certain foods, we should also be able to establish what may constitute insufficient evidence in such cases. The French authorities had also sought to rely on a report issued by the Conseil supérieur d'hygiène publique de France (French Public Health Authority – CSHPF) in defence of its refusal to authorise the marketing of food supplements and dietary products containing L-tartrate and L-carnitine. Their claim was that the addition of these substances to foods provided no significant nutritional benefit. The Court of Justice first made it clear, just as it had consistently done in the past, that the absence of nutritional need or benefit was not sufficient to justify a prohibition where the products were lawfully manufactured and marketed elsewhere in the EU. Products making nutritional or health claims are now subject to specific EU legislation.[69] The Court also stated here that aspects of the CSHPF report that were being relied upon were not the type or quality of evidence required by them to show that a restriction placed on the free movement of food was warranted. The report had cited 'digestive problems which affect 13 per cent of the population' without specifying their nature. It also mentioned the absence of proof supporting claims about the usefulness or benefits of adding L-tartrate and L-carnitine to supplements, but no detailed assessment of the effects which the addition of these substances could have on human health. It was found that this was not enough to support what amounted to a marketing ban. It was deemed to be more of a general opinion than a rigorous scientific survey. Article 36 TFEU could not, therefore, be successfully used by the French authorities in these circumstances. Something more substantial was required for this – something like the SCHN report on the use of taurine and glucuronolactone, which was sufficient to allow for similar action to be taken in the banning of Red Bull.

Comparing the response of the Court of Justice to the French CSHPF opinion on the one hand and the SCHN report on the other, could bring us to the conclusion that the EU institutions are favouring their own scientific investigations over those undertaken in the Member States. There are other examples of this

---

[69] Regulation (EC) No 1924/2006 of the European Parliament and of the Council of 20 December 2006 on nutrition and health claims made on foods [2007] OJ L 12/3. Nutrition and health claims are discussed in more detail in ch 7.

and these are discussed in the context of the use of the precautionary principle by the Council and the Commission in Chapter 5. However, the Court did also use the CSHPF opinion in support of the action on Red Bull. The difference between those aspects of the opinion which dealt with food supplements and those which set out the position on energy drinks was the Commission's own response to these. In relation to the former the Commission challenged the nature of the evidence submitted and the Court supported this. On the latter, the Commission did not adequately explain why the CSHPF opinion was insufficient to justify a prohibition on marketing energy drinks with a caffeine content higher than that which was authorised in France. It produced no evidence that called into question the French authorities' analysis of the dangers which these drinks could present to public health.[70] Coupled with the findings of the SCHN report on taurine and glucuronolactone use, this was enough to reverse the burden of proof requirements onto the Commission. It was then unable to stand over its claims about the illegitimate use by France of the Article 36 TFEU exception.[71]

The imposition of national compositional requirements, such as the inclusion or exclusion of certain ingredients, can potentially be justified by Member States on health protection grounds. A key feature of any such argument put forward by a State is the production of evidence that there is some threat posed to health by the inclusion or exclusion of substances in food production. As seen above, this came before the Court in cases such as *Milk Substitutes* and *Meat Purity* but, in these circumstances, there was little in the supporting documentation to show that there was any real safety or health concern.

In *Bellamy* the respondent argued that a national law setting a maximum salt content for bread was contrary to EU rules on the free movement of goods.[72] The State, in this case Belgium, contended that this was justifiable under the terms of Article 36 TFEU, as it was necessary to keep salt consumption low in the interests of protecting human health. Here, English Shop Wholesale imported foodstuffs from Britain for sale in Belgium, including bread with a salt content of 2.88 per cent. Belgian law prescribed that the salt content of bread sold there could not exceed 2 per cent. In considering whether prohibiting the sale of the bread imported from Britain was a measure equivalent to a quantitative restriction on trade, which it obviously was and if this could be justified as being necessary for

---

[70] The safety, or otherwise, of consuming energy drinks resurfaced following a 2013 report published by the French Food Safety and Environment Agency, which showed that these can have dangerous cardiovascular and psychological effects in some circumstances. For further discussion on this see E Amat and L Rihouey-Robini, 'A scientific report rekindles the controversy over energy drinks in France' (2013) 8 *European Food and Feed Law Review* 414.

[71] The fortification of foods is now legislated for by Regulation (EC) No 1925/2006 of the European Parliament and of the Council of 20 December 2006 on the addition of vitamins and minerals and of certain other substances to foods [2006] OJ L 404/26. This Regulation has since been amended by Art 50 of the newer Food Information Regulation 1169/2011 [2011] OJ L 304/18, which is discussed in much more detail in ch 7.

[72] Case C-123/2000 *Criminal Proceedings against Christina Bellamy and English Shop Wholesale SA* [2001] ECR I-2795.

the protection of human health, the Court, referring to its earlier judgment in *Van der Veldt*,[73] found that it was not compatible with EU obligations. No additional or different arguments in support of the maximum salt requirement were made, beyond those which had been offered in *Van der Veldt*. The rule remained likely to hinder trade between Member States and was not seen as justifiable by the Court. This line of reasoning has also made it more difficult for EU Member States to introduce maximum permitted quantities of added sugar in food products, meaning that they must resort to other health-promoting measures instead, such as the imposition of sugar taxes. Having said that, some EU Member States have successfully negotiated placing limits on the inclusion of trans fats in food. The possible reasons for and consequences of this difference in treatment is discussed in more detail in Chapter 9.

It is often presumed that the over-consumption of salt has a range of detrimental consequences for human health. There is sufficient evidence to show that it can lead to a high rate of blood pressure and also heart disease.[74] Despite this, the European Court of Justice in *Van der Veldt* refused to support a Belgian ban on salt content in bread above 2 per cent on the basis that it was a disproportionate response in the circumstances. The respondent in this case imported practically all its bread and other bakery products from the Netherlands. Food inspections discovered that the salt content of these products were at a level between 2.11 and 2.17 per cent. Charges were brought against the retailer.

The argument was made in *Van der Veldt* that the disputed Belgian rule was necessary to protect humans from the health implications of the over-consumption of salt. Rejecting this, the Court found that exceeding the maximum permitted levels by the small amounts which the imported bread did was not sufficient to pose the type of risk needed to justify a prohibition. It must be remembered that the baked products at issue only surpassed the 2 per cent salt content requirement by between 0.11 and 0.17 per cent. No scientific evidence was produced to show that this was a dangerous level. The Court also found that a more proportionate response was available to the Belgian authorities in the circumstances. According to it, the prescription of suitable labelling would have provided consumers with full information on the composition of the products concerned. It was stated that '[t]he protection of public health would thus have been ensured without such serious restrictions on the free movement of goods'.[75] This raises two questions on the suitability of the Court's approach to this issue, not only in its reasoning in *Van der Veldt*, but also that which was later based upon this in *Bellamy*.

It is certainly arguable that labelling disclosures may not have any real impact on health protection in the circumstances. The Court stated that disclosing the

---

[73] Case C-17/1993 *Criminal Proceedings against Van der Veldt* [1994] ECR I-3537.
[74] See, eg, P Meneton, X Jeunemaitre, H de Wardener and G Macgregor, 'Links between dietary salt intake, renal salt handling, blood pressure, and cardiovascular diseases' (2005) 85 *Physiological Reviews* 679.
[75] Para 19 of Case C-17/1993, n 73 above.

amount of salt in the bread would address any concerns about excessive sodium consumption. First, this fails to account for the fact that many bread and bakery products are exempt from all labelling requirements. It has always been the case that the EU framework labelling legislation, since first developed in 1979, does not apply to highly perishable freshly baked foodstuffs. Perhaps more significantly, however, is the failure to account for the fact that mere statements in the ingredients list, or nutrient declaration, about a 2.17 per cent salt level will mean little to the average consumer. There is unlikely to be much awareness of the recommended 2 per cent maximum permitted level. Providing indirect information about exceeding this provides no meaningful information at all. A requirement to include this in the nutrient declaration would not have been permitted under EU law at the time. The provision of any of this information was not even compulsory, except for those products about which some health or nutrition claim was being made. An obligation to include this for the products concerned would surely have been deemed a measure equivalent to a quantitative restriction itself, as the exporter would not have been met with the same requirement in their own State.

The second difficulty with the decision making in these cases relates to the manner in which the Court in *Bellamy* relies so heavily on its previous judgment in *Van der Veldt*, without any consideration of a key distinction between the two sets of circumstances involved. A key part of the reasoning for rejecting the Member State's claim that the measure was necessary to protect health related to the fact that the difference between the maximum level of salt permitted under national law and the actual amounts of salt contained in the breads was not very significant. It only exceeded the 2 per cent limit by around 0.15 per cent. In *Bellamy*, however, the salt content of the products concerned exceeded the maximum permitted level by nearly five times as much as that in *Van der Veldt*. Despite this, the Court in the former dismissed the Member State's claim on the basis that 'a ruling must be given in the same terms' as that in the latter. It did not consider it any further than this. It gave no consideration to the much higher levels of salt contained in the products at issue in *Bellamy*.

Finally, EU Member States have also attempted to use the health protection exception to argue that national laws restricting the sale of alcohol are necessary in the pursuit of this aim. Swedish law, for example, prescribed that only authorised wholesalers were permitted to import alcohol from other EU Member States. This rule was tested in *Rosengren* after several Swedish residents mail-ordered the importation of cases of Spanish wine.[76] The wine was confiscated by Swedish customs authorities and criminal proceedings were brought against those who had ordered the wine. The fact that private individuals were prohibited from importing alcoholic beverages was clearly a quantitative restriction on trade. One of the grounds on which the Swedish authorities argued that their authorisation system for alcohol importation was justifiable was the need to protect young people from the harmful effects of alcohol. This was rejected. Although the system included

---

[76] Case C-170/2004 *Klas Rosengren and others v Riksåklagaren* [2007] ECR I-4071.

provision for the granting of permission to applicants only if they are at least 20 years old and therefore did prevent some younger persons from purchasing alcohol, the ban at issue in the proceedings applied to everyone, of all ages. The Court therefore held that it was an effective health protection measure, but also a disproportionate one. It would, according to both the European Commission and the Court, be less of an impediment to trade if an effective age-checking system were put in place instead. The implications of this for Irish law on the marketing of alcohol are discussed in more detail in Chapter 9.

4.2.6. National Rules on Additive Use

Other substances may be added to foods for a variety of reasons. These additives can be used, for example, to preserve, colour, thicken or enhance the flavour of a foodstuff. All must be approved at EU level before use – usually indicated in the ingredient list by the presence of an assigned 'E' number.[77] Consumers are often averse to the inclusion of additives in food. Many are natural ingredients, extracted from other foods, such as E100 Curcumin, which is taken from the root of the turmeric plant, E162 Beetroot Red and E170 Calcium Carbonate, which is a natural chalk, or which can be extracted from eggshells. Their inclusion in production is usually therefore no more (and sometimes less) of a threat to the health or well-being of the consumer than any other ingredient used. Some additives may, however, have adverse consequences for some consumers and certainly may not be appealing to most. E153 Carbon Black or Vegetable Carbon, for example, can be obtained from charcoal, bones, blood oils or the incomplete combustion of natural gas. It is found in some concentrated fruit juices and jams. It has been banned in food production in the USA as it is suspected to be a carcinogenic agent. Non-vegetable varieties of this additive are also banned in Australia. It is recommended that it should not be consumed by children. E110 Tartrazine Yellow is also not recommended for consumption by children. It is a synthetic yellow dye that is often found in dilutable cordial and other soft drinks, or in the shells of medicine capsules. It can cause allergic reactions, in particular amongst asthmatics and those with an intolerance to aspirin. It is also suspected of causing hyperactivity in children.[78] Its use has been banned in both Norway and Austria, but it is commonly used in products available in Ireland.

---

[77] Originally set out in Art 8 of Council Directive 1989/107/EEC of 21 December 1988 on the approximation of the laws of the Member States concerning food additives authorised for use in foodstuffs intended for human consumption [1989] OJ L 40/27. This was transposed into Irish law by the European Communities (Labelling of Additives for Use in Foodstuffs) Regulations 1992, SI No 23/1992. It is now covered by Art 23 of Regulation (EC) No 1333/2008 of the European Parliament and of the Council of 16 December 2008 on food additives [2008] OJ L 354/16.

[78] See, eg, D McCann and Others, 'Food additives and hyperactive behaviour in 3-year-old and 8/9-year-old children in the community: A randomised, double-blinded, placebo-controlled trial' (2007) 370 *The Lancet* 1560. The website www.ukfoodguide.net provides an excellent assessment of, and information on, all additives approved for use in food production.

While the majority of additives pose no real threat to human health, they are often used to provide a cheap substitute for more wholesome or substantial ingredients. In *Commission v Germany* the Court of Justice examined a situation where the Member State tried to restrict the use of E160f in sauces and pastries as an alternative to eggs.[79] This colouring provided the finished product with a deep yellow appearance, suggesting that there had been plenty of eggs used in production, when in fact there could have been none used. This presents two possible problems. First, the consumer is presented with a product that appears to contain certain ingredients in significant quantities but, in reality, these have been substituted for additives specifically designed to mislead the purchaser. The product is presented as having a certain appearance but it is the additives, rather than the ingredients, that have given it this more appealing look or provided it with some other organoleptic property. Second, if additives are used to replace more wholesome ingredients, the nutritional value of the food is also misrepresented in its final appearance. It may look and taste more wholesome solely because of the use of colourings and flavour enhancers designed to present the product as having increased quantities of certain ingredients, which may only have been used at very low levels. In some cases, additives are used to replace an ingredient altogether, even possibly when the name of this ingredient has been used in the marketing of the product, such as 'chocolate flavoured' or 'strawberry flavoured'. This is all perfectly lawful. Neither chocolate nor strawberries need to be present in either of these two examples. Additives that present the products as being made with either chocolate or strawberries can have been used instead. As is discussed in Chapter 7, EU rules on food labelling allow this to happen. This legislation, coupled with EU rules on the free movement of food, prevent Member States from taking any action at national level to prevent it from happening.

The maintenance of national rules in EU Member States which prohibit the use of additives in certain foods is contrary to Article 34 TFEU. They are very difficult to justify. They almost always end up being withdrawn. The case law of the Court of Justice makes it very clear that laws which place limits on additive use can only be applied where this is necessary for the protection of human health or consumers. As has been discussed throughout this chapter, these are both very difficult arguments to make successfully, particularly if the same additives are permitted for use either in other foods or elsewhere in the EU. The decision in the *Beer Purity* case made it very clear that a general prohibition on additive use in these circumstances was not compatible with Article 34 TFEU obligations.[80] It could only be successfully argued that such a ban was necessary if it could be shown that there was a real risk to human health or that consumers could be misled, coupled with a demonstration that the additives in question served no technological function and could not be used in the production of other foods. These conditions still stand.

---

[79] Case C-51/1994 *Commission v Germany* [1995] ECR I-3599.
[80] See n 22 above.

However, there are some circumstances where the Court of Justice will permit the maintenance of national rules which place limitations on the use of certain additives.

An Italian law, for example, that prohibited the use of certain chemical additives, such as nitrates, in cheese production was found by the Court of Justice to be compatible with Article 34 TFEU. These rules could be allowed if they did not involve a total ban on additive use, as was the case in *Beer Purity* and if the authorisation process employed met certain conditions which were designed to ensure that appropriate additive use would be allowed. In *Commission v Italy* the Court held that national rules which require that an additive must be specifically authorised for use are in compliance with EU law if they are, as usual, readily accessible by applicants, if decisions on authorisation are made within a reasonable period of time and if resulting in a rejection then this decision must be open to a proper appeal process.[81] Also, applications could only be rejected if the additive in question did not meet any real need, in particular a technological need. The Court held that the Italian rules on additive use, in this case the addition of nitrate to cheese, were applied in the same way to both Italian producers and those from other Member States and were therefore compatible with EU provisions on free movement. Article 34 TFEU would only be breached if the national procedure unjustifiably rejected an application for the inclusion of a substance on the list of authorised additives.

The Court of Justice has, on occasions, allowed Member States to refuse the authorisation of some additives, even where their use has already been permitted elsewhere in the EU. In *Eyssen*, for example, the Court held that a Dutch ban on the addition of nisin to cheese was justifiable claiming it was necessary for the protection of human health.[82] This was decided despite the fact that this additive could be lawfully used in cheese production elsewhere in the EU. French restrictions on the use of sorbic acid in pastry products were also found to be justifiable on health protection grounds in *Bellon*.[83] Perhaps surprisingly, this allowance was made even though the First Preservatives Directive specifically permitted the use of sorbic acid in food production.[84] It was, however, subject to the condition that a Member State must have a suitable authorisation procedure in place before introducing any such ban. The Court also held in *Muller* that allowing Member States to prohibit or restrict the use of EU-listed additives is actually necessary to ensure that the Treaty provisions on free movement, in particular those contained in Article 36 TFEU designed to protect human health, are properly observed.[85]

[81] Case C-95/1989 *Commission v Italy* [1992] ECR I-4545.
[82] Case 53/1980 *Officier van Justitie v Kaasfabriek Eyssen BV* [1981] ECR 409.
[83] Case C-42/1990 *Criminal Proceedings against Jean-Claude Bellon* [1990] ECR I-4863.
[84] Council Directive 1964/54/EEC of 5 November 1963 on the approximation of the laws of the Member States concerning the preservatives authorised for use in foodstuffs intended for human consumption [1964] OJ L 12/161. English Special Edition Series I, Chapter 1963–1964, p 99.
[85] Case 304/1984 *Criminal Proceedings against Claude Muller* [1986] ECR 1511.

Some limitations on Member State actions in this regard were, however, set out in the decision in *Grunert*, where it was held that they could not introduce absolute prohibitions on additives approved for use under the terms of the Preservatives Directive.[86] They could, however, prohibit the use of approved additives in some circumstances, such as limiting this to pastry products, as was the case in the later decision in *Bellon*. While Member States have traditionally enjoyed some flexibility in their application of the legal requirements on authorised additive use, this is more limited where it can be shown that the substance in question meets a real need – either technological, physiological or economic.[87]

The issue of 'genuine or technological need' is controversial. The Court has interpreted this to mean that the possibility of using another substance,[88] or no substance at all,[89] to meet the same function as the banned or restricted additive does not mean that it does not serve a technological need. Also, an additive that significantly affects the appearance of a finished product does not necessarily serve a 'technological function' in that product, if its original function was to alter a characteristic of an ingredient.[90] Additives do not have to be listed as an ingredient on the labelling of a food product if they do not serve a technological function in the finished product.[91] The lists of additives permitted for use are now set out in Annex II to the EU Food Additives Regulation 2008,[92] the domestic application of which is now provided for by the European Union (Food Additives) Regulations 2015.[93]

4.3. Measures Equivalent to Customs Duties on Imported Food

There are three ways in which EU rules on the free movement of goods can impact on what can be done to regulate the food sector at national level. The first and by far the most significant, of these is that which has already been discussed at length in this chapter – the prohibition on quantitative restrictions on trade and measures of equivalent effect. As has been demonstrated, the application of this provision of EU law places plenty of limitations on the Government in relation to, for example, setting compositional or packaging requirements or the operation of authorisation procedures. As will be particularly evident from the discussion in Chapter 9, this

---

[86] Case 88/1979 *Criminal Proceedings against Siegfried Grunert* [1980] ECR 1827.
[87] Case 247/1984 *Criminal Proceedings against Léon Motte* [1985] ECR 1329.
[88] Case C-95/1989 *Commission v Italy* n 81 above.
[89] See n 22 above.
[90] Case C-144/1993 *Pfanni Werke Otto Eckart KG v Landeshauptstadt München* [1994] ECR I-4605.
[91] As stipulated by Art 20 of Reg 1169/2011, n 71 above. This is discussed in more detail in ch 7.
[92] See Reg 1333/2008, n 77 above.
[93] SI No 330/2015. As amended by the European Union (Food Additives)(Amendment) Regulations 2016, SI No 484/2016.

also severely curtails Government efforts to tackle significant public health issues like obesity and alcohol abuse through the introduction of clearer food labelling formats and warnings. The impact of this, on both human health and on the economy, is considerable.[94]

The other two ways in which EU rules on the free movement of goods can impact on what happens at national level are the prohibition on customs duties on trade between Member States and measures of equivalent effect and restrictions that are placed on the taxation of foods sold in the domestic market, in particular where these appear to discriminate against imported products in some way. The former is set out in Articles 28–30 TFEU. Article 28 TFEU sets out the general position that:

> [t]he Union shall comprise a customs union which shall cover all trade in goods and which shall involve a prohibition between Member States of customs duties on imports and exports and of all charges having equivalent effect and the adoption of a common customs tariff in their relations with third countries.

Article 30 TFEU more specifically provides that:

> [c]ustoms duties on imports and exports and charges having equivalent effect shall be prohibited between Member States.

The Common Customs Tariff referred to in Article 28 TFEU is important for the food sector for several reasons. It sets out the tariff rate for all foods, amongst other things, imported into the EU Member States from third countries – including, most significantly, the United Kingdom after it withdraws its EU membership, subject to any trade deal that may be struck prior to 2019. These tariffs can be set at a level that is deliberately designed to afford protection to EU producers. The rates set for foods like garlic offer a very good example of this.[95] There can also be different rates set for different times of the year, dependent on whether the

---

[94] According to Safefood-funded research carried out by researchers at University College Cork, health problems associated with being overweight or obese were estimated to cost Ireland €1.13 billion per year by 2012. This figure included direct healthcare costs of €398 million, as well as indirect costs, such as those arising out of lost productivity, of €728 million per year. See I Perry and others, 'The cost of overweight and obesity on the island of Ireland' (Safefood, 2012), ISBN: 978-1-905767-335. The HSE-funded group Alcohol Action Ireland has estimated that the minimum cost of alcohol abuse to the Irish health service is around €1.5 billion per annum, accounting for over 160,000 bed-days in public hospitals. This figure does not even include spending on emergency cases, GP visits, psychiatric admissions or alcohol treatment services. Up to 30% of all emergency department costs are thought to be alcohol related. See www.alcoholireland.ie. The impact of both food and alcohol abuse on the Irish economy and on Irish society and law more generally is discussed in more detail in ch 9.

[95] Commission Regulation (EU) No 1006/2011 of 27 September 2011 amending Annex I to Council Regulation (EEC) No 2658/1987 on the tariff and statistical nomenclature and on the Common Customs tariff [2011] OJ L 282/1 provides that almost all the import duty on garlic coming into the EU from third countries is to be set at 9.6% plus €120.00 per 100 kg. There is then a complex licensing mechanism to be employed to determine just how much of the garlic imported from countries such as Argentina and China is to be taxed at this higher rate. This can result in a tax rate as high as 232% on the importation of garlic from third countries. The same 2011 Regulation provides that similar foods, such as shallots and onions, are only to be taxed at the much lower rate of 9.6% across the board.

food in question is in production season in the Member States at that time. So, for example, apples imported from third countries during the months of January and February are met with a 6.4 per cent tariff, plus an additional tonnage charge. The same apples imported between April and June have this rate lowered to 4.8 per cent plus a tonnage charge as apples are not so in season across the EU at that time. Between August and December, prime harvesting time in Europe, the tariff rate jumps to 11.2 per cent plus tonnage charge. This is all set out in the Combined Nomenclature, which lists and defines all the goods most commonly imported into the EU and attaches a tariff rate to each of them.[96] The Common Customs Tariff is also used to help the EU institutions to come to decisions on other free movement of goods matters. For example, nomenclature definitions have been used to help the Court of Justice to establish whether a food name has become generic, or whether it remains firmly associated with production in a particular region or country, which can be a decisive factor in determining whether a State's laws are in compliance with EU obligations.[97] However, it is also usual for the Court to find that these definitions are not binding on them in any way and that they may be of a persuasive authority only.[98]

Treaty provisions provide that all food and drink traded between Member States must carry an importation and/or exportation duty of zero per cent. This is clear enough. However, the second part of the Article 30 TFEU prohibition can be more problematic. Charges imposed by Member States on imported or exported goods may be classified as 'charges of equivalent effect to a customs duty', even when they may appear to be something else entirely. Where the charge cannot be justified by the Member State, it must cease the imposition of the charge and make appropriate refunds. The real difficulty with the Article 30 TFEU prohibition is that a charge can be deemed incompatible with EU legal obligations even where domestic producers are met with a similar charge at a similar level. The charge must be imposed on all traders at the same stage and in the same manner for it to be deemed something other than of equivalent effect to a customs duty and to therefore escape further Court scrutiny.[99] The distinction between lawful and unlawful charges imposed by States in this way is not always immediately clear. It will often require a more detailed examination of the nature of the charge before it can be ascertained as to whether it is equivalent to a customs duty (prohibited) or merely a form of domestic taxation (allowed, provided it is not discriminatory against non-national produce).

---

[96] Commission Regulation 1006/2011, n 95 above.

[97] Joined Cases C-289/1996, C-293/1996 and C-299/1996 *Denmark, Germany and France v Commission* [1999] ECR I-1541. In this instance, this relates to the application of EU rules on protected geographical food names, which are discussed in much more detail in ch 8.

[98] Ibid. In para 71 of its judgment, the Court stated that 'the Community rules on export refunds and customs nomenclature relied on by the applicants reflect an approach specific to customs matters and are not in any way intended to govern industrial property rights relating to particular names or to reflect consumers' perceptions in that area, so that such rules are not relevant in determining whether a name is generic'.

[99] Case 87/1975 *Bresciani* [1976] ECR 129.

4.3.1. Unlawful Charges and Exceptions to the Rule

Put simply, any charge imposed by a Member State on a foodstuff imported from another Member State is deemed to be of equivalent effect to a customs duty if it is imposed at the point of importation or exportation. The purpose behind the imposition of the charge is irrelevant to this. It need not be protectionist in any way to still be caught by the Article 30 TFEU prohibition.[100] It need not have any revenue-raising purpose either.[101] It will be prohibited by Article 30 TFEU once it has a restrictive effect on trade. There are, of course, some exceptions to this, but they are very limited in both scope and application.

The first of these possible exceptions is that the charge was not imposed due to the importation or exportation of the products, but it was passed on to the importer as a payment due for a service provided. This was tested in *Commission v Italy*, where the Member State was placing a small charge on all exported goods.[102] The idea behind the charge was that its collection could be used to gather statistics on Italian export and trade patterns. The Court initially found that the purpose underlying the charge imposed was not relevant. The existence of the charge at all was enough to subject it to Court scrutiny. Article 30 TFEU contained an absolute prohibition. The low rate of the charge was also deemed irrelevant to any defence put forward in support of its imposition. However, the Member State also further claimed that the charge was effectively a payment for a service provided and should therefore be outside the scope of any Article 30 TFEU scrutiny. The Court disagreed, finding that the advantage conferred on exporters by the collection of the trade flow data was too general in nature and that it was too difficult to identify the service which individual payers of the charge were receiving. Consequently, the charge was deemed to be of equivalent effect to a customs duty, as prohibited by the State's EU Treaty obligations. It is clear, therefore, that for a Member State to successfully argue that the services exception to Article 30 TFEU applies, it must be able to show the specific, as opposed to a more general, benefit conferred on the importing or exporting payer of the charge.

There is a second possible exception to the application of this prohibition on charges of equivalent effect to customs duties. This applies in those circumstances where the fee is charged to cover the costs of meeting a specific obligation imposed on the Member State by EU law. A good example of this was seen in *Bauhuis*.[103] Here, Dutch exporters were met with charges imposed by the national authorities

---

[100] Cases 2 and 3/1969 *Diamond Workers* [1969] ECR 211. In para 18 of this judgment the Court encapsulated the essence of what constitutes a charge of equivalent effect to a customs duty when it stated that '[a]ny charge, however small and whatever its designation and mode of application, which is imposed unilaterally on goods by reason of the fact that they cross a frontier constitutes a charge having equivalent effect [to a customs duty] even if it is not imposed for the benefit of the State, is not discriminatory or protective in effect'.

[101] Case 7/1968 *Commission v Italy* [1968] ECR 423.

[102] Case 24/1968 *Commission v Italy* [1969] ECR 193.

[103] Case 46/1976 *Bauhuis v Netherlands* [1977] ECR 5.

to cover the cost of inspecting live animals. There were two charges at issue here. The first arose out of obligations placed on the Member State by the provisions of an EU directive.[104] This was not therefore based on unilateral action taken by the Member State. The Court decided that this would not be considered a charge of equivalent effect to a customs duty, provided that the amount charged was not more than the actual cost of carrying out the obligatory inspection. The second charge was for inspections that were not carried out pursuant to any specific provision of EU law. The Court did hold that the inspecting itself was justifiable under Article 36 TFEU as being necessary for the protection of human health, but also that the charge imposed to cover the cost of this was not justifiable as it related to the unilateral action of a Member State, placing an additional impediment in the way of the free movement of goods. The charge for the inspection carried out under national law was unlawful. The charge imposed for the execution of an obligation arising out of a specific provision of EU law was not. The Court later held that this exception could only be granted if four conditions were satisfied.[105] These are: (i) that the charge does not exceed the actual cost to the Member State; (ii) that the inspections, or other similar obligations, are obligatory across the Union; (iii) that the action that led to the cost is prescribed by Union law; and (iv) that the action promotes the free movement of goods in some way.

The third possible court-created exception to the prohibition set out in Article 30 TFEU is that the nature of the charge is such that it is really part of the national system of internal taxation, rather than any fee attached to the importation or exportation of food. Charges of equivalent effect to customs duties cannot, therefore, be 'justified' in the same way that measures of equivalent effect to quantitative restrictions can. Exceptions to the rule set out in Article 30 TFEU have been created by the Court of Justice. These determine that the status of the charge is outside the scope of Article 30 TFEU altogether, rather than providing grounds for Member States to argue that the fee imposed is necessary in some way. Customs duties and charges of equivalent effect can never really be justified. Where an additional cost is imposed by the Member State and the Court has determined that it is not within the scope of Article 30 TFEU, it is possible that the charge may be examinable under other provisions of the Treaty, usually those on discriminatory internal taxation, now set out in Article 110 TFEU.

4.4. Discriminatory Taxation on Food and Drink

As alluded to earlier, there are situations when it can be difficult to distinguish between charges imposed by Member States on importers and exporters which are

---

[104] Council Directive 1964/432/EEC of 26 June 1964 on animal health problems affecting intra-Community trade in bovine animals and swine [1964] OJ L 121/1977; English Special Edition Series I, Chapter 1963–1964, p 164.
[105] Case 18/1987 *Commission v Germany* [1988] ECR 5427.

to be classified as being of equivalent effect to customs duties and those which may instead be part of the internal taxation regime. While this can be a difficult distinction to make, it is also a very important one for the Member States and those who are met with the charge, as the consequences of being classified as one or the other can be very different.

A charge of equivalent effect is always prohibited and, once identified, must be abolished. A tax that is deemed to discriminate against products from other Member States does not have to be abolished; it just needs to be modified to remove the discriminatory element. The limitations placed on the way in which Member States can tax foodstuffs once they have come onto the market in a Member State are set out in Article 110 TFEU. Paragraph 1 of this provision states that:

> [n]o Member State shall impose, directly or indirectly, on the products of other Member States any internal taxation of any kind in excess of that imposed directly or indirectly on similar domestic products.

A national rate of tax must usually have three features for Article 110(1) TFEU to have any potential effect on it. First, there must be different rates of tax charged on different products. Charging a higher rate of tax on the same imported product would be blatantly discriminatory. Second, the higher rate of tax must be charged on the product that the imposing Member State does not produce at all or does not produce at any significant level. Third, the products on which the different tax rates are being compared must be in competition with each other. They must be 'similar products'.

It should be noted at this stage that it is not just the difference in a rate of taxation that can lead the Court to conclude that it is discriminatory. It can be the way in which the tax is imposed that can render it prejudicial to imports. In *Commission v Ireland*, the Court held that national rules which permitted national producers of alcoholic products to delay the payment of their tax were contrary to Article 110 TFEU.[106] Allowing domestic operators an additional period of up to six weeks to pay the taxes due on their products was seen by the Court to be a small, but obvious, advantage. The Irish authorities had tried to claim that the wording of Article 110 TFEU related to rates of tax only, but the Court disagreed. It is the effect of the tax that is decisive in determining whether Article 110 TFEU is applicable. The allowance made to Irish producers, which was not available to those from other Member States, was deemed to be directly discriminatory against non-nationals.

Unlike the prohibition on customs duties and measures of equivalent effect, there are circumstances where the Court accepts that seemingly discriminatory national taxes may, in fact, be justifiable. In *Commission v France*, for example, the higher rate of tax payable on the sale of liqueurs when compared to 'traditional natural sweet wines' was deemed justifiable, claiming the lower rate for the latter

---

[106] Case 55/1979 *Commission v Ireland* [1980] ECR 481.

was designed to support producers in areas which suffered from difficult environ-mental conditions.[107]

The French Government presented the argument that these wines were made in regions which were characterised by low rainfall levels and relatively poor soil quality, which limited the possibilities for growing other types of crop. Conse-quently, sweet wine production was vital to the agricultural economies of these areas. The tax advantage enjoyed by the producers of these wines was, accord-ing to the French authorities, designed to offset the more severe conditions under which they were being produced and to support the continued output of high-quality produce. This scheme of preferential taxation was, crucially, also extended to imported sweet wines. No evidence was produced by the Commission to show that the application of the scheme provided more favourable conditions for French wines than for those which possessed the same characteristics but which were produced in other Member States. The Court stated that:

> national provisions which cover both domestic and imported products without distinc-tion cannot be regarded as contrary to [EU] law merely because they might lend themselves to discriminatory application, unless it is proved that they are actually applied in that way.[108]

The Court, just as it did in *Commission v Ireland* above, therefore made it clear that it is always the effect of the national taxation measure that is key to determin-ing whether it is contrary to the Treaty or not. The effect must be discriminatory. Different rates of tax may be charged for similar products. Article 110 TFEU will only be breached where unjustifiable discrimination occurs.

The situation is more complicated, however, where the products that are subjected to different rates of tax are not necessarily 'similar' to each other, but they could be considered as being in, at least partial, competition with each other. Article 110(2) TFEU provides that:

> no Member State shall impose on the products of other Member States any internal taxation of such a nature as to afford indirect protection to other products.

Products are seen as being 'similar' where they 'have similar characteristics and meet the same needs from the point of view of consumers'.[109] 'Other' products include those which 'without being similar ... are nevertheless in competition, even partial, indirect or potential with certain products of the importing country'.[110]

Taxing different types of spirit drinks at different rates, depending on the raw materials used in their production, was tested for compatibility with Article 110 TFEU in *Commission v France*.[111] The Member State placed a higher rate of tax on

---

[107] Case 196/1985 *Commission v France* [1987] ECR 1597.
[108] Ibid, para 10.
[109] Para 12 of Case 45/1975 *Rewe-Zentrale des Lebensmittel-Grosshandels GmbH v Hauptzollamt Landau/Pfalz* [1976] ECR 181.
[110] Case 168/1978 *Commission v France* [1980] ECR 347, para 6.
[111] Ibid.

those spirits which had been made with cereals, such as whiskey, when compared to those made with fruit, like brandy. Other Member States had similar provisions in place and the Commission took issue with three of them on this.

The argument was made that this was an indirect way of protecting national producers, who produced the lower-taxed varieties in significantly larger quantities. The Member States contended that Article 110 TFEU was not applicable to the circumstances as each type of spirit operated in a distinct market. According to the Commission, all spirits, regardless of the raw materials used in their manufacture, possess similar characteristics and 'in essence meet the same needs of consumers'. Spirits should therefore be considered as operating in a single general market and taxation should be calculated based on a single rate for all products that is based on their alcohol content, rather than raw material type.

The Court found that three factors should be taken into consideration when determining whether all spirits were operating, at least partially, in the same market, which would be necessary for Article 110 TFEU to apply. The first was an assessment of the existence of common generic features. As all the spirits at issue were made by distillation procedure and were characterised by their high alcohol content, the Court found that it followed that, due to their similarities, these drinks formed an identifiable and unified group of products. However, on the second consideration, the assessment of more pronounced individual characteristics, the Court did accept that there were differences between spirit types. These were related to either the raw materials used in their production, be they cereals or fruits, the manufacturing processes employed, or the flavourings added. These characteristics were distinguishable to a level which entitled some of the drinks to registered designation status.[112] The third factor in the Court's assessment was related to the use to which these drinks were usually put. It stated that despite the distinctions that could be drawn between spirit types, it was impossible to disregard the fact that there were a range of unifying characteristics between them as well.

Two conclusions could be drawn from all of this. The first was that there was clearly a group of 'similar' products operating in the market for spirits. The tax on these was covered by Article 110(1) TFEU. Second, even where a sufficient degree of similarity between spirits was difficult to determine, there were still, in the case of all such drinks, common characteristics 'sufficiently pronounced to accept that in all cases there is at least partial or potential competition'. Article 110(2) TFEU would thus apply in such circumstances.

The Court deemed that it was unnecessary for the purposes of this dispute to determine whether the spirits were either wholly or partly similar products because there was at least partial competition between them, meaning that Article 110 TFEU would apply in the circumstances regardless. It was also clear to the Court that the French system of charging different rates of tax depending on

---

[112] See ch 8.

the raw materials used was deliberately designed to be protective of domestic spirit production. Spirits made from wine and fruit were within the most favourable tax category, whereas products that were usually imported from other Member States were subject to the higher rates. This was deemed to be a protective charge and the fact that there was one domestically produced drink, aniseed spirit, which was also subject to the higher rate did not, in the opinion of the Court, change this. Even the fact that whiskey's share of the market appeared to be on the increase did not alter the Court's findings in any way. The existence of at least partial competition between the types of product concerned, coupled with the fact that it was mostly imported products that were met with higher taxes, was sufficient to show the Court that the French methods of calculating charges on spirits was discriminatory, in a manner which was contrary to Article 110 TFEU.

Many of the key cases on the prohibition on discriminatory national taxes, in particular those on the issue of goods that are in partial competition with each other, concern alcoholic drinks. For example, the methods used to calculate the amount of tax paid by consumers when purchasing wine in the UK has also been the subject of Court scrutiny in the past.[113] The Commission was of the view that the higher rates charged on wine were deliberately designed to protect the domestic beer-producing industry. The government argued that there was no real competition between wine and beer as consumers would not readily substitute a preference for the former to the latter because of a difference in price. It was argued that any comparison should be between beer and wines with a lower alcohol content, which also tended to be less expensive. The Court agreed, finding that 'the decisive competitive relationship between beer, a popular and widely consumed beverage, and wine must be established by reference to those wines which are the most accessible to the public at large, that is to say, generally speaking, the lightest and cheapest varieties'.[114] The Court also considered that, to a certain extent at least, the two drinks in question were capable of meeting the same needs. There was, therefore, the potential for there to be some degree of 'interchangeability' between them, meaning that consumers would be willing to change their preference for one of the product types for the other, particularly if some other factor, such as price, were taken into consideration. The existence of 'interchangeability' is crucial in determining whether Article 110 TFEU is applicable. There must be a willingness, or at least a potential willingness, amongst consumers to alter their choice should the price of one product go up or down relative to that of another. It is only where there is interchangeability that the existence of some level of competition between products can be shown. The Court considered that there was some competition between beer and low-alcohol and cheap wines. It therefore compared the way in which these products were taxed, in assessing whether there had been a breach of the Treaty. Comparisons on the level of tax were difficult to make due to the different characteristics of wine and beer; comparisons relating

---

[113] Case 170/1978 *Commission v UK* [1983] ECR 2265.
[114] Ibid, para 12.

to the different volumes of each which would be normally drunk by a consumer were hard to quantify. Nevertheless, the Court did find that regardless of which method was used to determine the rates applied, it was clear that wine was taxed at a much higher level than beer. The cheaper wines, which were deemed to be those that were the most directly in competition with beer, were also subjected to this 'considerably higher tax burden'. This, according to the Court, afforded protection to domestic beer production to the detriment of wine imported from other EU Member States. It went on to state that:

> the effect of the United Kingdom tax system is to stamp wine with the hallmarks of a luxury product which, in view of the tax burden which it bears, can scarcely constitute in the eyes of the consumer a genuine alternative to the typical domestically produced beverage.[115]

The levying of taxes on wine at a relatively higher rate than beer was, therefore, contrary to the State's obligations, as set out in Article 110(2) TFEU.

4.4.1. Distinguishing between Customs Duties and Taxes

As mentioned above, there are cases where it can be difficult to determine whether the facts lend themselves to an examination of a national measure for its compliance with Article 30 TFEU prohibiting customs duties and charges of equivalent effect on the one hand and the restrictions placed by Article 110 TFEU on discriminatory internal taxation on the other.

Customs duties, or any equivalent charges, are unlawful under EU law and, where found to exist, must be abolished. Internal taxation is not unlawful and does not have to be abolished, but where it is found to discriminate against products from other Member States it may need to be modified to bring it into compliance with Treaty obligations to remove the discriminatory element.

There are, in general terms, two situations where it may be difficult to establish whether the charge at issue comes within the scope of Article 30 TFEU or Article 110 TFEU. The first is where the charge is imposed as part of a system of internal dues, applicable to all similar products at the same rate and at the same stage of production or marketing. An example of this type of charge was seen in *Denkavit*,[116] where proceedings were brought against the Danish Ministry of Agriculture by a Dutch manufacturer of animal feed over the imposition of a charge of an annual authorisation levy. It was queried whether charging importers this fee was compatible with what are now Articles 30 and 110 TFEU.

The annual authorisation levy that was at issue in *Denkavit* was also charged to national manufacturers of animal feed which contained additives. On first querying whether this levy was a charge of equivalent effect to a customs duty, the Court

---

[115] Ibid, para 27.
[116] Case 29/1987 *Dansk Denkavit ApS v Danish Ministry of Agriculture* [1988] ECR 2965.

noted that Article 30 TFEU was not applicable in those circumstances where any fee imposed on importers:

> relates to a general system of internal dues applied systematically and in accordance with the same criteria to domestic products and imported products alike, in which case it does not come within the scope of [Article 30 TFEU] but within [Article 110 TFEU instead].[117]

The fact that the levy was imposed on all traders in animal feed who were selling on the Danish market and given that it was charged in the same manner on all, regardless of nationality, made this authorisation levy a part of 'a general system of internal dues' and not something equivalent to a customs duty, that was being passed on to importers only. It would have to be examined as a part of the domestic system of taxation and tested for compatibility with Article 110 TFEU instead. On making this examination, the Court held that:

> [Article 110 TFEU] is complied with where an internal tax applies in accordance with the same criteria, objectively justified by the purpose for which the tax was introduced, to domestic products and imported products so that it does not result in the imported products bearing a heavier charge than that borne by the similar domestic product.[118]

The charge had to be paid by all operators, importers and domestic producers alike. It directly related to the costs incurred by the State in checking samples. It was neither within the scope of Article 30 TFEU, nor was it imposed in a manner that was contrary to Article 110 TFEU. While importers were met with this authorisation fee, they could not successfully claim that it should be abolished, provided it was charged to all traders at the same rate, at the same stage of marketing and for the same purpose – in this instance to cover the cost of the analysis of samples.

The situation can be a bit more complicated where a charge is payable on a type of food that is not widely produced by the imposing Member State. Obviously, if the Member State does not produce the good, the charge is being met by importers only. However, it is also obvious that such a charge cannot be automatically deemed incompatible with EU law as this would require that Member States could not impose any taxes or charges on foods that they do not produce themselves. The tax or charge could still be contrary to Treaty obligations, however, if a higher rate of tax was placed on imported foods that the State did not produce and a lower rate on those foods which it did and which were in at least partial competition with the imports.

Italy does not produce many bananas. However, its taxation of them was the subject of Court of Justice scrutiny in the case of *Co-frutta*.[119] The applicant imported bananas into the Benelux countries from Colombia, which it then exported to markets elsewhere in the Union. The goods were therefore subject to

---

[117] Ibid, para 33.
[118] Ibid, para 35.
[119] Case 193/1985 *Cooperativa Co-Frutta Srl v Amministrazione delle finanze dello Stato* [1987] ECR 2085.

the requirements of 'free circulation' once they had entered any EU Member State and were to be treated as if they had been produced in the EU. They were therefore entitled to the same free movement protections available after entering the Union, including the prohibition on customs duties and the elimination of discriminatory national taxes. Italian tax law had established a system of 19 consumer taxes, of which three were charged on goods which were classified as 'tropical products', including coffee, cocoa and bananas.

There were two key issues for the Court to determine here. First, it needed to be established if the tax was actually a customs duty given that, in practice, it really only applied to imported goods. If it were found to be a duty or a charge of equivalent effect then, as stated above, it would have to be abolished. Second, if the charge was alternatively found to be an internal tax, the Court would have to establish whether it was discriminatory against foods imported from other EU Member States.

On the first question, the Court recognised that a charge borne by imported goods only does not necessarily mean that it is a customs duty, as prohibited by Article 30 TFEU, if it:

> relates to a general system of internal dues applied systematically to categories of products in accordance with objective criteria irrespective of the origin of the products.[120]

This tax was seen to form part of 'a general system of internal dues'. The 19 categories of tax were charged on categories of products, regardless of their origin. The 'objective criterion' in this situation was the fact that the charge was imposed as the food in question, bananas, fell within a specific broader category, tropical products. The place of production of goods that were subjected to these taxes was not found by the Court to have any bearing on the rate charged, the basis of assessment or the manner in which the tax was being levied. Revenue generated by this system of taxation was used to finance State spending across all sectors. It was not being applied just because the goods at issue were imported. It was applied as part of a general system of revenue-raising for the State and it could also be applied to imported varieties of the products at issue, where these existed. The charge on bananas constituted internal taxation and would therefore be examinable for compatibility with Article 110 TFEU instead.

For the tax at issue to be deemed discriminatory, it would have to be shown that it favoured domestic production in some way. If the small quantity of bananas produced in Italy were taxed at a lower rate than those which reached the Italian market via another Member State, discrimination would be obvious and any difference in rates charged would have to be removed. The Court in *Co-frutta* examined this based on both Article 110(1) and 110(2) TFEU. The former was not seen to apply in this case. Looking to its deliberations in *Commission v Italy*,[121]

---

[120] Ibid, para 10.
[121] Case 184/1985 *Commission v Italy* [1987] ECR I-2013. See also Case 45/1975 *Rewe-Zentrale des Lebensmittel-Grosshandels GmbH v Hauptzollamt Landau/Pfalz*, n 109 above.

the Court reiterated that bananas were not 'similar' to those fruits which Italy did produce. Any test of similarity would have to be based on a comparison between a set of objective characteristics of the foods, such as their organoleptic properties (impact on the senses) and water content, as well as an assessment of whether they satisfy the same needs or wants of consumers.

Making this comparison, it was accepted that bananas differed from typical Italian-grown fruits in several ways. For example, it was agreed that fruits such as pears have a high water content which gives them a thirst-quenching property that bananas do not possess. Bananas were also recognised for their higher nutritional value and energy content. Article 110(1) did not therefore apply.

However, in its assessment in *Commission v Italy* and then supported by the Court in its judgment in *Co-frutta*, the Court did find that Article 110(2) TFEU could apply in the circumstances. Bananas present consumers with an alternative to other fruits and must therefore be regarded as being in partial competition with Italian-grown varieties.[122] The tax at issue could not therefore afford any indirect protection to domestic produce if it were to be deemed compatible with EU Treaty obligations.

Three factors were crucial here. First, the higher rate of tax did not apply to most typical Italian-produced fruit. Second, the tax on the imported bananas was so high that it could amount to half of the import price. Third, the difference in tax rates was significant enough to have an influence on the market and the purchasing preferences of consumers. Article 110(2) TFEU is breached, in circumstances like these, where it protects the domestic production of 'other' products. It would have to be amended to remove, or at the very least reduce, this protective element.

4.5. Conclusion

The impact of the TFEU requirements on the free movement of goods has been most significant. The way in which these provisions have been interpreted and applied by the European Court of Justice has led to (i) a reduction in the need for harmonising EU legislation, as the principle of mutual recognition means that the compositional requirements or production standards of a Member State must be accepted by all other Member States, reducing the need for the setting of these at EU level; (ii) the scrutinising of existing national measures for compliance, many of which have been deemed contrary to Treaty obligations and thus struck from the statute book; and (iii) perhaps most significantly, the prevention of the introduction by Member States of many new measures that they may feel are necessary to protect consumers, their health or that of the environment. The latter of these is most obviously presented in the Government's attempts to deal with health-risk

---

[122] Ibid, Case 184/1985 *Commission v Italy*, n 121 above. See Case 193/1985 *Co-frutta*, n 119 above.

factors, such as those arising out of poor diet and the over-consumption of alcohol. As will be discussed in Chapters 7 and 9, EU rules on free movement have placed limtations on the compulsory application of many of the most favoured methods of dealing, from a legal perspective, with the risks posed by non-communicable diseases caused by poor diet. The free movement of goods continues to be the most significant influence on the rules that must (and those which cannot) be applied at national level to the food and drink sector.

5

Food Safety

5.1. Introduction

Food should not be sold, in any form, if it is 'unsafe'.[1] It is not safe if it is 'injurious to health' or 'unfit for human consumption'.[2] The fact that the primary focus of food law is on safety is, however, problematic. Many other important considerations are often overlooked because of this emphasis on what is classified as 'unsafe'. There are other ways in which food can harm health, but these are not all directly related to or covered by the legal provisions on the marketing of safe food.

The consumption of nutritionally deficient food has a far greater impact on human health than unsafe food. Many more people die from the long-term consumption of a poor diet than from the contraction of a food-borne illness.[3] Despite this, the focus of both EU and domestic policy makers and legislators has been more fixed on those areas that are categorised as 'food safety' considerations. As outlined in Chapter 1, the narrow definition of 'injurious to health'

---

[1] Article 14(1) of Regulation (EC) No 178/2002 of the European Parliament and of the Council of 28 January 2002 laying down the general principles and requirements of food law, establishing the European Food Safety Authority and laying down procedures in matters of food safety [2002] OJ L 31/1. This legislation is more commonly referred to as 'the General Food Law Regulation'. For more on this see B van der Meulen, 'The core of food law' (2012a) 7 *European Food and Feed Law Review* 117.

[2] Ibid, Art 14(2).

[3] There is a lot of evidence supporting the claim that there is a strong link between poor diet and premature death. This includes a comprehensive study published in 2016 which showed that nearly one in every five premature deaths globally is caused by poor dietary habits, E. Gakidou and others, 'Global, regional and national comparative risk assessment of 84 behavioural, environmental and occupational, and metabolic risks or clusters of risks, 1990–2016: A systematic analysis for the Global Burden of Disease Study 2016' (2016) 390 *The Lancet* 1345. In the UK, the National Institute for Health and Clinical Excellence (NICE) estimates that there are 40,000 deaths per year in England related to the consumption of unhealthy foods. See 'Prevention of cardiovascular disease', NICE public health guidance 25 June 2012. Available at: www.nice.org. Compare this with the UK Food Standards Agency's estimate that there are around 590 deaths per year in the UK from food poisoning, or at least from infectious intestinal disease. See www.food.gov.uk. The World Health Organisation (WHO) Global Status Report on Non-Communicable Diseases 2010 estimated that around 2.8 million deaths per year across the EU were a result of people being overweight and obese. The 2014 edition of the report found that globally this figure is closer to 3.4 million deaths per year. The 2017 WHO Progress Monitor found that there were approximately 27,000 NCD deaths in Ireland per year, with 10% of the population at risk of premature death from target NCDs. These NCDs include those caused by smoking (around 5,500 according to the HSE) but also those contributed to by alcohol consumption (around 1,000) and poor diet. WHO reports available at: www.who.int. This is discussed in much more detail in Ch 9.

has formed the foundation of this serious shortcoming with the law and politics that dictate what happens in the food sector. The fact that this term traditionally covers 'dangerous' but not 'harmful' foods or ingredients has meant that many products which actually cause significant health problems, including premature death, often remain outside the scope of more appropriate regulation. This course, mostly directed at EU level, has a profound effect on Irish law and, consequently, national public health.

The EU General Food Law Regulation states that ascertaining whether food is 'injurious to health' is to be based upon an assessment of the probable immediate and/or short-term and/or long-term effects of that food on the health of a person consuming it, as well as on subsequent generations.[4] Account should also be taken of any probable cumulative toxic effects and/or the particular health sensitivities of a specific category of consumers where that food is intended for them. The Regulation makes specific reference to the effect on health, whether this is immediate, short-term or long-term. It is clear, however, that this is limited to the potential for food to spread disease, contaminate or toxify. Equally clearly, it does not include the potential for food to be a contributory factor in causing strokes, cancer, diabetes, heart disease or mental illness.

Many foods which have a serious long-term detrimental impact on human health are marketed, uninhibited by the law. They contain substances that, when consumed on an ongoing basis, can ultimately lead to premature death. As discussed in Chapter 7, food laws, such as those on labelling, facilitate this. Other regulations, which could control the use of these unhealthy substances in food production, are not introduced, despite overwhelming evidence of the damaging consequences of consumption. EU rules on the free movement of goods and those existing in related secondary legislation, prevent Member States, such as Ireland, from intervening. As seen in Chapter 4, the European Court of Justice has made it clear that national authorities cannot justify the maintenance of national laws on the ground that they are necessary for guaranteeing that food has any nutritional value. There can be no minimum standards for nutrition.

While the definition of a food that is 'injurious to health' has the potential to offer a framework for raising the nutritional qualities of food, it is not used in this way. Determining whether food is 'unfit for human consumption' is even less helpful in this regard. The Regulation states that assessment of whether food falls into this latter category should be based upon an examination of its intended use, any contamination, putrefaction, deterioration or decay.[5] Again, these considerations usually relate to the short-term consequences of eating rotting food. They clearly do not relate to harmful substances, such as trans-fats and fructose syrups, the long-term consumption of which can lead to the development of

---

[4] See Regulation (EC) No 178/2002, n 1 above, Art 14(4). For more on this see B van Der Meulen, 'The concept of unsafe food: A critical reflection on the tenet of EU food law' (2012b) 9 *Zeitschrift für Stoffrecht* 195.
[5] Ibid, Art 14(5).

terminal illness. These foods are 'fit for human consumption'. Yet, their impact on overall health is usually much more damaging than the consumption of milk or cheese that has passed its use-by date.

Since the BSE crisis, many new laws governing a range of issues related to 'food safety' have been introduced onto the Irish statute books, either in the form of directly applicable EU regulations or from the transposition of EU directives. The key problem with this is that the regulation of food safety has developed in a way that ignores many of the most unsafe aspects of food consumption. Efforts to make foods cheaper, longer-lasting and, in some cases, more palatable, has led to the increased use of unhealthy ingredients in production.

Yet this unwelcome result remains mostly outside the scope of the controlling legislation. As a consequence, those foods that contain these substances, often to dangerously high levels, are manufactured entirely within the law. The presence of these constituents is often kept concealed from consumers due to lax labelling requirements. These foods are made and marketed in compliance with the law. This, according to the General Food Law Regulation, makes them, legally, 'safe'.[6] As a consequence, they must also be deemed 'safe' under Irish law and specifically under the terms of the Food Safety Authority of Ireland Act 1998 and related legislation.

5.2. Food Safety Acts

The Food Safety Authority of Ireland Act 1998 provides much of the framework for Irish law on food safety. Some aspects of this were set out in Chapter 3, in particular those directly related to the establishment and the role of the Food Safety Authority of Ireland (FSAI). However, the Act now deals with many more of the primary matters of Irish food law. It is perhaps surprising that this 1998 Act presents us with only the second significant horizontal Act of the Oireachtas dealing with food law matters and the only one to be introduced since the Food Standards Act 1974.

The 1998 Act defines 'food' as including 'any substance used, available to be used or intended to be used, for food or drink by human persons and any substance which enters into or is used in the production, composition or preparation of these substances'.[7] This is relatively unchanged, if slightly simplified, from the definition of 'food' that was set out in the Food Standards Act 1974.[8] However, this definition

---

[6] Ibid, Art 14(7).

[7] Food Safety Authority of Ireland Act 1998, s 2(1).

[8] 'Food' was defined in s 1 of the 1974 Act as being 'any substance used for food or drink by man and any substance which enters into or is used in the composition or preparation of human food [or the] preparation of any such substance [and] chewing gum'.

is now surpassed by that which is set out in Article 2 of the EU General Food Law Regulation,[9] which provides that 'food' (or a 'foodstuff')

> [...] means any substance or product, whether processed, partially processed or unprocessed, intended to be, or reasonably expected to be ingested by humans [including] drink, chewing gum and any substance, including water, intentionally incorporated into the food during its manufacture, preparation or treatment.

'Food safety' is defined in the FSAI Act 1998 as meaning '[...] the steps taken to avoid risks to public health arising from food intended for human consumption'.[10] 'Food safety' is not actually defined in the EU General Food Law Regulation. However, the Regulation does provide that food will be deemed as 'unsafe' if it is considered to be injurious to health or unfit for human consumption.[11] The enforcement of standards related to food safety has already been set out in Chapter 3. The rest of this chapter will deal with what those standards are and where they have come from.

5.3. BSE Crisis

Bovine spongiform encephalopathy (BSE) or 'mad cow disease' is a neurodegenerative disorder affecting cattle. It has a fatal effect on the brain and central nervous system. There is no treatment and no cure. There is strong evidence that BSE can be transmitted to humans as variant Creutzfeldt-Jakob disease (vCJD). Those infected can suffer hallucinations, delusions and unpleasant physical sensations, such as pain and numbness in the limbs. This can develop into poor balance, uncontrollable muscle movements and dementia. Finally, patients may have eating and swallowing difficulties and an inability to function. Again, there is no treatment or cure available. Average life expectancy following infection is around one year.

According to the Southwood Report, the first cases of BSE were detected in British cattle during the 1970s.[12] This had risen to 10,000 confirmed cases by the end of 1989. The BSE Inquiry reported that cattle in Britain had died from BSE infection as early as 1987.[13] In all probability, the disease was being spread amongst herds there by the consumption of animal feed that contained infected bone meal. Early realisations about this led to the introduction of domestic legislation across Britain on the matter in 1988.

---

[9] Reg 178/2002, n 1 above.

[10] Food Safety Authority of Ireland Act 1998, s 2(1).

[11] Reg 178/2002, n 1 above, Art 14(2).

[12] Report of the Working Party on Bovine Spongiform Encephalopathy (Southwood Report) (London, Department of Health/MAFF, 1989).

[13] Report to the Minister of Agriculture, Fisheries and Food and the Secretary of State for Health. *The BSE Inquiry: The Report* (London, The Stationery Office, 2001).

5.3.1. Legal Response to the BSE Crisis

The British BSE Order 1988 was the first piece of domestic legislation to assist in dealing with the emergence and spread of the disease through contaminated animal feed.[14] It prescribed that anyone who was in possession of a cow or carcass that was suspected of being affected with the disease was obliged to notify an appointed veterinary inspector as soon as possible.[15] It also provided veterinary inspectors with the power to prohibit the movement of suspected animals.[16] Perhaps most significantly, the Order prohibited the use of animal feed that contained material derived from a carcass – but only between July 1988 and January 1989.[17] This Order was the first in a series of inadequate responses, at both UK and EU level, to the growing crisis.[18]

One of the conclusions of the British BSE Inquiry was that there was confusion during the period of the spread of the disease as to who had regulatory responsibility for dealing with the crisis. It was accepted, for example, that once definitive measures had been adopted by the European Commission, the UK authorities ceased to be entitled to adopt any unilateral action designed to deal with the risks posed by the disease. The first Decision taken by the Commission was in 1989.[19] This obliged the UK authorities to do two things. First, it prohibited the export to other EU Member States of all live cattle born before July 1988 – the date of the introduction of the animal feed ban by the BSE Order – and those born to female cattle suspected or confirmed as having the disease.[20] Second, the health certificate that had to accompany all other exports and which had been prescribed by EU Directive since 1964,[21] now had to include a statement that the BSE measures adopted by this Decision had been complied with.[22] The Commission undertook to monitor developments in the evolving crisis.[23] However, there was no recognition of the potential dangers posed to human health at this time.[24]

---

[14] SI No 1039/1988.

[15] Ibid, Art 4(1).

[16] Ibid, Art 6.

[17] Ibid, Art 7.

[18] The prohibition on using meat and bone meal in animal feed was officially recognised as being relatively ineffective in Recital 6, Preamble to Dec 1994/474, n 32 below.

[19] Commission Decision 1989/469/EEC concerning certain protection measures relating to bovine spongiform encephalopathy in the United Kingdom [1989] OJ L 225/51.

[20] Ibid, Art 1.

[21] Ibid, Art 3(2) and Annex F of Council Directive 1964/432/EEC of 26 June 1964 on animal health problems affecting intra-Community trade in bovine animals and swine [1964] OJ 121/1977. For further discussion on EU rules on meat inspection systems see J Lawless and K Wiedemann, 'European meat inspection: Continuity and change in building a (more) risk-based system of regulation' (2011) 6 *European Food and Feed Law Review* 96.

[22] Commission Decision 1989/469/EEC, n 19 above, Art 2.

[23] Ibid, Art 4.

[24] The Preamble to Dec 1989/469, n 19 above, only refers to the disease being considered as a 'new serious contagious or infectious animal disease whose presence may constitute a danger to cattle in other Member States' (recital 2).

The 1989 Commission Decision was amended soon after.[25] The limited ban on live cattle exports from the UK was altered, so that only those aged under six months old could be traded.[26] It was believed that these younger animals were unlikely to transmit the infection.[27] Obviously, the prohibition on the export of the offspring of infected cattle remained.[28] This Decision was supplemented in June 1990.[29] This extended the restrictions on exports of beef still attached to the bone which could not be certified as coming from holdings where there had been no cases of BSE for at least two years.[30] All nervous and lymphatic tissue had also to be removed.[31] Despite the fact that instances of BSE were now at a peak, there was no further legislative intervention until 1994. As will be discussed below, this lack of action was just one part of a whole range of negligent omissions, at both UK and EU level during the period.

By 1994 the crisis had deepened. In 1990, there were 14,181 confirmed cases of BSE in Britain, 12,611 of which were discovered in England. By 1994 this had risen to 23,943 and 20,322 respectively. The outbreak peaked at almost 37,000 confirmed cases in Britain in 1992, but 1993 was an almost equally bad year. Despite this, there was no significant legislative activity at EU level until the end of July 1994.[32] This extended the restriction on the export of 'bone-in' beef (meat attached to bone) to that which came from herds which had been BSE free for at least six years.[33]

It had been presumed that the measures already taken were a significant factor in reducing the levels of BSE incidents by 1994.[34] While the numbers of confirmed cases were in decline, these were still at very high levels – ten times what they had been when the BSE Order was introduced in 1988. The EU Commission did undertake to keep the situation under continual review.[35] The most significant development of all in this regard came with the Spongiform Encephalopathy Advisory Committee (SEAC) Report to the UK Government in 1996, which concluded that there was probably a link between the consumption of beef from BSE-infected cattle and the development of vCJD in humans. This resulted

---

[25] Commission Decision 1990/59/EEC of 7 February 1990 amending Decision 1989/469/EEC concerning certain protection measures relating to bovine spongiform encephalopathy in the United Kingdom [1990] OJ L 41/23.

[26] Ibid, Art 1.

[27] Ibid, recital 4 of Preamble.

[28] Ibid, Art 1.

[29] Commission Decision 1990/261 of 8 June 1990 amending Decision 1989/469/EEC concerning certain protection measures relating to bovine spongiform encephalopathy (BSE) in the United Kingdom and Decision 1990/200/EEC concerning additional requirements for some tissues and organs with respect to bovine spongiform encephalopathy [1990] OJ L 146/29.

[30] Ibid, Art 2.

[31] Ibid, Art 2(2).

[32] Commission Decision 1994/474/EC of 27 July 1994 concerning certain protection measures relating to bovine spongiform encephalopathy and repealing Decisions 1989/469/EEC and 1990/200/EEC [1994] OJ L 194/96.

[33] Ibid, Art 4(1).

[34] Preamble to Decision 1994/474, n 32 above, recital 3.

[35] Ibid, recital 4.

in the taking of highly interventionist action by both the EU Commission and the UK authorities.

In March 1996, the Commission decided to ban the export of all live cattle, all beef, all products obtained from slaughtered cattle and all animal feed containing meat and bone meal, with immediate effect.[36] The Commission obliged the UK to report every two weeks on the application of all protective measures taken to control the spread of BSE.[37] The UK would, however, also be provided with the opportunity to present further proposals to the Commission on alternative control measures.[38] While there was recognition that the outright ban on all UK exports was temporary,[39] the Decision was highly controversial and thought to be unnecessary, going beyond that which was required to control the spread of the disease. This belief that the prohibition on all exports was disproportionate would ultimately face examination by the European Court of Justice in two significant cases,[40] which are discussed in more detail later in this chapter.

While it continued to be accepted that infected meat and meat products could lead to the development of vCJD in humans, a position that was given further support by the conclusion of the UK Department of Health's Advisory Committee on Dangerous Pathogens (ACDP) in September 1997 that the BSE agent should be classified as a human pathogen, it was also acknowledged that the measures adopted by the EU and the UK were having some impact on reducing the spread of the disease. New findings also showed that the ban on exports could be lifted for some products, such as gelatin and tallow. Research suggested that the use of these, along with bovine semen, was safe.[41] However, a traceability system would have to be put in place for these products to ensure that they could be easily recalled from the market should any concerns about their use resurface.[42]

The ban on the exportation of British beef and cattle ended up lasting, in various forms, for an entire decade. The first partial resumption of the export of some beef products from the UK was permitted only from 1 August 1999.[43] Some EU

---

[36] Commission Decision 1996/239/EC of 27 March 1996 on emergency measures to protect against bovine spongiform encephalopathy [1996] OJ L 78/47.

[37] Ibid, Art 3.

[38] Ibid, Art 4.

[39] Art 1 of Decision 1996/239, n 36 above, states that the ban is introduced '[p]ending an overall examination of the situation'.

[40] Case C-180/1996 *United Kingdom v Commission* and Case C-157/1996 *Queen v National Farmers' Union*, n 120 below.

[41] Preamble to Council Decision 1998/256/EC of 16 March 1998 concerning emergency measures to protect against bovine spongiform encephalopathy, amending Decision 1994/474/EC and repealing Decision 1996/239/EC [1998] OJ L 113/32.

[42] Ibid, Art 5.

[43] Article 1 of Commission Decision 1999/514/EC of 23 July 1999 setting the date on which dispatch from the United Kingdom of bovine products under the date-based export scheme may commence by virtue of Art 6(5) of Council Decision 1998/256/EC [1999] OJ L 195/42. Initially, this partial resumption was to be for cattle born, reared and slaughtered in Northern Ireland only, but this was later amended to include other parts of the UK by Commission Decision 1998/692/EC of 25 November 1998 amending Decision 1998/256/EC as regards certain emergency measures to protect against bovine spongiform encephalopathy [1998] OJ L 328/28.

Member States, most notably France, refused to lift the ban and were consequently threatened with legal action by the Commission, the Court of Justice later deciding that they were in breach of their obligations under the relevant Decisions.[44] The ban on exporting 'bone-in' beef (meat attached to bone) and live cattle remained in place until 2006.[45] The decision to reverse the prohibition on exports was made following a unanimous opinion of the EU Standing Committee on the Food Chain and Animal Health, supporting a Commission proposal to lift the embargo. Two conditions had to be satisfied before the EU institutions would consider this course of action. First, there had to be an incidence of less than 200 BSE cases per million adult bovine animals. The European Food Safety Authority confirmed that this was the case in May 2004. Second, there would have to be a positive report from the EU Food and Veterinary Office (FVO) indicating that there was proper enforcement of BSE controls in the UK. An inspection carried out by the FVO in June 2005 confirmed that this was the case.

While there were many EU Decisions and Regulations established in the effort to restrict the spread of BSE during the 1990s and beyond, there was also a plethora of domestic UK controls designed to deal with this crisis introduced at the same time, dating back to the BSE Order in 1988, as discussed above. Further examples include the Beef (Emergency Control) Order 1996[46] and the Specified Bovine Material Order 1996,[47] both of which were published the day after the EU announced that it was banning British beef exports. This body of UK legislation introduced a further range of significant measures restricting the conditions under which beef could be produced and sold there.

The Specified Bovine Material Order was one of the most significant of the domestic measures introduced to deal with BSE in the UK. Under the Order, anything classified as 'specified bovine material' or anything containing any of this material, could not be sold by anyone.[48] This included all parts of the head (except for the tongue), spinal cord, spleen, thymus, tonsils and intestines of all cattle over six months old, or younger in some circumstances.[49] The Order also prohibited the use of meat recovered from the vertebral column by mechanical means, although it could be used for gelatine production.[50] A lot of these parts of the animal could not even be removed from the slaughterhouse, except for veterinary or scientific examination.[51] Incineration and rendering plants would face tighter controls.[52]

[44] Case C-1/2000 *Commission v France* [2001] ECR I-9989.
[45] Annex to Commission Regulation (EC) No 657/2006 of 10 April 2006 amending Regulation (EC) No 999/2001 of the European Parliament and of the Council as regards the United Kingdom and repealing Council Decision 1998/256/EC and Decisions 1998/351/EC and 1999/514/EC [2006] OJ L 116/9.
[46] SI No 961/1996.
[47] SI No 963/1996.
[48] Ibid, Art 4.
[49] Ibid, Art 2(1).
[50] Ibid, Art 5. The ban on the use of the vertebral column was originally introduced by the Specified Bovine Offal (Amendment) Order 1995, SI No 3246/1995.
[51] See, eg, SI No 963/1996, n 47 above, Arts 12 and 13.
[52] Ibid, Arts 17 and 18.

The Beef (Emergency Control) Order 1996 was used to introduce what is widely regarded as the most interventionist of all the UK's domestic legislative responses to the crisis. It prohibited the sale of all beef that came from cattle that were more than 30 months old at the time of slaughter.[53] This ban was to last until November 2005, when it was lifted by the Bovine Products (Restrictions on Placing on the Market) (England) Regulations.[54] The use of meat from cattle was now only limited to that coming from animals born before 1 August 1996,[55] provided they had had been slaughtered at an approved abattoir in accordance with the provisions of the EU Transmissible Spongiform Encephalopathy Regulation 2001, which is discussed in more detail below. The 'over 30-month' rule was only revoked after the UK's Food Standards Agency was satisfied that the system for testing cattle for disease was suitable and robust.

Huge volumes of domestic legislation were – and continue to be – introduced in the UK to first, deal with BSE at its most rampant and then to minimise the possibility of its devastating impact reoccurring.[56] The primary measures that continue to apply there include strict controls over slaughterhouses, animal feed and testing methods, including all of those set out in applicable EU regulations. The fact that the BSE crisis happened and the way that it was dealt with, has had a significant impact on Irish food law.

5.3.2. Transmissible Spongiform Encephalopathies Regulation 2001

By the time the ban on the exportation of beef from the UK was lifted in 2006, the cost to the sector was very significant. It has continued to rise ever since. According to the Report of the BSE Inquiry, domestic beef consumption in Britain declined by around 35 per cent,[57] although this rose again after the introduction of the 30-month rule. The Inquiry itself was estimated to have cost around £27 million. Beef prices fell by around 25 per cent. The total cost of aid and compensation was thought to stand at around £5 billion, in an industry that employed 130,000 workers.[58] Millions of cattle were slaughtered.[59] It is more difficult to estimate the

[53] SI No 961/1996, n 46 above, Art 2, as amended by the Beef (Emergency Control)(Amendment) Order 1996, SI No 1043/1996.

[54] SI No 2719/2005.

[55] Ibid, Reg 3.

[56] For example, cattle must carry 'passports' if they are to be moved around, or into or out of, Britain under the terms of the Cattle Passports Order 1996, SI No 1686/1996.

[57] See Report to the Minister of Agriculture, Fisheries and Food and the Secretary of State for Health. *The BSE Inquiry: The Report* n 13 above.

[58] The compensation scheme in Ireland discriminated between producers who exported cattle live and those who sold them for slaughter in Ireland. The High Court found that this was '[…] a very serious breach of Community law' and that compensation would be payable in much the same way to both. See *Maxwell v Minister for Agriculture, Food and Forestry* [1998] 8 JIC 1101.

[59] Most of this data comes from a report by Nigel Atkinson, Head of Economics (International) Division, Ministry of Agriculture, Fisheries and Food, entitled 'The impact of BSE on the UK economy' (1999).

actual cost to the beef sector in Ireland. Despite having very low incidence of BSE, demand and prices in Ireland dropped, the latter by around 12 per cent.[60] Many States outside the EU also placed long-term prohibitions on the importation of Irish beef and cattle. The Gulf Cooperation Council Food Safety Committee, for example, did not allow the importation of Irish beef again until 2013. China and the United States did not agree to lift these bans until 2015, although actual trade with the former did not recommence for some time after this.

There were two significant reports on the way that the BSE crisis was handled. The first of these, the British BSE Inquiry, chaired by Lord Phillips, found that there were a whole range of problems identifiable with the way in which the disease was dealt with during the 1990s. These ranged from the practical, such as using meat and bone meal as an ingredient of animal feed, to the legal, including both the lack of suitable measures and the failure to properly apply those restrictions that were introduced. A series of shortcomings were identified with the way in which EU law and UK domestic regulation interacted on the matter. It stated, for example, that it was generally accepted that the UK was not entitled to adopt unilateral measures to deal with BSE as soon as the EU Commission started taking action. National authorities were also constrained by the terms of secondary EU legislation, such as directives on veterinary checks[61] and zootechnical checks.[62] This, in turn, could call into question the lawfulness of those domestic measures that were adopted, such as the Specified Bovine Offal (Amendment) Order 1995.[63] The Inquiry concluded that this could all potentially have important consequences for the way in which any future food crises could be responded to at national level, although the significance of this is now probably reduced by the inclusion of safeguard clauses in the relevant EU legislation.[64]

The second report, the European Parliament Report, identified shortcomings with both the UK and the EU responses.[65] It noted how, despite the incidence of BSE being at peak levels in the early 1990s, EU legislative activity to control the spread of the disease was suspended during this period. The Council held

---

The figures presented here are revised to take account of other estimates. They are for indicative purposes only, as the estimates vary depending on the method of calculation used. The exact costs are substantial, but uncertain.

[60] S O'Neill, 'The implication of the BSE crisis on the demand for beef in Ireland: An econometric investigation' (1997) 11 *Student Economic Review* 222.

[61] Council Directive 1989/662/EEC of 11 December 1989 concerning veterinary checks in intra-Community trade with a view to the completion of the internal market [1989] OJ L 395/13.

[62] Council Directive 1990/425/EEC of 26 June 1990 concerning veterinary and zootechnical checks applicable in intra-Community trade in certain live animals and products with a view to the completion of the internal market [1990] OJ L 224/29.

[63] SI No 3246/1995; see also n 50 above.

[64] Such as that set out in Regulation (EC) No 999/2001 of the European Parliament and of the Council of 22 May 2001 laying down rules for the prevention, control and eradication of certain transmissible spongiform encephalopathies [2001] OJ L 147/1.

[65] European Parliament Report on alleged contraventions or maladministration in the implementation of Community law in relation to BSE, without prejudice to the jurisdiction of the Community and national courts, as established by EP Decision of 17 July 1996, OJ C 239/1.

no debates on the matter between 1990 and 1994. Ultimately, the Parliament found that the Council and the Commission, along with the UK authorities, had neglected their duties.

The framework legislation that was finally introduced to deal properly with the potential for BSE or similar diseases to create another crisis in the future, reducing the need for ad hoc and piecemeal legislative responses, is the Transmissible Spongiform Encephalopathies (TSE) Regulation 2001.[66] This Regulation sets classifications for EU Member States and third countries or regions, according to their BSE status.[67] A country or region can be deemed as having 'a negligible BSE risk', a 'controlled BSE risk' or an 'undetermined BSE risk'.[68] Categorisation is decided after a detailed risk analysis has been conducted, as well as other factors, such as the extent to which there is an education programme for veterinary practitioners, breeders and those who transport, trade in and slaughter cattle which seeks to encourage them to report all cases of neurological manifestations in adult animals. Account is also taken of whether there is compulsory reporting and examination of cattle showing signs of BSE, continuous surveillance and monitoring systems and laboratory testing.[69]

A country or region has a negligible BSE risk if it complies with all these conditions for at least seven years and it has had no reported cases of BSE or, where there have been reported cases, these were shown to have affected imported cattle only. Where there has been an indigenous case of BSE then it must be shown that the animal concerned was born more than eleven years ago, along with other conditions, like the production of evidence that shows that meat and bone meal have not been fed to ruminants for at least eight years. A country or region has a 'controlled BSE risk' where it complies with the conditions on risk analysis and risk management but cannot satisfy other conditions, such as those on prohibiting the use of meat and bone meal in ruminant feed for at least eight years. A country or region has an 'undetermined BSE risk' where a decision on its status has not yet been made or where it cannot meet the conditions of one of the other two categories, outlined above. Previously, there could be no trade in live cattle or beef products with States who had not had their BSE status classified by the European Commission.[70] However, since the new set of BSE status categories were introduced by the amending regulations, bovine animals and products can now be imported from those areas which have an 'undetermined' BSE risk, provided that these are accompanied by health certification which attests that the

---

[66] See Regulation (EC) No 999/2001, n 64 above.

[67] Ibid, Art 5(1).

[68] Annex II, Chapter C to Reg 999/2001, n 66 above. As amended by Commission Regulation (EC) No 722/2007 of 25 June 2007 amending Regulation (EC) No 999/2001 [2007] OJ L 164/7. Under Art 36 of the Animal Health Law, n 113 below, which will come into effect in 2021, EU Member States will apply to the EU Commission for approval of disease-free status for the diseases listed in the Regulation, either for the entire territory of the State, or for one or more zones thereof.

[69] Annex II, Chapter A to Reg 999/2001, n 66 above. Also amended by Reg 722/2007, n 68 above.

[70] Reg 999/2001, n 66 above, Art 5(1).

animals have not been fed meat and bone meal and that no 'specified risk material' is imported.[71] 'Specified risk material' for bovine animals includes:

> the skull [...] including the brain and eyes, and the spinal cord of animals aged over 12 months; the vertebral column [...] of animals aged over 24 months; and the tonsils, the intestines from the duodenum to the rectum and the mesentery of animals of all ages.

The degree to which a State can engage in cross-border trade in meat and live animals is determined on the basis of their BSE status.[72] For example, there can be imports of bovine animals from a country or a region with a negligible BSE risk provided that an animal health certificate is presented which shows that the animals were born and continuously reared in a country so classified; that the animals are identified by a permanent identification system enabling them to be traced back to the herd of origin and that they have not been exposed to BSE or potentially consumed contaminated feed. For imports from those countries where the BSE risk is undetermined, there must be a meat and bone meal ban in place there, along with the other conditions on animal health certification.

The TSE Regulation also introduces a monitoring system, to be systematically applied in each EU Member State.[73] Details are provided on how sampling is to take place, to test for incidence of one of the TSE diseases – scrapie – and BSE.[74] The results of this analysis must be submitted on an annual basis by the Department of Agriculture, Food and the Marine to the European Commission. There are two categories of surveillance of TSEs that take place in Ireland. The first is 'passive surveillance'. This involves the reporting of suspected cases of BSE and scrapie to the Department, after which the animal is examined by an inspector from the Regional Veterinary Office. Animals are also examined by veterinarians for diseases like BSE after slaughter in abattoirs. Any animal that is suspected of carrying BSE is killed and the herd in question is placed under official restriction and quarantine. The brain of the suspected animal is then sent for further testing at the TSE National Reference Laboratory.[75] If BSE is diagnosed, the carcass

---

[71] As amended by Reg 722/2007, n 68 above.

[72] Reg 999/2001, n 66 above, Annex IX. Commission Decision 2007/453/EC of 29 June 2007 establishing the BSE status of Member States or third countries or regions thereof according to their BSE risk, [2007] OJ L 172/84, sets out that Argentina, Australia, New Zealand, Singapore and Uruguay were all deemed to have a negligible BSE risk. Most EU Member States, including Ireland, were deemed to have a controlled BSE risk, along with EFTA countries Iceland and Norway and third countries Brazil, Canada, Chile, Taiwan and the United States of America. This is all set out in the Annex to Decision 2007/453. Any country or region not listed is automatically classified as having an 'undetermined BSE risk'. The lists change as countries are re-assessed. For example, Brazil, Chile and the United States of America, along with Australia, New Zealand, Japan and others were reclassified as 'negligible BSE risk' by Commission Implementing Decision 2013/429/EU amending Decision 2007/453/EC, [2013] OJ L 217/37. Some EU Member States have been designated as having only a negligible BSE risk by this Decision, including Belgium, Italy, Austria, Finland and Sweden.

[73] Reg 999/2001, above n 66, Art 6.

[74] Annex III, Chapter A to Reg 999/2001, n 66 above.

[75] As designated under the terms of Art 33 of Regulation (EC) No 882/2004 of the European Parliament and of the Council of 29 April 2004 on official controls performed to ensure the verification of compliance with feed and food law, animal health and animal welfare rules [2004] OJ L 165/1.

of the animal is destroyed and a full epidemiological investigation is undertaken. This includes an examination of farm records and a detailed inspection of the farm itself, primarily to determine whether there has been exposure to meat and bone meal. Other animals which are deemed to be cohorts of the diseased cow and which are traceable using the Department of Agriculture's Animal Health Computer System are also slaughtered and destroyed. This slaughter must take place at a facility that does not produce meat for human consumption. 'Cohorts' are those animals which would have shared the same farm as the BSE-infected animal when both animals were less than one year old because they are likely to have eaten the same contaminated feed. Studies have shown that cattle are most likely to be infected by BSE where they eat contaminated feed in the first few months of their life.

The second type of surveillance is 'active surveillance'. Under this programme, brain samples are taken from all cattle over 48 months of age that die on a farm. If an animal is shown to have been carrying BSE, then a process similar to that set out above for passive surveillance is undertaken. Most significantly, the specified risk materials, which are capable of transmitting BSE infection, are removed and destroyed from all bovine animals at abattoirs, regardless of BSE detection. This ensures that they cannot end up in the feed chain, potentially causing contamination in other animals.

The TSE Regulation specifically prohibits the use of protein derived from mammals in ruminant feed (that for cattle and sheep),[76] orders the removal and destruction of specified risk material,[77] restricts the use of ruminant material in the production of certain products,[78] restricts the movement of suspected animals[79] and sets out details of the measures to be taken following confirmation of the presence of a TSE.[80] All these requirements are incorporated into Irish law, as discussed above. Finally, the Regulation provides that the legislation and its implementation is to be kept under review by the European Commission, assisted by the Standing Committee on Plants, Animals, Food and Feed and is therefore subject to change at any time should circumstances dictate this.[81] The Regulation came into effect

[76] Ibid, Art 7. Despite this ban, the EFSA Panel on Biological Hazards has found that contaminated feed 'cannot be excluded as the origin of any of the [cases of BSE detected after its introduction]'. However, this contamination may have occurred by proximity to meal and bone stores, rendering plants, presence of feed intended for other species, farmyard disposal of carcasses or feed mills. See BIOHAZ, A Ricci and others, 'Bovine Spongiform Encephalopathy (BSE) cases born after the total feed ban' (2017) 15 *EFSA Journal* 4885.

[77] Reg 999/2011, n 66 above, Art 8. Specified risk material, for the purposes of Reg 999/2001, includes spinal cord, brain, eyes, intestines and spleen, amongst others, as listed in Annex V to the Regulation, and mentioned earlier in this chapter. Other details on the removal and destruction of these animal parts is also set out in this section of the legislation.

[78] Ibid, Art 9.

[79] Ibid, Art 12.

[80] Ibid, Art 13. Article 54 of the Animal Health Law, n 113 below, will further provide that national competent authorities must conduct investigations to confirm or to rule out the presence of a listed disease.

[81] Ibid, Arts 22–25. Alterations to the requirements set out in the Annexes to the Regulation are made using the comitology procedure (Art 23 in conjunction with Art 24(2)).

on 1 July 2001.[82] It is now given further effect in Irish law by the European Union (Transmissible Spongiform Encephalopathies) Regulations 2015.[83]

The Irish TSE Regulations establish how the EU requirements will be practically applied within the State. They make it clear, for example, that the only animal feed that can be stored, used, imported, manufactured or possessed is that which is specifically permitted by the EU Regulation.[84] Similar detail is provided on the movement of animals,[85] animal testing for disease,[86] registrations and authorisations,[87] enforcement[88] and the use of emergency measures where there are reasonable grounds for believing that there is an immediate risk to public health, animal health or the environment.[89] Authorised officers have a key role to play in the application of the practical measures to be employed when suspect cases of BSE or any other TSE arise.[90] They have the power to enter and inspect any premises where it is believed that animals, products, feed, equipment or records are or have been kept there.[91] Additional authority is granted under the Regulations where there are reasonable grounds for believing that there is a risk of disease or that a related offence has been committed. This includes the power to search, restrict or order the movement of vehicles, machinery and equipment, take samples and seize animals.[92] Compliance notices can be issued where an authorised officer comes to the opinion that there is a risk to health or that the TSE Regulation, or these domestic Regulations, have not been adhered to. The notice can compel the seizure and detaining of animals, meat or feed or the taking of any other actions deemed necessary in the circumstances.[93] A compliance notice may also require that an animal, feed or fertiliser is detained, disposed of or destroyed or prohibit or restrict the carrying on of any operations on the premises under suspicion.[94] This can also include prohibiting or restricting the transportation of

---

[82] Ibid, Art 26.
[83] SI No 532/2015. The TSE Regulation 999/2001 was originally given further effect in Irish law by the European Communities (Transmissible Spongiform Encephalopathies and Animal By-Products) Regulations 2006, SI No 612/2006.
[84] See the European Union (Transmissible Spongiform Encephalopathies) Regulations 2015, n 83 above, Reg 4. Very detailed provisions on the type of animal feed that can be used are set out in Annex IV to Regulation 999/2001, n 66 above. Reg 6 makes it clear that the ban on the feeding to ruminants of protein derived from animals, set out in Art 7 of the EU Regulation, applies.
[85] Ibid, Reg 3.
[86] Ibid, Regs 7–10.
[87] Ibid, Regs 16-19.
[88] Ibid, Regs 20–27.
[89] Ibid, Reg 28.
[90] Authorised officers, for the purposes of the application of the TSE Regulations, are appointed by the Department of Agriculture, Food and the Marine, as per s 37(1) of the Animal Health and Welfare Act 2013.
[91] See the European Union (Transmissible Spongiform Encephalopathies) Regulations 2015, n 83 above, Reg 21(1). Private dwellings should not be entered unless consent has been given or a warrant has been obtained.
[92] Ibid, Reg 21(4). Reg 23 provides that it is an offence to obstruct authorised officers in carrying out their functions.
[93] Ibid, Reg 25(1).
[94] Ibid, Reg 25(2).

animals or feed, requiring the return of animals or feed, requiring alterations be made to a premises or means of transport, or requiring the cleaning and disinfection of a premises. Compliance notices can be appealed to the District Court, where it can be confirmed, modified or annulled.[95] Conviction for contravention of the TSE Regulation carries potentially significant sentences, including up to three years imprisonment and/or a fine of up to €250,000,[96] with the burden of proof largely on the defendant to show that the legislative requirements on feed and containment were not breached.[97]

The BSE crisis marked a turning point for European Union food law and, consequently, for Irish food law as well. The focus prior to the late 1990s had primarily been on securing free movement through harmonising directives and the application of the mutual recognition principle developed by the Court of Justice in *Cassis*.[98] EU food law had been largely successful in this regard, creating plenty of possibilities for traders from all Member States to market their products elsewhere in the Union, mostly uninhibited. However, this relatively unfettered access brought its own difficulties, especially when it came to controlling the spread of disease between the free moving raw materials of the food industry. This, coupled with a lack of legislative attention being paid to food safety, meant that the Union was inadequately prepared for the outbreak of a disease as rampant and as devastating as BSE became.

5.4. White Paper on Food Safety

The need for a radical overhaul of food safety regulation became obvious during the BSE crisis. Existing legislation was shown to be inadequate, unable to deal with outbreaks of deadly transmissible disease. Ad hoc measures, when introduced, had two major flaws. First, they often fell some way short of achieving their stated aim by dealing with only one element of what really needed to be a more far-reaching and holistic response. This reduced public confidence in the efficacy of the entire regulatory system. The introduction of measure after measure suggests that those charged with controlling a crisis are not intervening at an appropriate level at any stage, otherwise there would be no need for a range of different responses or rules to be introduced over a protracted period of time – much the same way as the initial handling of the EU financial crisis from 2009 onwards failed to satisfy the markets that any of the steps taken to deal with sovereign debt would actually ever resolve the matter. Second, from a legal perspective, the failure to deal with BSE at the earliest possible stage led to the taking of questionable action by the

---

[95] Ibid, Reg 27.
[96] Ibid, Reg 31(1).
[97] Ibid, Reg 31(2).
[98] Case 120/1978, as discussed throughout ch 4.

Commission when introducing the ban on British exports in 1996.[99] This was contrary to Treaty provisions on the free movement of goods. The only support for this lay in principles that did not exist. This is discussed in more detail below, but for now it is sufficient to say that the Court of Justice, in upholding the ban, used reasoning that was based on aspects of environmental law and, given that the Treaty of Amsterdam had not come into existence, could not yet be applied to food law.

The proposals for amending EU-wide rules and systems for ensuring that food is safe were presented in 1997 in the Green Paper on the General Principles of Food Law[100] and in the White Paper on Food Safety in January 2000.[101] A 'radical new approach' was proposed, with a view to 'enabl[ing] food safety to be organised in a more co-ordinated and integrated manner'.[102] There would be an overhaul of the existing system at five different levels to ensure that this happened.

The first – and in some ways the most significant – proposal for change in the White Paper was the establishment of a new 'European Food Authority'.[103] This was deemed to be 'the most appropriate response to the need to guarantee a high level of food safety'. Second, food safety legislation would be amended to make it more coherent, 'covering all aspects of food products from farm to table'. This would involve over 80 separate alterations being made in the short term to existing legislation. The third area identified as needing reform was food controls. The evidence suggested that there were wide variations in the way in which EU food law was being implemented and enforced, meaning that consumers were not receiving the same level of protection across the Union. It was therefore proposed that, in co-operation with the Member States, a new framework for the development and operation of national control systems would have to be developed. It was also envisaged that there would be an increased role for consumers in the development of food safety policy. Lines of communication between the Commission and the public would have to be improved in times of crisis or concern. New labelling legislation that would bring about 'helpful and clearly presented' information would be introduced. Finally, the EU would undertake to play an active role in international bodies as 'an important element in explaining European developments in food safety'. All the other actions proposed would have to be effectively presented and explained to EU trading partners, especially considering that the Union is the world's largest importer/exporter of food.

---

[99] Commission Decision 1996/239, n 36 above. Some of the other reasons as to why BSE was able to spread in the way in which it did are discussed in H Pennington, *When food kills: BSE, E. coli and disaster science* (Oxford, OUP, 2003).

[100] COM (1997) 176.

[101] COM (1999) 719.

[102] Ibid, Executive Summary.

[103] For an insider's background into the formation of the European Food Safety Authority see D Byrne, 'The genesis of EFSA and the first 10 years of EU food law' in A Alemanno and S Gabbi (eds), *Foundations of EU food law and policy* (Farnham, Ashgate, 2013).

5.4.1. Principles of Food Safety

Chapter 2 of the White Paper set out a series of general principles that would be applied to 'transform EU food policy into a proactive, dynamic, coherent and comprehensive instrument to ensure a high level of human health and consumer protection'.

The first of these principles was that this policy should be based on a comprehensive and integrated approach. This meant that controls had to be systematically applied throughout the food chain, at all stages of production and across all food sectors, regardless of where any of the production activity takes place.

The second principle set out was that responsibility for safety would have to rest firmly with all stakeholders. Those involved in manufacturing feed, farmers, manufacturers, Member State and third country competent authorities, the Commission and consumers would all have a clearly defined role in ensuring that food was safe to eat.

The third principle was that traceability would be central to food safety policy. This would become central to ensuring that concerns could be properly addressed at the earliest opportunity and in the most effective way, as soon as issues arise.

The fourth principle would be transparency in decision making. All stakeholders would be allowed to make effective contributions to policy development. Publicising scientific opinions and inspection reports would be extended to more aspects of food safety.

The fifth principle espoused in the White Paper was to use systematic risk analysis as the foundation upon which food safety policy should be based. The best scientific information available would be used in developing new measures.

The sixth is the precautionary principle, which would now have to be applied in the taking of all risk management decisions.

Finally, the seventh general principle guiding food safety policy is that other legitimate factors relevant for the protection of consumer health and the promotion of fair practices in food trade should be considered. This includes consideration for the environment, animal welfare, sustainable agriculture, quality expectations and the provision of fair information on the essential characteristics of products and their method of production.

5.5. General Food Law Regulation

The White Paper on Food Safety was itself subject to the very type of stakeholder interest that the report itself saw as critical. A consultation process followed its publication. Comments and analysis were received from the European Economic and Social Committee, the European Parliament, Member States, select committees – including that of the House of Lords, as well as food and drink federations and associations. The final product of all of this was the publication of a new

General Food Law Regulation in January 2002,[104] which now forms the framework for all food safety law in the EU, including Ireland.

5.5.1. Key Provisions of Regulation 178/2002

The General Food Law Regulation 'provides the basis for the assurance of a high level of protection of human health and consumers' interest in relation to food'.[105] One of the main ways in which it will achieve this is through providing 'a strong science base, efficient organisational arrangements and procedures to underpin decision-making in matters of food and feed safety'.[106]

Defining 'Food' and 'Food Law'

As stated earlier in this chapter, the Regulation defines 'food' as 'any substance or product, whether processed, partially processed or unprocessed, intended to be, or reasonably expected to be ingested by humans'.[107] This includes drink, chewing gum and any other substance, including water, which was intentionally incorporated into food during manufacture or treatment. It does not include animal feed, which is defined elsewhere in the Regulation, live animals, plants prior to harvesting, medicinal products,[108] cosmetics,[109] narcotics,[110] or residues and contaminants. 'Food law' is defined as:

> [t]he laws, regulations and administrative provisions governing food in general, and food safety in particular, whether at [Union] or national level; it covers any stage of production, processing and distribution of food, and also of feed produced for, or fed to, food-producing animals.[111]

Finally, 'feed' is 'any substance or product, including additives, whether processed or unprocessed, intended to be used for oral feeding to animals'.[112]

General Principles of Food Law

The Regulation sets out several objectives for food law. These are listed as including the protection of human life and health, the protection of consumers' interests, fair practices in food trade, the protection of animal health and welfare and the

---

[104] Regulation (EC) No 178/2002 n 1 above.
[105] Ibid, Art 1(1).
[106] Ibid.
[107] Ibid, Art 2.
[108] As defined by Council Directives 1965/65/EEC, [1965] OJ L 22/369 and 1992/73/EEC, [1973] OJ L 297/8.
[109] Within the meaning prescribed by Council Directive 1976/768/EEC, [1976] OJ L 262/169.
[110] As classified by the United Nations Single Convention on Narcotic Drugs 1961.
[111] Regulation (EC) No 178/2002, n 1 above, Art 3(1).
[112] Ibid, Art 3(4).

protection of plant health and the environment.[113] In addition, food law is also to be designed in a way that facilitates free movement. International standards, where they exist or where their completion is imminent, should, according to the Regulation, be considered when food laws are being developed or adapted in any way, unless these are deemed to be inappropriate or sufficiently different from EU policy or norms.[114]

The principles of food safety, listed in the White Paper, are to be used to ensure that these general objectives of food law are met. This includes the use of appropriate risk analysis in the development and application of food law.[115] 'Risk analysis' is defined as 'a process consisting of three interconnected components: risk assessment, risk management and risk communication'.[116] The assessment element is to be based on available scientific evidence, considered in 'an independent, objective and transparent manner'.[117] A decision is then made on how best to deal with the nature and level of the risk identified as a result of this assessment. This is 'risk management'. The Regulation makes it clear that the opinion of the European Food Safety Authority is central to deciding on what steps to take to manage the risk.[118] A further consideration is that any measures taken should be based on the need to prevent identified risks from being fully realised. This is known as the 'precautionary principle' and it has become a central part of all food safety law, as well as other aspects of food law more generally.

Precautionary Principle

The General Food Law Regulation provides that:

[i]n specific circumstances where, following an assessment of available information, the possibility of harmful effects on health is identified but scientific uncertainty persists,

---

[113] Ibid, Art 5(1). For more on this see B van der Meulen, 'The function of food law: On the objectives of food law, legitimate factors and interests taken into account' (2010) 5 *European Food and Feed Law Review* 83. The issue of animal health more generally is now also dealt with by Regulation (EU) 2016/429 of the European Parliament and of the Council of 9 March 2016 on transmissible animal diseases and repealing certain acts in the area of animal health, [2016] OJ L 59/1. This Animal Health Law, which will come into effect in April 2021, is discussed further in Ch 10. Plant health is legislated for by Council Directive 2000/29/EC of 8 May 2000 on protective measures against the introduction into the Community of organisms harmful to plants or plant products and against their spread within the Community [2000] OJ L 169/1 as most recently amended by Commission implementing Directive (EU) 2017/1279 of 14 July 2017 amending Annexes I to V to Council Directive 2000/29/EC [2017] OJ L 184/33. The original plant health directive, Directive 1977/93 [1977] OJ L 26/20, was transposed into Irish law by the European Communities (Introduction of organisms harmful to plants or plant products)(Prohibition) Regulations 1980, SI No 125/1980, which was amended on numerous occasions, ultimately leading to the introduction of the European Communities (Introduction of organisms harmful to plants or plant products)(Prohibition)(Amendment) Regulations 2003, SI No 219/2003, which gave effect to EU Directive 2000/29, as amended.
[114] Regulation (EC) No 178/2002, above n 1, Art 5(3).
[115] Ibid, Art 6(1).
[116] Ibid, Art 3(10).
[117] Ibid, Art 6(2).
[118] Ibid, Art 6(3).

provisional risk management measures necessary to ensure the high level of health protection chosen in the [Union] may be adopted, pending further scientific information for a more comprehensive risk assessment.[119]

This is the formal legal presentation of the 'precautionary principle', as it applies to food law across the EU. It is a relatively simple proposition. Its application is fraught with difficulties.

Article 191 TFEU provides that 'Union policy ... shall be based on the precautionary principle and on the principles that preventive action should be taken'. This relates to environmental law only.

This is the first problem with the precautionary principle. Its application to food law has no legal basis in the Treaty. Despite this, the European Court of Justice formally extended the principle to food law based on this Treaty provision. When deliberating in the BSE cases,[120] the Court stated that '[w]here there is uncertainty as to the existence or extent of risks to human health, the institutions may take protective measures without having to wait until the reality and seriousness of those risks become fully apparent'.[121] This is merely a restatement of previous decisions, such as that in *Sandoz*.[122] It is, in essence, the precautionary principle and it had already been an accepted part of the Court's jurisprudence for some time. However, the Court then went on to formalise this as a principle of EU law derived from the Treaty. It stated that '[the purpose of Article 191 TFEU determines that Union] policy on the environment is to pursue the objective inter alia of protecting human health [and] that policy is to aim at a high level of protection and is to be based in particular on the principles that preventive action should be taken and that environmental protection requirements must be integrated into the definition and implementation of other [Union] policies'.[123]

Food safety and environmental protection are not connected in this way, in law or in fact. Using teleological interpretative techniques to make a connection between Article 191 TFEU and the BSE crisis, or matters of food safety more generally, is taking this to a new, unjustifiable level. It makes no sense. This is especially so when one considers that Treaty provisions on health protection did not even exist in their current, stronger form at the time. While the Treaty of Amsterdam did amend the Treaty to include the provision that '[Union] action ... shall be directed towards improving public health, preventing human illness and diseases, and obviating sources of danger to human health',[124] this did not happen until after

---

[119] Ibid, Art 7(1).

[120] Case C-180/1996 *United Kingdom v Commission* [1998] ECR I-2265 and Case C-157/1996 *Queen v National Farmers' Union* [1998] ECR I-2211.

[121] Para 99 of *UK v Commission* and para 63 of *Queen v NFU*, n 120 above.

[122] Case 174/1982 *Criminal proceedings against Sandoz BV* [1983] ECR 2445, where the Court stated, in para 16, that '[i]nsofar as there are uncertainties at the present state of scientific research it is for the Member States to decide what degree of protection of the health and life of humans they intend to ensure'.

[123] Para 100 of *UK v Commission* and para 64 of *Queen v NFU*, n 120 above.

[124] Former Art 152 EC. For more on this see ch 2.

the judgments in the BSE cases were delivered. There was not therefore any relevant Treaty provision in existence at the time that could be used in conjunction with Article 191 TFEU to formalise the application of the precautionary principle to human health protection. The real legal basis for the application of the principle to food safety matters is that which now appears in Article 7 of Regulation 178/2002. It continues to have no foundation for food law in the TFEU.[125]

The legislation remains open to serious criticism given that the real basis for the application of one of the most important principles of the entire food safety regime may be undermined because it is not found in any substantive Treaty provision. While this may seem like an academic point, it remains a significant one, despite the existence of Article 7 of the General Food Law Regulation. Use of the precautionary principle provides one of the most significant and potentially far-reaching exceptions to the free movement of goods between EU Member States. It allows the EU institutions to prohibit trade in goods where it has reason to believe that this is necessary to protect human health. However, this does not need to be conclusive. There must be a 'possibility of harmful effects on health'.

Despite the significance of this exception to a fundamental freedom enshrined in EU law, it continues to have no proper legal basis in the TFEU, unlike other grounds permitting derogation from this principle, such as that set out in Article 36 TFEU.[126] The key difference here is that Article 36 TFEU sets out when Member States, such as Ireland, can justify taking action or adopting measures that are contrary to the free movement of goods. The same right for the EU institutions is not provided for anywhere in the Treaty. It has not therefore been negotiated and/or accepted by the Member States on the same basis. No unanimity was required to introduce this vitally important exception to free movement into EU law. Instead, it was codified into the law using secondary legislation, relying on the Court's previous extension of the precautionary principle from environmental protection into food law, the reasoning for which was and has remained flawed. The EU institutions have become empowered to take precautionary action based on poor legal reasoning. The consequences of this type of action are potentially devastating, as many beef farmers are only too aware.

This brings us to the second problem with the precautionary principle. Neither the legislation, nor the related case law, makes it clear as to what is considered enough evidence supporting the taking of precautionary action. Article 7 of the General Food Law Regulation refers to 'an assessment of available information'. A European Commission Communication refers to three conditions that must exist before there can be recourse to the precautionary principle.[127]

First, there must be an identification of potentially negative effects. Some risk, or potential risk, to human health must be identified. This alone is not,

---

[125] For further discussion on this see C MacMaoláin, 'Using the precautionary principle to protect human health' (2003c) 28 *European Law Review* 723 at 732.

[126] As discussed in Ch 4.

[127] Communication from the Commission on the precautionary principle, COM (2000) 1.

of course, enough. The risk must be evaluated. This is the second condition. A scientific assessment of the potential adverse effects must be undertaken. There must be reliable scientific data presented which, on logical reasoning, leads to the conclusion that there is a possibility of negative impact on health. The potential severity of the risk must be evaluated, taking consideration of all relevant factors, including possible damage levels, persistency, reversibility and delayed effect. This assessment should be as comprehensive as the circumstances allow. The Communication states that it must consist of four components: hazard identification, hazard characterisation, appraisal of exposure and risk characterisation. An attempt should be made to complete these four steps before any decision to act is taken. The third condition that must exist before the precautionary principle can be invoked is that there must be some degree of scientific uncertainty. This may arise, for example, because the evidence is either incomplete or contested. The assessment indicates that the data is insufficient, inconclusive or imprecise, making it impossible to determine the level or nature of the risk with enough certainty.

If the three conditions are met and the precautionary principle is invoked, it will lead to the adoption of some sort of measure, unless, of course, it is determined that no measure is necessary. The decision to act is a political one. Decision makers are charged with weighing up the results of the assessment process with the degree to which the level of risk identified would be acceptable to society. It is then for the Court of Justice to determine whether action taken by the EU institutions, if challenged, is valid. The Commission Communication on the precautionary principle makes it clear that the Court accepts that its role at this stage is limited to examining whether the institution involved 'committed a manifest error or misuse of power or manifestly exceed[ed] the limits of its power of appraisal'. This should mean that measures adopted in an arbitrary fashion should not apply.[128]

This brings us to the third identifiable problem with the precautionary principle – it can be used to make arbitrary, political decisions that are unsupported by sufficiently sound scientific evidence. A clear example of this happening in practice is evident from the judgment in one of the most significant cases in this area, *Pfizer*.[129] Here, the applicant contested the validity of a 1998 Council Regulation which prohibited the use of four previously approved antibiotics in animal feed.[130] The applicant was, at the time, the only producer of one of the banned antibiotics, virginiamycin, in the world. They were thus able to bring an application under Article 263 TFEU to the General Court, seeking an annulment of this Regulation.

---

[128] Arbitrariness in precautionary decision making should also be avoided to prevent conflict with WTO obligations. For discussion on the operation of the precautionary principle in the international legal context see N Salmon, 'A European perspective on the precautionary principle: Food safety and the free trade imperative of the WTO' (2002) 27 *European Law Review* 138.

[129] Case T-13/1999 *Pfizer Animal Health SA v Council* [2002] ECR II-3305. A very similar judgment, based on similar facts, was delivered on the same day in Case T-70/1999 *Alpharma Inc v Council* [2002] ECR II-3495.

[130] Council Regulation (EC) No 2821/1998 of 17 December 1998 amending, as regards withdrawal of the authorisation of certain antibiotics, Directive 1970/524 concerning additives in feedingstuffs [1998] OJ L 351/4.

It was accepted by all parties to the case that the contested Regulation had been introduced as a precautionary measure, as neither the reality nor the seriousness of the risk had been scientifically proven. The main argument put forward by the applicant was that the risk assessment used to take this action was incomplete and erroneous. It was claimed that the Union institutions, in particular the Commission and the Council, had failed in two ways. First, they arbitrarily chose one body of evidence, supplied by Denmark, over another, which included a negative appraisal by the Scientific Committee for Animal Nutrition (SCAN) of this Danish dossier. Second, they re-interpreted the advice which suggested there was no risk posed to human health by continued use of the antibiotics. It is not within the scope of this book to evaluate whether the concerns raised about the studies and prompted the ban were valid. It is however, questionable as to whether the legislative institutions should take such interventionist action based on a re-interpretation of conclusions which stated that the evidence used in support of the ban was both misleading and artificial. The General Court even concluded that the institutions involved were aware of the methodological limitations of these studies. Despite this, it was considered acceptable for the Commission to ignore the opinion of SCAN, on the basis that sufficient reasons were not provided supporting their view that the Danish evidence failed to support the existence of any real risk. While the legislative institutions are not bound to follow the opinions of advisory committees, such as SCAN, it does leave them vulnerable to accusations of arbitrariness in the use of the precautionary principle, which is exactly what the Communication states they should seek to avoid.[131]

Public Consultation in Devising Food Laws

One of the beliefs about the way in which the BSE crisis was mishandled, at both domestic and EU levels, was that it led to reduced levels of confidence amongst consumers about the safety of food. Advice on the consumption of beef was mixed. Initial presumptions about the transferability of the disease to humans were later shown to be ill-founded. Neither science nor politics were shown to be capable of offering the type of reassurance that was sought.

Apart from the general overhaul of food safety rules and processes by the General Food Law Regulation, the legislation also seeks to regain the trust of consumers by actively involving them 'during the preparation, evaluation and revision of food law, except where the urgency of the matter does not allow it'.[132] This involves 'open and transparent public consultation, directly or through representative bodies'. This policy of involving stakeholders, including the general public, in the legislative process is now commonplace. Very few food law initiatives

---

[131] For more on the operations of the precautionary principle in food law see A Szajkowska, 'The impact of the definition of the precautionary principle in EU food law' (2010) 47 *Common Market Law Review* 173.
[132] Regulation (EC) No 178/2002, above n 1, Art 9.

come to the statute book without some prior dialogue with, amongst others, consumer groups. This is not limited to food safety laws. It has become the norm across almost all areas of food law. For example, the initial proposal to introduce a new EU food labelling regulation followed a series of public consultations on a range of related matters, including nutrition labelling and origin marking, as well as a general call for suggestions on how the framework legislation could be improved.[133]

The General Food Law Regulation also provides that the public should be properly communicated with and informed about any suspected or confirmed food safety concern. It provides that:

> where there are reasonable grounds to suspect that a food or feed may present a risk for human or animal health, then, depending on the nature, seriousness and extent of that risk, public authorities shall take appropriate steps to inform the general public of the nature of the risk to health, identifying to the fullest extent possible the food or feed, or type of food or feed, the risk that it may present, and the measures which are taken or about to be taken to prevent, reduce or eliminate that risk.[134]

This applies across all areas of food law. This 'risk communication' is a vital element of risk analysis and one of the three components identified by the Regulation. The other two elements of this, risk analysis and risk management, are dealt with in more detail above.

Food Business Operator Responsibilities

The General Food Law Regulation makes food businesses more accountable for failures to comply with the legislation and to prevent crises. The 'food business operator' is defined in the Regulation as 'the natural or legal persons responsible for ensuring that the requirements of food law are met within the ... business under their control'.[135] This applies across all stages of production, including any processing and distribution.[136] There are three main responsibilities placed on food business operators. The first is to ensure that they operate according to the applicable food safety regulations. The second is to ensure that they do all within their power to withdraw unsafe foods from the market.[137] The designated competent authorities, either the Food Safety Authority of Ireland or the Health Service Executive,[138] must be notified about the need to do this and the measures

---

[133] See DG SANCO, 'Labelling: competitiveness, consumer information and better regulation for the EU' Consultative Document, February 2006. Available at: ec.europa.eu/food.

[134] Regulation (EC) No 178/2002, above n 1, Art 10.

[135] Ibid, Art 3(6).

[136] Ibid, Art 17(1).

[137] Ibid, Art 19(1). The responsibilities of food business operators and national competent authorities in this regard are also set out in the European Communities (General Food Law) Regulations 2007, SI No 747/2007, in particular Regs 4–20 thereof.

[138] As set out in the European Communities (General Food Law) Regulations 2007, n 137 above, Reg 5(2).

that must be taken to achieve it, without delay.[139] Consumers must be informed about the reasons for the withdrawal of the product and they may, in some circumstances, be asked to return it to the place of purchase or to the producer or importer. This responsibility may be extended to include retailers and distributors in the process.[140] All are also under an obligation to collaborate with the designated competent authorities when action needs to be taken to avoid or reduce risks posed by a food which they have supplied.[141]

The third main responsibility of the food business operator is to ensure that it has a proper traceability system in place. This is defined as 'the ability to trace and follow a food, feed, food-producing animal or substance intended to be, or expected to be incorporated into a food or feed, through all stages of production, processing and distribution'.[142] Proper systems of traceability have become a feature of food law since the BSE crisis. The idea is that where a problem or safety concern with a particular food or ingredient is identified, all products which contain or have been associated with that food or ingredient can also be readily identified and withdrawn from the market if necessary. This is the practical development of the 'farm to fork' approach advocated in the White Paper on Food Safety. Those operating in the food sector are obliged to be in a position where they can identify any other operator who has supplied them with any food or ingredient.[143] They must, therefore, ensure that they have systems in place which guarantee that this information can be made available to the competent authorities on demand. Similarly, they must also be able to readily identify other businesses that they have supplied.[144] One of the best ways of ensuring that a proper system of traceability exists is through the use of proper labelling and documentation.[145] While the General Food Law Regulation provides the framework for developing traceability systems in the sector, other legislation establishes specific procedures and obligations related to foods for which this is deemed to be of particular importance. A good example of this can be seen in the GMO regulations.[146] These are discussed in more detail in Chapter 10.

5.5.2. European Food Safety Authority

One of the most heralded proposals put forward in the White Paper on Food Safety was the establishment of a 'European Food Authority'. This was claimed to

---

[139] Reg 178/2002, Arts 19(1) and 19(3).
[140] Ibid, Art 19(2).
[141] Ibid, Art 19(4).
[142] Ibid, Arts 3(15) and 18(1).
[143] Ibid, Art 18(2).
[144] Ibid, Art 18(3).
[145] Ibid, Art 18(4).
[146] Regulation (EC) No 1830/2003 of the European Parliament and of the Council of 22 September 2003 concerning the traceability and labelling of genetically modified organisms and the traceability of food and feed products produced from genetically modified organisms and amending Directive 2001/18/EC [2003] OJ L 268/24.

be central to the priority of the Commission to take effective measures designed to ensure a high level of consumer protection. The Authority, once established, would play a key role in this, having responsibility for risk assessment and communication on food safety matters. However, it was decided that at that particular stage in the development of EU law, it would be unwise to assign any risk management role to the Authority, especially where this involved the need to introduce legislation. It was thought that the transfer of regulatory powers to an independent body could lead to 'an unwarranted dilution of democratic accountability'. It would also have required for amendments to be made to the EU Treaties.

Chapter III of the General Food Law Regulation deals with the tasks and functioning of the European Food Safety Authority, which was established in 2002.[147] Its primary role is to provide scientific advice and scientific and technical support for the implementation of Union law and policy in all areas that have a bearing on the safety of food.[148] It is organised and functions in a way that, it is hoped, will ensure that it is widely regarded as a trustworthy point of reference for all in food safety matters, recognised for its independence, transparency and rigour.[149] It is responsible for the collection and analysis of data that can be used to evaluate risks within the food chain,[150] and the subsequent communication of noteworthy dangers to the public, when required.

The European Food Safety Authority is assigned a series of tasks to enable it to carry out these important functions properly. These include providing the EU institutions and the Member States with the best possible scientific opinions; promoting and co-ordinating the development of uniform risk assessment methodologies; providing scientific and technical support to the Commission and, when requested, interpreting and considering risk assessment opinions; commissioning scientific studies; collecting, analysing and summarising scientific and technical data; identifying and characterising emerging food safety risks; establishing a network of organisations operating within the sector; advising in crisis management procedures; improving co-operation between the Union, applicant countries, third countries and international organisations on food safety matters; and finally, providing independent conclusions on food safety or related concerns.[151]

The organisational structure of the European Food Safety Authority consists of a management board, an executive director, an advisory forum, a scientific committee, scientific panels and staff.[152] The management board consists of 14 members, who are appointed by the Council in consultation with the European

---

[147] Reg 178/2002, n 1 above, Art 22(1). For an assessment of the role of EFSA as set out in the Regulation see K Kanska, 'Wolves in the clothing of sheep? The case of the European Food Safety Authority' (2004) 29 *European Law Review* 711.

[148] Ibid, Art 22(2).

[149] Ibid, Art 22(7).

[150] Ibid, Art 22(4).

[151] Ibid, Art 23.

[152] Ibid, Art 24. Members of the Management Board, the Advisory Forum and the Executive Director are all obliged to act independently and in the public interest, under the terms of Art 37 of the General Food Law Regulation, n 1 above.

Parliament, from a list drawn up by the Commission.[153] At least four of the members of the management board must be representatives of consumer and other interest groups. The composition of the board should be structured in a way that ensures the presence of a high level of competence, a broad base of expertise and a good geographic distribution from within the EU Member States. Members of the Board serve a term of four years, renewable once. It meets at the request of the Chair or at least one-third of the members.[154] Its main role is to ensure that the rest of EFSA properly performs the tasks assigned to it by the Regulation.[155] It also sets a programme of work for the Authority, on an annual basis.[156]

The Executive Director is appointed by the Management Board, from a list of candidates proposed by the European Commission.[157] The Executive Director's responsibilities include the day-to-day administration of the Authority and over-seeing the implementation of the work programmes assigned by the Management Board;[158] and the annual production of a draft report on EFSA activities which, once adopted, is then circulated to the EU Commission, Council, European Parliament and the other Member States.[159]

The Advisory Forum is made up of representatives from the designated competent authorities of the Member States, including the Food Safety Authority of Ireland.[160] Its key role is to advise the Executive Director in his orchestration of EFSA.[161] It also provides a focus for the exchange of information of potential food safety risks and the pooling of information.[162] The Advisory Forum can also include representatives of the European Commission and the European Parliament in its work.[163]

The Scientific Committee and permanent Scientific Panels are more directly responsible for providing the scientific opinions issued by EFSA.[164] It is composed of the Chairs of each of the Scientific Panels, as well as six independent scientific experts.[165] Eight original panels were established at the time of the formation of EFSA. These included panels on additives (later included nutrient sources added to food), plants, genetically modified organisms, animal welfare, contaminants, biological hazards and dietetic products, nutrition and allergies.[166] The remits and

[153] Ibid, Art 25(1). Art 38(2) provides that EFSA Management Board meetings must be held in public.
[154] Ibid, Art 25(6).
[155] Ibid, Art 25(7).
[156] Ibid, Art 25(8). For further discussion on the governance of EFSA see S Gabbi, 'The scientific governance of the European Food Safety Authority: *Status quo* and perspectives' in A Alemanno and S Gabbi (eds), *Foundations of EU Food Law and Policy: Ten years of the European Food Safety Authority* (Ashford, Ashgate, 2014).
[157] Ibid, Art 26(1).
[158] Ibid, Art 26(2).
[159] Ibid, Art 26(3).
[160] Ibid, Art 27(1).
[161] Ibid, Art 27(3).
[162] Ibid, Art 27(4).
[163] Ibid, Art 27(7).
[164] Ibid, Art 28(1).
[165] Ibid, Art 28(3).
[166] Ibid, Art 28(4).

range of panels can be altered as and when required by EFSA and the European Commission, using the comitology procedure.[167] Two further panels were added, one dealing with food contact materials, enzymes, flavourings and processing aids and the other on additives and products or substances used in animal feed. Again, there is a strong link between the work of these panels and the Commission. Representatives of the latter, for example, can be present at both panel and committee meetings, but they may not 'seek to influence discussions'.[168] Smaller working groups of both the Committee and the Panels may be formed to deal with more specific matters.[169]

As stated, one of the key functions of EFSA is issuing scientific opinions. This can happen in one of three ways.[170] The first is where this is requested by the Commission. The majority of opinions are initiated in this way. Second, requests can also be made by the European Parliament or a Member State. Finally, EFSA may take the initiative and decide to deliver an opinion itself. Any request made for an opinion must include contextual information explaining the issue that needs to be addressed, as well as some reasoning as to why the investigation to be undertaken is of interest to the EU.[171] The Authority can refuse to issue an opinion where it is of the view that it has already delivered a similar, previously requested one and that there are no new scientific elements which justify a re-examination.[172]

EFSA is not the only point of reference on the scientific issues surrounding food safety matters. Other opinions are delivered by other bodies. EFSA is a significant point of reference, but it is obliged to consider the views and conclusions of others and seek to deal with any divergence of opinion that may exist.[173] It does this by contacting the other body involved with a view to sharing all relevant scientific information to properly identify potentially contentious scientific issues.[174] Where this other body is one of the EU's own agencies or that of a Member State, the two are obliged to co-operate with a view to either resolving the divergence or coming together to present a joint document to the Commission which clarifies the contentious points.[175] These documents must be made public.[176] EFSA can also commission others to undertake studies on its behalf.[177]

---

[167] Ibid, in conjunction with Art 58(2) of Reg 178/2002, n 1 above.
[168] Ibid, Art 28(8).
[169] Ibid, Art 28(9).
[170] Ibid, Art 29(1).
[171] Ibid, Art 29(2).
[172] Ibid, Art 29(5).
[173] Ibid, Art 30(1).
[174] Ibid, Art 30(2).
[175] Ibid, Art 30(3).
[176] Art 38 of the Regulation also provides that EFSA must carry out other activities with a high level of transparency. It must publicise all agendas and minutes of the Committee and Panel meetings, scientific opinions, reasons for any decisions taken and the annual report.
[177] Ibid, Art 32. For more on the role of EFSA in the provision of scientific advice on risks associated with the food chain see A Smith, S Terry and D Detken, '10 years of the European Food Safety Authority' (2012) 7 *European Food and Feed Law Review* 111.

Much of the work of EFSA involves the collection and analysis of relevant scientific and technical data from studies undertaken elsewhere.[178] It then uses these studies to assist it in identifying emerging risks, which are in turn communicated to the European Parliament, the Commission and the Member States.[179] Central to the proper functioning of these lines of communication is the 'rapid alert system'.[180] EFSA is a key figure in this process, being responsible for the analysis of the content of messages relayed through the system, providing the Commission and the Member States with any information that they need to make a proper risk analysis.[181] It is designated a similar role in the crisis management process.[182] The Authority can also, on its own initiative, communicate with the public on any risks that are identified.[183] It is also under an obligation to develop meaningful contact and dialogue with consumer and producer groups and representatives.[184]

Rapid Alert System

It is widely recognised that one of the best ways of dealing with a food safety crisis once it develops is to ensure that all affected parties are kept informed about the nature and extent of the problem so that they can act accordingly. The General Food Law Regulation maintains a network, designed to formalise these vital lines of communication and information. This is known as the 'Rapid Alert System'. Notification of all direct and indirect risks caused by food or feed to human health happens through this network. The main players in this are the EU Member States, the Commission and EFSA. All are required to have a designated contact point as part of the network, with the Commission having overall managerial control of the system.[185]

Members of the network must immediately notify the Commission where they have any information about a food safety risk.[186] The Commission then has responsibility for transmitting this information to the other members of the Rapid Alert System network. EFSA can intervene at this stage to provide additional scientific or technical information that can assist in the appropriate risk management decisions being taken. Member States have a clear obligation under the system. They must notify the Commission immediately about a risk, in the first place and about any management measures that they adopt, such as a restriction on marketing or

---

[178] Ibid, Art 33.
[179] Ibid, Art 34.
[180] For an appraisal of the functioning of the RAS see V Fuentes, 'The rapid alert system for food and feed: A critical approach' (2017) 12 *European Food and Feed Law Review* 121.
[181] Reg 178/2002, n 1 above, Art 35.
[182] Ibid, Art 56(2).
[183] Ibid, Art 40.
[184] Ibid, Art 42.
[185] Ibid, Art 50(1).
[186] Ibid, Art 50(2).

a product recall.[187] They must also provide a detailed explanation of the reasons underlying any course of action that they have taken.[188] The Commission must then notify the other members of the network about this risk management decision and the reasons for it, providing them with the opportunity to take their own action or, of course, to object to the measures adopted elsewhere where this affects their interests. Details of all further action taken by Member States must be relayed back through the network.[189] Participation in the Rapid Alert System is also open to EU applicant countries, third countries and international organisations.[190]

As with many other areas of food safety regulation and control, documents and information related to the Rapid Alert System must be made available to the public. Any information about food safety risks that is available to the network must also be available to consumers, including details of the products involved, the nature of the risk and any measures that have been, or which will be, taken.[191] This does not, however, extend to the disclosure of information that needs, for commercial reasons, to be kept secret. The only exception to this is that which must be made public to ensure that any risk posed to health is minimised or averted.

Emergencies and Crisis Management

In some circumstances, the use of the Rapid Alert System may not be sufficient to deal with the seriousness of the risk posed. These situations require the adoption of emergency measures instead.[192] The key distinguishing factor that identifies the risk as an 'emergency' is that it is thought that Member State intervention will not be sufficient to contain the risk.[193] The safety concern is deemed to be so serious that only Commission action, applicable across all EU Member States, will suffice. There are several different types of emergency measure that can be adopted, depending on the circumstances. The most obvious one is the suspension of marketing the food in question. Alternatively, 'special conditions' of use can be prescribed instead. The ban on British beef exports would be an example of the former. Bone-in beef restrictions would be an illustration of the latter. Emergency measures can apply with immediate effect. They are, however, subject to

---

[187] Ibid, Art 50(3)(a).
[188] Ibid, Art 50(3)(c).
[189] Ibid, Art 50(5).
[190] Ibid, Art 50(6).
[191] Ibid, Art 52(1) in conjunction with Art 10.
[192] Ibid, Art 53(1). Article 43 of the Animal Health Law, n 113 above, which comes into effect in 2021, provides that EU Member States are to draw up and keep up-to-date contingency plans and detailed instruction manuals that set out the measures to be taken in the Member State concerned in the event of an outbreak of a listed animal disease. There is more on the listed diseases in Ch 10. Under Art 45 of the same regulation, there should also be simulation exercises carried out in the Member States to ensure that the contingency plans function properly.
[193] Art 54 of Reg 178/2002 further provides that Member States can adopt interim protective measures where the Commission fails to take an emergency decision. These national interim protective measures can be maintained until the Commission does act.

review within 10 days of their passing, at which stage they should be confirmed, amended, revoked or extended.[194] Decisions on the continuance or otherwise of the emergency measure are made using comitology procedures. They should also be made public. Finally, the Commission is obliged, under the terms of the General Food Law Regulation, to have a proper crisis management plan in place to deal with wide-scale food safety concerns.[195] This should specify the practical procedures that should be followed to manage a crisis, including the principles of transparency to be applied and a communication strategy.[196] It should also establish a 'crisis unit', responsible for collecting and evaluating all information relevant to the crisis and for identifying the options that are available to minimise the risk to human health.[197] Details of the work and the conclusions of the crisis unit must also be made publicly available.[198]

5.5.3. European Communities (General Food Law) Regulations 2007

The 2007 Regulations were introduced to give full domestic applicability in Ireland to the provisions of the EU General Food Law Regulation. References are made throughout these Regulations to the Food Safety Authority of Ireland Act 1998, the provisions of which were set out in detail in Chapter 3. The enforcement of food safety requirements is still primarily dealt with by the 1998 Act. The European Communities (General Food Law) Regulations 2007 sets out how the general principles and requirements of food law and the procedures to be applied more specifically in matters of food safety are to be adhered to in Ireland. They also formally establish the Food Safety Authority of Ireland and the Health Service Executive as the national competent authorities for EU General Food Law Regulation purposes.[199]

The roles that are set by the Regulations for the competent authorities primarily relate to what is to be done where there is a suspicion that food is unsafe.[200] Where this is the case, measures may be adopted by either the FSAI or the HSE that impose restrictions on the marketing of these products, including withdrawal. Food business operators are guilty of an offence under the Regulations where they place unsafe food on the market, as categorised by Article 14 of the General Food Law Regulation.[201] Two main defences are available in such circumstances.

---

[194] Ibid, Art 53(2).
[195] Ibid, Art 55(1).
[196] Ibid, Art 55(2).
[197] Ibid, Arts 56 and 57.
[198] Ibid, Art 57(3).
[199] The European Communities (General Food Law) Regulations 2007, n 137 above, Reg 4(2).
[200] Ibid, Reg 5(2).
[201] Ibid, Reg 5(1). Art 14 of Reg 178/2002 has already been discussed earlier in this chapter, as well as in Ch 1.

The first relates to where the offence was due to a mistake or reliance on information supplied by, or the actions or inactions of, a third party, or some other factor beyond the accused's control.[202] However, the accused is obliged in these circumstances to inform the court as to the identity of this third party.[203] The second defence available is that the accused exercised due diligence, having taken all reasonable precautions available to avoid committing the offence.[204]

A significant portion of the 2007 Regulations deals in more detail with the role and the responsibilities of the food business operator in maintaining food safety.[205] To avoid committing other offences under the Regulations, the food business operator must also comply with other aspects of food law, including those related to labelling,[206] traceability,[207] withdrawal[208] or notification about a safety matter.[209] Finally, the 2007 Regulations formally authorise the Minister for Health, after consultation with the FSAI, to invoke the precautionary principle where required and facilitated by the provisions of the General Food Law Regulation.[210]

[202] Ibid, Reg 5(3)(a).

[203] Ibid, Reg 5(4)

[204] Ibid, Reg 5(4)(b).

[205] In parallel with the definition of the 'food business operator' set out in Art 3(3) of Reg 178/2002, n 1 above, Reg 2(1) of the 2007 Regulations, n 137 above, further provides that the 'food business operator' is as defined in the EU Regulation '[…] insofar as such operator has responsibility for any stage of production, processing or distribution of food of non-animal origin, food of animal origin sold directly to the final consumer [or supplied] from a retail establishment to other retail establishments where such supply is a marginal, localised and restricted activity as defined in national law, or food containing both products of plant origin and processed products of animal origin or the import or export of foods of non-animal origin or food containing both products of plant origin and processed products of animal origin, or any related activities'.

[206] The European Communities (General Food Law) Regulations 2007, n 137 above, Reg 6.

[207] Ibid, Reg 8.

[208] Ibid, Reg 9(1).

[209] Ibid, Reg 9(3).

[210] Ibid, Reg 11 in conjunction with the provisions set out in Arts 7 and 54 of EU Reg 178/2002 above n 1 on the precautionary principle and the use of emergency measures.

6

Chemical and Biological Safety of Food

6.1. Hormone Use in Food Production

The EU has been traditionally averse to the use of hormones in food-producing animals. These substances are often used in farming as growth-promoters, designed to create additional muscle in animals, leading to increased food production levels. Testosterone, progesterone, trenbolone acetate, melengestrol acetate and oestradiol can all be used for this purpose. While most of these substances can be used for veterinary medicinal purposes, the EU has banned their use for growth-promoting purposes since 1981.[1]

6.1.1. Hormones Directive

The original 1981 legislation, which had been transposed into Irish law by the Animal Remedies (Control of Sale) Regulations 1985,[2] was replaced by a new directive in 1996.[3] This Hormones Directive goes even further than its predecessor; amendments to it have reduced the circumstances in which certain listed substances can even be administered to farm animals for medicinal purposes. The ban on hormone use was introduced and later maintained due to the potential

---

[1] Council Directive 1981/602/EEC of 31 July 1981 concerning the prohibition of certain substances having a hormonal action and of any substances having a thyrostatic action [1981] OJ L 222/32. Art 2 of the Directive prescribed that 'Member States shall ensure that the following are prohibited: (a) the administering to a farm animal, by any means whatsoever, of substances having a thyrostatic or substances having (a) oestrogenic, androgenic or gestagenic action; (b) the placing on the market or slaughtering of farm animals to which [these] substances have been administered; (c) the placing on the market of meat [from such] farm animals; (d) processing of the meat referred to'.

[2] SI No 258/1985. This extended the provisions of the Animal Remedies Act 1956 to the hormones listed in Directive 1981/602, n 1 above. The 1956 Act was repealed with the introduction of the Animal Remedies Act 1993.

[3] Council Directive 1996/22/EC of 29 April 1996 concerning the prohibition on the use in stockfarming of certain substances having a hormonal or thyrostatic action and of beta-agonists, and repealing Directives 1981/602/EEC, 1988/146/EEC and 1988/299/EEC [1996] OJ L 125/3. It has since been amended by Directive 2003/74/EC of the European Parliament and of the Council of 22 September 2003 amending Council Directive 96/22/EC concerning the prohibition on the use in stockfarming of certain substances having a hormonal or thyrostatic action and of beta-agonists [2003] OJ L 262/17. Directive 1996/22/EC was transposed into Irish law by the Control of Animal Remedies and their Residues Regulations 1998, SI No 507/1998.

dangers that their residues could pose for human health. Under the terms of the Directive, all EU Member States are obliged to prohibit

> the placing on the market of stilbenes, stilbene derivatives, their salts and esters and thyrostatic substances for administering to animals of all species [and] the placing on the market of beta-agonists for administering to animals the flesh and products of which are intended for human consumption.[4]

Thyrostatic substances are administered to reduce or stabilise the production of thyroid hormones in animals. Beta-agonists can be used to enhance lean muscle gain and growth. The Directive also bans the importation of animals, meat or other products derived from animals which have been treated with listed substances.[5] The Hormones Directive 1996 has been transposed into Irish law by the Control of Animal Remedies and their Residues Regulations 1998.[6]

The ban on hormone use in food-producing animals is controversial as many of the prohibited substances have been approved for use in food production elsewhere, most notably by the Food and Drug Administration (FDA) in the USA. As discussed in Chapter 2, it has also created much disagreement at World Trade Organization level, where the Dispute Panel and the Appellate Body both found that prohibitions on importing products made from hormone-treated animals was inconsistent with the EU's WTO obligations, in particular those arising under the SPS Agreement.[7]

6.2. Pesticides

Pesticides can be used in the production of food for a variety of reasons. The term itself really covers a whole range of chemical compounds which are used to control pests that can damage crops, kill weeds and alter the growth rate of a plant. They include insecticides, herbicides, fungicides, plant growth regulators and biocides. Pesticides can only be used if they have been approved by the European Commission.

6.2.1. Pesticides Regulation

The key piece of legislation on the lawful use of pesticides in all EU Member States is the 2009 Regulation on the matter.[8] It is designed to take account of

---

[4] Art 2. Set down in Irish law by Reg 3 of the 1998 Regs, n 3 above.

[5] Dir 1996/22, n 3 above, Art 11.

[6] See n 3 above. Later amended by the Control of Animal Remedies and Their Residues (Amendment) Regulations 2004, SI No 827/2004.

[7] DS 26 and DS 48, *EC – Measures Concerning Meat and Meat Products (Hormones)*. For further discussion on this see J Pauwelyn, 'The WTO Agreement on Sanitary and Phytosanitary Measures as Applied in the First Three SPS Disputes: EC – Hormones, Australia – Salmon and Japan – Varietals' (1999) 2 *Journal of International Economic Law* 641.

[8] Regulation (EC) No 1107/2009 of the European Parliament and of the Council of 21 October 2009 concerning the placing of plant protection products on the market and repealing Council

all factors which can be affected by pesticide use, including the need to protect human health, animal health and the environment.[9] The Regulation defines 'plant protection products' as being those which contain, or which consist of, active substances intended to protect plants against harmful organisms, or influence the life processes of plants including their growth (other than as a nutrient), preserving plants or destroying undesired parts of plants.[10] Additional requirements are also set for the use of pesticides in the production of ingredients for specific products, such as baby foods. The European Communities (Processed Cereal-Based Foods and Baby Foods for Infants and Young Children) Regulations 2007 provide, for example, that much lower levels of permitted pesticide residues should be established for these products.[11]

The primary potential problem with pesticides is not necessarily their use but, as alluded to above, it is more that 'residues' of the substances will remain in the plants, in drinking water or in the environment, possibly causing pollution or causing harm to humans and/or animals. A pesticide can only be approved for use under the terms of the Regulation if it can be shown that

> [it] shall not have any harmful effects on human health, including that of vulnerable groups, or animal health, taking into account cumulative or synergistic effects ... or on groundwater [and] they shall not have any unacceptable effect on the environment.[12]

Not being harmful is not enough, however, to result in an approval for use. The substance must also be sufficiently effective, have no unacceptable effect on plants and it should cause no unnecessary suffering to the vertebrates it is designed to control.[13]

Applications for the approval of active substances are submitted by the producer to a rapporteur Member State, usually the State in which they are established.[14] A dossier of information related to the application is then assessed by the Member State, or a group of Member States in some circumstances,[15] before a

---

Directives 1979/117/EEC and 1991/414/EEC [2009] OJ L 309/1. Recital 8 of the Preamble to Reg 1107/2009 makes it clear that, as expected, the precautionary principle should be applied and that the Regulation seeks to ensure that industry demonstrate that substances or products produced or placed on the market do not have any harmful effect on human or animal health or any unacceptable effects on the environment.

[9] Including, most importantly, the protection of bees given their vital role in pollination. The importance of this aspect of Reg 1107/2009 was discussed and underlined by the General Court of the EU in Joined Cases T-429 and T-451, and Case T-584/2013 *Bayer, Syngenta, BASF Agro and Others v Commission* ECLI:EU:T:2018:279. It was noted by the Court that, according to the UN FAO, 84% of the 264 crop species in Europe are dependent on pollinators, including bees.

[10] Reg 1107/2009, n 8 above, Art 2(1).

[11] SI No 776/2007, reg 4(6). These Regulations give effect in Irish law to Commission Directive 2006/125/EC of 5 December 2006 on processed cereal-based foods and baby foods for infants and young children, [2006] OJ L 339/16.

[12] Reg 1107/2009, n 8 above, Art 4(2).

[13] Ibid, Art 4(3).

[14] Ibid, Art 7.

[15] Ibid, Arts 8 and 9.

'draft assessment report' on this is forwarded to the European Commission and the European Food Safety Authority.[16] The draft assessment report should also include the proposed set maximum residue levels to be permitted for the substance under review.[17] The Authority is responsible for making this report public, although some elements can be kept confidential at the request of the applicant.[18] There is then a period allowed for the submission of written comments from interested parties and the possible organisation of a consultation with experts on the content of the report and the suitability of the product for approval. At the end of this stage of the process, the European Food Safety Authority issues an opinion, which it is then up to the Commission to accept, reject or modify. This takes place by the issuing of a new Regulation by comitology, involving the Standing Committee on Plants, Animals, Food and Feed.[19] The Regulation either (i) approves the active substance, subject to conditions and restrictions; (ii) does not approve the use of the active substance; or (iii) amends the conditions previously attached to the approval for use.[20] First approvals are for a maximum period of 10 years.[21] These can then be re-approved for a further 5–15 years, depending on the type of substances at issue.[22] The Commission can, of course, also review any approval granted at any time, in particular where there is new scientific and technical knowledge and/or monitoring data available.[23]

Once an 'active substance' is approved for use under the procedure outlined above, it can then be used in plant protection products, which must then also be authorised for use. A plant protection product can only be authorised where its active substances have been approved and its overall technical formulation is such that user exposure or other risks are limited as much as possible without compromising the functioning of the product.[24] Its physical and chemical properties must have been determined and deemed acceptable for the appropriate uses and storage of the product. The maximum residue levels for the product must have previously been set by Regulation 396/2005.[25] The applications for plant protection products are examined by the Member State to which it was sent.[26] Member States are obliged under the terms of the Regulation to make an 'independent,

[16] Ibid, Art 11.
[17] Ibid, Art 11(2).
[18] Ibid, Art 12.
[19] Ibid, Arts 13 and 79.
[20] Ibid, Art 13(2). The different types of conditions and restrictions that can be set are listed in Art 6 of the Regulation. They include, for example, changes to the level of purity of the substance that can be used, the ways in which it is applied, limiting its use to professional users and additional post-approval monitoring.
[21] Ibid, Art 5.
[22] Ibid, Art 14.
[23] Ibid, Art 21.
[24] Ibid, Art 29.
[25] Regulation (EC) No 396/2005 on maximum residue levels of pesticides in or on food and feed of plant and animal origin and amending Council Directive 1991/414/EC [2005] OJ L 70/1.
[26] Reg 1107/2009, n 8 above, Art 35.

objective and transparent assessment in the light of current scientific and technical knowledge using guidance documents available at the time of application.[27] The Member State has 12 months to make a decision on authorisation, which it then communicates to the other EU Member States.[28] This authorisation, if granted, should then be recognised in the other Member States in the same region.[29] Some substances and products can be authorised for a temporary period, even where this would not normally be allowed, to deal with an emergency situation that cannot be treated in any other way.[30] Also, an approval or authorisation can be suspended at any time where there is a potential risk to human health, animal health or the environment from its continued use.[31] Approved products are also subject to additional packaging,[32] labelling,[33] and advertising controls.[34] Each EU Member State is obliged under the terms of the 2009 Regulation to designate a competent authority charged with carrying out the obligations arising under the terms of the legislation.[35] The Pesticide Registration and Controls Divisions and the Pesticide Control Laboratory of the Department of Agriculture, Food and the Marine are set as the competent authorities for this purpose in Ireland. They are also responsible for the exertion of controls over levels of pesticide residues in food. The provisions necessary for the application of the 2009 Regulation at national level are set by the European Communities (Plant Protection Products) Regulations 2012, which also set the terms for monitoring compliance with and enforcement of the EU provisions.[36] It should also be noted at this stage that all European and national authorities, manufacturers and importers of chemicals in all sectors must operate under the terms of REACH – the EU Programme and Regulation for the Registration, Evaluation, Authorisation and Restriction of Chemicals.[37]

---

[27] Ibid, Art 36.

[28] Ibid, Art 37.

[29] Ibid, Art 40.

[30] Ibid, Art 53.

[31] Ibid, Art 69. The General Court has been called upon to confirm, or otherwise, the validity of any such prohibitions. It is largely reliant on the findings of EFSA in support, or otherwise, of any such restrictions. The methods used by EFSA in reaching its persuasive opinion, and the use of the precautionary principle to justify a series of restrictions on the use of the insecticides clothianidin, thiamethoxam and imidacloprid because of the risks posed by these substances to bees was examined, and upheld by the General Court in 2018 in the Joined Cases T-429 and T-451, and Case T-584/2013 *Bayer, Syngenta, BASF Agro and Others v Commission*, n 9 above. It should be noted that the General Court did also annul the measures that had been introduced which restricted the use of the pesticide fipronil as it was imposed without a proper prior impact assessment.

[32] Ibid, Art 64.

[33] Ibid, Art 65.

[34] Ibid, Art 66.

[35] Ibid, Art 75.

[36] SI No 159/2012.

[37] Regulation (EC) No 1907/2006 of the European Parliament and of the Council of 18 December 2006 concerning the Registration, Evaluation, Authorisation and Restriction of Chemicals (REACH), establishing a European Chemicals Agency, amending Directive 1999/45/EC and repealing Council Regulation (EEC) No 793/1993 and Commission Regulation (EC) No 1488/1994 as well as Council Directive 1976/769/EEC and Commission Directives 1991/155/EEC, 1993/67/EEC, 1993/105/EC and 2000/21/EC [2007] OJ L 136/3.

6.3. Materials in Contact with Foodstuffs

Materials, such as packaging and containers that are used to store products during transit or before preparation or consumption can, of course, affect the composition or properties of the food. They also have the potential to contaminate food. Regulation of these materials is thus necessary to ensure that consumers and their health are protected.

Contact materials are legislated for through the application of a 2004 EU Regulation on the matter.[38] It covers both traditional food packaging and the more contemporary 'active food contact materials and articles'. The latter are defined in the Regulation as being those that:

> are intended to extend the shelf-life or to maintain or improve the condition of the packaged food [and which] are designed to deliberately incorporate components that would release or absorb substances into or from the packaged food or the environment surrounding the food.[39]

All materials and articles must be made and used in a way that neither endangers human health nor brings about an unacceptable change in the composition or organoleptic properties of the product that it is packaging.[40]

The Regulation also provides for more specific measures to be adopted for a range of contact materials, including cork, glass, ink, plastics, paper and metals.[41] As a result, legislation can be adopted that sets specific requirements for these materials on purity standards, conditions of use, migration limits (transferring components into food in unacceptable quantities), sampling and traceability. Consequently, there are specific additional legislative requirements in place for materials such as cadmium and lead,[42] cellulose film[43] and plastics,[44] amongst others. There is also a prohibition in place on the use of specified materials in plastic infant-feeding bottles.[45] Any provisions of the contact materials legislation

---

[38] Regulation (EC) No 1935/2004 of the European Parliament and of the Council of 27 October 2004 on materials and articles intended to come into contact with food and repealing Directives 1980/590/EEC and 1989/109/EEC [2004] OJ L 338/4.

[39] Ibid, Art 2(2).

[40] Ibid, Art 3.

[41] Ibid, Art 5(1).

[42] Council Directive 1984/500/EEC of 15 October 1984 on the approximation of the laws of the Member States relating to ceramic articles intended to come into contact with foodstuffs [1984] OJ L 277/12. Later amended by Commission Directive 2005/31/EC of 29 April 2005 amending Council Directive 84/500/EEC as regards a declaration of compliance and performance criteria of the analytical method for ceramic articles intended to come into contact with foodstuffs [2005] OJ L 110/36.

[43] Commission Directive 2007/42/EC of 29 June 2007 relating to materials and articles made of regenerated cellulose film intended to come into contact with foodstuffs [2007] OJ L 172/71.

[44] Commission Regulation (EU) No 10/2011 of 14 January 2011 on plastic materials and articles intended to come into contact with food [2011] OJ L 12/1. Most recently amended by Commission Regulation (EU) 2015/174 of 5 February 2015 amending and correcting Regulation (EU) No 10/2011 on plastic materials and articles intended to come into contact with food [2015] OJ L 30/2.

[45] Commission Implementing Regulation (EU) 321/2011 of 1 April 2011 amending Regulation (EU) No 10/2011 as regards the restriction of use of Bisphenol A in plastic infant feeding bottles [2011] OJ L 87/1.

that is liable to affect public health must involve consultation with the European Food Safety Authority.[46] This includes applications for the authorisation of new substances, where EFSA has a very significant role to play.[47]

The Contact Materials Regulation 2004 contains a range of provisions designed to best deal with situations where some risk with the substances used is identified. Traceability is required for materials and articles used at all stages in order to facilitate the recall of defective products, the provision of accurate consumer information and the attribution of responsibility where necessary.[48] As with many other areas of food law, Member States are entitled, under the terms of the Regulation, to adopt appropriate safeguard measures where they receive new information or following a reassessment of existing information that suggests a possible risk to human health.[49] This would usually involve the temporary suspension of the use of the substances identified. The usual procedures for such action apply, including immediate informing of the other EU Member States and the Commission. Any final decision on the appropriateness of the measure adopted is made by the Commission.

Member States must designate national competent authorities, such as the FSAI, as a contact point for authorisations and other matters arising under the 2004 Regulation. Also, the National Standards Authority of Ireland (NSAI) has been designated as an official agency of the Food Safety Authority of Ireland, with responsibility for exerting control over and monitoring compliance with food contact materials legislation.[50] National measures designed to give effect to the Regulations and Directives are now set out in the European Union (Plastics and other Materials)(Contact with Food) Regulations 2017.[51]

6.4. Ionisation

The use of ionising radiation could be considered as being either a chemical or a biological food safety issue. It usually involves the use of high-energy ionising radiation to destroy micro-organisms or bacteria in food. This can have a range of benefits, including killing off potentially harmful bacteria, preventing germination, slowing down ripening and prolonging shelf-life. Two directives on treating foods with ionising radiation were introduced by the EU in 1999.[52] These are

---

[46] Reg 1935/2004, Art 7, n 38 above.

[47] Ibid, Arts 9 and 10.

[48] Ibid, Art 17.

[49] Ibid, Art 18.

[50] The role and powers of such agencies in relation to monitoring and ensuring compliance with the contact materials legislation are set out in Reg 8 of the European Union (Plastics and Other Materials) (Contact with Food) Regulations 2017.

[51] SI No 49/2017.

[52] Directive 1999/2/EC of the European Parliament and of the Council of 22 February 1999 on the approximation of the laws of the Member States concerning foods and food ingredients treated with

transposed into Irish law by the European Communities (Foodstuffs Treated with Ionising Radiation) Regulations 2000.[53]

The directives provide that the use of ionisation is to be limited to certain types of foods and ingredients including dried herbs, spices and vegetable seasonings.[54] Only those foods or ingredients which appear on this positive list can be ionised. It is an offence to treat any non-listed foodstuff with ionising radiation.[55] Similarly, it is an offence to import ionised foods into Ireland from third countries,[56] unless these have been treated in accordance with the terms of the directives.[57] Foods must have been in a wholesome condition at the time that they were treated with ionising radiation to preserve them.[58] Competent authorities can authorise the use of irradiation in food production, but only where certain conditions have been met. For example, food irradiation can only be authorised if there is a reasonable technological need for it; if it presents no health hazard; if it is of benefit to consumers; or if it is not being used as a substitute for hygiene and health practices or for good manufacturing or agricultural practice.[59] The competent authorities in Ireland for the various aspects of ionisation regulation are the Food Unit at the Department of Health and Children (policy matters), the Radiological Protection Institute of Ireland (irradiation facilities) and the FSAI (irradiated food matters). Irradiation facilities used for the irradiation of food in Ireland must be licensed by the RPII.[60] Any person who wants to irradiate food must apply to the FSAI for a permit to do so.[61] The permit entitles to holder to irradiate food at the licensed facility. Permits and licences are usually valid for three years but can, of course, be revoked at any time should it be deemed necessary to do so.

A major review of the use of food irradiation undertaken by the European Food Safety Authority in 2011 led to a reassertion that the use of this treatment for these purposes continues to be safe.

6.5. Food Hygiene

Legislation on the hygienic production and marketing of food comes directly from three EU regulations, introduced in 2004.

---

ionising radiation [1999] OJ L 66/16; and Directive 1999/3/EC of the European Parliament and of the Council of 22 February 1999 on the establishment of a Community list of foods and food ingredients treated with ionising radiation [1999] OJ L 66/24.

[53] SI No 297/2000.
[54] Ibid, Reg 3(2)(c).
[55] Ibid, Reg 4(2).
[56] Ibid, Reg 8.
[57] See, in particular, Dir 1999/2/EC, Art 9, n 52 above.
[58] See SI No 297/2000, Reg 4(2), n 53 above.
[59] Dir 1999/2/EC, Annex I, n 52 above.
[60] SI No 297/2000, Reg 11, n 53 above.
[61] Ibid, Reg 12.

The first of these is the Food Hygiene Regulation.[62] This legislation lays down the general rules on the hygiene standards that must be met for all commercially traded foods. It is clear from the regulation that the primary responsibility for food hygiene rests with the food business operator.[63] The operator is required to ensure that all of the hygiene requirements set out in the regulation are met at every stage of the production, processing and distribution of his foods and products.[64] This includes compliance with microbiological criteria for foodstuffs, compliance with temperature control requirements for foodstuffs, maintenance of the 'cold chain' and sampling and analysis.[65] The only exceptions to the application of these rules are for those foods produced for private domestic use, or which are supplied in small quantities directly from the producer or local retailer to the consumer.[66] 'Food hygiene' is defined in the regulation as 'the measures and conditions necessary to control hazards and to ensure fitness for human consumption'.[67] The primary measure that must be employed to ensure that standards of hygiene are met is the use of the 'hazard analysis and critical control points' or 'HACCP' procedure.

6.5.1. Hazard Analysis Procedures

All food business operators must have a permanent hazard analysis and critical control points procedure in place.[68] This is to be based on a set of defined principles, which are to be used to identify hazards that must be prevented or reduced to acceptable levels, identifying the critical points at which action must be taken to minimise these hazards – the 'critical control points' in the process; establishing what level of hazard is acceptable at these points; implementing effective monitoring procedures at the critical control points; establishing what corrective action can be taken when required; setting up regular procedures to verify that the system is working; and documenting and recording, commensurate with the size of the food business, in a way that verifies that the other measures are working effectively.[69]

While there is clearly a responsibility placed on food business operators to ensure that they have suitable HACCP procedures in place as a key way of maintaining the hygienic and safe production and marketing of food, they are also

---

[62] Regulation (EC) No 852/2004 of the European Parliament and of the Council of 29 April 2004 on the hygiene of foodstuffs [2004] OJ L 226/3. For more on this see J Lawless, 'The complexity of flexibility in EU food hygiene regulation' (2012) 7 *European Food and Feed Law Review* 220.

[63] See Regulation (EC) No 852/2004, Art 1(1)(a).

[64] Ibid, Art 3.

[65] Ibid, Art 4. The targets and procedures referred to here are established and reviewed in consultation between the European Commission and the European Food Safety Authority, under the terms of Reg 852/2004, Arts 4(4) and 15, n 62 above.

[66] Ibid, Art 1(2)(c).

[67] Ibid, Art 2(1)(a).

[68] Ibid, Art 5(1).

[69] Ibid, Art 5(2).

obliged, under the terms of the Regulation, to provide all of this information to the competent authority when required.[70] The information must be recorded and it must be up-to-date and descriptive. National and EU guides must also be developed to assist in the promotion and uniform application of HACCP principles and hygienic practices.[71] Examples of these at national level include the HACCP guide produced by the FSAI, entitled 'Safe Catering – your guide to making food safely', which is ordered from the FSAI directly. The FSAI has also produced guidance notes on 'Assessment of HACCP Compliance', which are available in hard copy or on the Authority's website (www.fsai.ie.).

6.5.2. General Hygiene Provisions

The Food Hygiene Regulation provides that food business operators must comply with the general hygiene provisions laid down in Annex I (primary production) and Annex II (other operators) to the Regulation.[72] Primary production provisions also apply to all transportation, including that of live animals, as well as storage and handling of primary products, provided this does not substantially alter their nature or characteristics.

Primary Production Provisions

Food business operators must, under the terms of the Regulation, ensure that their products are protected from contamination, including that which may arise from exposure to the air, soil, water, feed, fertilisers, veterinary medicines, plant protection products and biocides. There is also provision in this part of the Regulation for the adoption of measures relating to animal health and welfare and plant health that have implications for human health, including programmes for the monitoring and control of zoonoses.

Other additional requirements are put in place for those food business operators who are rearing, harvesting or hunting animals or who are producing primary products of animal origin, such as milk or eggs. They are under an obligation to keep the animals, facilities, equipment and any vehicles that they use for this production clean, including those facilities that are used for the storage and handling of feed. This should include disinfecting where appropriate. Any staff used in this process must be in 'good health' and well trained on potential health risks.[73]

---

[70] Ibid, Art 5(4).

[71] Ibid, Art 7 and Annex I, Part B.

[72] Ibid, Arts 4(1) and (2).

[73] Annex II, Chapter XII further states that '[f]ood business operators are to ensure that food handlers are supervised and instructed and/or trained in food hygiene activities commensurate with their work activity; that those responsible for the development and maintenance of the [HACCP procedure] have received adequate training in the application of the HACCP principles; and compliance with any requirements of national law concerning training programmes for persons working in certain food sectors'.

All measures taken must be designed to keep the threat of contamination to a minimum level. This extends to taking any necessary steps designed to prevent the introduction and spread of contagious diseases transmissible to humans through food, including by taking precautionary measures when introducing new animals and reporting suspected outbreaks of disease to the relevant competent authority. Similar provisions apply for those food business operators who produce or harvest plant products or crops. Records should be kept of details related to the origin of animals kept, their feed, any veterinary medicines or plant protection products used, any incidence of health issues or disease and any results of sampling analyses undertaken.

General Hygiene Requirements for all Food Business Operators

Annex II to the Food Hygiene Regulation sets out the main requirements for those food business operators who are not engaged in what can be classified as 'primary production'. These apply across all stages of the production, processing and distribution of food. Conditions are set for food premises, preparation areas, temporary facilities such as market stalls and mobile sales vehicles and transportation.

Chapter I of Annex II provides that permanent food premises must be kept clean and maintained in good repair and condition. The layout, design, construction, siting and size of food premises must allow for adequate maintenance and cleaning, limit air-borne contamination and provide sufficient space for the hygienic performance of all operations. They must also be established in a way that protects against pests, contamination and the accumulation of dirt and which prevents contact with toxic materials, the shedding of particles onto food and the formation of condensation and mould. Requirements are also set on the positioning and availability of changing facilities for staff, storage for cleaning agents, lavatories, sinks, water, drainage, lighting and ventilation. Chapter II sets similar requirements for rooms which are used, on an ongoing basis, for the preparation, treatment and processing of food, excluding dining areas. Floor, door and wall surfaces are to be kept clean and disinfected. Ceilings and windows must be constructed in a way that prevents the accumulation of dirt, condensation and mould. Equipment and work surfaces must be maintained in good condition and be easy to clean and disinfect.[74] There must be a sufficient supply of hot and cold water and adequate provision for washing food.[75]

Chapter III of Annex II sets the requirements for those premises and rooms not covered by the other sections of this part of the Regulation. This includes all movable and/or temporary food premises, such as marquees, markets and mobile sales vehicles, as well as premises that are primarily used as a private residence

[74] Annex II, Chapter V provides further specific requirements on the hygienic use of equipment in the production and processing of food.
[75] Annex II, Chapter VII provides further detail on water supply and use, including more specific provision on the use of steam and ice in food preparation.

but which are also regularly used for commercial food preparation. All premises covered by this section must be sited, designed and constructed in a way that facilitates cleanliness and minimises the risk of contamination, particularly by animals and pests. There must be appropriate personal hygiene facilities, such as washbasins and changing facilities, available.[76] Surfaces and work utensils must be clean. There must be an adequate supply of hot and cold water. A system must be in place for the proper storage and disposal of waste. Foods must be stored at the appropriate temperatures.

Chapter IV deals with the transportation of food. All containers used for food transportation must be kept clean and be designed in a way that facilitates cleaning and disinfection. Any receptacles or containers used for the transportation of food cannot be used for any other purpose, or for the transportation of anything other than food, where this could lead to contamination. There must be an effective cleaning of these receptacles or containers where they have previously been used to transport something other than food. Different foods should be separated during transit where necessary. Foodstuffs transported in bulk that are in liquid, granulate or powder form should be contained in suitable receptacles or tankers that are clearly marked as being 'for foodstuffs only'. There should also be proper temperature control, appropriate to the foodstuff concerned, during transportation. The rules are designed to keep the risk of contamination or deterioration of the food to the minimum level possible.

The separation and disposal of food waste is dealt with in Annex II, Chapter VI. This provides that all food waste, non-edible by-products and other refuse must be removed from food preparation and storage areas as quickly as possible. This material should be deposited in closable containers, unless it can be demonstrated to the competent authorities that some other sort of disposal system is appropriate in the circumstances. Refuse stores must also be kept clean and, where possible, free from animals and pests. Waste should be destroyed or disposed of in a hygienic and environmentally friendly way. It should not itself become a direct or indirect source of contamination.

The final chapters of Annex II to the Food Hygiene Regulation set out more stipulations on the hygienic preparation, packaging and treatment of foods. Food business operators cannot accept raw materials or ingredients, other than live animals, if they are known to be, or might reasonably be expected to be, contaminated with parasites, pathogenic micro-organisms or toxic, decomposed or foreign substances to the extent that, even after the application of hygienic processes, the

---

[76] Annex II, Chapter VIII further provides that '[e]very person working in a food-handling area is to maintain a high degree of personal cleanliness and is to wear suitable, clean and, where necessary, protective clothing'. It also states that '[n]o person suffering from ... a disease likely to be transmitted through food or afflicted, for example, with infected wounds, skin infections, sores or diarrhoea is to be permitted to handle food or enter any food-handling area in any capacity if there is any likelihood of direct or indirect contamination'. Responsibility for the reporting of any such symptoms is, in the first instance, with the person affected, who must let the food business operator know about his illness or disease.

final product would be unfit for human consumption. All raw materials and ingredients should also be stored in conditions that prevent harmful deterioration or contamination. Food businesses that manufacture and wrap processed foods must have suitable rooms for these activities, which are large enough for the separate storage of raw and processed materials. Separate refrigeration space should also be available. Cooling, freezing and thawing should all be done in a way that poses minimal risk to health, including ensuring that material is thawed to minimise the growth of pathogenic micro-organisms or the formation of toxins in the foods. Finally, materials used for wrapping and packaging should not themselves be a source of contamination.

6.5.3. Specific Hygiene Rules

The second of the three hygiene regulations, all introduced in April 2004, lays down more specific hygiene rules for foods produced from animals.[77] The need for this regulation was identified as being related to the fact that incidence of microbiological and chemical hazards tends to be reported more frequently for foods of animal origin.[78] 'Products of animal origin' includes the obvious, for example eggs, dairy, meat and fish, but also foods such as honey and those produced containing blood.[79] The rules laid down in this regulation are designed to supplement those set out in the Food Hygiene Regulation.[80] This Regulation does not apply to food production for private domestic use or to the direct supply of small quantities by producers to consumers or local retail establishments.[81] The Regulation does not define what is meant by 'small quantities' or 'local retail establishments' but instead leaves this up to national authorities, provided that the relevant domestic laws are drafted in a way that ensures that the objectives of the EU Regulation are achieved.[82]

The Animal Hygiene Regulation sets out more specific obligations for food business operators.[83] These include applying the required identification mark to products of animal origin. The mark can only be applied if the product has been manufactured in accordance with this Regulation and in a registered and approved establishment.[84] Food business operators who run slaughterhouses must

---

[77] Regulation (EC) No 853/2004 laying down specific hygiene rules for food of animal origin [2004] OJ L 226/22.

[78] Ibid, Preamble, Recital 2.

[79] Reg 853/2004, Annex I, n 77 above.

[80] Reg 852/2004, n 62 above.

[81] Reg 853/2004, Art 1(3), n 77 above.

[82] Ibid, Art 1(4).

[83] Ibid, Art 3 in conjunction with Annexes II and III.

[84] Ibid, Art 5. The mark itself is dealt with in more detail in Regulation (EC) No 854/2004 of the European Parliament and of the Council of 29 April 2004 laying down specific rules for the organisation of official controls on products of animal origin intended for human consumption [2004] OJ L 226/. Establishments must have been approved and registered under the terms of Reg 852/2004, n 62 above.

comply with the HACCP provisions of the Food Hygiene Regulation,[85] as well as more specific requirements tailored to meet the additional needs of producing food from animals.[86] This includes a range of stipulations on animal welfare, both during transportation to and arrival at, the abattoir. Animals brought into the slaughter hall must be slaughtered as soon as possible thereafter.[87] Parts of the animal that are to be used for human consumption must be treated in a way that minimises the risk of any contamination.[88] Those parts that are not to be used must be removed from the clean sector at the first available opportunity. Carcasses and offal must not come into contact with floors, walls or work stands. Cutting, boning, storage and later transportation must take place in an environment with a set maximum temperature. As is usual with this type of Regulation, the European Commission is assisted by the Standing Committee on Plants, Animals, Food and Feed,[89] and the European Food Safety Authority where necessary.[90]

The second of the more specific EU Food Hygiene Regulations and the third part of the overall corpus of rules on the hygienic production and marketing of food, is the Organisation of Official Controls Regulation.[91] This Regulation is designed to establish a framework for EU Member States to establish and apply national rules for the implementation of the hygiene rules set out in the other regulations. Again, it only applies to products of animal origin.[92] 'Official controls' are defined in the Regulation as being 'any form of control that the competent authority performs for the verification of compliance with food law, including animal health and animal welfare rules'.[93] As will be seen here, this Regulation links up with the other two hygiene regulations discussed above, setting out how Member States such as Ireland should practically apply the requirements set out therein. For example, the other regulations provide that food establishments must be 'approved' before they can operate legitimately.

This Regulation states that where such approval is required, the competent authority must first make an on-site visit to assess the establishment.[94] It can only then approve the establishment if the food business operator can demonstrate that he has met all the requirements of the Food Hygiene Regulation and the Animal Hygiene Regulation. In some cases, conditional approval can be granted if it appears from the on-site visit that the establishment does meet all the infrastructure and equipment requirements. It can then only grant full approval if a demonstration is made during a second on-site visit, which must take place within

---

[85] Reg 852/2004, Art 5, n 62 above.
[86] Reg 853/2004, Annex II, n 77 above.
[87] Ibid, Annex III.
[88] Full detail of this is set out in Annex III.
[89] Reg 853/2004, Art 12.
[90] Ibid, Art 13.
[91] See Regulation (EC) No 854/2004.
[92] Ibid, Art 1(1).
[93] Ibid, Art 2(1)(a).
[94] Ibid, Art 3(1)(a).

three months of the first one, that all the other requirements set by those Regulations have also been met.[95] Member States must then keep up-to-date lists of approved establishments.[96]

The Regulation also sets out a series of general principles for official controls in respect of all products of animal origin. These include that Member States must ensure that food business operators provide all assistance necessary to enable the national competent authorities to carry out their investigative tasks effectively.[97] This means that there must be facilitation, through national law, of access to all food establishment buildings, premises and installations.[98] There should, in the same way, be full disclosure of documentation and records that enable the authorities to properly judge any given situation or business that they are investigating. All investigations carried out under the terms of this Regulation must be related to the Food Hygiene Regulation, the Animal Hygiene Regulation and the Animal By-products Regulation.[99] These official controls should include audits of good hygiene practices and HACCP procedures in general, as well as the more specific examinations related to different types of animal-based foodstuffs.[100] The general hygiene practice audits should verify that food business operators continuously apply the proper procedures related to the design and maintenance of premises and equipment, personal hygiene, employee training, pest control, water quality, temperature control and documentation.[101] The HACCP audits should verify that food business operators are also applying the correct procedures related to this on a continuous basis.[102]

The more specific official controls take account of the type of food produced by the food business operator. There are requirements set by the Regulation for fresh meat,[103] molluscs,[104] fish,[105] and milk and dairy products.[106] The national competent authority is obliged to take action where any of these audits show that there has been non-compliance with the Regulations.[107] This action should include the imposition of any necessary sanitation procedures.[108] However, it may also include marketing restrictions or prohibitions, product recalls or closure of the business.[109]

---

[95] Ibid, Art 3(1)(b).

[96] Ibid, Art 3(6).

[97] Ibid, Art 4(1).

[98] As set out in Ch 3 of this book. More specifically, Reg 9 of the European Communities (Food and Feed Hygiene) Regulations 2005, SI No 910/2005, provides authorized officers with the powers necessary to address this provision of the EU Regulations.

[99] Regulation (EC) No 1774/2002 of the European Parliament and of the Council of 3 October 2002 laying down health rules concerning animal by-products not intended for human consumption [2002] OJ L 273/1.

[100] Ibid, Art 4(3).

[101] Ibid, Art 4(4).

[102] Ibid, Art 4(5).

[103] Ibid, Art 5.

[104] Ibid, Art 6 in conjunction with Annex II.

[105] Ibid, Art 7 in conjunction with Annex III.

[106] Ibid, Art 8 in conjunction with Annex IV.

[107] Ibid, Art 9(1).

[108] Ibid, Art 9(2)(a).

[109] Ibid, Art 9(2)(b), (c) and (e).

The 2005 Food Hygiene Regulations deal with the domestic aspects of the interpretation and implementation of the three main EU Regulations in this area, outlined above.[110] As we have seen from the EU regulations, the national competent authority is central to the application of the hygiene rules at national level. The Irish Food Hygiene Regulations designate the Food Safety Authority of Ireland as the body responsible for maintaining the register of food businesses.[111] Inspections of food businesses are carried out by Environmental Health Officers under a service contract between the HSE and the FSAI. The range of powers, procedures and outcomes was discussed in Chapter 3.

---

[110] SI No 910/2005.
[111] Ibid, Reg 6(1).

7

Food Labelling and Advertising

7.1. Framework Food Labelling Legislation

Compulsory indications that must appear on the labelling of all pre-packaged foods have been standardised at EU level since the late 1970s.[1] This legislation first appeared in Irish law as the European Communities (Labelling, Presentation and Advertising of Foodstuffs) Regulations 1982.[2] Although there have been multiple amendments to the original EU directive, including a re-draft in 2000,[3] current provisions have remained almost identical to those first set out in 1979. Some new additions have been included in the list of mandatory particulars but, by and large, food labelling requirements have remained relatively unchanged for several decades. However, the most significant changes were brought about when the much-heralded proposals for a new EU 'food information' regulation came into effect during the period 2014–2016.[4]

7.1.1. Labelling Definitions

The labelling and advertising of food is regulated in Ireland by the European Union (Provision of Food Information to Consumers) Regulations 2014,[5]

---

[1] Council Directive 1979/112/EEC of 18 December 1978 on the approximation of the laws of the Member States relating to the labelling, presentation and advertising of foodstuffs for sale to the ultimate consumer [1979] OJ L 33/1.

[2] SI No 205/1982.

[3] Directive 2000/13/EC of the European Parliament and of the Council of 20 March 2000 on the approximation of the laws of the Member States relating to the labelling, presentation and advertising of foodstuffs [2000] OJ L 109/29.

[4] Proposal for a Regulation of the European Parliament and of the Council on the provision of food information to consumers, COM (2008) 40, which became Regulation (EU) No 1169/2011 of the European Parliament and of the Council of 25 October 2011 on the provision of food information to consumers, amending Regulations (EC) No 1924/2006 and (EC) No 1925/2006 of the European Parliament and of the Council and repealing Commission Directive 1987/250/EEC, Council Directive 1990/496/EEC, Commission Directive 1999/10/EC, Directive 2000/13/EC of the European Parliament and of the Council, Commission Directives 2002/67/EC and 2008/5/EC and Commission Regulation (EC) No 608/2004 [2011] OJ L 304/18. For more on its initial implementation and the changes that it was expected to introduce see, eg, L González Vaqué, 'The new European regulation on food labelling: Are we ready for the "D" day on 13 December 2014?' (2013b) 8 *European Food and Feed Law Review* 158.

[5] SI No 556/2014.

which give full domestic applicability to EU Food Information Regulation 2011.[6] Labelling is defined in the Irish regulations as being

> any words, particulars, trade mark, brand name, pictorial matter or symbol relating to the food and appearing on the packaging of the food or on any document, notice, label, ring or collar accompanying the food.[7]

Although the legal definition is clearly a broad one, it is not all encompassing. The European Court of Justice has clarified that details provided on the packaging will only be classified as forming part of the labelling if its purpose is 'specifically intended to inform the consumer as to the characteristics of the product in question'.[8] A national cheese mark, essentially a serial number, designed to demonstrate to the authorities that the product had been made in compliance with certain rules, does not satisfy this 'consumer information' requirement. It is not, therefore, 'labelling' within the legal definition of the term.[9] The information imparted to the consumer should therefore be related to the nature, identity, properties, composition, quality, durability, origin or manufacturing method of the foodstuff for it to constitute 'labelling'.[10]

The Food Information Regulation and the Irish Regulations, also establish the new legal term of 'food information'. This is defined as:

> [...] information concerning a food and made available to the final consumer by means of a label, other accompanying material, or any other means including modern technology tools or verbal communication.[11]

This has broadened the scope of application of the legislation further, accounting for other forms of communication with consumers, such as the internet and social media. 'Labelling' is now a component of 'information'. The Regulations, however, apply to all 'information' provided to the 'final consumer' and not just the 'labelling'.

The 'final consumer', which the legislation is primarily designed to protect, is not defined in the Irish Regulations. However, Article 3(18) of the EU General Food Law Regulation states that the:

> 'final consumer' means the ultimate consumer of a foodstuff who will not use the food as part of any food business operation or activity.[12]

---

[6] See Food Information Regulations, reg 1169/2011, n 4 above. For more on the protracted process of introducing this regulation, see P Dévényi, 'The new regulation on the provision of food information to consumers: Is new always better?' (2011) 6 *European Food and Feed Law Review* 210.

[7] See SI No 556/2014, n 5 above, reg 2(1). It is similarly defined in SI 1169/2011, Art 2(2)(j).

[8] Case C-285/1992 *Criminal Proceedings against Coöperatieve Zuivelindustrie 'Twee Provinciën' WA* [1993] ECR I-6045.

[9] Ibid, paras 16–18 of the judgment.

[10] SI 1169/2011, Art 7(1)(a), n 4 above and Case 298/1987, *Proceedings for Compulsory Reconstruction against Smanor SA* [1988] ECR 4489, para 30.

[11] Reg 2(1) of the Irish Regulations 2014 and Art 2(2)(a) of the EU Food Information Regulation.

[12] As discussed throughout this book, the General Food Law Regulation is Regulation (EC) No 178/2002 of the European Parliament and of the Council of 28 January 2002 laying down the general principles and requirements of food law, establishing the European Food Safety Authority and laying

It appears that in EU law and in Irish law the terms 'final consumer' and 'ultimate consumer' are somewhat interchangeable. The definition of the 'final consumer' set out above is significant because it removes some of the ambiguity that has existed in the past when the legislation made clear references to the 'purchaser', when these should really have been made to the 'consumer'.[13] This is an important consideration to make in the context of food labelling because the information imparted is as significant for the person who actually prepares or consumes the food as for the one who has bought it, a point also clearly recognised by the European Court of Justice.[14] The Food Labelling Directives of 1979 and 2000 consistently made references to both the 'purchaser' and to the 'consumer', in circumstances where the two were not clearly interchangeable.[15] This is something that is now addressed by the introduction of the Food Information Regulation, which specifically refers to 'consumers' throughout, making only two references to 'purchasers'. Article 7(1) of the EU Food Information Regulation provides that '[f]ood information shall be accurate, clear and easy to understand for the consumer'.

The compulsory indications that must appear on all food labels, apart from those which are excluded from specified provisions of the Food Information Regulation, such as carbonated water,[16] or those which have their own labelling requirements set out in other legislation,[17] are as established by the Food

down procedures in matters of food safety [2002] OJ L 31/1. The 'ultimate consumer' is not defined, in either the EU or the Irish Regulations. Regulation 2(1) of the English Food Labelling Regulations SI No 1499/1996 defines the 'ultimate consumer' as 'any person who buys other than for the purpose of resale, for ... a catering establishment or for ... a manufacturing business'. This UK definition, however, fails to account for the fact that the purchaser and the consumer are often not the same person.

[13] Dir 1979/112, n 1 above, Art 2(1)(a), for example, stated that '[t]he labelling and methods used must not be such as could mislead the purchaser to a material degree'. Article 5 of the same Directive provided that, when using a description for a foodstuff then this '[...] shall be [...] sufficiently precise to inform the purchaser of its true nature and to enable it to be distinguished from products with which it could be confused'. Article 14 provided that the language used on food labelling must be '[...] easily understood by purchasers'.

[14] Case C-85/1994, *Groupement des Producteurs, Importateurs et Agents Généraux d'Eaux Minérales Etrangères, VZW (Piageme) and others v Peeters NV* [1995] ECR I-2955, paras 24 and 25; Case C-385/1996, *Criminal Proceedings against Hermann Josef Goerres* [1998] ECR I-4431, para 24. The use of the term 'consumer' (which obviously can also include the 'purchaser') is much more pragmatic than the previous use of both the term 'consumer' and the term 'purchaser', even when not fully appropriate. The term 'ultimate consumer' is not specifically defined in either the EU General Food Law Regulation or the Irish Food Information Regulations, so it remains potentially problematic but not to the same extent as when the term 'purchaser' was being used where 'consumer' would have been a more accurate reflection of what the directives were striving to achieve.

[15] Dir 1979/112, n 1 above and Directive 2000/13/EC of the European Parliament and of the Council of 20 March 2000 on the approximation of the laws of the Member States relating to the labelling, presentation and advertising of foodstuffs [2000] OJ L 109/29.

[16] Reg 1169/2011, Art 19(1)(b) for example, removes carbonated water from the requirement to bear a list of ingredients. Article 7 of Dir 2009/54/EC of the European Parliament and of the Council of 18 June 2009 on the exploitation and marketing of natural mineral waters sets out more detailed provisions on the labelling of natural mineral waters. The 2009 Directive is now transposed into Irish law by the European Union (Natural Mineral Waters, Spring Waters and Other Waters in Bottles or Containers) Regulations 2016, SI No 282/2016.

[17] Eg honey, which is dealt with by the European Communities (Marketing of Honey) Regulations 2003, SI No 367/2003; chocolate, which is regulated by the European Communities (Marketing of

Information Regulation. These include the name of the food, a list of ingredients, the appropriate durability indication, any special storage conditions or conditions of use, the name or business name and an address or registered office of either or both of the manufacturer or packer or a seller established within the EU, particulars of the place of origin or provenance of the food if failure to provide this might mislead a purchaser as to the true origin of the food and, finally, instructions for use where necessary.[18] One of the most obvious changes to be made by the introduction of the EU Food Information Regulation is that nutrient declarations would be included in this list of compulsory indications from December 2016 onwards.[19] This is discussed in more detail in Chapter 9.

7.1.2. Labelling Format

All of the labelling particulars must be easily accessible and must appear either on the packaging or on a label attached to the packaging.[20] All particulars must be provided in a manner that is easy to understand.[21] It must be clearly legible and indelible.[22] It must also be clearly visible to the consumer.[23] It cannot be hidden or obscured in any way. There is no provision made in the Irish Regulations for providing information at catering establishments via temporary media such as chalk and blackboards.[24] There is an obligation on food business operators to place some of the compulsory indications into the same field of vision on the labeling. This includes the name of the food, the net quantity of the food and the alcohol content where required.[25]

7.1.3. Food Names

Food names that appear on labelling should be as prescribed by law,[26] such as a 'recipe' law,[27] or some other form of set compositional or quality-based

---

Cocoa and Chocolate Products) Regulations 2003, SI No 236/2003; and coffee, which is covered by the European Communities (Marketing of Coffee Extracts and Chicory Extracts) Regulations 2000, SI No 281/2000.

[18] Reg 1169/2011, Art 7.

[19] Art 54 in conjunction with Art 9(1)(l) of Reg 1169/2011, n 4 above.

[20] Reg 9.

[21] Reg 5(1).

[22] Reg 10(1).

[23] Reg 10(2).

[24] There is provision made for this in other jurisdictions, for example Reg 38(3) of the English Food Labelling Regulations 1996, n 12 above.

[25] Reg 10(5).

[26] Reg 7(1)(a). The name of the food should be in accordance with Art 17(1) to (4) of the Food Information Regulation, n 4 above.

[27] Eg those set for honey, chocolate and coffee, as set out in n 17 above.

requirements.[28] These are known as 'legal names'.[29] If no name is prescribed for a food by a specific law, the name that is customarily used where the food is sold should be on the label.[30] This is known as a 'customary name' and it is defined as being:

> [...] a name which is accepted as the name of the food by consumers in the Member State in which that food is sold, without that name needing further explanation.[31]

Where neither a legal nor a customary name exists, then a 'descriptive name' should be used. This is a name:

> [...] providing a description of the food, and if necessary of its use, which is sufficiently clear to enable consumers to know its true nature and distinguish it from other products with which it might be confused.[32]

Trademarks, brand names or 'fancy names' should not be substituted for the name of a food.[33] The latter are not defined in either the Irish or the EU legislation. Indications of physical condition or treatment, such as dried, frozen, concentrated or smoked, should be provided alongside the name of the food where necessary.[34]

7.1.4. Ingredients

The list of ingredients, which must be included on all food products,[35] subject to some exceptions,[36] must be headed or preceded by an appropriate heading which

---

[28] Such as that which was set for 'butter' by Council Regulation (EC) No 2991/94 of 5 December 1994 laying down standards for spreadable fats [1994] OJ L 316/2, but which has since been replaced by Art 83 of Regulation (EU) No 1308/2013 of the European Parliament and of the Council of 17 December 2013 establishing a common organisation of the markets in agricultural products [2013] OJ L 347/671, which allows Member States to maintain national rules laying down different quality levels for spreadable fats provided that this is done in a non-discriminatory manner and also by Appendix II to the 2013 Regulation which sets sales descriptions for, amongst other things, 'butter'. This category of food name also includes that which was set for 'sugar' by Council Directive 2001/111/EC of 20 December 2001 relating to certain sugars intended for human consumption, [2001] OJ L 10/53, transposed into Irish law by the European Communities (Marketing of Sugar Products) Regulations 2003, SI No 289/2003.

[29] Legal names are reserved for foods that meet the standard definitions, subject to some possible exceptions. These exceptions do not extend to plant-based products which describe themselves in a manner that suggests a similarity to animal-based dairy products. The CJEU has ruled that purely plant-based products cannot, in principle therefore, be marketed using designations such as 'milk', 'cream', 'cheese', or 'butter' where these names are reserved by EU law for animal products. It is only where some listed exception to this rule exists that such names can be used. There are currently no such exceptions for tofu or soya products. See Case C-422/2016, *Verband Sozialer Wettbewerb eV v TofuTown.com GmbH* ECLI:EU:C:2017:458.

[30] Art 17(1) of the Food Information Regulation, set by Reg 7(1)(a) of the Irish Food Information Regulations, n 5 above.

[31] Art 2(2)(o) of the Food Information Regulation, n 4 above.

[32] Ibid, Art 2(2)(p).

[33] Ibid, Art 17(4).

[34] Annex VI to the EU Reg.

[35] See Reg 7(1)(b) of the Irish Food Information Regulations, n 5 above.

[36] The exceptions are set out in Art 19 of EU Reg 1169/2011, n 4 above and are discussed in more detail later in this section.

consists of or includes the word 'ingredients'.[37] The ingredients should usually be listed in descending order of weight used in the preparation of the product.[38] The main exception to this ordering of ingredients occurs when water is used, as its position in the list is calculated on the basis of the quantity of it present in the finished product, rather than on the quantity used in preparation.[39] Water does not have to be listed as an ingredient at all where it is used to reconstitute an ingredient or it is not consumed as part of the product or if it does not exceed 5 per cent of the finished foodstuff.[40] Ingredients themselves are defined as being:

> any substance or product, including flavourings, food additives and food enzymes, and any constituent of a compound ingredient, used in the manufacture or preparation of a food and still present in the finished product, even if in an altered form.[41]

Residues are not considered as being ingredients.

Compound ingredients, mentioned above, are '[...] an ingredient that is itself the product of more than one ingredient'.[42] In some circumstances, the names of all of the ingredients of a compound ingredient are to be listed, usually in a way that makes it clear that they are the ingredients of the compound ingredient.[43] However, the list of ingredients is not compulsory for compound ingredients where the composition of the compound ingredient is defined in EU law, or is not required under EU law, or is a mixture of herbs and/or spices and the compound ingredient constitutes less than 2 per cent of the finished product. This exception does not apply in the case of additives.

While vegetable oils and fats may be grouped together in the list of ingredients under the name 'vegetable oils' or 'vegetable fats', followed by the phrase 'in varying proportions', the expressions 'fully hydrogenated' or 'partly hydrogenated', as appropriate, must also be used.[44] Similar requirements exist for the labelling of hydrogenated and partially hydrogenated animal oils and fats in the list of ingredients.[45] Hydrogenated oils and fats have had their chemical structure altered

---

[37] Art 18(1) of EU Reg 1169/2011, n 4 above. It has been held in the Irish High Court that the ingredients list and other particulars provided on food labelling is not a legally binding warranty. It is, of course, still subject to the labelling legislation. See *East Coast Area Health Board v O'Kane Foods (Ireland)* [2002] 4 IR 377.

[38] Art 18. Ingredients used in concentrated or dehydrated form and later reconstituted during preparation of the food should be placed in the list of ingredients according to the pre-concentration or pre-dehydration condition, Annex VII to the EU Reg. Also, where a food is sold in concentrated or dehydrated form and is usually reconstituted by the addition of water, its ingredients may be listed in descending order of their weight post-reconstitution. When this is the case, the list of ingredients should be preceded by the heading 'ingredients of the reconstituted product' or similar.

[39] Annex VII to the EU Reg. Also, any ingredient constituting less than 2% of the finished product can be listed in any order after listing all the other ingredients used.

[40] Ibid.

[41] Art 2(2)(f) of Reg 1169/2011, n 4 above.

[42] Ibid, Art 2(2)(h).

[43] EU Reg, Annex VII, Part E. The ingredients of a compound ingredient should normally immediately follow the name of the compound ingredient in the ingredients list.

[44] EU Reg, Annex VII, Part A.

[45] Ibid, Annex VII, Part B.

to delay perishability. There are concerns over the increased use and presence of hydrogenated oils and fats in foods, especially processed foods like biscuits and cakes with a longer shelf-life. However, the consumption of partially hydrogenated oils and fats is considered to be an even bigger risk for human health. Trans-fatty acids, or 'transfats', can occur naturally in foods, such as meat and dairy products, usually at relatively low levels. Partially hydrogenated oils are an artificial source of transfats and their consumption is deemed to have a very negative impact on human health. The United States Food and Drug Administration (FDA) has now moved to ban the inclusion of these artificial transfats in foods, following a phasing-out period. They are not deemed to be 'generally recognised as safe'. This determination has been reached based on '[...] extensive research into the effects of partially hydrogenated oils, as well as input from stakeholders during the public comment period'.[46] The labelling and use of transfats in the European Union and in EU Member States is discussed in more detail later in this chapter.

Other ingredients, including many of those which consumers have tended to have the most interest in being properly informed about, must appear in the list of ingredients by the name of their category, followed by their specific name or E number. This includes, some food additives and enzymes, such as acidity regulators, colours, sweeteners and thickeners.[47] Flavourings, however, need only be designated by the generic term 'flavouring(s)' or 'smoke flavouring(s)'. Use of the term 'natural' in association with flavourings listed as ingredients is subject to the requirements of Article 16 of Regulation 1334/2008, which states that:

> [i]f the term 'natural' is used to describe a flavouring in the sales description [then it] may only be used if the flavouring component comprises only flavouring preparations and/or natural flavouring substances.[48]

The term 'natural' may only be used with reference to the food more generally where the flavouring component has been obtained exclusively or by at least 95 per cent from the source material referred to.[49]

The list of ingredients cannot be used as a mechanism for correcting other misleading aspects of the food label.[50]

---

[46] As stated on www.fda.gov.ie. Sections 201(s) and 409 of the Federal Food, Drug and Cosmetic Act 1938, as amended by the Food Additives Amendment 1958, provides that additives that are 'Generally Recognised as Safe' (GRAS) by recognised experts can be added to foods without the usual authorisation requirements. Partially hydrogenated vegetable oils no longer satisfy the conditions of this exemption.

[47] EU Reg, Annex VII, Part C. This is only a small sample of the types of additives and enzymes that included in this obligation, with 24 separate categories being listed in the Regulation.

[48] Regulation (EC) No 1334/2008 of the European Parliament and of the Council of 16 December 2008 on flavourings and certain food ingredients with flavouring properties for use in and on foods [2008] OJ L 354/34.

[49] Ibid, Art 16(4). The use of additives in food is discussed in more detail in ch 4.

[50] See Case C-195/2014, *Bundesverband der Verbraucherzentralen und Verbraucherverbände – Verbraucherzentrale Bundesverband eV v Teekanne GmbH & Co KG* ECLI:EU:C:2015:361. Despite this and despite the general obligation to ensure that food labels do not mislead consumers, many products continue to be labelled in a misleading manner. Consider, for example, the high-sugar breakfast cereal

Ingredients Listing Exceptions

All the above requirements on the listing of ingredients are subject to two important exceptions. First, some ingredients do not need to be named. Second, some foodstuffs do not need to bear a list of ingredients at all.

The most significant exclusion from the ingredients listing requirement is the additive that is contained in an ingredient and serves 'no technological function' in the finished product.[51] This means that any additive used in the production of an ingredient does not have to be listed on the label, once it does not affect the nature of the finished product. This is a complicated matter, perhaps best explained by reference to the European Court of Justice's assessment of what constitutes an additive in an ingredient that serves no technological function in the finished product.

In its decision in *Pfanni Werke*,[52] the Court of Justice discussed the fact that EU law provides that additives serving no technological function are not considered to be ingredients. A German manufacturer of dehydrated potato products had added diphosphate (E450a) to one of its products, potato purée flakes, to prevent discoloration during the manufacturing process. Local authorities warned the manufacturer that failing to list this additive as an ingredient was contrary to labelling laws and could lead to the imposition of a fine. The company subsequently brought an action against the authorities, claiming that the additive in question did not play any role in the finished product and did not need to be listed. It was, they claimed, added to potato pulp to prevent it from changing colour and that the production of this pulp was only one stage in the manufacture of 'potato purée flakes'. After the dehydration of that pulp the colour of the potato flakes could not change. Initial domestic judgment went against the applicant, the local court considering that the inclusion of an additive that ultimately altered the appearance of a product had to be included in the list of ingredients. On second appeal, on a point of law, to the Federal Administrative Court, the case was referred to the Court of Justice to establish whether an additive such as this, used to prevent the discoloration of an ingredient, continues to serve a technological function in the finished product. The Court accepted that the purpose of the labelling legislation was to inform consumers by, inter alia, requiring producers to list ingredients. However, derogations from this provision, such as that on the technological function of additives, exist to ensure that information provided to consumers is effective. Requiring the publication of an exhaustive list of ingredients used would, according to the Court, deprive the legislation of its substance.

---

that displays pictures or images of fruit on the packaging that are not contained in the product and which are used to suggest a wholesomeness for the product that does not exist. This combined with the misleading nature of many nutrient declarations discussed in Chapter 9, has come to mean that it is often only the list of ingredients that can be relied upon by the consumer when it comes to being properly informed about the constituents of a product. This itself is also subject to the consumer actually being able to properly decipher all of the information in the ingredients list.

[51] Reg 1169/2011, n 4 above, Art 20(b)(i).

[52] Case C-144/1993 *Pfanni Werke Otto Eckart KG v Landeshauptstadt München* [1994] ECR I-4605.

In this particular case, the fact that discoloration was no longer possible in the finished product meant that the presence of diphosphate E450a was no longer necessary in the finished product. Accordingly, this additive 'no longer serves a technological function in the finished product so that, if the consumer is not to be misled, it should not be included in the list of ingredients.'[53] Diphosphate E450a did not, therefore, have to be listed as an ingredient used in the manufacture of potato purée flakes.

This 'no technological function' exemption from the list of ingredients as interpreted by the Court of Justice in *Pfanni Werke* raises several concerns. First, the Court accepted that the purpose of the original Framework Food Labelling Directive, as transposed into Irish law by the European Communities (Labelling, Presentation and Advertising of Foodstuffs) Regulations 1982,[54] was to 'inform and protect the consumer.'[55] The Directive further stated that 'labelling ... must not be such as could mislead the purchaser ... as to the characteristics of the food-stuff and, in particular, as to its ... composition.'[56] The Court went on to accept that the additive is present in the finished product. However, having served its irreversible function, it does not have to be listed as an ingredient. This misleads the consumer about the composition of the product. If an additive is contained in a foodstuff, the fact that the function that it serves is irreversible should not mean that it does not have to be listed as an ingredient. Should several additives contained in the finished product serve no ongoing 'technological function', the list of ingredients may deceptively portray the product as containing relatively few additives. This appears entirely at odds with the declared purpose of informing the consumer.

Second, the Court does present one good argument for removing the need to list all additives – the 'de-cluttering' of the ingredients list to make the information provided more effective. However, if we work on the basis that consumers tend to see additives as a group of constituents to be avoided, or at worst to be taken in minimal quantities, then an ingredients list that reveals less than the total quantity of additives present could be considered simple, but very misleading. Effectively, product A could contain fewer additives than product B, but it must be labelled in a way that makes it appear as if it contains more of them, depending on whether the additives present in product A serve a reversible or an irreversible function in the finished foodstuff.

Other ingredients that do not need to be listed on the label include additives used solely as a processing aid,[57] some carriers and substances which are not

---

[53] Ibid at para 18.

[54] SI No 205/1982.

[55] See *Pfanni Werke*, n 52 above, para 15. Recital 6 of the Preamble to Directive 2000/13, n 3 above, also stated that '[t]he prime consideration for any rules on the labelling of foodstuffs should be the need to inform and protect the consumer'.

[56] Dir 1979/112, n 1 above, Art 2(1)(a). Now contained in Art 7(1) of Reg 1169/2011, n 4 above.

[57] Reg 1169/2011, n 4 above, Art 20(b).

considered to be additives,[58] and water where it is used during the manufacturing process for the reconstitution of an ingredient used in concentrated or dehydrated form or where it is not normally meant for consumption.[59]

The second key exception to the ingredients listing requirement is that some foods do not need to bear a list of ingredients at all. This includes fresh fruit and vegetables, including potatoes, that have not been peeled or cut; carbonated water that contains no other ingredients; fermentation vinegar produced from a single basic product; cheese, butter, fermented milk and fermented cream where no ingredients other than lactic products, enzymes, micro-organism cultures or, in the case of cheese, salt essential to manufacture have been added; single ingredient foods where the name of the food is identical to the ingredient name or the name of the food enables the nature of the ingredient to be clearly identified; and drinks with an alcoholic strength above 1.2 per cent by volume.[60]

Quantitative Ingredient Declarations

When a food is marketed by 'special emphasis' on the inclusion of a specific ingredient, the actual percentage quantity of this ingredient that is used in the production of this foodstuff must be stated on the label.[61] This is known as the 'quantitative ingredient declaration' or 'QUID'. The Food Information Regulation prescribes that:

> [t]he indication of the quantity of an ingredient or category of ingredients used in the manufacture or preparation of a food shall be required where the ingredient or category of ingredients concerned appears in the name of the food or is usually associated with that name by the consumer; is emphasized on the labelling in words, pictures or graphics; or is essential to characterise a food and to distinguish it from products with which it might be confused because of its name or appearance.[62]

This quantity declaration should be listed as a percentage, appearing next to the name of the food or next to the name of the ingredient as it appears in the list.[63] Therefore, for example, if a label makes reference to the inclusion of strawberries in a cereal bar, either by stating this in words or by some sort of pictorial reference, like a photograph of a strawberry, then the overall quantity of strawberries contained in that bar must be listed beside the name of that ingredient in the ingredients list, or in the description of the product.[64] References to the

---

[58] Ibid, Art 20(c) and (d).
[59] Ibid, Art 20(e)(i) and (ii).
[60] Ibid, Art 19(1).
[61] Ibid, Art 22.
[62] Ibid, Art 22(1).
[63] Annex VIII to the Food Information Regulation.
[64] Pictures of ingredients can only be used on labels if the ingredient is present in the product. The fact that the list of ingredients makes no reference to the ingredient that has been presented on the label does not mean that the label is not misleading. The CJEU has found that the labelling of a foodstuff

use of an ingredient which is only used in a small quantity as a flavouring does not constitute 'emphasis' and is not, therefore, subject to the quantitative ingredient declaration requirements.[65] Any ingredient which is covered by the indication 'with sweeteners' or 'with sugars and sweeteners' does not need to have the actual quantity of this component disclosed in the ingredients list. Nor does any added vitamin or mineral quantity have to be specifically disclosed in the ingredients if that substance is already subject to a nutrition declaration.[66]

7.1.5. Date of Durability

The 'date of minimum durability of a food' means 'the date until which the food retains its specific properties when properly stored'.[67] Under the terms of the Food Information Regulation, several types of 'date of minimum durability' exist, determined by the level of perishability of the foodstuff. The date must be included in the labelling of all prepackaged foods, subject to some exceptions.[68]

Highly perishable foods must carry a 'use by' date. This applies to those foods which, from a microbiological perspective, are likely to constitute a danger to human health if consumed after the stated date.[69] They are deemed to be 'unsafe' after this date.[70] Otherwise, the durability date is expressed as a 'best before' date. The 'use by' date must include the words 'use by' and the date by which the product should be consumed. This should also include recommended storage conditions where necessary. It should consist of a day, month and possibly a year, in that order and in an uncoded form.[71]

The 'best before' date can consist of either a specific day or as a 'best before end', which indicates the end of a specified time period, such as a year. If necessary, the durability date should be accompanied by the storage conditions that should be observed for the product to last until the end of the specified period of

cannot mislead the consumer by giving the impression that an ingredient is present when in fact it is not. The fact that the list of ingredients may be truthful and comprehensive is not sufficient to correct the erroneous impression imparted by pictures on the label which suggest the presence of a particular ingredient, such as a fruit or vegetable. See Case C-195/2014 *Bundesverband der Verbraucherzentralen und Verbraucherverbände*, n 50 above.

[65] Annex VIII to the Food Information Regulation.

[66] Ibid.

[67] Reg 1169/2011, n 4 above, Art 2(2)(r). The durability date is set as one of the mandatory particulars by Art 9(1)(f) of the Regulation.

[68] See the European Union (Provision of Food Information to Consumers) Regulations 2014, n 5 above, Reg 7(1)(f).

[69] Reg 1169/2011, n 4 above, Art 24.

[70] Under the terms of the General Food Law Regulation, n 12 above, Art 14(2)–(5).

[71] Annex X.2 to the Food Information Regulation. The English courts have held that while a food is no longer 'highly perishable' after it has been frozen, the 'use by' date stipulations continue to apply. The sale of previously frozen food after this date was held to be an offence under the terms of the UK Food Labelling Regulations 1996, SI No 1499/1996. See *Torfaen Borough Council v Douglas Willis Limited* [2012] EWHC 296.

perishability. Only the day and month needs to be included for any durability date which is within three months of the date of production. Those products which will retain their specific properties for between three and 18 months need only present a month and year as the durability date. An indication of the year only is sufficient for those products that will keep these properties for more than 18 months.[72]

The 'best before' date and the 'use by' date may also be printed separately from the words 'use by', if this is followed by a reference to the place where the date and storage conditions do appear, such as 'for use by date see lid'.[73] There is an obvious practical reason for allowing this. It means that the producer does not need to alter the label on the main form of all his packaging, just on one element of it, such as the lid. This is likely to be more convenient and more cost-effective.

Several food types do not need to present an indication of minimum durability at all. These include fresh fruit and vegetables, including potatoes, that have not been peeled, cut or similarly treated, wines, drinks with an alcohol content of 10 per cent or more, baked foods such as breads and pastries that are normally consumed within 24 hours of production, vinegar, some salts and sugars, some confectionery products and chewing gums.[74]

The 'date of freezing' has also been introduced into food labelling requirements, in particular for frozen meat, frozen meat preparations and frozen unprocessed fishery products.[75] This indication should be preceded by the words 'frozen on …', accompanied by the date itself, consisting of the day, month and year of freezing, in that order and in uncoded form.

7.1.6. Indications of Origin

There are two main types of origin marking on food labels. Both are controversial. The first, which is examined in more detail here, relates simply to the place of production. Statements on the label, such as 'Irish smoked salmon' or 'EU honey' are both examples of this first type of origin indication. They are contentious because they are often deceptive. 'Irish smoked salmon' may not actually have been mostly produced in Ireland. It could come from elsewhere and may only have been 'smoked' in Ireland. Shortcomings in the law as it stands facilitate the deception of consumers who may prefer locally or nationally produced food in some circumstances.[76] However, this has now been addressed to a significant degree by

---

[72] All these stipulations are set out in Reg 1169/2011, n 4 above, Annex X.1(a)–(c).

[73] Ibid, Annex X.

[74] Ibid, Annex X.1(d). The exemption for fresh fruit and vegetables does not apply for sprouting seeds and similar products. These must display a durability date.

[75] Reg 1169/2011, n 4 above, Annex X.3 in conjunction with Annex III.6.

[76] For example, in 2016, Aldi supermarkets were found to be marketing farmed Scottish smoked salmon as wild Irish smoked salmon which, according to the retailer's Christmas brochure had been 'caught in the estuaries of Ireland'. The retailer later admitted to this deceptive description and it was reported that they claimed that they had made 'a descriptive error'. See www.irishtimes.com,

the introduction of new meat origin labelling requirements by the Food Information Regulation. This is discussed further below.

The second type of origin indication on food, the geographical indication, is
assessed in much more detail in the next chapter. All that needs to be said here,
therefore, is that this type of labelling disclosure relates to foods that have been
registered for protection throughout the EU and potentially beyond, because they
have satisfied the decision-making authorities that they possess special characteristics that distinguish them from other similar products. Registered geographical
food names can only be used by those producers who are covered by the terms
of the registration. This is usually a group of producers who all obtain their
ingredients and operate within a clearly defined geographical area, possibly manufacturing their wares using traditional or alternative methods of production. There
are relatively few Irish food names protected under this scheme.

The first type of origin marking, which is within the scope of this chapter and
which is directly legislated for in the Food Information Regulation, is the statement about where a foodstuff has been produced, such as 'Made in …' or 'Product
of …'. This can often be the most misleading piece of information to appear on
food labels, either by giving the false impression that a product has been made in
a place and/or with ingredients from that place, or by the total absence from the
label of any meaningful information about the place of provenance at all.[77]

The Food Information Regulation provides that indication of the country of
origin or place of provenance shall only be mandatory

> where failure to indicate this might mislead the consumer as to the true country of
> origin or place of provenance of the food, in particular if the information accompany-
> ing the food or the label as a whole would otherwise imply that the food has a different
> country of origin or place of provenance [and] for meat falling within the Combined
> Nomenclature codes listed in Annex XI.[78]

These meats referred to in the latter part of this extract include that from pigs,
poultry, sheep and goats. To be clear about this, origin labelling is therefore only
mandatory, under the terms of the Regulation, where the product is either a

---

19 December 2016. There are many reports about the presentation of fish, in particular, as being
'produced in Ireland', when in reality only one part of the production process, such as packaging, actually took place in Irish territory. Fish are often also presented as being both 'fresh' and 'Irish' when,
in reality, they may be from as far away as Asia or South America, frozen and later defrosted to be
marketed as if 'fresh'. Displaying Irish symbols or the Irish flag in a prominent position on the labelling is a particularly deceptive practice used in the marketing of some products as Irish when only
one, often relatively insignificant, part of the process has taken place in Ireland. This situation persists
despite the existence of some labelling requirements for fish set by Art 4(1) of Council Regulation (EC)
No 104/2000 of 17 December 1999 on the common organisation of the markets in fishery and aquaculture products [2000] OJ L 17/22.

[77] It has been held in the English courts that the sale of American-made 'Greek' yoghurt in England
and Wales 'plainly involves a material misrepresentation' and was therefore passing off. A permanent
injunction against the sale of this product was thus granted by the court in *FAGE UK Ltd v Chobani
UK Ltd* [2013] EWHC 630.

[78] Reg 1169/2011, n 4 above, Art 26(2).

particular type of meat or where the labelling and/or packaging would be misleading otherwise. Since the BSE crisis, beef has already had its own specific labelling requirements.[79]

Meat and Dairy Origin Labelling Requirements

The Preamble to the Food Information Regulation states that '[…] the origin of meat appears to be consumers' prime concern'.[80] It was therefore decided to introduce more stringent rules on origin labelling for pig, sheep, goat and poultry meat. The Food Information Regulation also included an undertaking for the Commission to submit reports on the introduction of mandatory rules for origin labelling for meats, milk and other products,[81] as well as conducting impact assessments on the requirements already introduced for pig, sheep, goat and poultry meat, leading to the introduction of implementing acts providing more, or possibly fewer, origin labelling requirements for meats from these latter sources.[82] All of these changes and possible future changes, are discussed below.

While the Food Information Regulation introduced the general obligation to provide origin indications on the meat from specified animals, it also provided for the necessary introduction of implementing acts which would set out what these new labelling obligations would involve.[83] A Regulation was thus introduced in 2013, with an application date of April 2015, to provide for this.[84] The Regulation obliges all food business operators involved in the production and marketing of the specified meats to have full traceability systems in place, to ensure that the link between each meat and the animals from which it has been produced can be readily identified at each stage in the process.[85] Article 5 of the Regulation sets different origin labelling requirements for each type of animal covered by the legislation. This includes details about the country that the animal was 'reared in',[86]

---

[79] Reg (EC) 1760/2000 of the European Parliament and of the Council establishing a system for the identification and registration of bovine animals and regarding the labelling of beef and beef products and repealing Council Regulation 820/1997 [2000] OJ L 204/1 (in conjunction with Commission Regulation (EC) 1825/2000 laying down detailed rules for the application of Regulation 1760/2000 as regards the labelling of beef and beef products [2000] OJ L 216/8, as amended by Commission Regulation (EC) 275/2007 [2007] OJ L76/12).

[80] Recital 31 of the Preamble to Reg 1169/2011, n 4 above. However, a 2015 Commission Report and a 2013 Eurobarometer taken in advance of this Report, both suggest that there is little appetite for additional mandatory origin indications for either meat or dairy products where this leads to price increases. Both the 2013 Eurobarometer and the 2015 Report are discussed below.

[81] Reg 1169/2011, n 4 above Art 26(5).

[82] Art 26(8).

[83] Art 26(2)(b).

[84] Commission Implementing Regulation (EU) No 1337/2013 of 13 December 2013 laying down rules for the application of Regulation (EU) No 1169/2011 of the European Parliament and of the Council as regards the indication of the country of origin or place of provenance for fresh, chilled and frozen meat of swine, sheep, goats and poultry [2013] OJ L 335/19.

[85] Reg 1337/2013, Art 3.

[86] For pigs, where the animal slaughtered was older than six months then this country should be that in which the last rearing period of at least four months took place; where it is younger than six months

the country that it was 'slaughtered in' and the batch code. Where the minimum period requirements for rearing have not been met in any one State then a disclosure should appear on the label that indicates that the animal was 'reared in several Member States of the EU' or 'reared in several non-EU countries', or a combination of the two where appropriate.[87] The indications on place of rearing and slaughter can be combined into a simple expression of 'origin', followed by the name of the State in question, where the food business operator can prove to the competent authority that the meat referred to has been obtained from animals born, reared and slaughtered in a single EU Member State or third country.[88] Due to their nature, a range of derogations are set for minced meat and trimmings, which may come from several different animals, from several different locations. Designations like 'Origin: EU' or 'Reared and slaughtered in EU' can therefore be used where these products have been produced from meat obtained from animals from several different countries.[89] Any of these disclosures on the origin of meat can be supplemented by food business operators with some additional indications concerning the provenance of the product.[90] Where this option is taken up, any additional disclosures must, of course, comply with the more general food labelling requirements established by the Food Information Regulation, in particular that it should not mislead the consumer in any way,[91] nor should it cause ambiguity or confusion.[92] These provisions of the Food Information Regulation and the related implementing Regulation, are given full applicability in Irish law through the European Union (Origin Labelling of Meat) Regulations 2015.[93] The Irish Government also intends to extend these origin labelling requirements to non-prepackaged meats covered by the Regulations as well, such as those which are sold across the counter in butchers' shops and supermarkets, as it is permitted to do under the terms of Article 44 of the Food Information Regulation.

Since the coming into force of the Food Information Regulation, the Commission has followed-up on its obligation to report on the possibilities available for providing additional mandatory information on the provenance of other types of

---

but weighing at least 80kg, then the country listed should be that where it was reared after reaching 30kg in weight; or where under six months of age at time of slaughter and under 80 kg live weight, then the country listed on the label should be that where the entire rearing took place. For sheep and goats, the rearing country is that where the last rearing period of at least six months took place, unless the animal was younger than six months at slaughter, in which case it should be the country where all rearing took place. Finally, for poultry the rearing country is that in which the last rearing period of at least one month took place, unless the bird was younger than one month at time of slaughter, in which case the State listed should be that in which the whole rearing period after the animal was placed for fattening took place. This is all set out in Reg 1337/2013, Art 5(1)(a)(i)–(iii).

[87] Ibid, Art 5(1). Alternatively, the actual States may be listed if the food business operator can prove this to the national competent authorities, usually the Department of Agriculture, Food and the Marine.

[88] Ibid, Art 5(2).

[89] Ibid, Art 7.

[90] Ibid, Art 8.

[91] As established by Reg 1169/2011, Arts 7 and 36(2)(a).

[92] Ibid, Art 36(2)(b).

[93] SI No 113/2015.

meat and dairy produce.[94] According to this report, a Eurobarometer survey from 2013, published in 2014, found that most EU citizens consider it necessary to indicate the origin of milk, either when sold as such or when used as an ingredient in other dairy products.[95] An even higher amount of those interviewed (88%) were of the opinion that the origin of meats, other than those already accounted for by the Food Information Regulation, should be labelled. However, opinion was divided as to what sort of information should be provided to address this, such as whether the place indicated on the label should be that where the milk was transformed into dairy produce (77%) or whether it should relate to where the milking was actually done (68%) – meaning that consumers, perhaps surprisingly, are more interested in the place of transformation than in the place of milking.[96] The types of information preferred by consumers was even more diverse for meats, with the majority seeing disclosures on the place where the animal was raised (83%), followed by the place where it was slaughtered (62%) and the place where the animal was born (47%). Overall, for milk and dairy, 73 per cent of EU consumers felt that country of origin was important, rising to 80 per cent for Irish consumers specifically. For other meats, 88 per cent of EU and 89 per cent of Irish consumers felt that it was necessary to be able to identify the origin of these products. There is clearly a stated desire amongst consumers, both in Ireland and across the EU, to have origin indications on food produced from animals. The preference is also clearly for the country of origin rather than the more specific region of origin.[97]

Eurobarometer and similar types of survey have, across the years, suggested that many consumers have a strong interest in the quality of foodstuffs. The Eurobarometer on origin indications, for example, found that the quality of a product was a significantly more determining factor than either price, origin or brand. For dairy products, 54 per cent (45% for Ireland specifically) of those surveyed stated that quality was the primary factor which influenced their purchasing decisions, followed by price (22%; 29% for Ireland) and origin (16%; 17% for Ireland). The quality of a product was an even more pronounced factor in purchasing decisions for meat, with 56 per cent (48% for Ireland) of those questioned stating that this was the most significant issue for them, followed by origin (20%; 25% for Ireland)

---

[94] Report from the Commission to the European Parliament and to the Council regarding the mandatory indication of the country of origin or place of provenance for milk, milk used as an ingredient in dairy products and types of meat other than beef, swine, sheep, goat and poultry meat. COM (2015) 205.

[95] Special Eurobarometer 410 on Europeans, Agriculture the Common Agricultural Policy, March 2014. Available at: ec.europa.eu/public_opinion. According to the survey, 84% of those interviewed felt that the origin of milk and dairy should be indicated on food labels and 91% of Irish consumers felt that there should be origin indications of some kind on milk and dairy products.

[96] Having said this, in some EU Member States, including Ireland, consumers were more interested in the place of milking (79%) than in the place of transformation (67%).

[97] 81% of Irish respondents thought that the country of origin indications for milk and dairy were important, with only 33% seeing the region of origin as significant. 75% of EU consumers felt that the country of origin was an important disclosure (83% for Ireland), falling to 52% wanting information more specifically on the region (41% for Ireland).

and price (18%; 19% for Ireland). The origin of meat and dairy could not really be described as a highly significant factor for most consumers, with quality being clearly the key consideration. Having said that, this is not always borne out in actual purchaser decision-making. The evidence often suggests that price may be a far more significant issue than the Eurobarometer suggests. For example, the sale of 'free range' and 'organic' chickens in Ireland accounts for only around 2 per cent of the market when compared with those produced on intensive holdings. It is possible also that the origin of meats and dairy are more influential than the surveys suggest. But cost and price remain key. The Eurobarometer also found that only half of consumers would be willing to pay an additional 1–2 per cent to cover the cost of more comprehensive origin information on meat and dairy products.

Having assessed the various options for additional labelling on the origin of foods and the costs and regulatory burdens attached to the implementation of these, the Commission Report found that in many cases it may not be worth the effort and effect of introducing the suggested provenance requirements.[98] Voluntary origin information was already presented on many food labels and consumers could, it was suggested, already opt for these products if they so wished. This would impose no additional burden on industry. Key to this finding was the fact that consumers' overall willingness to pay for this information was modest, despite their stated interest in its presentation. This would be further complicated in those areas where there was little milk production, either as a primary product or for use as a food ingredient, as this could lead to escalating costs due to increased traceability requirements. Finally, the Report also found that consumers did have a preference for Member State level mandatory origin labelling, if it were to be introduced, rather than these disclosures being made on an EU/non-EU basis, despite the higher cost of implementing the former. Overall, consumers say that they want more, specific, information – but they do not want to have to pay, possibly even modest amounts, for it. It is likely, therefore, that meat and dairy origin labelling requirements will mostly remain as they are until these priorities change, or until a food safety crisis demands it.

7.1.7. Labelling Exemptions

Despite the relatively comprehensive coverage of food labelling regulations, the way in which these laws are often applied means that food labels can regularly omit, conceal or mislead on the significant information that they are supposed to impart. In some circumstances, the law provides that certain foods sold to consumers do not have to disclose anything on the label at all. This can lead to difficulties, especially when many of those foods that are exempt from some of the labelling requirements are often high in fat, sugar and/or salt content. National authorities may wish to reduce the consumption of these in the interests of improving health.

---

[98] COM (2015) 205, n 94 above.

However, the law may not readily facilitate them in ensuring that this inclusion is disclosed to consumers. A properly informed choice cannot therefore be made in the circumstances.

Most of the provisions of the Food Information Regulation do not apply to non-prepackaged foods – for the obvious reason that if they have no packaging then they can have no label attached. Article 44 of the Regulation provides that only those ingredients that are likely to cause allergic reactions in vulnerable consumers must by clearly identified, whether included in packaged or non-prepackaged form.[99] Nutrient declarations are not required for these products, meaning that many unhealthy foods automatically escape the need to disclose a high sugar, fat or salt content, particulrly foods produced for immediate consumption, such as those produced and sold in bakeries, cafés and restaurants. Where a nutrition declaration is provided for non-prepackaged food then, under the terms of Article 30(5) of the Food Information Regulation, this can be limited either to information on the energy value or the energy value together with the amounts of fats, saturates, sugars and salt present. However, as stated, Article 44 of the Regulation makes it clear that only allergen information has to be provided.[100] For all of the other mandatory labelling requirements, such as the ingredients, the durability date and the nutrient declaration, there is no obligation on food business operators to provide this information '[…] unless Member States adopt national measures requiring the provision of some or all of those particulars or elements of those particulars'.[101] While in some ways consumer empowerment is limited by the omission of non-prepackaged foods from those which are obliged to carry all, or at least the most significant, labelling requirements, the inclusion of this opportunity for Member States to introduce their own measures on this marks a significant and deliberate loosening of the rules. The Food Information Regulation specifically provides that:

> [m]ember States may adopt national measures concerning the means through which the particulars specified […] are to be made available and, where appropriate, their forms of expression and presentation.[102]

Member States must still inform the Commission about any such measures that they wish to adopt but, most significantly, the option is open to them to introduce information obligations for non-prepackaged foods.[103] Similar provision was not made in the original framework food labelling directives.[104]

---

[99] This is set out in Art 44(1)(a) of the Regulation. The importance of including this allergen information for all foodstuffs is highlighted by Recital 48 of the Preamble to the Regulation, which states that '[e]vidence suggests that most food allergy incidents can be traced back to non-prepacked food [and] therefore information on potential allergens should always be provided to the consumer'.

[100] Food Information Regulation, n 4 above, Art 44(1)(a).

[101] Ibid, Art 44(1)(b).

[102] Ibid, Art 44(2).

[103] Ibid, Art 44(3).

[104] Art 24 of Dir 2000/13 did provide that '[m]ember States shall ensure that the Commission receives the text of any essential provision of national law which they adopt in the field governed by this Directive'. However, the Directive was quite specifically limited in scope to prepackaged foods and

Some prepackaged foods are also exempt from some of the mandatory labelling requirements set out in the Food Information Regulation. Two of these exemptions have been set out earlier in this chapter – those related to ingredient listing and durability dates. A number of other foods are also exempt from the obligation to include the mandatory nutrition declaration on the label. This includes unprocessed single-ingredient products, processed single-ingredient products where the only process undergone has been maturing, waters including those that have been carbonated and/or have only had flavourings added, herbs, spices, salts, tabletop sweeteners, coffees, teas, fermented vinegars, flavourings, additives, processing aids, enzymes, gelatine, jam-setting compounds, yeast, chewing gum, foods in packages that have a largest surface area of 25 cm squared and local or handcrafted foods produced in small quantities and supplied directly to consumers.[105] Controversially, it also includes alcoholic drinks containing more than 1.2 per cent by volume of alcohol.[106] This controversy and the steps that are being taken to address it, is discussed in more detail in Chapter 9.

7.2. Nutrition Labelling and Claims

Requirements relating to the disclosure of the nutritional value of foods did not exist until the introduction of an EU directive on the matter in 1990.[107] Nutrition and health claims made on foods were not the subject of specific regulation until 2006.[108] Prior to this, they were only subject to the general and less certain, requirement that they should not be misleading in any way.[109] Nutrition labelling remained voluntary, unless a nutrition or health claim was made. However, as already alluded to earlier in this chapter, this changed during 2016 when the presentation of nutrient declarations became compulsory for the labelling of all pre-packaged foodstuffs, subject to some limited exceptions.

7.2.1. Nutrition and Health Claims

One of the more significant legislative developments to have taken place in relation to food labelling has been the introduction of regulations controlling the

---

no mention is made of applying any of the mandatory labelling requirements to non-prepackaged food. Provision was not made for labelling requirements disclosing the presence of allergens in non-prepackaged food in the terms of amending Directive 2003/89, [1989] OJ L 308/15, either.

[105] Reg 1169/2011, n 4 above, Annex V.

[106] Reg 1169/2011, n 4 above, Art 16(4).

[107] Council Directive 1990/496/EEC of 24 September 1990 on nutrition labelling for foodstuffs [1990] OJ L 276/40.

[108] Regulation (EC) No 1924/2006 of the European Parliament and of the Council of 20 December 2006 on nutrition and health claims made on foods [2007] OJ L 12/3.

[109] As originally set out in Art 2(1) of Dir 1979/112, n 1 above.

use of nutrition and health claims. It was recognised that an increasing number of foods for sale across the EU bore some sort of statement indicating that the product possessed properties that may be beneficial to health.[110] This absence of specific legal provisions designed to address the use of spurious claims meant that there was plenty of scope for these statements to remain either deliberately false of without substantiation. Consumers needed protecting from unscrupulous producers who were using concerns over the link between diet and health to create new or additional markets for their products. Some of these products had no or negligible additional health benefits.

Apart from the need to protect consumers, who may be deceived into purchasing and possibly paying a premium for products that carried nutrition or health claims, there was also a threat posed to the free movement of goods across the EU as Member States applied their own, often differing, laws to counter misleading claim-making. This could have a direct impact on the functioning of the internal market. It would also distort competition. A combination of these factors led to the belief that harmonised EU rules were thus required to regulate the use of claims.[111]

Defining 'Claims'

The Nutrition and Health Claims Regulation covers a broad range of statements or suggestions made on food labelling. 'Claims' are defined in the Regulation as:

> any message or representation, which is not mandatory under [EU] or national legislation, including pictorial, graphic or symbolic representation, in any form, which states, suggests or implies that a food has particular characteristics.[112]

A 'nutrition claim' is that which:

> states, suggests or implies that a food has particular beneficial nutritional properties due to [the energy (calorific value) it provides; provides at a reduced or increased rate; or does not provide; and/or the nutrients or other substances it contains; contains in reduced or increased proportions; or does not contain].[113]

Essentially, a nutrition claim is made where there is any suggestion on the label that the food contained inside has an altered calorie or nutrient content. 'Health claims', on the other hand, are those which suggest that there is a relationship between a food and good health.[114] Nutrition and health claims may only be used if they comply with the terms of the Regulation.[115] They may never be false, ambiguous or misleading; give rise to doubts about the safety and/or the nutritional adequacy of other foods; encourage or condone excess consumption of a food; suggest or imply

[110] Preamble to the Nutrition and Health Claims Regulation, n 108 above, Recital 1.
[111] Ibid., Recital 2.
[112] Reg 1924/2006, n 108 above, Art 2(2)(1).
[113] Ibid, Art 2(2)(4).
[114] Ibid, Art 2(2)(5).
[115] Ibid, Art 3.

that a balanced or varied diet cannot provide appropriate quantities of nutrients in general; or refer to changes in bodily functions which could cause fear amongst consumers.[116]

Nutrient Profiles

The Nutrition and Health Claims Regulation works on the basis that the Commission, using comitology, establishes a set of 'nutrient profiles' with which foods must comply before a claim can be made.[117] These are meant to be calculated after consideration of the quantities of nutrients and other substances, such as fats and sugars, that are contained in the food. Nutrient profiles are to be based on scientific knowledge about the relationship between diet and health. They are to be set following consultation with the European Food Safety Authority, food business operators and consumer groups. They can, of course, be updated based on scientific developments. Again, comitology is to be used to make any necessary amendments. Unfortunately, this aspect of the Nutrition and Health Claims Regulation has still not been properly addressed at this time of writing. Nutrient profiles were due to be set by January 2009. This did not happen. A review of the Regulation was formally launched in October 2015. It was due to be completed by June 2017.[118]

Nutrition claims that make reference to reduced levels of fat, trans-fat, sugar or salt are allowed without reference to a profile for the nutrient concerned.[119] Controversially, nutrition claims can also be made where a single nutrient, such as fat or sodium, exceeds that permitted by the profile, provided that a statement to this effect appears beside the claim.[120] This means, for example, that a food

---

[116] Ibid.

[117] Ibid, Art 4(1).

[118] See European Commission, 'Evaluation of (a) Regulation (EC) No 1924/2006 on nutrition and health claims made on food with regard to nutrient profiles and health claims made on plants and their preparations and of (b) the general regulatory framework for their use in foods'. Available at: http://ec.europa.eu/smart-regulation/roadmaps/docs/2015_sante_595_evaluation_health_claims_en.pdf.

[119] Reg 1924/2006, n 108 above, Art 4(2)(a). The CJEU has found that natural mineral waters cannot mention that they are low in sodium or salt, or that they are suitable for a low-sodium diet, if the sodium content is above 20mg/l, regardless of the chemical form of the sodium contained in the product. The sodium content of water must be calculated on the basis of sodium chloride, added to the amount of sodium bicarbonate present. In reaching this conclusion, the Court was of the opinion that consumers could be misled where only one chemical form of sodium was used in making these calculations. See Case C-157/2014 *Neptune Distribution v Ministre de l'Economie et des Finances* ECLI:EU:C:2015:823.

[120] Reg 1924/2006, n 108 above, Art 4(2)(b). The EU Commission can, however, refuse to authorise a health claim where the product for which an application is made carries significant unhealthy properties or the appearance of the claim on the product would portray a contradictory and ambiguous message, as was the case for the application made by Dextro Energy for its glucose tablets. Both the General Court, in the first instance and the Court of Justice, on appeal, upheld the Commission's decision, despite an initial positive opinion provided by EFSA. To allow the health claim to be made here would, in the opinion of both courts, be contrary to generally accepted nutrition and health principles due to the high sugar content of the glucose tables. See Case C-296/2016 *Dextro Energy GmbH & Co KG v Commission* ECLI:EU:C:2017:437.

that is high in sugar may still carry a nutrition claim if it is also high in some other nutrient, such as vitamin C. This is controversial because it means that foods that overall may be considered as being 'unhealthy' can, in some circumstances, still carry nutrition claims, which suggest that it is actually 'healthy' to consume them.[121] This mostly unsatisfactory situation has been allowed to persist on the basis that full nutrient declarations on the labelling of foods carrying nutrition or health claims will disclose the fact that these products contain high levels of potentially undesirable nutrients, where this is the case. However, it should be noted that it would probably be very difficult to make the system for nutrition and health claims fully workable if this sort of allowance was not facilitated, but it should also be stated that this does inevitably lead to the inappropriate use of claims on some food products. Any drink that has an alcohol content above 1.2 per cent can never carry a health claim.[122] They may, however, carry nutrition claims, such as 'low alcohol', 'reduced alcohol' or 'reduced calories'. The Commission, using comitological procedures, is free to add to the list of foods upon which restrictions on the use of claims may be placed.

Conditions for the Use of Claims

The use of nutrition and health claims is only permitted if certain conditions are fulfilled. First, the presence or absence of a nutrient about which a claim is made must have been shown to have some beneficial nutritional or physiological effect. This must be supported by generally accepted scientific evidence.[123]

Second, the nutrient concerned must also be contained in the finished product in a quantity that is enough to provide the defined benefit to the consumer. This level is determined by that set in EU legislation, where such exists. Otherwise, scientific evidence must show that the amount of the nutrient contained in the food will have a positive effect on human health.[124] Of course, claims can also be made about the absence of a particular nutrient such as fat or energy and the benefits that this may have for consumers. Similar evidence must also be provided to support these claims, showing that the level by which this nutrient has been reduced is beneficial.[125]

---

[121] For other criticisms of the way in which the Nutrition and Health Claims Regulation has come to work, see A Bast et al, 'Scientism, legalism and precaution: Contending with regulating nutrition and health claims in Europe' (2013) 8 *European Food and Feed Law Review* 401; P Coppens, 'Regulation (EU) No 432/2012 establishing a list of permitted health claims' (2012) 7 *European Food and Feed Law Review* 162; and B Haber and A Meisterernst, 'Proposals for a revision of Regulation (EC) 1924/2006' (2011) 6 *European Food and Feed Law Review*.

[122] Reg 1924/2006, n 108 above, Art 4(3).

[123] Ibid, Art 5(1)(a). For further discussion on the types of health claims that can be made, see B Klaus, 'Restriction of use for health claims in regard to water: Interpretation in conformity with the EU law' (2012) 7 *European Food and Feed Law Review* 251.

[124] Reg 1924/2006, n 108 above, Art 5(1)(b)(i).

[125] Ibid, Art 5(1)(b)(ii).

The third condition is that nutrients that are the subject of a claim must be present in the food in a form that can be properly used by the body.[126] It must be capable of being absorbed and transformed in a manner that benefits health. Another requirement relates to the fact that the quantity of the product that can reasonably be expected to be consumed must provide sufficient amounts of the nutrient about which the claim is made.[127] These first four conditions are set for the valid use of all claims. Additional requirements are also established for health claims specifically. These include prescribed statements that must appear on the labelling.[128] For example, there must be a statement indicating the importance of a varied and balanced diet. The quantity of the food that must be consumed for a benefit to be derived should be indicated. Where required, there should also be disclosures about the dangers of excessive consumption of the food in question. Some types of health claim can never be made.[129] Producers are prohibited from making a statement to the effect that health could be affected by not consuming the food. References to amounts of weight loss are not permitted.

Finally, the use of nutrition and health claims is only permitted if the 'average consumer', as defined in EU law, can be expected to understand the beneficial effects as expressed in the claim.[130] The 'average consumer' is categorised as being 'reasonably well informed and reasonably observant and circumspect'.[131] Nutrition and health claims must always relate to the food as it is to be consumed, according to the manufacturer's instructions.[132]

Scientific Substantiation and Authorisation

All nutrition and health claims must be based, in one way or another, on generally accepted scientific evidence.[133] Any 'food business operator' who makes a claim about their products must be able to justify this use.[134] It is up to the competent authorities in each EU Member State to require that these operators produce all of the necessary data to support any claims that they make and to ensure that they comply with their other obligations set out in the Regulation.[135] The competent

---

[126] Ibid, Art 5(1)(c).

[127] Ibid, Art 5(1)(d).

[128] Ibid, Art 10.

[129] Ibid, Art 12.

[130] Ibid, Art 5(2).

[131] As most recently set out by the Court of Justice in para 22 of its judgment in Case C-421/2013 *Apple Inc v Deutsches Patent- und Markenamt*, ECLI:EU:C:2014:2070. Also set out previously in, amongst many others, para 41 of the judgment in Cases C-53–55/2001 *Linde and others* [2003] ECR I-3161. For further discussion on the classification of 'consumers' in food law see M Zboralska, 'Trap of stereotypes: The EU model of a consumer' (2011) 6 *European Food and Feed Law Review* 283.

[132] Reg 1924/2006, n 108 above, Art 5(3).

[133] Ibid, Art 6(1).

[134] Ibid, Art 6(2).

[135] Ibid, Art 6(3).

authority responsible for this is the Food Safety Authority of Ireland.[136] The conditions that must be met before a claim can be made depend on the type of claim that is being made.

Nutrition claims can be made if they are one of those listed in the Annex to the Regulation and if they comply with all of the other terms of the legislation as well.[137] Examples of this type of nutrition claim include 'low fat' which, under the terms set out in the Annex, can only be used where the product contains no more than 3 g of fat per 100 g for solids, or 1.5 g of fat per 100 ml for liquids (with the exception of semi-skimmed milk, which can contain up to 1.8 g of fat per 100 ml). A product can only claim to be 'fat-free' where it contains no more than 0.5 g of fat per 100 g or 100 ml. Most significantly, claims that a product is 'X per cent fat-free' are now, quite rightly, prohibited. Foods that were relatively high in fat content could previously carry such a claim – they could have a fat level of 10 per cent yet could be marketed as being '90 per cent fat-free'! Other examples of permitted nutrition claims set out in the Annex to the Regulation include 'high fibre', which can only appear where the product contains at least 6 g of fibre per 100 g. A food can be described as a 'source of fibre', however, if it contains only 3 g of fibre per 100 g.

The list set out in the Annex can be amended under the comitology procedure, usually after consultation with EFSA.[138] The Commission can also call upon interested parties, such as food business operators and consumer groups, to assist it in establishing perceptions about nutrition claims and evaluating the degree to which they are readily understood.

Health claims, which must be based on generally accepted scientific evidence and which must also be easily understood by the average consumer,[139] may only be made if authorised. This can happen in two ways. First, under the terms of the Regulation, Member States were free to provide the Commission with lists of health claims and accompanying scientific substantiation by 2008.[140] Once received and following consultation with EFSA and use of the comitology procedure, these lists would be combined to form a 'Community list' of permitted claims and any conditions of use.[141] Changes can, of course, be made to this list, again using comitology and following consultation with EFSA, either on the initiative of the Commission or following a request by a Member State.[142] However, health claims that make

[136] Regulation 4 of the European Union (Nutrition and Health Claims made on foods) Regulations 2014, SI No 11/2014.
[137] Reg 1924/2006, n 108 above, Art 8(1).
[138] Ibid, Art 8(2).
[139] Ibid, Art 13(1).
[140] Ibid, Art 13(2).
[141] Ibid, Art 13(3).
[142] Ibid, Art 13(4). Under the terms of Art 18 of Reg 178/2002, n 12 above, a food business operator who wishes to have a health claim included on the approved list can make an application for this through their national competent authority, such as the FSAI. The request is then made by the Member State where the competent authority deems it appropriate to do so. EFSA assesses the application. The Commission then decides whether to include the claim on the list, usually based on the EFSA opinion.

reference to a reduction in the risk of contracting a disease, or which refer to the health or development of children, may not avail of the list scheme.[143] This type of claim is strictly subject to the second way in which these can be authorised – the formal procedure set out in the Regulation.

Formal Authorisation Procedure for Health Claims

All health claims that are not on the pre-approved list must first be authorised for use following a Commission decision, usually based on an EFSA opinion. Applications for any such authorisation must initially be made to the national competent authority of a Member State; the FSAI in Ireland. The FSAI, or other relevant authority, must then inform EFSA about this application.[144] EFSA is then obliged to relay this information to all other Member States, to the Commission and to the public.[145] Applications should contain information relating to the applicant, the beneficial nature of the health claim, copies of all relevant studies and proposed wording for the claim.[146] Both the Commission and EFSA are obliged, under the terms of the Regulation, to provide technical assistance to food business operators and in particular small and medium-sized enterprises, in preparing applications for authorisation.[147]

It must be remembered that EFSA does not authorise the use of health claims, it only provides an opinion prior to formal authorisation by the Commission in consultation with the Standing Committee on Plants, Animals, Food and Feed.[148] This opinion must be provided within a time limit of five months from the date of receipt of a valid application.[149] This can be extended by up to two months where the provision of additional information is requested by EFSA from the applicant. EFSA must verify that the health claim is properly substantiated by scientific evidence and that the wording of the proposed claim is in compliance with the criteria laid down in the Regulation.[150] Once made, the opinion of EFSA is then forwarded to the Commission, the Member States and the applicant.[151] This should be accompanied by a report describing the assessment that was made of the application and the reasons and information upon which it was based. The opinion

[143] Ibid, Arts 13 and 14.
[144] Ibid, Art 15(2)(a).
[145] Ibid, Art 15(2)(b).
[146] Ibid, Art 15(3).
[147] Ibid, Art 15(5).
[148] For more on this relationship between EFSA and the Commission in the context of health claims, see M Hagenmeyer and A Hahn, 'EFSA's secret health claims' (2013) 8 *European Food and Feed Law Review* 10.
[149] Reg 1924/2006, n 108 above, Art 16(1).
[150] Ibid, Art 16(3).
[151] Ibid, Art 16(5).

must also be made public.[152] The applicant or the public may make comments on the opinion to the Commission within 30 days of its publication.[153]

As stated above, the actual decision on whether to authorise the use of the health claim rests with the Commission, although it usually follows the opinion presented by EFSA.[154] The Commission has two months from the date of the EFSA opinion to provide the Standing Committee with a draft decision.[155] It must also provide an explanation of its decision where this differs from that of EFSA.[156] A final decision on the application must then be adopted using comitology.[157] The Commission must then immediately inform the applicant of the decision taken.[158] It must also be published in the Official Journal. Once approved, a health claim can be used by any food business operator,[159] subject to data protection provisions.[160] All approved health claims can, of course, be modified, suspended or revoked at any time following an EFSA opinion and Commission decision.[161] Records of all approved and authorised nutrition and health claims and the conditions attached to their use, are detailed on a community register.[162] These are listed online (nutrition claims, authorised health claims and rejected health claims),[163] in the annex to Regulation 1924/2006 (nutrition claims) and in individual regulations, such as Regulation 665/2011 (health claims).[164]

Most EU food legislation introduced after the publication of the White Paper on Food Safety in 2000 carries safeguard measures. The Nutrition and Health Claims Regulation is no different in this regard. It permits Member States to suspend the use of any claim where it has grounds for considering that it does not comply with the terms of the Regulation, or that it has been validated with insufficient supporting scientific evidence.[165] Of course, it must inform the other

---

[152] Ibid, Art 16(6). This must happen with all such EFSA opinions in accordance with the terms of Art 38(1) of Reg 178/2002, n 12 above.

[153] Ibid, Art 16(6).

[154] For a more detailed analysis of this, see A Alemanno, 'The European Food Safety Authority before European Courts: Some reflections on the judicial review of EFSA scientific opinions and administrative acts' (2008) 5 *European Food and Feed Law Review* 320.

[155] Reg 1924/2006, n 108 above, Art 17(1).

[156] Ibid.

[157] Reg 178/2002, n 12 above, Arts 17(3) and 25(2).

[158] Ibid, Art 17(4).

[159] Ibid, Art 17(5).

[160] Ibid, Art 21.

[161] Ibid, Art 19.

[162] As established by Reg 1924/2006, n 108 above, Art 20.

[163] Available at: http://ec.europa.eu/food/food/labellingnutrition/claims/community_register/index_en.htm.

[164] Commission Regulation (EU) No 665/2011 of 11 July 2011 on the authorisation and refusal of authorisation of certain health claims made on foods and referring to the reduction of disease risk [2011] OJ L 182/5. This Regulation authorised the use of health claims related to the beneficial effects of chewing sugar-free gum. Annex I to the Regulation permits use of the claim that 'sugar-free chewing gum helps neutralise plaque acids'.

[165] Reg 1924/2006, n 108 above, Art 24(1).

Member States and the Commission about any such action and the reasons for it. As with other aspects of this Regulation, an EFSA opinion is sought before a Commission decision is made on the appropriateness of the action taken by the Member State.[166] However, the Commission may also initiate this procedure on its own initiative when it so chooses.[167] The Member State is entitled to maintain the suspension until any decision has been made and notified by the Commission.[168]

European Union (Nutrition and Health Claims Made on Foods) Regulations 2014

It was emphasised in Chapter 2 that EU directives must be formally transposed into Irish law, but EU regulations do not require this. They automatically become part of Irish law once published and from the date that they enter into force.[169] They are thus directly applicable in the Member States. However, some form of domestic legislation is often required to provide further detail on those aspects of the application of the Regulation that are particular to the individual Member State concerned. The European Union (Nutrition and Health Claims made on foods) Regulations 2014 provide such details here.[170]

These 2014 Regulations weave and contextualise the EU Nutrition and Health Claims Regulation into Irish law. They link the EU Regulation to various provisions of the Food Safety Authority of Ireland Act 1998.[171] They establish the Food Safety Authority of Ireland as the designated national competent authority.[172] Penalties are set.[173] Offences are outlined,[174] as is the role of authorised officers ensuring that the terms of the Nutrition and Health Claims Regulation are complied with.[175]

7.3. Labelling Codes of Conduct and Practice

There are a series of codes of practice and standards that directly impact upon food labelling and food advertising in Ireland. These codes set non-binding parameters within which various operators in the food sector should act. They provide guidelines for producers and retailers about the ways in which they should go about producing and marketing their wares. They are often created in the hope

---

[166] Ibid, Art 24(2).
[167] Ibid.
[168] Ibid, Art 24(3).
[169] Article 29 of the Nutrition and Health Claims Regulation provides that it is to enter into force from 1 July 2007, approximately six months after its publication in December 2006.
[170] SI No 11/2014.
[171] Reg 2(1) of the Irish Regulations 2014.
[172] Ibid, Reg 4.
[173] Ibid, Reg 33.
[174] Ibid, Regs 5–18 and 30–32.
[175] Ibid, Regs 22, 23 and 25–28.

that they will lead to a modification in behaviour that reduces or eliminates the need to introduce binding legislation. They may also exist because EU law prevents domestic legislators from introducing new laws that create some direct or indirect impediment to the free movement of food.

7.3.1. Advertising Standards

The European Communities (Misleading Advertising) Regulations 1988 set the legal boundaries within which goods, amongst other things, can be represented to potential buyers.[176] An advertisement is deemed to be misleading if it

> deceives or is likely to deceive the persons to whom it is addressed or whom it reaches and which, by reason of its deceptive nature, is likely to affect their economic behaviour or which, for those reasons, injures or is likely to injure a competitor.[177]

Advertising in Ireland is largely self-regulated. The Advertising Standards Authority of Ireland (ASAI), whose core objective is ensuring that all commercial marketing communications are 'legal, decent, honest and truthful', as set out in the seventh edition of the Code of Standards for Advertising and Marketing Communications in Ireland,[178] is a self-regulatory body that was set up and financed by, the advertising industry. All members of the ASAI are required to abide by the Advertising Code. The ASAI Code acknowledges that '[c]hildren lack adults' knowledge, experience and maturity of judgement [and therefore] marketing communications addressed directly or indirectly to children, or [which are] likely to be seen or heard by a significant proportion of them, should have regard to the special characteristics of children and the ways in which they perceive and react to marketing communications'.[179] Section 8 of the Code deals specifically with the advertising and marketing of food and non-alcoholic beverages. It states that the rules set out in this section of the Code must be read in conjunction with the EU Food Information Regulation,[180] and the Nutrition and Health Claims Regulation,[181] noting that the use of these claims is therefore already subject to meeting the conditions set

---

[176] SI No 134/1988.
[177] As originally set out in Art 2(2) of Council Directive 1984/450/EEC of 10 September 1984 relating to the approximation of the laws, regulations and administrative provisions of the Member States concerning misleading advertising, [1984] OJ L 250/17. The 1988 Irish Misleading Advertising Regulations, n 176 above, state in the Explanatory Note that the Regulations should be read together with Directive 1984/450. The 1984 Directive has since been replaced by Directive 2006/114/EC of the European Parliament and of the Council of 12 December 2006 concerning misleading and comparative advertising, [2006] OJ L 376/21. Art 2(b) of the 2006 Directive defines misleading advertising in exactly the same way as in the original version.
[178] Section 3.2. thereof.
[179] Section 7.2 of the ASAI Code of Standards for Advertising and Marketing Communications in Ireland, 7th edn, which came into effect on 1 March 2016. Available at: www.asai.ie.
[180] Reg 1169/2011, n 4 above.
[181] Reg 1924/2006, n 108 above.

out in the latter regulation.[182] However, the Code also notes that the use of some types of claims continue to operate in a transitional phase and that these should be subject to the provisions of the 2006 Regulation and this edition of the Code. As a result, all marketing communications for food, including those related to nutritional and/or health advice, should not encourage or condone excess consumption or unhealthy habits.[183] While there is further discussion on the use of portion sizes as an indicator of nutrient content in Chapter 9 of this book, it should be noted here that section 8.7. of the ASAI Code goes some way to addressing how quantity declarations should be made on food products in stating that:

> [m]arketing communications for food representing any material characteristics of the product, including size and content, should be accurate and should not mislead consumers concerning any of those characteristics, or the intended use of the product.

This presents us with the requirement that labelling should not be misleading in any way in another format yet, as will be seen from the discussion on this issue in Chapter 9, this remains an underused obligation that, if properly utilised, could go some way to addressing some of the health-related and legal difficulties that arise when using food labelling as part of the package of measures needed to address ongoing concerns about obesity and diet-related disease. Rules on the labelling, marketing and advertising of alcoholic drinks and the role of this in dealing with non-communicable disease, are also discussed in more detail in Chapter 9.

In general, advertising can be controlled in two ways – either it is unlawful because it is misleading and therefore contravenes the 1988 Regulations, or it is presented in a manner that is contrary to the Advertising Standards Authority of Ireland code. There is also a role here for the Broadcasting Authority of Ireland (BAI). The BAI has, for example, developed the Children's Commercial Communications Code, as part of its statutory obligations set by the Broadcasting Act 2009.[184] This Code, which is discussed in more detail below, applies to the commercial promotion of products that are deemed to be of particular interest to children, including foods that are high in fat, sugar or salt. The BAI is also obliged to undertake statutory reviews of the effectiveness of the Children's Code.[185] The first of these is due during 2018–2019.

An obligation is also set out in the Television Without Frontiers Directive,[186] requiring EU Member States such as Ireland to take positive action to protect

---

[182] Section 8.8 of the Code makes it clear that only those claims that are authorised by and listed in, the Nutrition and Health Claims Regulations can be used in food marketing communications in Ireland. Section 8.10 further provides that any claims that are legitimately made must also be '[....] presented clearly and without exaggeration'.
[183] Section 8.4. of the Code, n 179 above.
[184] Section 42 of the Broadcasting Act 2009 provides that: '[t]he Authority shall prepare and from time to time as occasion requires, revise, in accordance with this section, a code or codes governing standards and practice to be observed by broadcasters'.
[185] As also set out in s 42 of the Broadcasting Act 2009, n 184 above.
[186] Council Directive 1989/552/EEC of 3 October 1989 on the coordination of certain provisions laid down by law, regulation or administrative action in Member States concerning the pursuit of television broadcasting activities [1989] OJ L 298/23.

children from the harmful effects of advertising.[187] This is, of course, subject to the requirement established in EU law that any restriction on the freedom to provide services must be both necessary and proportionate.[188]

Advertising of Food and Drink to Children

Obesity is a growing problem. Research suggests that many cases of adult obesity are determined by habits developed during childhood.[189] While this epidemic is dealt with in more detail in Chapter 9, the fact that the Department of Health has clearly identified television advertising as an area where action should be considered to restrict the promotion of foods with a high fat, salt and/or sugar content to children, is more appropriately considered here.

A national Obesity Policy and Action Plan was launched by the Department of Health in 2016.[190] This plan covers the period up to 2025. Its primary aim is to reduce growing rates of obesity, non-communicable diseases and other negative consequences arising out of diet and activity-related poor health. The Plan includes the establishment of a number of bodies and areas of action which, it is hoped, will help to achieve these aims. The Department of Health has, for example, set up an Obesity Policy Implementation Oversight Group, which also includes representatives of the Departments of Agriculture, Children and Youth Affairs, Employment and Social Protection, Education, Housing, Planning and Local Government, University College Cork, the Food Safety Authority of Ireland, the Health Service Executive and Safefood. Practical measures adopted include the introduction of an additional tax on sugar-sweetened drinks, the launch of a childhood obesity campaign, the adoption of new healthy eating guidelines, setting new nutrition standards for foods and developments in the HSE that are designed to facilitate early intervention in childhood obesity. Accompanying all of this is the Healthy Ireland Campaign, which was briefly discussed in Chapter 3. A key part of this overall strategy, designed to combat ever-rising rates of obesity in Ireland, has been the delivery of codes of practice on the advertising and marketing of food and non-alcoholic beverages. The most recent of these was launched in February 2018.

First published in December 2017, the voluntary codes of practice on the marketing of food and non-alcoholic drinks, cover a broad range of advertising media, including sponsorship and retail product placement, digital media,

---

[187] Ibid, Art 16.

[188] As held in cases such as Case 33/1974 *Van Binsbergen v Bestuur Van de Bedrijfsvereniging voor de Metaalnijverheid* [1974] ECR 1299; Case C-180/1989 *Commission v Italy* [1991] ECR I-709; and Case C-198/1989 *Commission v Greece* [1991] ECR I-727.

[189] See, eg, T Parsons, C Power, S Logan and C Summerbell, 'Childhood predictors of adult obesity: A systematic review' (1999) *International Journal of Obesity* 23; and W Dietz 'Health consequences of obesity in youth: Childhood predictors of adult disease' (1998) 101 *Pediatrics* 518.

[190] Department of Health, 'A healthy weight for Ireland: Obesity policy and action plan 2016–2025', ISBN: 9781406429268. Also available at: www.health.gov.ie.

print media and cinemas.[191] These codes do not extend to most broadcast media, which are covered by other, pre-existing, codes.[192] The Codes are all voluntary arrangements, which are to be entered into freely by those companies and partner organisations who choose to do so.[193] By their voluntary nature and by their content, the Codes can remain outside the scrutiny of any legal challenge related to the fact that they may present an impediment to the free movement of goods, as prohibited by Article 34 TFEU. The Codes primarily relate to 'selling arrangements', meaning that they should not in the first instance come within the remit of Article 34 TFEU, following the decision of the European Court of Justice in *Keck* ([1993] ECR I-6097). However, it should also be noted that any feature of the Codes that can give rise to an impediment to access to the Irish market, be this through limitations placed on advertising or perhaps sponsorship, that prejudices producers from other EU Member States, then this could potentially give rise to legal issues under Article 34 TFEU,[194] which may also, of course, be justifiable under the terms of Article 36 TFEU on the grounds that the Codes are necessary for the protection of human health.[195] The Codes are to be monitored for both compliance and effectiveness by a monitoring body, designated by the Minister for Health. This Body should also hear complaints raised in relation to the operation of the Codes.[196]

Children are defined by the Codes as being anyone under the age of 18. However, children's media are deemed to be those which are created specifically for people under the age of 15 and/or those whose audience or user profile consists of 50 per cent or more of this age group. As far as advertising and sponsorship aimed at children are concerned, the Code sets voluntary requirements for all 'HFSS' foods.

HFSS foods are those which are deemed to be high in fat, sugar and/or salt, as determined by the nutrient profile set out in the BAI General and Children's Commercial Communications Codes. As far as these foods are concerned, all marketing communications should not be made through children's media. The Code goes on to state that:

> [i]n circumstances where the marketing/media platform is not self-evidently targeted at children or where adequate audience data is not available, every reasonable effort should be made to act with a sense of responsibility to both the consumer and society

---

[191] Department of Health, 'Non-broadcast media advertising and marketing of food and non-alcoholic beverages, including sponsorship and retail product placement: Voluntary codes of practice', December 2017. Available at: www.health.gov.ie.

[192] Most significantly, the ASAI Code of Standards for Advertising and Marketing Communications in Ireland, n 179 above and the BAI Children's Commercial Communications Code, August 2013.

[193] Section 10.1. of the 2017 Code, n 191 above.

[194] As originally set out by the Court of Justice in Cases C-34, 35 and 36/1995 *De Agostini* [1997] ECR I-3843.

[195] For more on this see ch 4.

[196] Section 10.2. of the 2017 Code, n 191 above.

[while] account should [also] be taken of such factors as the channels of placement, the content and the overall impression of the marketing communication.[197]

Underlining the call to refrain from some forms of marketing HFSS foods to children is the extension of restrictions to marketing communications that are carried outside of children's media but which are still targeted at children. These should never include: '[l]icensed characters and celebrities popular with children in any communication for a HFSS food', nor should they involve promotions or competitions. In addition to this, age-filters should be used on internet websites and social media applications where they exist to ensure, as far as is possible, that HFSS foods are not advertised to children under the age of 15.[198] Nor should e-mails or short message services be used in this way. In general, social media should not be used to communicate marketing of HFSS foods to children under 15. Even where the marketing of these foods is permitted it should not exceed 25 per cent of the total advertising space. Finally, as far as electronic media are concerned, the websites of food businesses should not carry content that is designed to engage children with HFSS brands, be this through, for example, videos, cartoons or interactive features.

The 2017 Non-broadcast Media Code also places a number of restrictions on the use of 'out of home media', including billboards, hoardings, public transport shelters, the interior or exterior of buses or trains and building banners. A maximum of 33 per cent of the available space in these forms of media should be used for communications and advertising of HFSS foods.[199] Large roadside billboards advertising these foods should not appear within 100 meters of a school gate.[200] This is deemed to be even more pertinent for those billboards that are advertising HFSS foods to children. There is an outright restriction on the use of marketing communications for HFSS foods on building banners.

The Codes contain relatively extensive provisions of the advertising and marketing of HFSS foods. In addition to the clear requirements set out above on the use of electronic and out of home media, there are also a range of stipulations set for print media. These include an obligation to refrain from advertising HFSS foods in any publications that are not overwhelmingly read by adults. Marketing communications for HFSS foods should only be carried in consumer publications where the adult readership is 75 per cent or greater.[201] This extends to any supplements or advertising inserts circulated with publication. Those publications which can carry HFSS advertisements should limit these to 25 per cent of the total advertising space.[202] Similarly, where marketing communications for HFSS food

---

[197] Ibid, Section 7.1.
[198] Ibid, Section 7.2.
[199] Ibid, Section 7.3.1.
[200] 'Large' billboards are deemed to be those that are over 48 sheet (1.2m x 1.8m) sizes. This 100-metre restriction is reduced to 60 metres where 60 sheets are used in the advertisement. This is all set out in section 7.3.2. of the 2017 Code.
[201] Ibid, Section 7.4.1.
[202] Ibid, Section 7.4.2.

is permissible on cinema screens, this also should not exceed a maximum of 25 per cent of the total advertising space per film screening.[203] HFSS food sponsorship of sports pages or sports supplements is not allowed.[204]

Extensive restrictions on the use of sponsorship by HFSS products are also set out in the 2017 Code. These include outright prohibitions on the such sponsorship at any setting dedicated to use by children of primary school age or of events of particular appeal to this cohort.[205] The Code is also quite prescriptive on the product placement of HFSS foods in Irish retail outlets, including the provision, where possible, of HFSS food free cash register checkout lanes; active promotion of the consumption of adequate amounts of fruit and vegetables; providing offers that promote a healthy and balanced diet; and the use of calorie labelling information for food that is not packaged, such as that made available at delicatessens and hot food counters.[206]

The ASAI Code also deals with the advertising of food and non-alcoholic drinks to children. It provides that marketing communications for food and beverages that are addressed to children should not denigrate a healthy lifestyle, nor should they encourage an unhealthy one, always indicating clearly the role of the product concerned within the framework of a balanced diet.[207] They should not mislead children as to the potential benefits from consumption of the product, either physically, socially or psychologically. Marketing that features a promotional offer should '[...] be prepared with a due sense of responsibility'.[208] Promotional offers should not be targeted directly at pre-school or primary school children, except where these are for fresh fruit and vegetables, or where they are permitted under the terms of the BAI Children's Commercial Communications Code, or they are made at point of sale displays, or on packages, labels, tickets or menus.[209] Promotions aimed at children under the age of 16 should not encourage children to eat or to purchase excessively.[210] Finally, licensed characters and celebrities who are popular with children should only be used in marketing where they meet a similar set of conditions to those listed for promotions.[211]

The Broadcasting Authority of Ireland (BAI) Children's Commercial Communications Code sets out a series of standards to be implemented when advertising, sponsorship, product placement and any other forms of commercial promotion are aimed at children, or which are delivered during commercial advertising breaks between children's programmes. It also includes rules on the promotion of HFSS foods that are high in fat, salt or sugar. As stated, the development of this

[203] Ibid, Section 7.5.1.
[204] Ibid, Section 7.4.3.
[205] Ibid, Section 8.
[206] Ibid, Section 9.
[207] Ibid, Sections 8.16–8.18. Nutrition and health claims aimed at child development and the advertising of vitamin and mineral supplements are permitted, provided these comply with the relevant EU legislation.
[208] Ibid, Section 8.19.
[209] Ibid, Section 8.20.
[210] Ibid, Section 8.21.
[211] Ibid, Section 8.22.

Code forms part of the BAI's statutory obligations under the terms of the Broadcasting Act 2009.

The objectives of the BAI Code are deemed to be the protection of children from inappropriate and/or harmful communications, especially considering the special susceptibilities of children, ensuring that this is not exploited and ensuring that commercial communications are fair and present products and services in an easily interpreted and realistic way. While the Code defines a 'child' as anyone under the age of 18, it also recognises that children of different ages require different levels of protection.

Part 11 of the Code deals specifically with diet and nutrition. It provides a range of requirements for children's commercial communications in this regard, including that these should be responsible in the manner in which food is portrayed; they should not encourage an unhealthy lifestyle, eating or drinking habits; they should not contain any misleading or incorrect information about the nutritional value of a product; and they should not imply that particular foods are a substitute for fruit and/or vegetables. Stricter guidelines are set for commercial communications for HFSS foods, including placing prohibitions on their appearance in children's programmes; on the use of licensed characters in their promotion; on the use of nutrition and health claims; and the use of promotional offers. The former two prohibitions are set for all commercial communications for HFSS foods aimed at children under the age of 18; the latter two are set for those aimed at children under the age of 13.

Separate requirements are also set by the Code for fast food and confectionery. All commercial communications for fast food products and which are aimed at children must carry a message stating that this food 'should be eaten in moderation and as part of a balanced diet'. Similarly, advertisements for confectionery products and sugar-based soft drinks should include a message that 'snacking on sugary foods and drinks can damage teeth'.

There are a series of general obligations that apply to all food and drink advertisements aimed at children. These include a prohibition on the use of sports stars and celebrities in such promotions, unless the communication is part of a public health or education campaign. Celebrities are defined as being '[…] persons who are widely acclaimed, or honoured and/or known to children' but this does not extend to persons or characters that have become known to children directly because of their appearance in commercials. Characters and personalities from children's programmes should not be used to promote HFSS foods to children either.

7.4. Quality and Composition Labelling

Food laws, since the very earliest times, have prescribed what can and cannot be used as ingredients in the manufacturing of certain products.[212] Some of the initial

---

[212] See ch 1.

EU laws specified the minimum compositional requirements for some foods. These are known as 'recipe laws' and their application in Irish law is discussed in more detail below. Setting harmonised EU-wide minimum standards for food has, however, become much less commonplace since the famous decision of the Court of Justice in *Cassis*.[213] Despite this, some important vertical compositional and quality standards remain, applying to a single food, such as honey, or to a single category of food, such as fruit juices.

7.4.1. European Communities (Marketing of Honey) Regulations 2003

During the 1970s, the EEC, as it then was, introduced a series of directives setting compositional requirements for a list of specified foodstuffs. These directives were designed to harmonise standards across all Member States for each of the products concerned in order to facilitate the free movement of these foods and, to a lesser extent, to ensure that consumers were protected by setting absolute minimum standards. This list of foods included chocolate,[214] coffee,[215] jams,[216] fruit juices[217] and honey.[218] All of these original directives have since been updated and transposed into Irish law.

The European Communities (Marketing of Honey) Regulations 2003 set domestic compositional requirements,[219] giving effect to harmonised EU law in this area.[220] 'Honey' is defined as:

> the natural sweet substance produced by ... bees from the nectar of plants or secretions of living parts of plants or excretions of plant-sucking insects on the living parts of plants, which the bees collect, transform by combining with specific substances of their own, deposit, dehydrate, store and leave in honeycombs to ripen and mature.[221]

---

[213] Case 120/1978 *Rewe-Zentral AG v Bundesmonopolverwaltung für Branntwein* [1979] ECR 649, as discussed in ch 4.

[214] Council Directive 1973/241/EEC of 23 July 1973 on the approximation of the laws of the Member States relating to cocoa and chocolate products intended for human consumption [1973] OJ L 228/23.

[215] Council Directive 1977/436/EEC of 27 June 1977 on the approximation of the laws of the Member States relating to coffee extracts and chicory extracts [1977] OJ L 172/20.

[216] Council Directive 1979/693/EEC of 24 July 1979 on the approximation of the laws of the Member States relating to fruit jams, jellies and marmalades and chestnut pureé [1979] OJ L 205/5.

[217] Council Directive 1975/726/EEC of 17 November 1975 on the approximation of the laws of the Member States concerning fruit juices and certain similar products [1975] OJ L 311/40.

[218] Council Directive 1974/409/EEC of 22 July 1974 on the harmonisation of the laws of the Member States relating to honey [1974] OJ L 221/10.

[219] SI No 367/2003. These Regulations replace the Food Standards (Honey) (European Communities) Regulations 1976, SI No 155/1976. They have also been amended by the European Communities (Marketing of Honey)(Amendment) Regulations 2015, SI No 261/2015 to take account of the amendments introduced at European Union level by Directive 2014/63/EU, [2014] OJ L 164/1.

[220] As now set out in Council Directive 2001/110/EC of 20 December 2001 relating to honey [2002] OJ L 10/47, as amended by Dir 2014/63, n 219 above.

[221] As set out in Annex I to Directive 2001/110, n 220 above. Regulation 2(2) of the Irish Regulations, n 219 above, provides that '[a] word or expression which is used in these Regulations and which is also

Under the terms of these Regulations use of the name 'honey' is limited to those who comply with the compositional and labelling requirements set out. These include providing labelling particulars that accurately describe the product and give details of its origin.[222] The fact that much of the honey that is sold to consumers is blended is also reflected in the origin labelling requirements. These provide that 'the country or countries of origin where the honey has been harvested' must be listed.[223] However, where the honey originated in more than one EU Member State or third country, this can be replaced with a statement that it is a blend of EC, or non-EC, or a combination of EC and non-EC, honeys. Several different types of honey are defined in Directive 2001/110.[224] These include 'comb honey', 'blossom honey', 'baker's honey' and 'filtered honey'. The sale of 'baker's honey', which 'may have a foreign taste or odour, have begun to ferment or have fermented, or have been overheated', must be accompanied by a labelling disclosure that it is 'intended for cooking only' and it must be listed in the ingredients of a finished product as such. Fines can be imposed on those who contravene the labelling provisions of the 2003 Irish regulations.[225] Offences can be prosecuted by the office of the Minister for Agriculture, Food and the Marine, the Competition and Consumer Protection Commission (originally done by the Director of Consumer Affairs, then by the National Consumer Agency, both since replaced) or the Health Service Executive.[226]

7.4.2. European Communities (Marketing of Cocoa and Chocolate Products) Regulations 2003

Just what can be called 'chocolate' and its other forms such as 'milk' and 'dark', has been the subject of much debate since EU legislators first introduced a directive on the matter in 1973.[227] The problem first arose because Ireland, along with the UK and Denmark, were about to become members of the European Economic Community. Chocolate produced these new Member States tended to be made with a higher milk content and lower cocoa content than that traditionally produced in existing Member States, such as Belgium and France. Irish and British chocolate was also often made with vegetable fats instead of cocoa butter, which was used

---

used in the Council Directive has, unless the contrary intention appears, the same meaning as it has in the Council Directive'. This is the case for the transposition of most EU food directives into Irish law. In English law, the domestic transpositions there tend to apply their own, modified, definitions. In Irish Law, the transpositions are much more likely to simply make a direct reference to the relevant EU directives.

[222] Dir 2001/110, n 220 above, Art 2 and the Irish Regulations 2003, n 219 above, Reg 4(1).
[223] Dir 2001/110, n 220 above, Art 2(4)(a).
[224] Annex 1 thereto.
[225] Fines of up to €3,000 can be imposed under the terms set out in the Irish Regulations 2003, n 219 above, Reg 9(1).
[226] Ibid, Reg 9(2).
[227] Dir 1973/241, n 214 above.

elsewhere. These other States insisted that the Irish variety of 'milk chocolate', for example, should instead be called 'milk chocolate with high milk content'. Ireland, along with the UK, disagreed and were granted an exemption.[228] Thirty years of debate and proposed compromise ensued.

The controversy over the high milk, low cocoa and vegetable fat content of Irish and British chocolate was finally resolved with the introduction of a new EU directive in 2000.[229] This allowed for the derogation provided for the UK and Ireland in the 1973 directive to be maintained. However, the name 'milk chocolate with high milk content' was to be replaced with the name 'family milk chocolate', when this product (20 per cent dry cocoa, 20 per cent dry milk) was sold elsewhere in the EU. It could still be labelled as 'milk chocolate' when sold in Ireland.[230] The use of vegetable fats other than cocoa butter would also be permitted, subject to a maximum of 5 per cent of the finished product.[231]

The EU Chocolate Directive 2000 is transposed into Irish law by the European Communities (Marketing of Cocoa and Chocolate Products) Regulations 2003.[232] The Directive defines 'chocolate' as:

> [...] the product obtained from cocoa products and sugars which ... contains not less than 35% total dry cocoa solids, including not less than 18% cocoa butter and not less than 14% of dry non-fat cocoa solids.[233]

'Milk chocolate' is defined as:

> [...] the product obtained from cocoa products, sugars and milk or milk products which ... contains not less than 25% total dry cocoa solids ... 14% dry milk solids ... 2.5% dry non-fat cocoa solids, 3.5% milk fat [and] 25% total fat (cocoa butter and milk fat).[234]

'Family milk chocolate' has the exact same compositional requirements as 'milk chocolate' except for the fact that the total cocoa solids quantity can be reduced to 20 per cent, the milk solids increased to 20 per cent and the milk fat increased to 5 per cent. The Annex to the Directive clarifies that the names 'milk chocolate' and 'family milk chocolate' are interchangeable in Ireland once the minimum compositional requirements for family milk chocolate (the 20/20 formula) are met.[235]

---

[228] Ibid, Art 3(1).

[229] Directive 2000/36/EC of the European Parliament and of the Council of 23 June 2000 relating to cocoa and chocolate products intended for human consumption [2000] OJ L 197/19. For discussion on more recent updates in the case law in this area, see F Capelli and B Klaus, 'Chocolate can also be made from pure cocoa but one should be careful how to communicate this on the label' (2011) 6 *European Food and Feed Law Review* 88.

[230] Dir 2000/36, n 229 above, Annex I.

[231] Ibid, Art 2(1).

[232] SI No 236/2003. These Regulations replace the Food Standards (Cocoa and Chocolate Products) (European Communities) Regulations 1975, SI No 180/1975.

[233] Dir 2000/36/EC, n 229 above, Annex 1(a)(3). As with the Honey Regulations, the Irish Chocolate Regulations simply refer us to the Directive for these legal definitions.

[234] Ibid, Annex 1(a)(4).

[235] Ibid, Annex 1(a)(4)(d). This provides that: '[t]he United Kingdom and Ireland may authorise the use in their territory of the name 'milk chocolate' to designate [family milk chocolate] on condition

While vegetable fats other than cocoa butter may be used in chocolate products, this is limited to those which are specifically listed in Annex II to the Directive. Vegetable fats permitted for use are therefore restricted to oils from palm, shea, mango kernel, illipe, sal and kokum gurgi, only up to 5 per cent of the finished product. Coconut oil can be used in the manufacture of ice cream and other similar frozen products. Chocolate can only be marketed as such if it complies with the domestic Regulations,[236] in conjunction with the provisions of the EU Directive. Failure to comply with this can lead to the imposition of a fine on summary conviction.[237] Again, the office of the Minister for Agriculture, Food and the Marine, the Competition and Consumer Protection Commission and the Health Service Executive are charged with prosecuting under these Regulations.[238]

7.4.3. European Communities (Marketing of Coffee Extracts and Chicory Extracts) Regulations 2000

The Coffee Regulations are really only designed to deal with compositional and labelling requirements for extracts, such as instant coffee.[239] Only water can be used to extract the product from roasted coffee beans.[240] 'Instant coffee' (dried coffee extract), as defined in the Annex to Directive 1999/4/EC, must contain '[…] coffee-based dry matter [which] is not less than 95% by weight [and] no substances other than those derived from the extraction of coffee'. As with the other compositional regulations, coffee extract products must be labelled and described in accordance with the provisions of these rules,[241] and failure to do so can lead to the imposition of a fine.[242] Finally, the ways in which the decaffeination of coffee is permitted are set out in the Health (Extraction Solvents in Foodstuffs) Regulations 1995.[243] Part 2 of the Schedule to the Regulations provides that the substances methyl acetate, ethylmethylketone and dichloromethane can

---

that the term is accompanied in both cases by an indication of the amount of dry milk solids laid down for each of the two products, in the form of 'milk solids: … %minimum'. This allowance is also specifically referred to in Regulation 4(3) of the European Communities (Marketing of Cocoa and Chocolate Products) Regulations 2003, n 232 above.

[236] SI No 236/2003, Reg 4.

[237] Ibid, Reg 7(3).

[238] Ibid, Reg 7(2).

[239] SI No 281/2000 transposes Directive 1999/4/EC of the European Parliament and of the Council of 22 February 1999 relating to coffee extracts and chicory extracts [1999] OJ L 66/26 into Irish law. These Regulations replace the European Communities (Coffee Extracts and Chicory Extracts) Regulations 1982, SI No 295/1982, as amended by SI No 102/1988.

[240] Annex to Dir 1999/4/EC, n 239 above.

[241] SI No 281/2000, n 239 above, Regs 4 and 5.

[242] Ibid, Reg 8.

[243] SI No 283/1995, replacing the Health (Extraction Solvents in Foodstuffs) Regulations 1993, SI No 387/1993.

all be used in the decaffeination of coffee, subject to set maximum residue limits of 20 mg per kg, or just 2 mg per kg in the case of dichloromethane.[244]

7.4.4. European Union (Marketing of Fruit Juices and Certain Similar Products) Regulations 2013

These 2013 Irish Regulations give effect to a 2001 EU directive on standards for fruit juices and nectars.[245] The EU directive was itself amended on several occasions, most recently in 2012.[246] These EU Directives define 'fruit juice' as:

> [t]he fermentable but unfermented product obtained from the edible part of fruit which is sound and ripe, fresh or preserved by chilling or freezing of one or more kinds mixed together having the characteristic colour, flavour and taste typical of the juice of the fruit from which it comes.[247]

Juice used must come from the endocarp, or inner part, of the fruit. Where fruit juice is 'concentrated', at least 50 per cent of the water content must have been removed. However, 'fruit juice from concentrate' is:

> [t]he product obtained by reconstituting concentrated fruit juice [...] with potable water that meets the criteria set out in Council Directive 98/83/EC on the quality of water intended for human consumption. Flavour, pulp and cells obtained by suitable physical means from the same species of fruit may be restored to the fruit juice from concentrate. The mixing of fruit juice and/or concentrated fruit juice with fruit purée and/or concentrated fruit purée is authorised in the production of fruit juice from concentrate.

Authorised vitamins, minerals and, in some cases, sugar or honey may be added to fruit juice.[248] Fruit juice cannot be sold in Ireland unless it meets these standards set out in the EU Directives and the 2013 Irish Regulations.[249] Any offence

---

[244] These requirements and those for the use of extraction solvents in food production more generally, are now also set out in Directive 2009/32/EC of the European Parliament and of the Council of 23 April 2009 on the approximation of the laws of the Member States on extraction solvents used in the production of foodstuffs and food ingredients, [2009] OJ L 141/3. This Directive is transposed into Irish law by the European Communities (Extraction Solvents used in the Production of Foodstuffs and Food Ingredients) Regulations 2010, SI No 119/2010, as amended by SI No 129/2011.

[245] Council Directive 2001/112/EC of 20 December 2001 relating to fruit juices and certain similar products intended for human consumption [2002] OJ L 10/58, as amended by Directive 2009/106 [2009] OJ L 212/42.

[246] By Directive 2012/12/EU of the European Parliament and of the Council of 19 April 2012 amending Council Directive 2001/112/EC relating to fruit juices and certain similar products intended for human consumption, [2012] OJ L 115/1.

[247] Ibid, Annex I.

[248] Ibid, Annex I.II.2. Any vitamins and/or minerals added would have to have been authorised for such a purpose under the terms of Regulation (EC) No 1925/2006 of the European Parliament and of the Council of 20 December 2006 on the addition of vitamins and minerals and of certain other substances to foods, [2006] OJ L 404/26.

[249] European Union (Marketing of fruit juices and certain similar products) Regulations 2013, SI No 410/2013, Reg 3.

committed under the domestic regulations can be prosecuted by the Minister, the FSAI or the HSE,[250] with the possible imposition of a Class A fine.[251]

7.4.5. European Communities (Marketing of Fruit Jams, Jellies, Marmalades and Sweetened Chestnut Purée) Regulations 2003

Another category of foods covered by the original 'recipe laws' is jams, jellies and marmalades. The last to be introduced before the Court of Justice decision in *Cassis*, the 1979 directive related to these products followed a similar format to that used for honey and chocolate.[252] This was transposed into Irish law in 1982,[253] and later replaced by these new regulations in 2003.[254]

'Jam' is defined as:

> […] a mixture, brought to a suitable gelled consistency, of sugars, the pulp and/or purée of one or more kinds of fruit and water […] the quantity of pulp and/or purée used for the manufacture of 1000 g of finished product must not be less than 350g as a general rule, 250g for redcurrants [and] blackcurrants, 150g for ginger [or] 60g for passion fruit.[255]

To be called 'extra jam' the minimum compositional requirements are set at 450 grams for most fruits, such as strawberries and raspberries. 'Marmalade' must contain a minimum of 200 grams of citrus fruit per 1,000 grams of finished product, with at least 75g of this coming from the fruit's endocarp. Minimum compositional standards are also set for chestnut purée and jelly.[256] Only those products that are produced in accordance with the requirements set out in the Regulations can be labelled using any of the names specified.[257] Failure to adhere to these requirements can result in the imposition of a fine, along similar lines to that which was set out in the other Irish transpositions of the EU 'recipe laws'.[258]

---

[250] Ibid, Reg 13(1).

[251] Ibid, Reg 12.

[252] Dir 1979/693, n 216 above. Since replaced by Council Directive 2001/113/EC of 20 December 2001 relating to fruit jams, jellies and marmalades and sweetened chestnut purée intended for human consumption, [2002] OJ L 10/67.

[253] European Communities (Fruit jams, Jellies and Marmalades and Chestnut Purée) Regulations 1982, SI No 250/1982.

[254] SI No 294/2003.

[255] Annex I.I to Dir 2001/113/EC, n 252 above.

[256] This highlights one of the disadvantages of the Irish method of transposing by direct reference to the EU Directive. The transposing English Regulations, for example, use the opportunity to also set standards for similar products that are more commonly available on their market, such as curds and mincemeat. The Directive was transposed into English law by the Jam and Similar Products (England) Regulations 2003, SI No 3120/2003. No similar standards are set by the Irish Regulations.

[257] See the 2003 Irish Regulations, n 254 above, Reg 4.

[258] Ibid, Reg 9.

7.4.6. Baby and Infant Foods

Processed baby and infant foods are subject to a range of additional legislative requirements beyond the usual framework of labelling and compositional rules.[259] The specific hygiene and contaminant provisions relating to these products have already been mentioned in Chapter 6. In Ireland, the European Communities (Infant formulae and Follow-on formulae) Regulations 2007 were designed to give effect to other EU directives in this area.[260] These have since been superseded by a new EU Regulation on food intended for infants and young children, amongst other types of specialised foods.[261] Here, 'Infant formula' is defined as:

> [...] food intended for use by infants during the first months of life and satisfying by itself the nutritional requirements of such infants until the introduction of appropriate complementary feeding.[262]

'Follow-on formula' means:

> [...] food intended for use by infants when appropriate complimentary feeding is introduced and which constitutes the principal liquid element in a progressively diversified diet of such infants.[263]

Finally, 'baby food' is that which is:

> [...] intended to fulfil the particular requirements of infants in good health while they are being weaned and of young children in good health as a supplement to their diet

---

[259] Voluntary advertising restrictions for these products are set out in sections 8.30–8.33 of the ASAI Code, n 179 above. Primarily, the Code provides that these should be read in conjunction with the European Communities (Infant Formulae and Follow on Formula) Regulations 2007, n 260 below. They also provide that marketing communications for infant formula are prohibited unless they appear in scientific publications, pre-retail trade publications or publications which are not really intended for general readership. Follow-on formulae can be advertised to the general public, but only where this is designed to provide information about their use and where this does not discourage breast-feeding. These products should also never use terms such as 'humanised', 'maternalised', 'adapted' or similar words or phrases in their descriptions.

[260] SI No 852/2007, giving partial effect to Commission Directive 2006/141/EC of 22 December 2006 on infant formulae and follow-on formulae and amending Directive 1999/21/EC, [2006] OJ L 401/1. Also giving further effect to Council Directive 92/52/EEC of 18 June 1992 on infant formulae and follow-on formulae intended for export to third countries, [1992] OJ L 179/129.

[261] Regulation (EU) No 609/2013 of the European Parliament and of the Council of 12 June 2013 on food intended for infants and young children, food for special medical purposes and total diet replacement for weight control and repealing Council Directive 92/52/EEC, Commission Directives 96/8/EC, 1999/21/EC, 2006/125/EC and 2006/141/EC, Directive 2009/39/EC of the European Parliament and of the Council and Commission Regulations (EC) No 41/2009 and (EC) No 953/2009, [2013] OJ L 181/35. 'Infants' are defined in Art 2(2)(a) of the Regulation as being '[...] a child under the age of 12 months'. Art 2(2)(b) provides that 'young children' are those '[...] aged between one and three years'.

[262] Reg 609/2013, n 261 above, Art 2(2)(c). It was similarly defined in the previous applicable legislation, as set out in Art 2(c) of Commission Directive 2006/141/EC of 22 December 2006 on infant formulae and follow-on formulae and amending Directive 1999/21/EC, [2006] OJ L 401/1.

[263] Reg 609/2013, n 261 above, Art 2(2)(d).

and/or for their progressive adaptation to ordinary food [but] excluding processed cereal-based food and milk-based drinks and similar products intended for young children.[264]

All foods, including infant, follow-on and baby foods, which are covered by Regulation 609/2013 must also comply with all other relevant aspects of EU food law.[265] However, the requirements set down for these foods in this Regulation prevail over any other conflicting provision of EU food law.[266] These include a series of specific additional labelling, presentation and advertising requirements for infant and follow-on formulae. The new EU Regulation on infant and special foods, replacing the previous body of directives, was formally incorporated into Irish law by the Food Safety Authority of Ireland Act 1998 (Amendment of First and Second Schedules) Order 2014.[267] Regulation 609/2013 is itself directly applicable in Irish law.

An 'infant' is defined, under the terms of Regulation 609/2013 as '[...] a child under the age of 12 months',[268] while a 'young child' is that which is aged between one and three years.[269] The additional labelling requirements for formulae that are meant for consumption by infants and young children are set out in Article 10 of the Regulation. The first of these is that the [...] labelling, presentation and advertising of infant formula and follow-on formula shall be designed so as not to discourage breast-feeding'.[270] Nor should the labelling of either type of product '[...] include pictures of infants, or other pictures or text which may idealise the use of such formulae'.[271] However, graphic presentations that enable the easy identification of these products, as well as those which illustrate how these products are to be prepared, are allowed. Article 11 of the Regulation provides for the adoption of additional delegated acts setting out more specific requirements on the labelling, presentation and advertising of all products covered by the legislation, including infant foods, foods for special medical purposes and those for diet replacement and weight control.[272] Most of the requirements for the labelling,

---

[264] Ibid, Art 2(2)(f). 'Processed cereal-based foods' are themselves defined in Art 2(2)(e) as those which are '[...] intended to fulfil the particular requirements of infants in good health while they are being weaned and of young children in good health as a supplement to their diet and/or for their progressive adaptation, to ordinary food and [which are one of] simple cereals [...] reconstituted with milk or other appropriate nutritious liquids, cereals with an added high protein food [...], pastas [or] rusks and biscuits which are to be used either directly or, after pulverisation, with the addition of water, milk or other suitable liquids'.
[265] Reg 609/2013, n 261 above, Art 6(1).
[266] Ibid, Art 6(2).
[267] SI No 390/2014.
[268] Regulation 609/2013, Art 2(2)(a).
[269] Ibid, Art 2(2)(b).
[270] Ibid, Art 10(1).
[271] Ibid, Art 10(2).
[272] Ibid, Art 11(1)(c).

presentation and promotion of infant and follow-on formulae are now set out in this Delegated Regulation.[273]

While infant formula is subject to all the usual labelling requirements as set out in the Food Information Regulation, a set of additional compulsory indications must also always appear. These include a statement that the product is suitable for infants from birth when they are not breast fed; instructions for the appropriate preparation, storage and disposal of the product; and a statement concerning the superiority of breast feed and a recommendation that the product should only be used on the advice of an independent and medically-qualified, or similar, person.[274] This latter statement must be preceded by the words 'important notice' or something similar.

For follow-on formula, the labelling must include a statement that the product is only suitable for infants that are over six months old, that it should only be used as part of a diversified diet, that it should not be used as a substitute for breast milk during the first six months of a baby's life and that any decision to being using this product as part of complementary feeding should only be made on the advice of suitably qualified persons.[275] In an exception to the rules set out for nutrition information set out in the main Food Information Regulation, this information must be presented on all infant and follow-on formulae, regardless of the size of the packaging or container.[276] There is no exemption for small packages. In another derogation from the Food Information Regulation, the energy value and the amount of nutrients in formulae must be expressed per 100 ml of the food as it is ready for use after proper preparation.[277] Nutrition and health claims can never be made on infant formula.[278] It may, however, as may follow-on formula, be labelled as 'lactose free', provided that the lactose level is less than 10 mg per 100 calories.[279]

Several restrictions continue to be placed on the advertising and marketing of infant and follow-on formula, as was the case under the EU Directives and the transposing European Communities (Infant formulae and Follow-on formulae) Regulations 2007. For example, the advertising of infant formula continues to be restricted to scientific publications and those that specialise in baby care.[280] Member States are also free to introduce additional restrictions or prohibitions on

---

[273] Commission Delegated Regulation (EU) 2016/127 of 25 September 2015 supplementing Regulation (EU) No 609/2013 of the European Parliament and of the Council as regards the specific compositional and information requirements for infant formula and follow-on formula and as regards requirements on information relating to infant and young child feeding, [2016] OJ L 25/1. Similar delegated regulations were introduced for diet replacement and weight control foods (Reg 2017/1798, [2017] OJ L 259/2) and food for special medical purposes (Reg 2016/128, [2016] OJ L 25/30).
[274] Reg 2016/127, n 273 above, Art 6(2).
[275] Ibid, Art 6(3)(a).
[276] Ibid, Art 7(4).
[277] Ibid, Art 7(6).
[278] Ibid, Art 8.
[279] Ibid, Art 9(2).
[280] Ibid, Art 10(1).

such advertising if they choose to do so. Regardless of whether they do or not, any advertising of infant formula can only contain scientific information and facts. It cannot suggest or imply that bottle-feeding is in any way equivalent or superior to breast feeding.

Prohibitions also continue on the use of point-of-sale advertising, the giving of samples or any other promotional device designed to induce sales of infant formula directly to the consumer at retail level.[281] This includes the use of special displays, discount coupons, special sales, loss-leaders and tie-in sales. This is extended to include a prohibition on giving out free or low-priced products, samples or promotional gifts, either directly or indirectly through the health care system or health workers.[282] These provisions, set out in the 2016 Delegated Regulation on Infant and Follow-on Formulae, mostly come into effect from February 2020 onwards.[283] As stated, they continue along the same lines as those which existed previously in Ireland, as set out in the 2007 domestic regulations.[284]

7.5. Conclusion

Most of our food labelling laws in Ireland now come from the direct transposition of an ever-growing body of European Union legislative initiatives on the matter. Many of the general compulsory indications applicable for all prepackaged foodstuffs have, however, remained relatively unchanged since the first framework labelling directive of the late 1970s and later transposed into Irish law by the European Communities (Labelling, Presentation and Advertising of Foodstuffs) Regulations 1982.[285] Some significant changes were introduced into Irish law by the EU Food Information Regulation, especially those on origin indications. However, the use of labels to help address public health problems, such as those caused by obesity, have not been so effective. While this issue is discussed in much more detail in Chapter 9, it can still be noted here that one of the primary reasons for introducing the Food Information Regulation was to create compulsory labelling obligations that could assist in improving this issue. In this regard, the Regulation has mostly failed to achieve this objective.

EU food labelling requirements tend to be transposed into Irish law verbatim. This differs from the approach adopted in other EU Member States. While still a member of the Union, the UK has tended to take the primary obligations of EU food labelling directives and adopt them in a more tailored fashion, creating additional obligations and modified definitions where this better suits their own legal system.

---

[281] Ibid, Art 11(2).
[282] Ibid, Art 11(3).
[283] Ibid, Art 14.
[284] See European Communities (Infant formulae and Follow-on formulae) Regulations 2007, n 260 above, in particular Art 8.
[285] SI No 205/1982.

The Irish approach, coupled with EU rules on the free movement of food, creates a difficulty for the State where some public health concern needs addressing through labelling laws. More recently, legislation has been introduced to deal with some of these problems, as is the case with the Public Health (Alcohol) Bill 2015. This unilateral initiative, which is also discussed in more detail in Chapter 9, has proven to be necessary because alcoholic drinks remain largely outside the remit of our other labelling laws. These products do not have to carry some of the indications that are compulsory for other 'foods', such as those on ingredient listing and nutrition information. This continues to be the case, despite recognition at EU level that this would need to be addressed as far back as 1978.

Finally, it could be argued that a combination of EU rules on free movement, international legal obligations and national legislation make it difficult for a State such as Ireland to introduce new labelling laws designed to address national or local concerns. These measures must now usually be adopted at EU level and withstand international scrutiny, before making it on to the statute books. The rules on infant and follow-on formula have shown that this can be done where the will to do so exists. Nowhere in any of the EU regulations does it state, suggest or imply that infant formula and follow-on formula are dangerous products. Yet stringent labelling and marketing conditions have been created for both products. Recital 3 of the Preamble to Regulation 2016/127 states that '[i]nfant formula [...] wholly satisfies the nutritional requirements of infants during the first months of life until the introduction of appropriate complementary feeding'. However, the same stringency is not applied once children move on to 'complementary feeding'. Once the child starts to eat other processed foods he is instantly more susceptible to much of the deliberate misinformation and deception that takes place through the exploitation of gaps which exist in our labelling laws. The labelling on many processed foods is designed to suggest to the purchaser and to the consumer that the product possesses qualities or characteristics that either it does not possess, or which are greatly exaggerated. The labelling laws have always included a general provision that labelling should not be 'misleading' in any way – regardless of which other, more specific, obligations also exist. Yet, despite being more regulated than ever, much of our food labelling is more deliberately deceptive than ever. This is also discussed in more detail in Chapter 9, primarily in the context of the role of labelling in the prevention of non-communicable disease.

8

Protected Food Names

8.1. Geographical Indications

The main European Commission study on geographical indications, published in March 2013, found that foods and drinks produced in the EU that are protected from production or imitation by producers other than those who have registered their products were worth around €54 billion annually.[1] Around one-third of this figure was for foods and agricultural products, the other two-thirds being accounted for by wines and spirits. These protected products account for 15 per cent of the EU's total food and drink exports. The same study found that annual sales of protected geographical foods and drinks were calculated to be worth over €600 million across Ireland. However, unlike many other EU Member States, this figure was based primarily on the sale of protected spirits, with foods accounting for only 5 per cent of the total. To date, Ireland has underused the EU-created scheme for protecting geographical food names, with only seven products gaining protection by 2018.[2] Three of these are Protected Designations of Origin (PDO), with Oriel Sea Salt and Oriel Sea Minerals registered in 2016 and Imokilly Regato in 1999, while the other four are Protected Geographical Indications (PGI), including Waterford Blaa, which was registered in 2013, Connemara Hill Lamb/ Uain Sléibhe Chonamara (2007), Timoleague Brown Pudding (2000) and Clare Island Salmon (1999).[3] Ireland has no registered Traditional Specialities Guaranteed (TSG). The United Kingdom has registered 71 food names for protection, 67 of which are PDOs or PGIs, 4 are TSGs.[4] Some other EU Member States have registered many more than this.

---

[1] AND-International report for the European Commission, 'Value of production of agricultural products and foodstuffs, wines, aromatised wines and spirits protected by a geographical indication'. Available at: ec.europa.eu/agriculture/external-studies.

[2] While this is a relatively low number when compared with some other EU Member States it is similar to some others. Denmark has 7 registered PGIs, Cyprus has 5 registered PGIs and PDOs, while Finland has 10 names registered, 3 of which are TSGs. Neither Estonia nor Malta had registered any names by May 2018. Some of the 'newer' EU Member States have enthusiastically embraced the scheme, with Slovenia, for example, registering 24 names since 2007 and Poland having registered 39 names since 2008. The EU's newest Member State, Croatia, registered 19 names between 2015 and 2018.

[3] Several foods from Northern Ireland have also been registered, including Lough Neagh Pollan (PDO, 2018), Armagh Bramley Apples (PGI, 2012) and Lough Neagh Eel (PGI, 2011).

[4] English foods that have been registered as protected designations of origin (PDO) include Yorkshire forced rhubarb, which was registered in March 2010, Staffordshire cheese, which was registered in

The system devised at EU level for protecting these 'geographical indications' and 'designations of origin' was first established in 1992.[5] When the Court of Justice developed the principle of mutual recognition in February 1979,[6] declaring that a product 'lawfully produced and marketed in one of the Member States' should be marketable in all of the Member States,[7] it essentially created an inter-State market without restrictions as to compositional requirements or methods of manufacture. A producer in one Member State could make cheese, call it whatever he liked, including a geographical name with which his product had no connection, and sell it using that name in any EU Member State. Edam cheese could be made in an EU Member State other than the Netherlands and then trade off the good name of the Dutch version. Provided the producer could call the cheese 'Edam' in the country where it was originally marketed, he could call it that in other States as well – even where the two versions of the product differed from each other in composition, texture and taste. Producers of the original version would have to share, and risk, their goodwill. Consumers could be deceived into purchasing a product, believing that it was, in fact, something else. The introduction of a register for geographical food names sought to remedy this. It arrived, however, too late for some foods, like Edam, where the name had come into such common usage that it would now be deemed to be 'generic' and therefore outside of the preconditions necessary for registration and protection. Many geographical or traditional names, such as Waterford Blaa and Imokilly Regato, are not considered generic. As a result, around 1,500 names had been registered by 2018.

The operation of the scheme for registering geographical and traditional food names has not been without its own difficulties. In 2005 the World Trade Organization found that elements of the EU system for registering and protecting geographical food names were contrary to the Agreement on Trade Related Aspects of Intellectual Property Rights (TRIPs).[8] As was discussed in Chapter 2, it was decided that the equivalence and reciprocity conditions for access to the system established by Regulation 2081/1992 violated the national treatment obligations set out in TRIPs and the General Agreement on Tariffs and Trade (GATT).[9] As a result of this, a new Regulation on the protection of geographical food names had to be introduced by the EU, to replace the original offending legislation.

September 2007, Cornish clotted cream, which was registered in October 1998 and Stilton, which was registered in June 1996. Cornish pasties (2011), Cumberland sausages (2011), Melton Mowbray pork pies (2009), Welsh beef (2002) and Exmoor Blue cheese (1999) have, amongst others, all been registered as protected geographical indications (PGIs). Post-Brexit, these registered foods should still retain their protected status in the EU given (i) the rules provide for the registration of foods from third countries; and (ii) WTO rules under the TRIPs Agreement. There is more on this throughout this chapter.

[5] Council Regulation (EEC) No 2081/1992 of 14 July 1992 on the protection of geographical indications and designations of origin for agricultural products and foodstuffs [1992] OJ L 208/1.

[6] Case 120/1978 *Rewe-Zentral AG v Bundesmonopolverwaltung für Branntwein* (Cassis) [1979] ECR 649.

[7] Ibid, para 14 of the judgment.

[8] DS 174, 290, *European Communities – Protection of Trademarks and Geographical Indications for Agricultural Products and Foodstuffs*.

[9] Art 3.1 TRIPs and Art III:4 GATT.

This 2006 Regulation addressed the concerns that had been raised at WTO level.[10] Otherwise the system remains substantially the same as that originally developed in 1992. The key provisions of the 2006 Regulation have themselves since been incorporated into a new EU Quality Schemes for Agricultural Products Regulation 2012.[11] The law remains relatively unchanged by this newer Regulation, most of which came into effect at the end of 2012. The 2006 regulations have thus been repealed.

8.1.1. Geographical Food Names Regulation

The preamble to the EU Quality Schemes for Agricultural Products Regulation 2012 states that '[c]itizens and consumers in the Union increasingly demand quality as well as traditional products'.[12] This then 'generates a demand for agricultural products or foodstuffs with identifiable specific characteristics, in particular those linked to their geographical origin'.[13] With the introduction of the compulsory indication of the protected status of registered foodstuffs, it is now easier for discerning consumers to make choices that can be based on a consistent level of quality.[14] The presence of the related symbol on labelling informs the consumer, in a clear way, that the product has been manufactured to set minimum standards, and in a specific place. Products must first be registered for protection under the terms of the Regulation before this symbol, or other indication, can be used.

Categories of Protected Geographical Food Name

The EU Quality Schemes for Agricultural Products Regulation 2012 sets out two types of protected geographical food name. These are the designation of origin and the geographical indication. The former is defined as being

> [a] name which identifies a product originating in a specific place, region or, in exceptional cases, a country, whose quality or characteristics are essentially or exclusively due

---

[10] Council Regulation (EC) No 510/2006 of 20 March 2006 on the protection of geographical indications and designations of origin for agricultural products and foodstuffs [2006] OJ L 93/12.

[11] Regulation (EU) No 1151/2012 of the European Parliament and of the Council of 21 November 2012 on quality schemes for agricultural products and foodstuffs [2012] OJ L 343/1, referred to throughout this chapter as the 'EU Quality Schemes for Agricultural Products Regulation 2012'. For a more detailed analysis of this Regulation see M Gragnani, 'The EU Regulation 1151/2012 on quality schemes for agricultural products and foodstuffs' (2013) 8 *European Food and Feed Law Review* 376.

[12] Recital 2 of the Preamble to Reg 1151/2012, n 11 above.

[13] Ibid.

[14] Art 8 of Reg 510/2006 provided that the symbol and/or indication of protected status should appear on the labelling of registered foodstuffs. This was not, under the terms of Art 20 of the Regulation, a compulsory indication until 1 May 2009. The symbols that had to be used were set out in the Annex to Commission Regulation (EC) No 628/2008 of 2 July 2008 amending Regulation (EC) No 1898/2006 laying down detailed rules of implementation of Council Regulation (EC) No 510/2006 on the protection of geographical indications and designations of origin for agricultural products and foodstuffs [2008] OJ L 173/3. Art 12 of Reg 1151/2012 now provides for the establishment of a new symbol, designed to publicise PDOs and PGIs. This provision took full effect in 2016.

to a particular geographical environment with its inherent natural and human factors, and the production steps of which all take place in the defined geographical area.[15]

These 'steps' were identified in the previous regulations as being 'the production, processing and preparation'.[16] The second category, the geographical indication, is mostly the same as the designation of origin except that only the production and/or processing and/or preparation must take place in the defined geographical area, described in the 2012 Regulation as being 'at least one of the production steps'.[17] Non-geographical names, such as feta, can also be registered as designations of origin or geographical indications where there is a clear link between the traditional place of production and the characteristics of the foodstuff. This was stated explicitly in the original Protected Geographical Food Names Regulations,[18] but is indicated in the 2012 Regulation by an alteration of the definitions of PDO and PGI to being 'a name which identifies a product', rather than limiting this to the name of a region or place.[19]

Generic Names

While the EU Quality Schemes for Agricultural Products Regulation goes some way to promoting and protecting minimum quality standards for foodstuffs and the property rights of those who produce them the majority of products can never be registered as a PDO or a PGI. As alluded to above, any name that has become 'generic' cannot be registered or protected.[20] As a result, some of the most well-known geographical food names are excluded from the scope of the Regulation. Cheddar, for example, can never be registered. Although originally produced in Somerset in England, its reputation well established by the twelfth century, use of the name 'cheddar' to describe many varieties of cheese, produced in many different places, means that the name, although geographical, is also generic. Its use has become so commonplace that it cannot now be registered for protection. However, if the application for registration is made more specific, and tailored to a defined geographical area, protection is still possible. 'Cheddar' cannot be registered, but 'West Country Farmhouse Cheddar' can.[21] 'Regato' has not been registered for protection, but Imokilly Regato, produced in county Cork, is a protected designation of origin.[22]

---

[15] Reg 1151/2012, n 11 above, Art 5(1).

[16] Reg 510/2006, n 10 above, Art 2(1).

[17] Reg 1151/2012, n 11 above, Art 5(2).

[18] Eg Reg 510/2006, n 10 above, Art 2(2).

[19] Reg 1151/2012, n 11 above, Art 5(1) and (2).

[20] Ibid, Art 6(1).

[21] West Country Farmhouse Cheddar cheese was registered as a protected designation of origin under the terms of Commission Regulation (EC) No 1107/1996 of 12 June 1996 on the registration of geographical indications and designations of origin under the procedure laid down in Art 17 of Council Regulation (EEC) No 2081/1992 [1996] OJ L 148/1.

[22] Imokilly Regato was added to the register of protected food names by Commission Regulation (EC) No 2107/1999 of 4 October 1999 supplementing the Annex to Regulation (EC) No 2400/96 on the

This previous example helps to illustrate some of the complications that exist in determining which names are generic. This is a constant source of deliberation – most famously debated in relation to the status of feta cheese. Cheddar is clearly a generic name. It is the most widely eaten cheese in the world. It is produced in the UK, Ireland, USA, Canada, New Zealand, Australia and elsewhere. The Regulation provides that generic names are those which are 'the names of products which, although relating to the place, region or country where the product was originally produced or marketed, have become the common name of a product in the Union'.[23] A range of factors must be taken into account when determining whether a name satisfies this definition and has consequently become generic for the purposes of the Regulation. The situation in the Member States and in areas of consumption must be considered, as must any relevant national or Union laws.[24] This is a flexible and objective test, requiring the examination of evidence to support a claim that the name has not, in fact, become generic and is therefore potentially eligible for protection as a PDO or a PGI. The Court of Justice has stated that:

> [t]he way in which the name of a product becomes generic is the result of an objective process, at the end of which that name, although referring to the geographical place where the product in question was originally manufactured or marketed, has become the common name of that product.[25]

Tests of this nature are often problematic and open to accusations of arbitrary decision making. Flexible objectivity can sometimes lead to more subjective decision making. Never was this more evident than in relation to the long-running saga which centered on attempts to have Greek feta cheese registered as a protected designation of origin.

Assessing Names

As noted above, certain considerations must be taken into account when deciding whether a geographical food name is generic. These are broad assessment criteria related to the name, its history, consumer preference for the food, the existence of relevant laws and their application and public perception. Essentially, the criteria set out in the Regulation, that there must be an examination of the situation in the Member States and of the relevant national or Community rules, facilitates the presentation of a vast variety of supporting evidence for any claim that a name is either generic, or non-generic and therefore potentially suitable for registration and protection.

entry of certain names in the 'Register of protected designations of origin and protected geographical indications' provided for in Council Regulation (EEC) No 2081/92 on the protection of geographical indications and designations of origin for agricultural products and foodstuffs, [1999] OJ L 258/3.
[23] Reg 1151/2012, n 11 above Art 3(6).
[24] Ibid, Art 41(2).
[25] Case C-466/2007 *Alberto Severi v Regione Emilia-Romagna* [2009] ECR I-8041, para 50.

The case law of the Court of Justice, and the legislation that has developed out of it, presents significant elaboration on what is meant by the ambiguous assessment criterion of 'the situation in the Member States'. In June 1996, the Greek cheese 'feta' was registered as a protected designation of origin, along with around 19 varieties of Greek cheese and many different foodstuffs from the other EU Member States.[26] However, three Member States, Denmark, Germany and France, took exception to this, claiming that the name 'feta' was generic and should not, therefore, have been registered. They sought to have the decision to register feta as a PDO annulled.[27]

In *Denmark, Germany and France v Commission*,[28] it was noted that prior to making the decision to register feta as a PDO there was acceptance that 'extreme caution' would be required when determining whether the name had become generic. 'Convincing evidence' would need to be presented to support whichever decision was made.

A 'Eurobarometer' study was therefore commissioned, to gauge public perceptions about the name 'feta', and in particular to ascertain, as far as possible, whether it had become the common name for a product, detached from its original geographical connotation.[29] This study found that, on average, around one in five EU citizens had heard of feta, rising to almost everybody in Greece and Denmark. Of those who had heard the name, the majority associated it with cheese, and the majority of those associated this cheese with Greece. Three-quarters of those surveyed who were familiar with the name 'feta' saw it as having a geographical connotation. More interviewees considered 'feta' to be a common name rather than one which related exclusively to a particular place of origin.[30] While the range of questions posed in the study appear confusing and mostly superfluous to the aim of ascertaining consumer perceptions about feta, the results of the survey were clear. Most of those questioned had never heard of feta. Of those who were familiar with it, many considered it to be a common name. Just over half of Greeks considered it to be a geographical name. Despite this, the Commission concluded that 'feta' had not become generic. Even the Scientific Committee for Designations of Origin and Geographical Indications could only determine by the slimmest of majorities, four votes to three, that 'feta' met the conditions for registration as a

[26] Commission Regulation (EC) No 1107/1996 of 12 June 1996 on the registration of geographical designations and designations of origin under the procedure laid down in Art 17 of Council Regulation (EEC) No 2081/1992, OJ L 148/1.

[27] This application for the annulment of that part of Reg 1107/1996 which listed feta as a PDO was brought under Art 263 TFEU (formerly Art 230 EC, but which was Art 173 EC at the time of this case). For further discussion on the relevance of Art 263 TFEU to Irish food law see Ch 2.

[28] Joined cases C-289/1996, C-293/1996 and C-299/1996 *Kingdom of Denmark, Federal Republic of Germany and French Republic v Commission of the European Communities* [1999] ECR I-1541.

[29] This Eurobarometer survey was based on interviews with 12,800 nationals of the then 12 Member States. It was published on 24 October 1994.

[30] These findings were presented in para 37 of the judgment in *Denmark, Germany and France v Commission*, n 28 above.

protected name, although they were convinced that it was not a generic name.[31] Denmark, Germany and France contested these conclusions.

It is important to dwell on these feta cases for a while as they exemplify so much about the system of protection for registered geographical food names. They make it clear that a name need not be 'geographical' to be accepted onto the register. They illustrate the range and type of data that must be presented where there is contention over eligibility for registration. They also clearly show us how that data is then interpreted, arguably arbitrarily, in the decision-making process. The Commission was effectively accused of this arbitrariness by both the applicant Member States and the Court of Justice in *Denmark, Germany and France v Commission*. When deciding that 'feta' was not generic, the Commission had not given proper consideration to 'the situation in other Member States', as it was obliged to under the terms of the Regulation. The name had been used for a considerable time in other Member States, not just in Greece. A product called 'feta' had been lawfully produced and marketed in those States. None of this potentially persuasive evidence was considered by the Commission when deciding that 'feta' was not a generic name. The registration of feta as a PDO was thus annulled by the Court.[32]

The Court of Justice did not decide in *Denmark, Germany and France v Commission* that the name 'feta' was generic. All they had decided was that the Commission had erred in its decision-making process by not taking the existing situation in other Member States into consideration. It could be argued, of course, that the Commission also erred in interpreting the results of the Eurobarometer study, so central to its finding that the name should be eligible for registration as a PDO, in the way that it did. But the Court did not make any declaration on this aspect of the Commission's assessment. The possibility therefore existed for the Commission to go through the process again. It could collate data on the existing situation in other Member States and use this, along with its existing interpretations of the Eurobarometer and the Scientific Committee findings, to support its registration of 'feta' as a PDO. This is exactly what the Commission then did.

A new Regulation was introduced in 2002 to reinstate 'feta' onto the PDO register.[33] The Commission organised another poll in 1999, this one more directly related to the 'situation' regarding feta cheese in all the Member States. The data

---

[31] This Committee was established by Commission Decision 1993/53/EEC of 21 December 1992 setting up a scientific committee for designations of origin, geographical indications and certificates of specific character [1993] OJ L 13/16. In particular the Committee was not unanimously convinced that 'feta' met the terms of Art 2(3) of Reg 2081/1992, that it was a '[c]ertain traditional geographical or non-geographical [name] designating an agricultural product or a foodstuff originating in a region or a specific place, which fulfils the conditions [for a designation of origin]'.

[32] 'Feta' was removed from the PDO register by Art 1 of Commission Regulation (EC) No 1070/1999 amending the Annex to Regulation (EC) No 1107/1996 on the registration of geographical indications and designations of origin under the procedure laid down in Art 17 of Council Regulation (EEC) No 2081/1992 [1999] OJ L 130/18.

[33] Commission Regulation (EC) No 1829/2002 of 14 October 2002 amending the Annex to Regulation (EC) No 1107/1996 with regard to the name 'feta' [2002] OJ L 277/10.

at the time suggested that specific rules governing the production and marketing of feta cheese existed in three places: Greece, since 1935; Denmark, since 1963; and the Netherlands, between 1981 and 1998. Feta cheese had been produced, at varying levels, in at least 13 of the then 15 Member States. Feta production was described as 'substantial' in four of these States: Greece (since ancient times), Denmark (since the 1930s), France (since 1931) and Germany (since 1972). Much of this cheese was exported around the world. Greek feta tended to be produced using ewe's and goat's milk. The Danish, French and German varieties were usually made with ewe's milk (especially in France) or cow's milk. The poll also showed that when Greece had joined the EU in 1981, it had accounted for around 92 per cent of feta consumption amongst all the Member States. Consumption had increased in the other States since then, to a level where Greece now only accounted for 73 per cent of the total rate. Crucially, however, the replies to the questionnaire sent by the Member States to the Commission showed that many of the cheeses that were marketed as 'feta' tended to make some sort of reference to Greece on the label. Text, symbols or pictures suggesting a link between the product and Greek territory, culture or tradition were used to market the product – regardless of where the cheese had been produced. Practically all the feta produced in the EU was being marketed in this way. Dictionary definitions of 'feta' usually specified a Greek cheese made from ewe's and goat's milk, but there was some recognition that production was now more widespread than this. The Scientific Committee unanimously concluded that 'feta' was not a generic name. It gave several reasons for this: the concentration of both production and consumption in Greece; the usual difference in the type of milk used (cow's) and the method of manufacture (ultra-filtration) in other Member States; the evocation of the Greek origin of the product amongst consumers; and the absence of specific legislation setting compositional requirements in most Member States other than Greece (Denmark being the only exception at the time).

It must be remembered that the Commission is not obliged to follow the Scientific Committee's opinion. It may, however, be of persuasive authority. Taking account of this and an 'exhaustive overall analysis of the legal, historical, cultural, political, social, economic, scientific and technical information,'[34] the Commission concluded that 'feta' is not a generic name. It is, instead, a traditional non-geographical name, eligible for protection under what is now Article 5 of Regulation 1151/2012.[35] The name 'feta' would now therefore be included in the register of protected designations of origin and geographical indications.[36]

The assessment by EU institutions and Member States of whether the name 'feta' is generic was described earlier as being something of a saga. This is because despite everything that has been outlined already – the regulations, the court cases,

---

[34] Preamble to Reg 1829/2002, n 33 above, recital 33.
[35] Formerly Art 2(3) of Reg 2081/1992, n 5 above.
[36] Reg 1829/2002, n 33 above, Art 1(1).

the surveying – the decision to register feta for protection came before the Court of Justice again in *Germany and Denmark v Commission*.[37]

The Court now looked at what at had been done and discovered by the Commission since deliberations about the generic nature of the name 'feta' had last come before it. Looking at the preamble to the reinstatement of feta on the PDO register,[38] the Court noted that information provided by the Member States indicated that products called 'feta' tend to make some explicit or implicit reference to Greece on the labelling.[39] The link between feta and Greece was being deliberately suggested on almost all of the cheese of that type being produced in other countries as part of a sales strategy aimed to capitalise on the reputation of the original Greek product.[40] This, combined with all of the data gathered by the 1999 Commission poll, suggested to the Court that 'feta' was not a generic name. This time, the Court was satisfied that the Commission had taken all relevant factors taken into consideration in their assessment – the existing situation in the Member State in which the name originates and in arrears of consumption; the existing situation in other Member States; and the relevant national or Union laws – as was required by Article 3(1) of Regulation 510/2006. The action brought by Germany and Denmark was consequently dismissed.

It is clear from the wording of Article 3(1) of the Regulation, and the related case law, such as the feta cases discussed above, that a full assessment of all the listed factors is essential in determining whether a name is generic. This was further clarified by the Court in *Commission v Germany*,[41] where it stated that:

> [w]hen assessing the generic character of a name, the Court has held that it is necessary, under Article 3(1) of [the Regulation,] to take into account the places of production of the product concerned both inside and outside the Member State which obtained the registration of the name at issue, the consumption of that product and how it is perceived by consumers inside and outside that Member State, the existence of national legislation specifically relating to that product, and the way in which the name has been used in [Union] law.[42]

Essentially, the Court was summarising the range of factors taken into consideration in *Germany and Denmark v Commission*. It has also been found that a food name should not be presumed to be generic until declared otherwise.[43] To do so

---

[37] Joined cases C-465/2002 and C-466/2002 *Germany and Denmark v Commission* [2005] ECR I-9115.

[38] Reg 1829/2002, n 33 above.

[39] Preamble to Reg 1829/2002, n 33 above, recital 20.

[40] Similarly, the Court found in para 55 of Case C-132/2005 *Commission v Germany*, [2008] ECR I-957, that 'Parmesan' cheese sold in Germany tended to be marketed with labels that referred to Italian culture and landscapes, and from this it could be inferred that German consumers perceived Parmesan as an Italian product, even if it had been produced elsewhere. What is sometimes marketed as 'Parmesan' cheese was actually registered as the PDO 'Parmigiano Reggiano' in 1996 by Reg 1107/96, n 21 above.

[41] See *Commission v Germany*, n 40.

[42] Ibid, para 53 of the judgment.

[43] Case C-446/2007 *Alberto Severi v Regione Emilia-Romagna* [2009] ECR I-8041.

would jeopardise the application, as generic names cannot be registered. It would also be contrary to the objectives pursued by the Regulation, namely the protection of both consumers and producers.[44]

Applications for Legal Protection

Geographical food names must be registered with the European Commission before they can be legally protected in all Member States and potentially throughout the member countries of the World Trade Organization. Applications for protection commence with the completion of a product specification.[45] This should provide the Commission with details about the foodstuff for which protection is sought, including the name of the product; a description of the product, including information about the raw materials used in production and the key characteristics of the food, such as its physical, chemical, microbiological and organoleptic qualities (texture, taste, smell, appearance); a definition of the geographical area where the food is traditionally produced; evidence that the product originates in that defined geographical area; a description of the method of production; and packaging details.[46] All of this information may not be required for all applications. For example, the foodstuff under consideration may not traditionally have any specific type of packaging, making the provision of details on this superfluous to this application. Finally, information must be furnished which demonstrates that there is a link between the characteristics of the foodstuff and its traditional place of production.[47] The product specification can be amended, even after protected status has been finalised.[48]

Only groups are entitled to apply for registration under the terms of the Regulation.[49] A 'group', for the purposes of the Regulation, is an association of producers or processors working with the same agricultural product or foodstuff. A natural or legal person may be treated as a group in some circumstances.[50] This can be the case where the person concerned is the only producer in the defined geographical area who is willing to submit an application and the defined geographical area in question possesses characteristics which differ appreciably from those of neighbouring areas or the characteristics of the product for which registration is sought differ from those produced in neighbouring areas.[51] Applications may also be lodged by several groups joined together seeking the registration of a trans-border geographical name.[52] The application must

[44] Ibid, para 53 of the judgment.
[45] Reg 1151/2012, n 11 above, Art 7.
[46] Ibid, Art 7(1)(a)–(e).
[47] Ibid, Art 7(1)(f).
[48] Ibid, Art 53.
[49] Ibid, Art 49.
[50] Ibid, Art 49(1).
[51] Ibid, Art 49(1)(a) and (b). Both criteria must be satisfied.
[52] Ibid, Art 49(1).

include the specification details, outlined above, as well as the name and address of the applicant group or groups, and a single document that sets out details on the main points of the specification and the link between the product and its area of production – basically a clear and summarised version of all relevant information.[53]

Where an application relates to a product made or processed within a single Member State, the dossier of evidence supporting the request for registration should be addressed to that Member State. The application must then be scrutinised by the relevant authority within the State to check that it is justified and meets the conditions necessary for registration as a protected geographical food name. In Ireland, applications are made to the Department of Agriculture, Food and the Marine as the designated competent authority.[54] There is also an obligation placed on the relevant authority to establish a national objection procedure. This involves publishing details of applications made, providing a reasonable period for potential objectors to lodge a claim that the application should not proceed.[55] Any natural or legal person who has a legitimate interest in the application and who is established within the State may lodge an objection to an application. The Department of Agriculture, Food and the Marine must consider the admissibility of any objections lodged, taking into account whether the foodstuff for which an application has been made is in compliance with the terms of the Regulation, in particular whether it is the type of name that is eligible for protection, whether it is a generic name or whether registration would jeopardise an existing trade mark.[56]

A final decision is then to be taken by the Department on the eligibility of the application. If this is favourable, the application is forwarded to the European Commission, alongside further publication of the details of the application, giving potential objectors one more opportunity to try to stall the process. Once all outstanding issues have been resolved, the Commission then considers the application lodged by the Department. Objections from other Member States and/or third countries are dealt with at a later stage in the process. Member States may grant transitional protection, extending to the host State only, while the application is considered.[57] This interim status must cease as soon as the Commission has made its decision on eligibility for protection.

It is the European Commission that makes the ultimate decision on whether to include a foodstuff on the protected designations of origin or protected geographical indications register. The Department of Agriculture, Food and the Marine sends the details of applications that it has pre-assessed on to the Commission for EU approval. Only the summarised version of the product specification must

[53] Ibid, Art 8(1).
[54] Under Reg 1151/2012, n 11 above, Art 36, Member States are responsible for designating competent authorities. In Ireland this is set by Art 3 of the European Union (Quality Schemes for Agricultural Products and Foodstuffs) Regulations 2015, SI No 296/2015.
[55] Reg 1151/2012, n 11 above, Art 49(3).
[56] Ibid, Art 10.
[57] Ibid, Art 9.

be included in this submission, along with details of the name and address of the applicant group and details of its own publication and declaration that it considers that the foodstuff in question is eligible for protection.[58] The Commission then has a maximum of six months in which to consider the application.[59] A list of applications received should be published on a monthly basis, as well as including details of applications that are being considered for registration in the Official Journal of the European Union.[60] The application is then subject to Commission scrutiny.

Objections to Protection

Objections to the registration of geographical food names may be made by any Member State or third country within six months after publication of the details, mentioned above, in the Official Journal.[61] In order to do so, the Member State or third country must lodge a document of objection with the Commission. This right to object is also extended to natural or legal persons who have a legitimate interest in the application that has been made, whether resident in an EU Member State or a third country.[62] This does not extend to residents of the Member State from which the application has been made, as they have already had the opportunity to object when the application was initially under the consideration of the relevant national authority, such as the Department of Agriculture, Food and the Marine, as outlined above.

The objection by others from within the EU is made through the relevant body in their own Member State. Attempts to block the registration by interested parties from third countries are made by way of application to the Commission, either directly by themselves or through their national authority. All statements of objection, regardless of where they come from, have to be made within the set three-month time period.[63] Objections are only admissible where they can demonstrate that the product for which registration is sought does not fall within the definitions of designation of origin or geographical indication, or that its registration would jeopardise an existing trade mark, or that the name is generic or potentially misleading to consumers. Admissible objections are then considered, with a view to agreement being reached between all the interested parties on how to proceed or if that fails to produce a result the Commission will make a decision on the basis of the evidence presented to it.[64] If no admissible objections are received, the name is registered for protection.[65] Protected names can be

---

[58] Ibid, Art 8(2).
[59] Ibid, Art 50(1). It was allowed 12 months for this under Art 6(1) of Reg 510/2006, n 10 above.
[60] Ibid, Art 50(2).
[61] Ibid, Art 51(1)(1).
[62] Ibid, Art 51(1)(2).
[63] Ibid, Art 10. Again, this time frame has been reduced by Reg 1151/2012. It was set at six months under the terms of Reg 510/2006, Art 7(3).
[64] Ibid, Art 52(3).
[65] Ibid, Art 52(2).

cancelled at a later date, should circumstances change in a way that warrants this course of action.[66]

Effects of Protection

Once registered, the protected name can be used by any operator who markets a product that conforms to the standards set out in the specification.[67] Obviously, this will only extend to those who produce or process within the specified region. Member States may not use national law to alter the nature or the terms of the protected designation of origin after registration.[68] A statement that the product is a protected designation of origin or designation of origin must appear on the labelling, and since May 2009 the standard EU PDO or PGI symbol, as appropriate, must also be included.[69]

Registered food names are accorded a high level of legal protection under the scheme.[70] Primarily, they are protected against any use of the name by operators who are not covered by the terms of the product specification,[71] or any other practice that is liable to mislead the consumer about the true origin of the product.[72] They are specifically protected from any 'misuse, imitation or evocation', even where the actual origin of the product has been indicated on the label.[73] Prohibiting 'evocation' of registered food names means that the producers of

---

[66] Ibid, Art 54.

[67] Ibid, Art 12(1). The General Court has also held that a registered product does not have to be well known amongst consumers to be able to avail of all the protections available. It was stated at para 48 in Case T-510/2015 *Mengozzi v European Union Intellectual Property Office* ECLI:EU:T:2017:54 that '[…] the reputation of a PGI is not a condition for its protection'.

[68] Joined Cases C-129/1997 and C-130/1997 *Chiciak, Chiciak and Fol* [1998] ECR I-3315.

[69] As originally established by Regulation 510/2006, Art 8(2) in conjunction with Art 20. The approved symbols are, until 2016, set out in Annex V to Regulation 1898/2006 [2006] OJ L 369/1.

[70] While the level of protection accorded to registered names is generally high, it is exhaustive in nature, and does not extend to geographical indications for which no application for registration has been made. This was seen most clearly in case C-478/2007 *Budějovicky Budvar v Rudolf Ammersin GmbH* [2009] ECR I-7721, where use of the name 'Bud' was not prohibited by the protected status of three Czech beers which included this designation within the PGIs Budějovické pivo, Českobudějovické pivo and Budějovicky měšťansky var. This was the case despite the fact that the designation 'Bud' had previously been protected under a bilateral agreement between Austria and Czechoslovakia. An application for the protection of the designation 'Bud' would have to be successfully made before restrictions could be placed on others' use of that name for marketing their beer.

[71] Reg 1151/2012, n 11 above, Art 13(1)(a).

[72] Ibid, Art 13(1)(d).

[73] Ibid, Art 13(1)(b). More recently, the Court of Justice of the EU has held that the use of the name 'Champagne Sorbet' could be perfectly legitimate, provided that the product contains the PDO 'Champagne' and provided that it also possesses a taste that is primarily attributable to champagne. To call a product made with champagne as one of its ingredients, and possessing the flavour of Champagne would not, in the opinion of the Court, take undue advantage of the protected designation of origin 'Champagne', nor would it constitute 'misuse, imitation or evocation' – provided, as stated, that it actually contains champagne and retains sufficient characteristics, such as taste. See Case C-393/2016, *Comité Interprofessionnel du Vin de Champagne v Aldi Süd Dienstleistungs-GmbH & Co.* ECLI:EU:C:2017:991. For more on this see A Mahy and F d'Ath, 'The case of the Champagner sorbet: Unlawful exploitation or legitimate use of the protected name Champagne?' (2017) 12 *European Food and Feed Law Review* 43.

another similar product cannot use a similar name to that of its protected counterpart. This is so even where the other, similar name has been in use for some time and predates the registration of the protected geographical indication or designation of origin.

In *Gorgonzola*,[74] for example, it was held that the name 'Cambozola' was an evocation, even though it was itself protected by an existing registered trade mark. The soft blue Italian cheese, Gorgonzola, had been registered as a protected designation of origin since 1996.[75] The German soft blue cheese, Cambozola, had been protected by a trade mark there since January 1983. The consortium for the protection of Gorgonzola applied to the Commercial Court in Vienna seeking an order prohibiting the marketing of Cambozola in Austria using that name, contending that the designation of origin status was compromised due to the similarity between the two names. While leaving the ultimate decision on continued use of the trade mark name to the national court, the European Court of Justice did decide that there was evocation of a protected name because similar names were being used to describe similar products. This created the possibility of creating confusion amongst consumers. During its deliberations, the Court described 'evocation' as covering those situations

> where the term used to designate a product incorporates part of a protected designation, so that when the consumer is confronted with the name of the product, the image triggered in his mind is that of the product whose designation is protected.[76]

Since the products at issue here were both soft blue cheeses which were similar in appearance, it would be reasonable, according to the Court, to conclude that the protected name 'Gorgonzola' was being evoked where the other name, 'Cambozola', ends in the same two syllables and contains the same number of syllables, resulting in a 'phonetic and visual similarity between the two'.[77] While the European Court of Justice was clearly of the opinion that the circumstances at issue here gave rise to probable evocation, the Protected Geographical Food Names Regulation still allowed certain trademarks to continue in their application, even where they would run contrary to the terms of a protected designation of origin or protected geographical indication. Article 14(2) states that:

> a trademark the use of which corresponds to one of the situations referred to in Article 13 [such as evocation] which has been applied for, registered or established by use ... in good faith within the territory of the [Union] before either the date of

---

[74] Case C-87/1997, *Consorzio per la tutela del formaggio Gorgonzola v Käserei Champignon Hofmeisted GmbH & Co KG and Eduard Bracharz GmbH* [1999] ECR I-1301.

[75] Reg 1107/1996, n 21 above, Annex.

[76] See *Gorgonzola*, n 74 above, para 25.

[77] Ibid, para 27. There can still be evocation in the absence of any likelihood of confusion between goods, all that is actually required is '[...] an association of ideas regarding the origin of the products [...] in the mind of the public and that a trader does not take undue advantage of the reputation of the PGI', para 31 of Case T-510/2015, n 67 above. See also para 45 of Case C-75/2015 *Viiniverla* ECLI:EU:C:2016:35.

protection of the designation of origin or geographical indication in the country of origin or before 1 January 1996, may continue to be used ... provided that no grounds for its invalidity or revocation exist.

In other words, where a trade mark was registered in good faith in a Member State prior to protection being accorded under the Regulation 510/2006 scheme, then use of the trade mark should continue, unless there is some other good reason for preventing this. In *Gorgonzola*, it was noted that 'Cambozola' was registered as a trade mark before Gorgonzola was accorded PDO status. It would have been 'in good faith' had it been done 'in compliance with the rules of law in force at the time'.[78] Assessment of this is left to the national court.[79]

In *Commission v Germany*,[80] where an action was brought against the Member State for failing to prevent the abuse of a protected designation of origin, it was held that there was a phonetic and visual similarity between the names 'Parmesan' and the registered 'Parmigiano-Reggiano'. Both products are hard cheeses, usually grated or intended to be grated. Both are of similar appearance. This, according to the Court, made it irrelevant that one was not a direct linguistic translation of the other. The similarities were deemed to be such that consumers could think of Parmigiano-Reggiano when confronted with Parmesan. The latter was thus found to be an evocation of the former.[81]

Where a food name has been classified as a protected designation of origin or protected geographical indication, other products cannot be marketed as being similar. This means that the use of terms such as 'style', 'type' or 'imitation' cannot be used in conjunction with the protected name by producers not covered by the registration specification.[82] Registered food names are also protected from:

> any other false or misleading indication as to the provenance, origin, nature, or essential qualities of the product, on the ... packaging, advertising material or documents relating to the product concerned, and the packing of a product in a container liable to convey a false impression as to its origin.[83]

It must be remembered that the use of a PDO or a PGI is conditional upon full compliance with the terms of the specification. This can mean that all or specific aspects of the production process must take place in the region covered by the registration, even where this has little impact on the nature of the protected

---

[78] *Gorgonzola*, n 74 above, para 34.

[79] Ibid, para 36. For more on this see V Rubino, 'From Cambozola to Toscoro' (2017) 12 *European Food and Feed Law Review* 326. The CJEU, in para 48 of Case T-510/2015, n 67 above, has put assessments by national courts of whether there is evocation as being based upon '[...] the phonetic and visual relationship between those names and any evidence that may show that such a relationship is not fortuitous, so as to ascertain whether, when the average European consumer, reasonably well informed and reasonably observant and circumspect, is confronted with the name of the product, the image triggered in his mind is that of the product whose geographical indication is protected'.

[80] *Commission v Germany*, n 40 above.

[81] Ibid, para 49.

[82] Reg 1151/2012, Art 13(1)(b).

[83] Ibid, Art 13(1)(c).

product itself. Slicing, grating and/or packaging may all have to happen in the same place before a registered name can be lawfully used in the marketing of a foodstuff. In *Bellon*, for example, it was held that all stages of production, including the grating and packaging of Grana Padano cheese, could be included as conditions for the use of a protected designation of origin.[84] Limiting the use of this PDO to cheese that had been grated and packaged in the region covered by the specification was deemed a measure equivalent to a quantitative restriction on exports, as prohibited by Article 35 TFEU. However, this could be justified on the basis that the quality and authenticity of the product as presented to consumers could be compromised if these stages of production took place outside the region covered by the registration. The Court also stated that no alternative, less restrictive measures could be used to achieve this aim of guaranteeing quality – recognised as being one of the key aims of the original Protected Geographical Food Names Regulation, and of the framework of the Common Agricultural Policy more generally.[85] A condition like this, insisting that grating and packaging must take place in the region of production, can, however, only be relied upon against other food business operators if it has been brought to their knowledge by adequate publicity in EU legislation, such as making specific reference to it in the relevant regulation.[86] It can be relied upon, but only against those who could reasonably have been expected to know about it.

The Court of Justice came to similar conclusions on the condition that Parma ham could only be sold as such if it had been sliced in the region of production. This matter first came before the English courts as the respondent company, Asda, had been selling packets of pre-sliced Parma ham in its supermarkets.[87] There was no dispute over whether the ham was genuine 'Prosciutto di Parma', which was registered as a protected designation of origin.[88] However, the fact that the product was sliced and packaged in England did give rise to a dispute – the producers' association claiming that the ham in question was not lawfully marketable due to the fact that the product specification stipulated that all stages of production must take place in the registered region. The House of Lords, on appeal from the Parma ham producers, referred the matter to the European Court of Justice, asking whether the Regulations, combined with the registered product specification, created a valid EU right, directly enforceable in the court of a Member State.[89]

Under the terms of Italian national law, Parma ham must be marked with a distinguishing five-pointed coronet (corona ducale).[90] Article 6 of this law

---

[84] Case C-469/2000 *Ravil SARL v Bellon Import SARL and Biraghi SpA* [2003] ECR I-5053.

[85] Ibid, para 48.

[86] In this case, Reg 1107/1996, n 21 above.

[87] *Consorzio del Prosciutto di Parma v Asda Stores Ltd and Hygrade Foods Ltd* [1999] ETMR 319, CA.

[88] Registered by Reg 1107/1996, n 21 above.

[89] Pre-ECJ determination opinion in the House of Lords was that the respondents were infringing a valid EU right, directly enforceable in the English courts. See n 87 above.

[90] Law No 26 on protection of the designation of origin Prosciutto di Parma of 13 February 1990, GURI No 42 of 20 February 1990, p 3.

provides that the mark must be applied and kept on the ham, indelibly stamped if necessary. It also states that the packaging operations must take place in the typical production area, to ensure that the mark is only affixed to genuine products. Other related Italian legislation prescribes that the slicing and packaging of Parma ham must take place at plants in the typical production area, which have been approved by the producers' association and in the presence of representatives of the association.[91] Having taken all of this into consideration, the European Court of Justice confirmed that the Protected Geographical Food Names Regulation (now the Quality Schemes for Agricultural Products Regulation) could be used to create a condition that operations, such as the slicing and packaging of a designation of origin, must take place in the region of production, where this is set out in the specification used to register the product.[92] It also held that the enforcement of this condition was a measure equivalent to a quantitative restriction on exports. It continued to point out, however, that this could be justified on the basis that the resulting restriction on trade and commercial operations was necessary to ensure preservation of the reputation of Parma ham. Despite all of this, however, it was ultimately held that the producers could not rely on the slicing and packaging elements of the registered product specification. The specificity of the conditions attached to this had not been properly publicised. Similar to its decision in *Bellon*, the Court had found that all the terms of a registered specification are enforceable, provided that they are necessary, proportionate and have been brought to the attention of other operators. Setting out all the conditions attached to the use of a PDO in the relevant EU legislation is deemed to be sufficient for the satisfaction of the latter.

The existence of a protected food name cannot be used by national authorities to restrict the activities of operators who produce unregistered similar foods in the region covered by the product specification on the basis that such limitations are necessary to preserve the status of the protected name.[93] Complete protection is not always immediate on registration.[94] Existing producers of the protected product, who are not covered by the product specification, may be permitted to continue to use the name for a period of time after registration.[95] Finally, protected

---

[91] Decree No 253, Arts 25 and 26 implementing Law No 26, GURI No 173 of 26 July 1993, p 4.

[92] Case C-108/2001 *Consorzio del Prosciutto di Parma and Salumificio S Rita SpA v Asda Stores Ltd and Hygrade Foods Ltd* [2003] ECR I-5121.

[93] Case C-161/2009 *Kakavestos-Fragkopoulos kai v Korinthias* [2011] ECR I-915.

[94] Reg 1151/2012, n 11 above, Art 15(1) provides that 'the Commission may adopt implementing acts granting a transitional period of up to five years to enable products originating in a Member State or a third country the designation of which consists of or contains a name that contravenes Art 13(1) to continue to use the designation under which it was marketed [where] such products have been legally marketed with that name in the territory concerned for at least five years preceding the [registration]'.

[95] For example, in England, several producers were permitted to continue their production and marketing of Melton Mowbray pork pies for five years after the registration of that name as a protected geographical indication, despite operating outside the terms of the product specification, as set out in Art 1 of Commission Regulation (EC) No 566/2009 of 29 June 2009 entering a name in the register of protected designations of origin and protected geographical indications [2009] OJ L 168/20.

food names cannot, subject to one exception, ever become legally 'generic'.[96] The only circumstances in which a protected food name can later become generic is if the Regulation which entered the PDO or PGI onto the register is annulled by the Court of Justice under the Article 263 TFEU procedure, as discussed in Chapter 2.

8.2. Traditional Specialities

Foods that owe their qualities or characteristics to their raw materials or composition, but which are not 'geographical' within the terms of Regulation 1151/2012, may still be accorded protection under EU law if they satisfy the conditions for registration as a 'traditional speciality guaranteed' or 'TSG'.[97] The system for registering TSGs was also originally developed in 1992,[98] updated and amended in 2006,[99] and again in 2012.[100] It is stated that the creation of TSGs was necessary as '[t]he promotion of traditional products with specific characteristics could be of considerable benefit to the rural economy … by improving the income of farmers and by retaining the rural population in these areas'.[101] By 2018, Ireland had no registered Traditional Specialities Guaranteed. Four UK products have been registered as a TSG. These are 'Traditional Farmfresh Turkey', which was granted TSG status in 2000, 'Traditionally Farmed Gloucestershire Old Spots Pork', registered in 2010, 'Traditional Bramley Apple Pie Filling', registered in 2015 and 'Traditionally Reared Pedigree Welsh Pork', registered in 2017. The UK authorities also applied to have 'Watercress' registered as a TSG, but this application, first lodged in 2010, has not been successful. Traditional specialities from other EU Member States that have been entered on the TSG Register include 'Pizza Napoletana' (Italy, 2010), 'Mozzarella' (Italy, 1998), 'Faro' beer (Belgium, 1997) and 'Jamón Serrano' (Spain, 1999). Very few TSGs have been registered across the EU. It is a very much underused system for registering traditional food names as compared to the PDO/PGI procedure.[102] It is also, however, a potentially very valuable process for producers.

---

[96] Reg 1151/2012, n 11 above, Art 13(2).

[97] The 'traditional speciality guaranteed' was previously known as the 'certificate of specific character', but this changed with the introduction of the new TSG Regulation in 2006, Regulation 509/2006 of 20 March 2006 on agricultural products and foodstuffs as traditional specialities guaranteed [2006] OJ L 93/1.

[98] Council Regulation (EEC) No 2082/1992 of 14 July 1992 on certificates of specific character for agricultural products and foodstuffs [1992] OJ L 208/9.

[99] Reg 509/2006, n 97 above.

[100] Reg 1151/2012, n 11 above.

[101] Recital 2 of the Preamble to Reg 509/2006, n 97 above. Recital 34 of the Preamble to Reg 1151/2012 states that '[t]he specific objective of the scheme for traditional specialities guaranteed is to help the producers of traditional products to communicate to consumers the value-adding attributes of their product'.

[102] This was also formally recognised in recital 34 of the Preamble to Reg 1151/2012, where it was stated that 'as only a few names have been registered, the current scheme for traditional specialities

Only a handful of EU Member States have sought registration for TSGs in more recent years, with only three applications being made in 2016, four in 2017, rising to five in the first half of 2018. A total of 58 TSGs were registered across the EU between 1997 and 2018.

'Traditional speciality guaranteed' was very simply defined in the 2006 Regulation as 'a traditional agricultural product or foodstuff recognised by the [EU] for its specific character through its registration under this Regulation'.[103] 'Specific character' was deemed to be 'the characteristic or set of characteristics which distinguishes an agricultural product or a foodstuff clearly from other similar products or foodstuffs of the same category'.[104] A product was deemed to be 'traditional' when it has been in existence for at least 25 years.[105] This has now been extended to 30 years.[106] The characteristics of a foodstuff that can be considered in determining whether the product is eligible for registration as a TSG include the physical, chemical, microbiological or organoleptic features, or the method or conditions of production.[107] Presentation is not in itself an examinable characteristic. One of the key differences between the TSG system and that for PDOs and PGIs is that the use of a registered TSG may not necessarily become the exclusive preserve of those who apply for the name to be registered, or for those who meet the conditions set out in the product specification, which must be submitted as part of the application for registration. As a result, there have to date been two TSG registers: one for those names the use of which is reserved for certain producers, and one for those TSGs which can be used by other producers as well.[108]

An agricultural product or foodstuff must be produced using traditional raw materials or be characterised by a traditional composition or production method before it is eligible for registration as a traditional speciality guaranteed.[109] A name could be either 'specific in itself', as would be the case for Neapolitan pizza, or it could clearly identify the specific character of the foodstuff – such as a reference to being 'traditionally farmed'.[110] Under the terms of the EU Quality Schemes for Agricultural Products Regulation 2012, names are now eligible for registration as a traditional speciality guaranteed where they describe a specific product or foodstuff that:

> results from a mode of production, processing or composition corresponding to traditional practice for that product or foodstuff; or is produced from raw materials or ingredients that are those traditionally used.[111]

guaranteed has failed to realise its potential [and it] should therefore be improved, clarified and sharpened in order to make the scheme more understandable, operational and attractive to potential applicants'.
[103] Reg 509/2006, n 97 above, Art 2(1)(c).
[104] Ibid, Art 2(1)(a).
[105] Ibid, Art 2(1)(b).
[106] Reg 1151/2012, n 11 above, Art 3(3).
[107] Ibid, Art 19(1).
[108] As previously established by Reg 509/2006, n 97 above, Art 3.
[109] Reg 1151/2012, n 11 above, Art 19(1).
[110] Reg 509/2006, n 97 above, Art 4(2). Now contained in Art 18(2) of Reg 1151/2012, n 11 above.
[111] Reg 1151/2012, n 11 above, Art 18.

A name cannot be registered if it is merely referring to claims of a general nature used for a set of products.[112] Names already registered under the 1992 and 2006 Regulations can continue to use their TSG status. They are to be automatically entered into the new register, as established by Article 22 of Regulation 1151/2012.[113]

The TSG name cannot be used unless the product carrying it complies with the terms of the 'specification'.[114] The product specification itself should include details of the name by which it is proposed to be registered, a description of the foodstuff and its characteristics, a description of the ingredients and production method, the aspects of the product that give it a distinguishing character and evidence to support the claim that the product is 'traditional'.[115] Individuals cannot apply for the registration of a TSG. This must be done by a 'group',[116] defined in the Regulation as 'any association, irrespective of its legal form, mainly composed of producers or processors working with the same product'.[117] Several groups from different Member States or third countries may submit a joint application.[118] Applications for the registration of a TSG can only be made by those who actually produce the product or foodstuff in question.[119] This removes the possibility of opportunistic applications being made by those with no existing interest in the traditional product. Applications should include information about the group applying and the details in the product specification.[120]

Applications should be initially lodged with relevant authorities in the Member State where the group is based. They, in turn, scrutinise the application to ensure that registration may be possible under the terms of the Regulation, and to check that the information and supporting documentation meets the requirements set out therein.[121] Applications for TSG registration can, of course, be objected to by others. It is up to the Member States to ensure that a proper national objection procedure is established and facilitated.[122] This should include ensuring that there is adequate publicising of any applications made, along with the provision of reasonable periods within which those with a legitimate interest can lodge their objections. The Member State authorities then forward the application to the Commission for consideration.[123] The Commission is then charged with

---

[112] Ibid, Art 18(4).
[113] Ibid, Art 25(1).
[114] Ibid, Art 19(1).
[115] Ibid, Art 19(1)(a)–(d).
[116] Ibid, Art 49(1). As is the case for PDO and PGI applicants, a single natural or legal person may be treated as a 'group' in some circumstances.
[117] Ibid, Art 3(2).
[118] Ibid, Art 49(1).
[119] Ibid.
[120] Ibid, Art 20(1).
[121] Ibid, Art 49(2).
[122] Ibid, Art 49(3).
[123] Ibid, Art 49(4).

publicising applications,[124] providing others with a legitimate interest with the opportunity to raise an objection to the registration of a TSG.[125]

Objections must be made within three months of the details of the application being publicised in the Official Journal. They must demonstrate that the name should not be eligible for registration as a TSG, within the terms of the Regulation. If no such objection or demonstration is made, the name is registered. Where a legitimate concern is raised, the Commission tries to facilitate consultations between the parties concerned, in the hope of reaching an acceptable agreement between them.[126]

The Commission makes the final decision on registration where no such agreement can be reached between the parties. Any registered name can have its TSG status cancelled by use of the comitology procedure if the Commission considers that it should not continue to be protected under the terms of the Regulation.[127] The Commission is assisted by the Agricultural Product Quality Policy Committee.[128]

8.2.1. Benefits of Traditional Speciality Guaranteed Status

A name that is successfully registered as a TSG can be used by any operator who markets a product that conforms to the terms of the specification.[129] Those products that meet the standards set out in the specification also benefit from being able to display the TSG symbol on the labelling.[130] This is similar to the symbol used in the marketing of PDOs and PGIs. The whole system for using the TSG has thus been opened up by the introduction of Regulation 1151/2012. Any producer, including those from third countries can use a registered name, provided that their product complies with the requirements of the specification. Their use remains reserved for those who meet the standards set, but the system does now provide a good opportunity for both the producers of 'traditional' products and consumers, who know that the foods they purchase, if carrying the TSG symbol, have been made according to prescribed conditions related to distinctive qualities or characteristics.

Member States are obliged, under the terms of the Regulation, to ensure that legal protection is put in place against any misuse or misleading use of the traditional speciality guaranteed term or symbol on food labelling.[131] They must also

[124] Ibid, Art 50(2).
[125] Ibid, Art 51(1).
[126] Ibid, Art 51(3).
[127] Ibid, Art 54.
[128] Ibid, Art 57(1). For TSGs it used to be assisted by the Standing Committee on Traditional Specialities Guaranteed.
[129] Ibid, Art 23(1).
[130] Ibid, Art 23(2) and (3).
[131] Ibid, Art 24(1).

take steps to prevent the imitation of registered names by others who are not covered by the product specification, or anything else related to the misuse of registered TSGs that may cause confusion amongst consumers.[132]

8.2.2. Control of Traditional Speciality Guaranteed Use

As is the case for designations of origin and geographical indications, the Department of Agriculture is the designated national competent authority for dealing with traditional speciality applications. However, under the terms of the Regulation, responsibility for verifying compliance with registered product specifications can be passed to a product specification body,[133] which must first be accredited in accordance with the 'General Requirements for Bodies Operating Product Certification Systems'.[134]

It is stipulated in these requirements that inspection bodies must act independently and with impartiality when carrying out their checks. So, for example, when the Gloucestershire Old Spots Pig Breeders' Club in the UK sought to have their product registered for its specific character, a private body, the Product Authentication Inspectorate Limited, was appointed, charged with verifying compliance with the product specification. This same body is also responsible for checking the authenticity of the protected designations of origin Stilton cheese and West Country Farmhouse Cheddar, as well as the protected geographical indication Melton Mowbray pork pies in the UK.[135] As stated, Ireland has not, at the time of writing, registered any TSGs. Were any to be registered then their use would be monitored by the Department of Agriculture, Food and the Marine. Prosecutions for failure to comply with the terms of the EU Quality Schemes for Agricultural Products Regulation 2012 can be brought by either the Department, the HSE or the FSAI.[136]

8.2.3. Optional Quality Terms

Finally, Regulation 1151/2012 also establishes a new type of food name, the 'optional quality term'. This is described as a 'second tier of quality systems, based on quality terms which add value, which can be communicated on the internal

---

[132] Ibid, Art 24(2).
[133] Ibid, Art 37(1).
[134] European standard EN 45011, ISBN: 0580294153, as set out in Reg 1151/2012, n 11 above, Art 39(2).
[135] Reg 1151/2012, n 11 above, Art 37 also provides that product certification bodies can be used to verify compliance with the product specifications for protected designations of origin and protected geographical indications.
[136] Reg 24(1) of the European Union (Quality Schemes for Agricultural Products and Foodstuffs) Regulations 2015, n 54 above.

market and which are to be applied voluntarily'.[137] They are descriptive terms used for products that are related to farming methods or processing techniques. An optional quality term must relate to a distinguishing characteristic, such as a method of production, it must add value when compared to its non-use for similar products, and it should have a European dimension.[138] This suggests that names previously registered as a TSG, such as 'Traditional Farmfresh Turkey', should now be considered as a quality term rather than a speciality guarantee, although the 'European dimension' is still questionable.

Regulation 1151/2012 specifically identifies two quality terms. The first of these is the 'mountain product'. This term can only be used to describe foods where both the raw materials and any animal feed used come from mountain areas.[139] Any processing should also take place in the mountains.[140] 'Mountain areas' are themselves defined by Article 18 of Regulation 1257/1999.[141] The second quality term recognised by Regulation 1151/2012 is the term 'product of island farming'.[142] Again, the raw materials used in production should come from islands, and use of the term should really be limited to those foods which are substantially affected by being produced in such places. The Commission is charged with introducing more detailed rules in this area.[143] Member States should ensure that these terms are used appropriately.[144]

8.3. Wine and Spirits Protection

The EU Member States combined form the world's largest producer, exporter and consumer of wine. A common market organisation (CMO) for wine, which was reformed in 1999[145] and again in 2008,[146] is used to support this important part of the agricultural and manufacturing sectors. The idea behind having a CMO for wine is that it can be used to make EU producers more competitive in the global market. To achieve this, simpler, clearer and more effective rules governing the sector should be introduced and applied. This would result in the lifting of some

---

[137] Reg 1151/2012, n 11 above, Preamble, recital 44.

[138] Ibid, Art 29(1).

[139] Ibid, Art 31(1)(a).

[140] Ibid, Art 31(1)(b).

[141] Council Regulation (EC) No 1257/1999 of 17 May 1999 on support for rural development from the European Agricultural Guidance and Guarantee Fund (EAGGF) and amending and repealing certain Regulations [1999] OJ L 160/80.

[142] Reg 1151/2012, n 11 above, Art 32.

[143] Ibid, Art 33.

[144] Ibid, Art 34.

[145] Council Regulation (EC) No 1493/1999 of 17 May 1999 on the common organisation of the market in wine [1999] OJ L 179/1.

[146] Council Regulation (EC) No 479/2008 of 29 April 2008 on the common organisation of the market in wine, amending Regulation (EC) No 1493/1999, 1782/2003, 1290/2005, 3/2008 and repealing Regulations (EEC) No 2392/1986 and 1493/1999 [2008] OJ L 148/1.

existing restrictions on the planting of new vines across all EU Member States by 1 January 2016.[147] Many restrictions remain.[148]

8.3.1. Common Organisation of the Market in Wine

As was stated above, a system of registering and protecting the geographical status of wines was originally excluded from the scope of both the 1992 and 2006 food names regulations.[149] This continues to be the case with Regulation 1151/2012.[150] However, a variation on the PDO/PGI registration scheme had been in existence for wines since 1970, predating Ireland's accession to the Treaty of Rome.[151] It was revised and updated in 1979.[152] Under this system, 'quality wines produced in specified regions' could be protected on the basis of satisfying a range of production factors and product characteristics. Determining whether a wine or a sparkling wine could be considered to be of a certain 'quality' would follow an assessment of the production area, vine varieties used, cultivation methods, wine-making methods, yields and analysis of organoleptic characteristics.[153] Member States could also set additional conditions of production and characteristic

---

[147] Debate over vine-planting rights have been going on in Europe for some time. In 1726, for example, the French philosopher Montesquieu made a complaint to the King of France, Louis XV, about the prohibition on the planting of new vines, but his appeal was unsuccessful. It was not until the French revolution of 1789 that these planting rights became more liberalised. For further discussion on this see G Meloni and J Swinnen, 'L'Histoire se répète: Why the liberalisation of the EU vineyard planting rights regime may require another French Revolution' (2015) LICOS Discussion Paper Series, No. 367. Available at: www.econstor.eu. Meloni and Swinnen link the impact of this debate with Montesquieu's influential work in 'De l'Esprit des Lois' (The Spirit of the Laws), where he argued for the separation of powers into the executive, the legislative and the judicial, which has had such a significant impact on national constitutional laws around the World, including Bunreacht na hÉireann.

[148] Now set out in Commission Delegated Regulation (EU) 2018/273 of 11 December 2017 supplementing Regulation (EU) No 1308/2013 of the European parliament and of the Council as regards the scheme of authorisations for vine plantings, the vineyard register, accompanying documents and certification, the inward and outward register, compulsory declarations and publication of notified information and supplementing Regulation (EU) 1306/2013 of the European Parliament and of the Council as regards the relevant checks and penalties, amending Commission Regulations (EC) No 555/2008, 606/2009, 607/2009 and repealing Commission Regulation (EC) no 436/2009 and Commission Delegated Regulation (EU) No 2015/560, [2018] OJ L 58/1.

[149] Reg 2081/1992, n 5 above, and Reg 510/2006, n 10 above, respectively.

[150] Reg 1151/2012, n 11 above, Art 2(2) states that it does not apply to spirits, aromatised wines or grapevine products.

[151] Council Regulation (EEC) No 817/1970 of 28 April 1970 laying down special provisions relating to quality wines produced in specified regions [1970] OJ L 99/20. No English language version of this Regulation exists. Earlier attempts had been made to organise the EEC wine market with the introduction of Regulation 24/1962, Règlement No 24 portant établissement gradual d'une organisation commune du marché viti-vinicole [1962] OJ 989/62. Article 4 of this Regulation presents the first attempt to introduce an EU-wide quality control system for wines. Under Irish law, the original EEC Wine Regulations were given full domestic applicability by the European Communities (Wine) Regulations 1978, SI No 154/1978.

[152] Council Regulation (EEC) No 338/1979 of 5 February 1979 laying down special provisions relating to quality wines produced in specific regions [1979] OJ L 54/48.

[153] Reg 338/1979, Art 2(1).

requirements.[154] Essentially, assessment of eligibility for protection under the terms of the Regulation was left to the Member States themselves. This resulted in nearly 3,000 wines being listed as a 'quality wine produced in specified region' prior to the establishment of the more structured PDO/PGI registration system for wines in 2008.[155] This includes, amongst others, any wine or sparkling wine with an 'Appellation d'origine contrôlée', 'Appellation contrôlée', 'Champagne' designation or 'Vin délimité de qualité supérieure' made in France or those awarded a 'Denominazione di origine controllata' in Italy.[156]

A new wine regulation, creating a registration system for wine similar to that which exists for food, was published in 2008.[157] This Regulation defines a 'designation of origin' for wines as

> the name of a region, a specific place or, in exceptional cases, a country used to describe a product that complies with the following requirements: (i) its quality and characteristics are essentially or exclusively due to a particular geographical environment with its inherent natural and human factors; (ii) the grapes from which it is produced come exclusively from this geographical area; and (iii) its production takes place in this geographical area.[158]

A 'geographical indication' differs from this in that only 85 per cent of the grapes used for production must come from the defined geographical area.[159] Generic names cannot be protected.[160] Issues that are considered when assessing whether a name is generic includes an examination of the existing situation in EU Member States in areas where the food is most commonly consumed. An assessment is also made of whether there are any existing relevant national or EU legal provisions which could offer some guidance on whether the name has traditionally been reserved for foods produced in defined areas. It should also be established whether these rules have been properly applied and adhered to by national authorities in the past.

Geographical names that are liable to mislead consumers because, for example, they are similar to a well-known existing trade mark, cannot be registered either.[161] Similarly, names cannot be registered as trademarks where they are similar to protected geographical names.[162]

---

[154] Ibid, Art 2(2).
[155] The Preamble to Reg 479/2008, n 146 above recognised that up to that stage, the system identifying quality wines using protected designations of origin and geographical indications was 'not fully developed in this respect'. A new regime was thus required to 'allow for a transparent and more elaborate framework underpinning the claim to quality by the products concerned'. This would, according to Preamble recital 27, 'be established … in line with the approach followed under the [Union's] horizontal quality policy applicable to foodstuffs other than wine and spirits in Council Regulation (EC) No 510/2006'.
[156] Reg 338/1979, Art 16.
[157] Reg 479/2008, n 146 above.
[158] Ibid, Art 34(1)(a).
[159] Ibid, Art 34(1)(b).
[160] Ibid, Art 43(1).
[161] Ibid, Art 43(2).
[162] Ibid, Art 44(1).

The 'technical file' is the key component of the application for the registration of a wine as a designation of origin or geographical indication. It should include details about the name to be protected, the applicant's details and a detailed, as well as summarised, product specification.[163] The 'product specification' lists information related to the name of the wine, a description of the wine – including an evaluation of its organoleptic properties, the production method, the geographical area of production, yields, grape varieties and compliance verification authority details.[164] Applicants are usually the representative of a group of producers of the wine but may, in exceptional cases, be a single producer.[165] Initial applications are made to the designated national authorities.[166] The Department of Agriculture, Food and the Marine, which would be the designated competent authority for Ireland, would then examine the application to assess whether it is in compliance with the terms of the Regulation. If it is, the application is published, providing those with a legitimate interest with the opportunity to object to registration.[167] If no justifiable objections are received, the application is forwarded to the Commission for their scrutiny.[168] Further objections can be received by the Commission,[169] following publication of the details of the application in the Official Journal of the European Union.[170] A decision on registration, using the comitology procedure, is then made.[171] Registered product specifications can be amended at a later date.[172] Protected status can be cancelled by the Commission where necessary.[173]

Once registered, the protected designation of origin or protected geographical indication can be used by any operator who complies with the terms of the product specification.[174] Registered wines are protected against direct or indirect commercial use of the name by comparable products that are not in compliance with the specification where this exploits the reputation of the PDO or PGI.[175] They are also protected against any misuse, imitation or evocation, even where the true origin of the product is indicated.[176] Finally, the usual protections against 'any other false or misleading indication' apply, as does that which prevents the registered name from becoming 'generic'.[177] Member States are obliged to prevent the unlawful

---

[163] Ibid, Art 35(1).
[164] Ibid, Art 35(2).
[165] Ibid, Art 37.
[166] Ibid, Art 38(2).
[167] Ibid, Art 38(3).
[168] Ibid, Art 38(5).
[169] Ibid, Art 40.
[170] Ibid, Art 39(3).
[171] Art 41 in conjunction with Art 113(2). A public electronic register of all protected designations of origin and geographical indications for wine is maintained by the Commission (Art 46).
[172] Ibid, Art 49.
[173] Ibid, Art 50.
[174] Ibid, Art 45(1).
[175] Ibid, Art 45(2)(a).
[176] Ibid, Art 45(2)(b). For discussion on what is meant by 'evocation' see also C MacMaoláin, 'Reforming European Community Food Law: Putting quality back on the agenda' (2003a) 58 *Food and Drug Law Journal* 549. See also para 43 of Case T-510/2015, n 67 above.
[177] Reg 479/2008, Arts 45(2)(c) and 45(3).

use of protected wine names;[178] while they are responsible for designating their competent authorities for controlling the PDO/PGI system for wines,[179] verifying compliance with the terms of a registered name can also be designated to a private 'control body'.[180] The costs of verification are borne by the producers.[181]

The system for registering wines according to their regional qualities or production characteristics has historically been very different from that which exists for foodstuffs. There are nearly three times as many wines registered for protected status in the EU as there are registered foods. The use of PDOs and PGIs for wines is not nearly as reliable as it has become for foodstuffs. This is primarily because 'traditional terms' used to classify wines in Member States entitle the user to claim that the product is a PDO or a PGI, even though the product has not undergone the same rigorous assessment of quality as that prescribed for food. There has been no meaningful Commission involvement in the process and there have been fewer opportunities for objections to the registration to be raised. There is also confusion over the fact that 'traditional terms' cannot become generic,[182] even though they are general in nature, for example the 'Appellation d'origine contrôlée' and have been used to describe thousands of products. There is the possibility that the comitology procedure can be used to restructure this system for wines so that only those producers who make applications to the Commission through their own State authorities will be eligible for protection in the future. This would greatly assist quality wine producers as it would probably mean that fewer producers in other EU Member States would be able to make legally verifiable claims about the quality of their product, leaving the producers of quality sparkling and non-sparkling wines facing less competition in this field.

8.3.2. Spirits Protection

Permitted definitions, descriptions, presentation formats and labelling content for spirit drinks are also set by EU regulations.[183] 'Spirit drinks' are defined as alcoholic beverages:

> intended for human consumption; possessing particular organoleptic qualities; having a minimum alcoholic content strength of 15% vol.; having been produced either

---

[178] Ibid, Art 45(4).
[179] Ibid, Art 47.
[180] Ibid, Art 48. 'Control bodies' that can operate as product certifiers are defined in Reg 882/2004, Art 2 as 'an independent third party to which the competent authority has delegated certain control tasks' [2004] OJ L 165/1.
[181] Further details on how the whole process works are set out in Commission Regulation (EC) No 607/2009 of 14 July 2009 laying down certain detailed rules for the implementation of Council Regulation (EC) No 479/2008 as regards protected designations of origin and geographical indications, traditional terms, labelling and presentation of certain wine sector products [2009] OJ L 193/60.
[182] Reg 479/2008, n 146 above, Art 55(2).
[183] Regulation (EC) No 110/2008 of the European Parliament and of the Council of 15 January 2008 on the definition, description, presentation, labelling and protection of geographical indications of spirit drinks and repealing Council Regulation (EEC) No 1576/1989 [2008] OJ L 39/16.

directly by [distillation, maceration or similar processing] or by the mixture of a spirit drink with one or more other spirit drinks and/or ethyl alcohol of agricultural origin or distillates of agricultural origin, and/or other alcoholic beverages, and/or drinks.[184]

Spirit drinks are further categorised in Annex II to the Regulations. This provides more detailed definitions for drinks such as rum, whisky, brandy, vodka and gin. Most are required to have a minimum alcohol content of 37.5 per cent. 'London gin', for example, is defined as being:

obtained exclusively from ethyl alcohol of agricultural origin ... whose flavour is intro-duced exclusively through the re-distillation in traditional stills of ethyl alcohol in the presence of all the natural plant materials used ... which does not contain added sweet-ening exceeding 0.1 gram of sugars per litre of the final product nor colorants, which does not contain any other added ingredients other than water. The minimum alcoholic strength by volume of London gin shall be 37.5%. The term London gin may be supple-mented by the term "dry".

'London gin' is a type of distilled gin that is not considered to be a geographical name. It can be produced anywhere, provided the product specification is adhered to. 'Whiskey' is defined in Annex II to the Regulation as:

... a spirit drink produced exclusively by (i) distillation of a mash made from malted cereals with or without whole grains or other cereals, which has been saccharified by the diatase of the malt contained therein, with or without natural enzymes, fermented by the action of yeast [with] one or more distillations at less than 94.8% vol., so that the distillate has an aroma and taste derived from the raw materials used [and] maturation of the final distillate for at least three years in wooden casks not exceeding 700 litres capacity.

In addition to this, the final distillate can only be diluted with water, and with plain caramel for colour. The minimum alcohol content of the finished product must be 40%. No sweeteners or flavourings, other than the caramel for colour, should be added.

The sales names of spirit drinks can, subject to satisfaction of set conditions, be protected as geographical indications. EU regulations define geographical indications for spirits as:

an indication which identifies a spirit drink as originating in the territory of a country, or a region or locality in that territory, where a given quality, reputation or other charac-teristic of that spirit drink is essentially attributable to its geographical origin.[185]

Spirits registered with a geographical indication are listed in Annex III to the Regulations. These include Cognac (France), Grappa (Italy), Kirsch d'Alsace (France), Swedish Vodka, Scotch Whisky, and Plymouth Gin. As noted above, the inclusion of 'London gin' in the Annex II definitions categorises this as a generic name. Under the terms of the Regulation, generic names, or those which have

---

[184] Ibid, Art 2(1).
[185] Ibid, Art 15(1).

come into common usage, cannot be registered as geographical indications.[186] Three Irish spirits are listed as geographical indications in Annex III to Regulation 110/2008. These are Irish Whiskey,[187] Irish Cream and Irish Poitín.

Applications for the registration of spirit drinks are always to be made by the Member State of origin to the Commission.[188] Again, the technical file forms the key component of any application. Technical files were submitted by the Department of Agriculture, Food and the Marine to the European Commission for each of the three types of Irish spirit drinks registered, setting out the geographical links between the products and Ireland and their geographical areas of production, details of key product characteristics, organoleptic properties and production method details. The Commission then has 12 months to consider the application.[189] If it considers that the name is eligible for protection, it publishes the technical file in the Official Journal of the European Union, allowing six months for possible objections to registration to be raised by others.[190] Finally, if the Commission decides to proceed with the registration of the geographical indication, it should use the comitology regulatory procedure with scrutiny in making this decision. This decision is also to be publicised through its announcement in the Official Journal.[191] It is then up to the Member States and their designated authorities to ensure that the specifications set out in the technical file are complied with.[192]

Once registered, geographical indications for spirit drinks are protected against any direct or indirect commercial use by those not covered by the registration; any misuse, imitation or evocation, even where the real origin of the product is indicated; any other false or misleading indication; or any other practice liable to mislead the consumer as to the true origin of the product.[193]

Other products that have been registered as trademarks that contain or consist of a registered geographical indication must be invalidated, or refused for registration in the first place, if their use is likely to impinge upon the protection accorded to the PGI under the terms of the Regulation.[194] Some limited exceptional circumstances that may facilitate continued use of the trade mark are set out in the Regulation.[195] Registered geographical indications for spirits can, of course,

[186] Ibid, Art 15(3).
[187] Alternatively, the name 'Uisce Beatha Eireannach' can be used for Irish Whiskey or Irish Whisky. 'Poteen' is also interchangeable with Poitín.
[188] Regulation (EC) No 110/2008, Art 17(1) and (2).
[189] Ibid, Art 17(5).
[190] Ibid, Art 17(6) and (7).
[191] Ibid, Art 17(8).
[192] Ibid, Art 22(1) in conjunction with Art 24(1). The technical file can be altered, using the same procedure as that used for the initial application for registration, as set out in Reg 110/2008, Art 21. In Ireland, verification is often done by the Revenue Commissioners.
[193] Regulation (EC) No 110/2008, Art 16.
[194] Ibid, Art 23(1).
[195] Ibid, Art 23(2). These limited exceptions include those circumstances where the trademark was registered in good faith in an EU Member State prior to either the date of protection of the geographical indication in the country of origin or before 1 January 1996.

be cancelled by the Commission where it is of the opinion that the specifications set out in the technical file can no longer be ensured.[196] Again, any decision made in this regard must follow use of the correct comitology procedure, involving the (EU) Committee for Spirit Drinks.[197] The same procedure is also to be used for any amendments to the Annexes to the Regulation, such as those involving an alteration to the legal definitions of the spirit drink categories or the listing or de-listing of geographical indications.[198]

---

[196] Ibid, Art 18.
[197] As established by Reg 110/2008, Art 25.
[198] Ibid, Art 26.

9

Nutrition, Obesity and Health

9.1. Introduction

It has been illustrated in earlier chapters in this book that there has been a significant legislative and political emphasis on food safety matters since the BSE crisis of the 1990s, leading to the neglect of other concerns, in particular those related to the nutritional value and quality of food. While new directly applicable regulations have been introduced on quality,[1] and on food labelling,[2] it is here argued that these will contribute little, certainly in the short to medium term, to dealing with the biggest of all food concerns – those related to nutrition. Studies referred to previously have highlighted the figures which illustrate this point.[3] The Organisation for Economic Co-operation and Development (OECD) reports that 23 per cent of Irish adults are classified as obese.[4] At national level, government policy can be directed towards trying to improve the health of the nation. Safefood have reported that 69 per cent of Irish men and 52 per cent of Irish women are overweight and these figures were continuing to rise.[5] While the most recent studies suggest that rates of overweight amongst children are stabilising, they are doing so at a very high level. The Childhood Obesity Surveillance Initiative,

---

[1] Regulation (EU) No 1151/2012 of the European Parliament and of the Council of 21 November 2012 on quality schemes for agricultural products and foodstuffs [2012] OJ L 343/1.

[2] Regulation (EU) No 1169/2011 of the European Parliament and of the Council of 25 October 2011 on the provision of food information to consumers, amending Regulations (EC) No 1924/2006 and (EC) No 1925/2006 of the European Parliament and of the Council, and repealing Commission Directive 1987/250/EEC, Council Directive 1990/496/EEC, Commission Directive 1999/10/EC, Directive 2000/13/EC of the European Parliament and of the Council, Commission Directives 2002/67/EC and 2008/5/EC and Commission Regulation (EC) No 608/2004 [2011] OJ L 304/18.

[3] As noted in Chapter 5, the National Institute for Health and Clinical Excellence (NICE) in the UK estimates that there are 40,000 deaths per year in England alone related to the consumption of low-quality foods. See 'Prevention of cardiovascular disease', NICE public health guidance, 25 June 2012. Available at: www.nice.org. The Food Standards Agency in the UK estimates that there are around 590 deaths per year there from food poisoning. See www.food.gov.uk. See also S Mayor, 'Regulation has not reduced food poisoning in Britain' (1997) 315 *British Medical Journal* 1111. Over 80 times as many people are estimated to die from coronary heart disease resulting from poor diet in England alone as die from food poisoning across the entire UK, on an annual basis.

[4] OECD, Obesity Update 2017. Available at: www.oecd.org.

[5] Safefood, Weight Status of the Population in the Republic of Ireland, National Adult Nutrition Survey 2010–2011. Available at: www.safefood.eu.

published in 2017, indicates that nearly one in five children in Ireland is either overweight or obese.[6] However, legally, there is little that can be done at national level to change this. As is discussed throughout this chapter and as has already been alluded to in this book, EU rules on the free movement of food prevent Member State governments from introducing some of the legally binding national measures that have been identified as offering one of the best ways of reducing obesity and rates of overweightness in society. As is also discussed here, harmonising EU food labelling requirements have not adequately addressed this – despite clear recognition at institutional level that there is a problem and that labelling can be used to help to resolve it.

The EU Commission has produced a White Paper outlining a strategy on nutrition and obesity.[7] Understanding the stance that the EU may adopt on these matters is crucial to determining just what can be done at national level. Where legislative intervention is concerned, it is only where the EU acts that similar rules or regulations can be introduced into Irish law. It is recognised that a system of colour coding, graded-labels, or at least clearer, more user-friendly, nutrient declarations may be one of the best ways of ensuring that consumers are informed about the composition and potential positive and detrimental effects of the food they consume.[8] However, as is also noted, it is only where there is specific standardisation at EU level that any rules on the use of these alternative labelling schemes can be properly applied at national level. To date, EU law does not provide for the use by Member States of binding labelling templates that have been shown to improve consumer understanding and decision making. This is a significant shortcoming in the law. Member States cannot act to take what they may deem to be the appropriate measures unless EU law permits this. EU legislators have not acted either to introduce or facilitate these alternative labelling schemes, which could go some way to addressing concerns about the relationship between diet and health, when considered as part of a package of measures that needs to be employed.[9]

---

[6] S Bel-Serrat, MM Heinen, CM Murrin, L Daly, J Mehegan, M Concannon, C Flood, D Farrell, S O'Brien, N Eldin, CC Kelleher [2017]. The Childhood Obesity Surveillance Initiative (COSI) in the Republic of Ireland: Findings from 2008, 2010, 2012 and 2015, Dublin: Health Service Executive. Available at: www.hse.ie. This detailed report finds that the rates of overweight and obese for all children for the years 2008, 2010, 2012 and 2015 respectively were 21.6%, 20.8%, 16.8% and 16.9%. More girls are overweight that boys, For the year 2015, for example, 20.4% of girls and 13.2% of boys were found to be overweight or obese.

[7] Commission White Paper on a strategy for Europe on nutrition, overweight and obesity related health issues, COM (2007) 279. This is discussed in more detail below. However, for much more detailed analysis of this see Chapter 2 of A Garde, *EU Law and Obesity Prevention* (Alphen aan den Rijn, Kluwer Law International, 2010).

[8] By, eg, I Borgmeier and J Westenhoefer, 'Impact of different food label formats on healthiness evaluation and food choice of consumers: Aa randomised-controlled study' (2009) 9 *BMC Public Health* 184.

[9] Reg 1169/2011, n 2 above, Art 35 does allow for the use of additional labelling types if certain conditions are met. However, their use cannot be made compulsory by Member States and therefore they remain subject to the same problems as already exist for the enforcement of such schemes, as identified later in this chapter.

9.2. Nutrition Labelling Requirements

No significant legal changes were made to nutrition labelling requirements between the introduction of the first directive on this matter in 1990[10] and the enactment of a new regulation in 2011.[11] Originally, all nutrition labelling was optional,[12] except for those products where a nutrition claim appeared on the label.[13] Where nutrition labelling was used, there was only an obligation to provide information on the energy value, protein level, carbohydrate and fat.[14] A different set of particulars, known as 'group two particulars', would only have to appear if a nutrition claim was made specifically about the sugar, saturated fat, fibre or sodium level in a foodstuff. In this case additional information on all these nutrients would also have to be provided.[15] The 2011 Food Information Regulation changed all of this.

The Preamble to the Food Information Regulation noted that the nutrition labelling legislation was in need of updating.[16] It also stated that the Commission White Paper on a Strategy for Europe on Nutrition, Overweight and Obesity related health issues had highlighted that nutrition labelling was an important method of informing consumers about the composition of foods and of helping them to make informed choices.[17] A Commission Communication, entitled 'EU Consumer Policy Strategy 2007–2013 – Empowering consumers, enhancing their welfare, effectively protecting them' had underlined how facilitating informed choice was essential to creating effective competition in the market and protecting consumer welfare.[18] Crucially, there was recognition that:

> [k]nowledge of the basic principles of nutrition and appropriate nutrition information on foods would contribute significantly towards enabling the consumer to make … an informed choice.[19]

The ultimate result was the repeal of the Nutrition Labelling Directive and the creation of a new set of provisions, setting revised requirements for the presentation of this information and increasing its ubiquity and prominence on virtually all prepackaged foods, including, for the first time, those which are not subject to any nutrition or health claim.

---

[10] Council Directive 1990/496/EEC of 24 September 1990 on nutrition labelling for foodstuffs [1990] OJ L 276/40. Transposed into Irish law by the Health (Nutrition Labelling for Foodstuffs) Regulations 1993, SI No 388/1993.

[11] Reg 1169/2011, n 2 above on the provision of food information to consumers.

[12] Directive 1990/496, n 10 above, Art 2(1).

[13] Ibid, Art 2(2).

[14] Ibid, Art 4(1).

[15] Ibid.

[16] See Preamble to Reg 1169/2011, n 2 above, recital 7.

[17] Ibid, recital 10.

[18] Communication from the Commission to the Council, the European Parliament and the European Economic and Social Committee; EU Consumer Policy strategy 2007–2013; Empowering consumers, enhancing their welfare, effectively protecting them, COM (2007) 99.

[19] See Preamble to Reg 1169/2011, n 2 above, recital 10.

As outlined in Chapter 7, the Food Information Regulation has provided that the inclusion of details on the nutritional characteristics of products would be mandatory on all labelling in order to enable consumers to make more informed choices from 2016 onwards.[20] Section 3 of the Regulation presents us with the detail on what this compulsory requirement now entails. It states that the mandatory nutrient declaration should include details on the energy value (usually calories), the fat content and quantity of this which is in saturated form, carbohydrate level, as well as that for sugars, protein and salt.[21] This minimum level of mandatory detail can also be supplemented with information on monounsaturated fats, polyunsaturated fats, polyols, starch, fibre and vitamins and minerals which are present in significant amounts.[22]

9.2.1. Use of Portion Sizes

The Food Information Regulation states that nutrient values should be expressed per 100 g or 100 ml as required[23] or as a percentage of the recommended intake for vitamins and minerals,[24] but also that:

> the energy value and the amounts of nutrients [present] may be expressed per portion and/or per consumption unit, easily recognisable by the consumer, provided that the portion or the unit used is quantified on the label and that the number of portions or units contained in the package is stated.[25]

The use of nutrition labelling on a per portion basis can only be done if it is in addition to the expression per 100 g or per 100 ml. The use of portion sizes as a basis for the presentation of information on nutrient values is often problematic. Most specifically, the Regulation makes no reference to the fact that self-determined 'portion' sizes must at least be reasonable. It only states that that where the portion size is used as a method for expressing this important information, the total number of portions contained in the package must also be provided on the label. This does little to protect the consumer. It also facilitates deception. It allows the portrayal of a product as having a much lower fat or sugar content than it actually does. By reducing the portion size on which the information is based to half the quantity that we could reasonably expect to be consumed, the fat, salt, sugar and calorie levels are also halved, to a level that is based on an unrealistic and dishonest assessment of what the reasonable consumer actually consumes.

---

[20] See Reg 1169/2011, n 2 above, Art 4(1)(c). Specific provision is then made for this inclusion by Art 9(1)(l) of the Regulation.

[21] See Reg 1169/2011, n 2 above, Art 30(1).

[22] The quantity which constitutes a 'significant amount' is set out in Part A of Annex XIII to the Regulation. This usually means that there must be at least 15% of the daily reference intake (based on set nutrient reference values) supplied by 100 g or 100 ml of a food or 7.5% per 100 ml of a drink.

[23] See Reg 1169/2011, n 2 above, Art 32(1) and (2).

[24] Ibid, Art 32(3) and (4).

[25] Ibid, Art 33(1).

There is, however, the potential for the Food Information Regulation to make a significant change in this area if Article 33(5) thereof is properly applied. It provides that:

> [i]n order to ensure the uniform implementation of the expression of the nutrition declaration per portion or per unit of consumption and to provide for a uniform basis of comparison for the consumer, the Commission shall, taking into account actual consumption behaviour of consumers as well as dietary recommendations, adopt, by means of implementing acts, rules on the expression per portion or per consumption unit for specific categories of foods.

The revised comitology examination procedure is to be used to introduce any measure designed to set these uniform portion sizes.[26] Doubts remain, however, about the ability of the use of this provision to satisfy concerns about the exploitation by producers of the 'per portion' allowance. First, the Commission's general acceptance that it cannot introduce specific legislative requirements for each individual food type, as exemplified by its decision to cease introducing recipe laws relatively early in the development of EU food law, suggests that it would be equally reluctant and/or unable to provide similar provision here. Second, Article 33(5) of the Food Information Regulation explicitly states that dietary recommendations will be taken into account in determining portion sizes. This essentially means that the higher the quantity of fats, sugars and salt contained in the foodstuff, the lower the 'recommended' portion size may be. This could then continue to facilitate the setting of the unrealistic 'two squares' of chocolate or 'one-sixth of a bag of crisps' portion. While this could assist in creating consistency across portion sizes, it would not tally with the consumption behaviour of the average peckish consumer.

9.2.2. Mandatory Nutrient Declarations

The mandatory nutrient declaration, which has been applicable to practically all prepackaged foods since 2016,[27] must be presented 'in the principal field of vision',[28] and in a set minimum font size.[29] Negligible amounts of a nutrient need not be listed, other than as being 'negligible amounts'.[30]

---

[26] See Reg 1169/2011, n 2 above, Art 33(5) in conjunction with Art 48(2). The revised comitology examination procedure is set out in Art 5 of Regulation (EU) No 182/2011 of the European Parliament and of the Council of 16 February 2011 laying down the rules and general principles concerning mechanisms for control by Member States of the Commission's exercise of implementing powers [2011] OJ L 55/13. The entire revised comitology procedure is discussed in more detail in ch 2.

[27] Reg 1169/2011, n 2 above, Art 55.

[28] Ibid, Art 34(3)(a).

[29] Ibid, Art 34(3)(b) thereof. Minimum font sizes are set out in Art 13(2) of the Regulation, which stipulates that 'the mandatory particulars ... shall be printed on the package or on the label in such a way as to ensure clear legibility, in characters using a font size where the x-height ... is equal to or greater than 1.2 mm'. It was originally proposed that this minimum should be set at 3 mm, but this was later deemed excessive following extensive lobbying and appeals.

[30] Reg 1169/2011, n 2 above, Art 34(5).

The first key change made to the presentation of nutrient declarations on food-stuffs is, of course, this alteration from an optional requirement to a compulsory one in most circumstances and insistence that the information is laid out in a set format or formats in a prominent position on the label. Many, if not most, producers were already providing this information, whether they were obliged to do so or not.[31] So, it is arguable, this will make little difference to the use of labelling as a mechanism for informing consumers in a way that facilitates informed decision making in a manner that improves diet. The Food Information Regulation does, however, also recognise the potential value of using additional forms of presentation of the same information in a manner that improves the imparting of this to and the understanding of it amongst, consumers. Article 35(1) provides:

> [i]n addition to the forms of expression [and presentation] referred to in [this legislation, information on] the energy value and the amount of nutrients ... may be given by other forms of expression and/or presented using graphical forms or symbols in addition to words or numbers provided that the following requirements are met: (a) they are based on sound and scientifically valid consumer research and do not mislead the consumer ...; (b) their development is the result of consultation with a wide range of stakeholder groups; (c) they aim to facilitate consumer understanding of the contribution or importance of the food to the energy and nutrient content of a diet; (d) they are supported by scientifically valid evidence of understanding of such forms of expression or presentation by the average consumer; (e) ... they are based either on the harmonised reference intakes [or] on generally accepted scientific advice on intakes for energy or nutrients; (f) they are objective and non-discriminatory; and (g) their application does not create obstacles to the free movement of goods.

In other words, signpost or similar labelling schemes, such as the 'traffic lights' in the UK or 'Nutri-score' in France, may be used, but only alongside the tabular form prescribed by the Food Information Regulation and provided that it can be shown that the method chosen for presenting in this additional way is both genuine and readily understood by consumers.

Member States can recommend the use of a form of presentation for this additional nutrition labelling but, as is clear from the wording of the Regulation, they remain unable to prescribe a set format or template for this.[32] This fact is further highlighted by the inclusion of the requirement that no such scheme can 'create obstacles to the free movement of goods' which, of course, a compulsory labelling format would do. They must also provide the EU Commission with the details on any such scheme which is introduced – primarily to ensure that it does not breach any of these, or other, free movement of goods rules.[33] A new labelling

---

[31] See S Bonsmann et al, 'Penetration of nutrition information on food labels across the EU-27 plus Turkey' (2010) 64 *Journal of Clinical Nutrition* 1379, which finds that, on average, 85% of products presented nutrition labelling or related information, rising to as high as 97% in Member States such as Ireland.

[32] Reg 1169/2011, n 2 above, Art 35(2).

[33] Such as that set out in TFEU, Art 34, as discussed in detail in Ch 4.

scheme announced by the UK Government in late 2012 could not therefore be any less voluntary than its predecessor, introduced by the UK Food Standards Agency in 2006 and which did not operate in the way that they had hoped. In these circumstances, a new template could be recommended to the food sector there, but it not have to be followed by producers or retailers. EU Member States are also obliged, under the terms of the Food Information Regulation, to monitor the use of any additional labelling scheme that they may introduce.[34] Member States may, however, also require that food business operators from other EU Member States notify the national authorities of the host State about any signpost or similar labelling that they wish to use in the host State. An assessment can then be made as to whether the requirements set out in the Regulation on the use of such schemes have been met.

The EU Commission provides a focal point for the collection and exchange of information on the use of these alternative labelling systems. Article 35(4) provides that it:

> shall facilitate and organise the exchange of information between member States, itself and stakeholders on matters relating to the use of any additional forms of expression or presentation of the nutrition declaration.

While it has been made clear here and throughout this book, that the implementation of labelling, or similar, schemes such as these are outside the control of the individual Member State authorities, the Food Information Regulation does at least provide the possibility for the setting of a harmonised form of alternative presentation in the future. Article 35(5) has provided that:

> [b]y 13 December 2017, in light of the experience gained, the Commission shall submit a report to the European Parliament and the Council on the use of additional forms of expression and presentation, on their effect on the internal market and on the advisability of further harmonisation of those forms of expression and presentation. For this purpose, Member States shall provide the Commission with relevant information concerning the use of such additional forms of expression or presentation on the market in their territory. The Commission may accompany this report with proposals to modify the relevant Union provisions.

This creates an undertaking to evaluate (i) the success of alternative labelling mechanisms; and (ii) the ubiquitousness of such schemes across the EU and, on the basis of this evaluation, to consider the introduction of a harmonised EU standard for signpost or traffic-light labels. At the time of writing, this report had not yet been produced. However, subject to the findings of the report, this undertaking could eventually lead to the development of a harmonised EU alternative labelling format, creating a standard way in which nutritional information is to be presented, perhaps even supplanting the traditional tabular form. Alternatively, it may be decided that Member States could be given more flexibility in the

---

[34] Reg 1169/2011, n 2 above, Art 35(3).

development of national schemes. Only then could the UK Food Standards Agency, Santé Publique France, or the FSAI possibly prescribe that a set template is used for alternative labelling on all foodstuffs to which this would apply.

9.3. EU Nutrition Policy and Obesity

In December 2010, what was then DG SANCO (now SANTE) produced the implementation progress report on the 'Strategy for Europe on nutrition, overweight and obesity related health issues'.[35] The data presented highlighted the prevalence of weight-related health issues across the EU. In seven countries that carried out measurements on adults, between 53.5 and 68.5 per cent of men and 47.2 and 61.8 per cent of women were deemed to be overweight. Those who were 'obese' ranged from 14.2 to 26 per cent of men and from 13.3 to 30 per cent of women. The figures for men for each of the Member States for which there was comparable data, bar one – Finland, showed that those affected by the epidemic continued to rise. The graphs presented also indicated that there was a rise in the rate of overweight adult males in Ireland during the period under review (2002–2007), from 53 to 58 per cent. Similar figures were reported for women, although in Ireland the rate of overweight and obese adult females fell slightly, from 43 to 42 per cent. Around the same time, the World Health Organization (WHO) European Childhood Obesity Surveillance Initiative (COSI), the first round of which took place in 2007–2008, found that, on average, 24 per cent of children aged between six and nine years were overweight or obese.

The data available all suggests that there are serious and ongoing concerns about weight and obesity issues across the EU. Yet little was done at EU level in the years that followed the publication of the White Paper on Obesity. The same position was maintained in the implementation progress report of late 2011 as had been put forward in the White Paper of 2007 and the Green Paper two years before that. Despite rising obesity rates and the serious consequences for human health that this entailed, existing and widely criticised, nutrition labelling and nutrition and health claims requirements would, it was claimed, be sufficient to deal with the detrimental contribution that food was making to the spread of this epidemic. As already noted, the revamped Regulation on the Provision of Food Information to Consumers does now, however, at least pave the way for more meaningful legislative intervention at a later stage. This itself is, however, not certain and subject to a range of factors developing in the years following the introduction of this Regulation.

The White Paper on nutrition and obesity sets out a starting point for any integrated EU approach to assist in reducing incidence of ill health arising out of poor diet. It noted that levels of overweight and obese children and adults have

[35] See n 7 above.

risen dramatically in recent decades. It was also noted that there were repeated calls from the Council for the Commission to develop action plans in the fields of both nutrition and physical activity levels to deal with this.[36] The publication of a previous Green Paper on promoting healthy diets had already led to the finding that there was a broad consensus on the need for the Union to contribute in a meaningful way to tackling this epidemic by engaging with relevant stakeholders at national, regional and local levels.[37] Respondents to the content of the Green Paper highlighted the need for a meaningful and coherent EU-wide approach to tackling obesity.

Provisions of the EU Treaties on health policy have consistently envisaged that measures designed to promote physical wellbeing should be complementary to national policies in this area. Article 168 TFEU now provides that:

> [a] high level of human health protection shall be ensured in the definition and imple- mentation of all Union policies and activities. Union action, which shall complement national policies, shall be directed towards improving public health, preventing physi- cal and mental illness and diseases and obviating sources of danger to physical and mental health. Such action shall cover the fight against the major health scourges, by promoting research into their causes, their transmission and their prevention, as well as health information and education and monitoring, early warning of and combating serious cross-border threats to health.

While the latter part of Article 168(1) TFEU refers more specifically to contami- nation and disease, efforts made by both the Union and by Member States are clearly covered by those references in the remainder of the provision to physical health. As will be discussed in more detail later in this chapter and as has already been alluded to in Chapter 4, a significant obstacle exists within EU law itself which prevents the co-operative and complementary nature of action referred to in tackling health-related issues from being realised. This is, of course, the exist- ence of Article 34 TFEU, prohibiting Member States such as Ireland from adopting or applying any national measures that inhibit trade and which cannot be justi- fied. Member States can take action designed to protect human health; Article 168 TFEU even supports this, but they may only do so within the parameters set else- where in the Treaty, namely where the action taken does limit, in any way, the sale or marketing of food from other States, even where these may have a detrimental effect on health. This essentially means that it is only the EU institutions which are able to introduce enforceable labelling or other types of similar, legislation designed to combat obesity and nutrition-related illness. It cannot be a comple- mentary process of the type envisaged in Article 168 TFEU.

The White Paper identified four strands to the Union-wide approach to tackling obesity. The first was that actions should aim to address the root causes of

---

[36] Council Conclusions of 2 December 2002 on Obesity [2002] OJ C 11/3.
[37] Commission Green Paper on promoting healthy diets and physical activity: a dimension for the prevention of overweight, obesity and chronic diseases, COM (2005) 637.

health-related risks, extending to those associated with both poor diet and limited physical activity. The over-consumption of food, or the excessive consumption of the wrong food, is, of course, only one of the factors that can lead to obesity. Second, the actions identified in the White Paper should apply horizontally across government policy areas and at different levels of government, local and national, using a range of instruments including legislation, networking, public–private approaches and to engage the private sector and civil society. Third, action will need to be taken by private actors, such as the food industry and civil society, including local actors such as schools and community organisations.

Finally, there would have to be close monitoring of the impact that these measures adopted and approaches taken were having on diet and physical activity levels, with a view to assessing that which would need to be refined in any way or even changed fundamentally. There would have to be broad stakeholder involvement, ranging from industry and researchers to civil society, community groups and the media, to make any proposals ultimately effective. This, it was hoped, would lead to better informed consumers who would be capable of making the right choices if given 'access to clear, consistent and evidence-based information when deciding which foods to buy' following exposure to 'the wider information environment [as] shaped by cultural factors, such as advertising and other media'.

Following on from this, the White Paper identified three ways in which already existing EU-developed laws could be used to help tackle nutrition-related illness and disease. The first was through the development of the nutrition labelling requirements. This, it was noted, could be used to support consumers in their efforts to make decisions that would benefit their health. At the time of the White Paper, it was suggested that this could possibly lead to mandatory nutrition labelling for all foods. As noted, the new Regulation on the Provision of Food Information to Consumers has now introduced provision for this.[38] From 2016 onwards this information would have to be presented in a clear position on the food packaging. As stated, while 'signpost' nutrition labelling was not made compulsory, there is scope in the Regulation for this to possibly be made the subject of EU-wide legislation at a later stage.[39] The merits or otherwise of compelling producers and/or retailers to use this system on their labels is discussed in more detail below.

The second way in which existing laws could assist in combating obesity was envisaged as being through exerting proper controls over the use of nutrition and health claims. As previously noted, these types of statement only became the subject of specific Union regulation in 2006.[40] This was seen in the White Paper as presenting the opportunity of ensuring that claims made on foods about their nutritional values and/or health-promoting properties would be based on reliable scientific evidence only, ensuring that consumers would not be misled by inaccurate or confusing claims.

---

[38] See Reg 1169/2011, n 2 above, Art 9(1)(l). For further discussion see Ch 7.

[39] Ibid, Art 35(5). This review was to take place by December 2017. For further discussion see Ch 7.

[40] Regulation (EC) No 1924/2006 of the European Parliament and of the Council of 20 December 2006 on nutrition and health claims made on foods [2007] OJ L 12/3.

Finally, it was stated in the White Paper that some form of tailored regulation of the advertising and marketing of food would have to be introduced to control the ways in which these could be used to influence consumers into acting in a manner that may be detrimental to their health. It was stated that there was strong evidence that advertising aimed at children could be particularly influential in this regard. As a result, the Commission initiated an Advertising Round Table to explore whether self-regulatory approaches could be used to develop best practice models for industry. Voluntary measures that have been adopted in Ireland to address this problem, which were discussed in Chapter 7 of this book, were set out in the resulting report as an example of measures that could be adopted at national level to address these sorts of concerns. This DG SANCO (now SANTE) report set out a model for the sector and assessed whether it could present an effective method for controlling advertising aimed at children.[41] The Report found that there was a broad consensus that self-regulation in the advertising sector would only be able to work properly if there was a clear legislative framework which facilitated this. Self-regulation within the sector would be delivered, primarily, through the adoption and application of codes rather than legally binding rules. However, it was noted that for this mechanism to be effective, there would have to be meaningful contribution from stakeholders to the development of these codes, including consumer groups, parent associations and academics. The European Commission made it clear in the White Paper on Obesity that it was to keep the existing voluntary approach. This was due to the fact that this method possessed the potential 'to act quickly and effectively to tackle rising overweight and obesity rates', subject to a reassessment of this position in 2010. This ultimately resulted in the publication of the progress report on the White Paper strategy in December of that year.

The 2010 implementation progress report also referred to the fact that the EU has introduced the Audiovisual Media Services Directive, which obliges the Member States and the Commission to encourage media service providers to establish codes of conduct on commercials aimed at children that are advertising unhealthy foods.[42] The directive encourages self-regulation of the advertising sector in a manner that contributes to the promotion of healthy lifestyles among children. There is a reporting system established in the Directive which facilitates the monitoring of the application of these aims within the Member States.[43]

---

[41] DG SANCO Report on Self-Regulation in the EU Advertising Sector, July 2006. Available at: www. ec.europa.eu/dgs/health_consumer/self_regulation/docs/report_advertising_en.pdf.

[42] Art 9(2) of Directive 2010/13/EU of the European Parliament and of the Council of 10 March 2010 on the coordination of certain provisions laid down by law, regulation or administrative action in Member States concerning the provision of audiovisual media services [2010] OJ L 95/1. For an assessment of the EU's role in using the directive to prevent children from being targeted by the alcohol and food industries see O Bartlett and A Garde, 'Time to seize the (red) bull by the horns: The European Union's failure to protect children from alcohol and unhealthy food marketing' (2013) 38 *European Law Review* 498 and Chapter 5 of A Garde, *EU Law and Obesity Prevention*, n 7 above.

[43] The 2013 report recognised the 'efforts made by the advertising industry and members of the EU pledge to respond to the [Directive's] call for codes of conduct for commercial communications,

The White Paper itself also recognised that responses to nutrition-related ill health could not be limited to legislative or self-regulatory measures alone. It stated that the Commission, in conjunction with the Member States and relevant stakeholders, would undertake to develop and support scientific information and education campaigns to raise awareness of the health problems that are now associated with poor diet.

It also undertook to promote the consumption of healthier food options through its own campaigns and within the framework established by the Common Agricultural Policy. It proposed allowing surplus fruit and vegetable production to be distributed to children through schools and increasing financial support provided by the Commission for healthy eating projects aimed at young consumers. It was also noted that the Commission would initiate a study to examine the potential for more food reformulation, designed to reduce the levels of fat, saturated and trans-fats, salt and sugar in manufactured products. This study could then be used to gauge the extent to which self-regulation was working in relation to this aspect of improving the nutritional value of food.

There were other ways envisaged in the White Paper that the EU, in co-operation with the Member States, could assist in reducing rates of obesity. These included encouraging physical activity through sport, outdoor activities and active commuting. Targeting vulnerable groups, such as children and those in low socio-economic groups, was also prioritised. Developing the evidence base to support policy and decision making designed to combat obesity and using EFSA advice in relation to nutrition and health claims were also set as key ways in which the EU institutions could have a role to play.[44] There would also have to be an improvement in and harmonisation of national systems for monitoring data on food consumption levels, overweight and obesity rates. This would, it was suggested, have to happen at three levels.

First, there would have to be monitoring at the macro level to ensure the consistent gathering of comparable data on progress indicators. This should happen with reference to European Community Health Indicators (ECHI), assessing weight, diet and physical activity levels across the Union.

Second, there would need to be a systematic identification of action already undertaken in the Member States and an evaluation of its impact and effectiveness.

Third, there should be an assessment of individual projects and programmes, or micro monitoring. Support for all of this would be available through the Commission-developed European Health Interview Survey (EHIS), which became operational in 2007 and is managed by Eurostat. This system of data collection takes place in five-year cycles and gathers information on participants' BMI,

---

accompanying or included in children's programmes, of foods and beverages high in fat, sugar and salt'. Report No 2132/2012 on the Implementation of the Audiovisual Media Services Directive, 28/02/2013.

[44] For a detailed examination of EFSA's role in nutrition policy formulation see M Friant-Perrot and A Garde, 'From BSE to obesity: EFSA's growing role in the EU's nutrition policy' in A Alemanno and S Gabbi (eds), *Foundations of EU Food Law and Policy* (Farnham, Ashgate, 2013).

smoking behaviour, alcohol consumption and perceptions of personal health. The DG also launched the European Health Examination Survey in 2010. All the information produced by these systems is then collated to inform policy making and action taking on obesity prevention.

While much of what happens to combat nutrition-related illness must take place at EU level, there is recognition that Member State action is essential to addressing overweight and obesity issues. The White Paper clearly states that EU activity in this area is designed to support and complement that of the Member States. Diet and the extent to which it affects health, varies from State to State, meaning that the type of action to be taken is often best determined at local level.

Despite this recognition, however, one outstanding and very significant legal problem remains. Member States cannot take some forms of legislative action designed to minimise the ill-effects of poor diet, such as the introduction of clearer and binding food labelling requirements. To do so would be contrary to EU Treaty rules on the free movement of food. Any measures adopted would be deemed equivalent to a quantitative restriction on trade which, as discussed in Chapter 4, we know to be prohibited by Article 34 TFEU, with little chance of justification available under Article 36 TFEU.

We can conclude from this that while EU policy documents support policy decision making at Member State level, EU law prevents this national policy metamorphosing into national law, where this would inhibit, directly or indirectly, actually or potentially, interstate trade.[45] We must therefore trust that existing EU food labelling legislation is sufficient to deal with diet-related contributors to the prevalence of overweight people in society.

There is recognition at EU level that one of the best ways that this can be achieved is through the adoption of more meaningful and comprehensible forms of nutrition labelling. Despite this, the Food Information Regulation does not provide for compulsory alternative labelling schemes. Article 34 TFEU also prevents Member States from properly implementing their own policies aimed at addressing this.

9.4. National Nutrition Policy in EU Member States

9.4.1. Alternative Labelling Formats

Concerned at the ineffectiveness of the nutrition labelling requirements set out in the Nutrition Labelling Directive 1990 and the Food Labelling Regulations 1996,[46] the development of 'a clear straightforward coding system ... in common use ... that busy people can understand at a glance' was one of the central proposals put

---

[45] For a more in-depth discussion on the importance of defining the relationship between 'local' and 'European' ideals and notions of 'risk' see D Chalmers, 'Food for thought: Reconciling European risks and traditional ways of life' (2003) 66 *MLR* 532.

[46] SI No 1499/1996.

forward by the UK Government in its Public Health White Paper, published in November 2004.[47] It further stated that:

> [f]ood is a prime example of an area where there needs to be clear and consistent information to help people make healthy choices. A lot of information is provided on packaged and processed foods. Many people understand the importance of thinking about how much salt, fat and sugar they eat. But lists expressed in terms that few of us can understand are not enough. What we need to know is where a particular food fits in a healthy balanced diet so that we can make informed choices.

The UK Government undertook, therefore, to 'press vigorously for progress during the UK presidency of the EU in 2005 to simplify nutrition labelling and make it mandatory on packaged foods'.[48] The latter part of this would require a revision of the EU Nutrition Labelling Directive which, as we know from the discussion above, only set compulsory nutrition labelling requirements for those foods which carried a nutrition or health claim on the packaging, at that time.

Making this change would prove relatively straightforward given that most foodstuffs carry this information anyway, regardless of whether a claim has been made or not.[49] It has, of course, now been made mandatory to provide nutrition information for all products through the introduction of the Food Information Regulation.[50] The former part, the simplification of nutrition information, would be more difficult to achieve. This would require agreement amongst EU Member States that the system for presenting this information required a significant overhaul. It would essentially mean the introduction of an EU-wide scheme for the presentation of nutrition information in the 'signpost', 'traffic-light', or similar, format.

This particular amendment is not contained in the Food Information Regulation. In the meantime, national authorities in EU Member States must continue to rely on the use of voluntary codes and the support of producers and retailers to make any such scheme workable. Initial attempts to achieve this in the UK in 2006 failed. New proposals in this regard were thus put forward in late 2012 in the hope of developing a scheme that would result in increased adherence rates. These would, however, like their predecessor, remain entirely unenforceable by law, despite their recognised value in dealing with the problems of poor diet, overweightness, obesity and related illness and disease, such as type 2 diabetes, heart disease and cancer.[51]

---

[47] White Paper on Public Health, *Choosing health: Making health choices easier*, Department of Health, London, 2004.

[48] Ibid.

[49] See Bonsmann et al, n 31 above.

[50] See Reg No 1169/2011, n 2 above, Art 9(1)(l).

[51] The level of influence that these types of nutrition labels have on consumer decision-making is, of course, open to debate. This debate was really started by G Sacks, M Rayner and B Swinburn, 'Impact of front-of-pack traffic-light nutrition labelling on consumer food purchases in the UK' (2009) 24 *Health Promotion International* 344. The arguments for and against the use of these types of labelling format

9.4.2. Signpost Labelling

It has long been contended that traditional tabular forms of nutrition labelling are difficult for most consumers to comprehend.[52] We must therefore present this important information in a format that is easier to understand. This is even more imperative where the consumer must evaluate the data on nutrition values in addition to all the other details presented, including that on durability dates, ingredients, allergens, price, value, content and so on. It must therefore appear in a way that imparts the relevant particulars in a manner which facilitates consumer decision making in a quick, yet informed, way. The use of a well-considered 'signpost' or 'traffic-light' labelling scheme is, it is contended, the best way of achieving this dual aim. However, the system is not without its flaws. Crucially, existing alternative nutrition labelling schemes have two main shortcomings – and both relate to the fact that the templates developed by national bodies, such as the UK Food Standards Agency or Santé Publique France are not enforceable by law. The first of these shortcomings is that retailers and producers can often modify the templates provided to suit their own needs and marketing priorities. The second relates to the fact that the portion sizes upon which the colour-coded information provided is usually based can be doctored to present the product as having less detrimental nutritional values than that which is in fact the case. This former makes the scheme unworkable and confusing. The latter facilitates the deception of the consumer. This is, of course, problematic in a system initially designed to create clarity, consistency and certainty. Ongoing and flagrant abuse of the system leads to the directly opposite result. The operation of the French nutri-score scheme is possibly less vulnerable to this type of misleading practice than the UK traffic light.[53]

The idea behind UK signpost nutrition labelling is that it presents the relevant information in an easily understandable format. The colours used in traffic lights are also used for the key nutrients. The label expresses the quantity of the nutrient, such as fat level, present in the product. A green background to this information indicates that a safe or relatively healthy amount of fat is present in a portion of

---

and the evidence in support of these positions, is discussed throughout this chapter. It should be noted at this stage, however, that different versions of the traffic-light or signpost label can have different levels of impact on consumers.

[52] For further discussion on consumers' ability to understand these labels see, eg, G Cowburn and L Stockley, 'Consumer understanding and use of nutrition labelling: a systematic review' (2005) 8 *Public Health Nutrition* 21; and A Shine, S O'Reilly and K O'Sullivan, 'Consumer attitudes to nutrition labelling' (1997) 99 *British Food Journal* 283. It has also been suggested that understanding of nutrition information seems to be more widespread than use, suggesting that there is a lack of motivation amongst consumers as well as a failure, in many cases, to understand. It is hoped that 'signpost' labels, discussed in this chapter, could address the apparent apathy issue by clearly highlighting foods of poor nutritional benefit. See K Grunert et al, 'Use and understanding of nutrition information on food labels in six European countries' (2010) 18 *Journal of Public Health* 261.

[53] For more on the development of Nutri-score in France see I Carreño, 'Developments on front-of-pack nutrition declarations in the EU' (2017) 12 *European Food and Feed Law Review* 321.

the food in question. The use of an amber background for this suggests that the quantity contained in the product is at a higher level. The use of a red background signifies that there is a high level of fat or other nutrient in the food. Similar information is usually provided for saturated fats, sugar and salt. Determining which colour should be used is made by reference to the definitions set out in the EU Nutrition and Health Claims Regulation.[54] The Annex to this Regulation provides that a food can be classified as 'low-fat' where it contains a maximum of 3 g of fat per 100 g of solids, or 1.5 g of fat per 100 ml of liquids. Similar categorisation is provided for 'low-saturated fat', 'low sugar' and 'low salt', the latter description being retained for those foods that contain a maximum of 0.12 g of salt per 100 g or per 100 ml. The Regulation does not, however, set any range for medium or high levels of fats, salt, sugar or saturated fats. The UK Food Standards Agency has therefore determined that the amber (medium level) and red (high) classifications for these should be based on the recommendations of the UK Scientific Advisory Committee on Nutrition (SACN) and the Committee on Medical Aspects of Food and Nutrition Policy (COMA). These scales base 'high' levels for fat, saturated fat, sugar and salt on the calculation of 25 per cent of the recommended daily intake level per 100 g, or 30 per cent (40 per cent for salt) per portion. The nutritional information provided should be based, according to the UK FSA, on the product 'as sold', except for dried foods, where it should be expressed 'as reconstituted'.[55]

The first of the shortcomings with the FSA-developed signpost labelling scheme identified above is that producers and retailers can modify the template provided. This is as a direct result of the fact that EU law prohibits the national authorities from introducing any labelling requirement other than that directly introduced by the EU. As has been discussed in some detail in Chapter 4, this relates to the fact that EU rules on the free movement of goods, in particular the prohibition on the implementation of national measures that are of equivalent effect to quantitative restrictions on trade, prevent the adoption of any national law that restricts the flow of products between Member States. Labelling laws are clearly within the scope of this provision, set out in Article 34 TFEU. As a consequence, lack of legal effect, UK producers and retailers adopted their own versions of the FSA-backed scheme, soon after its introduction. This resulted, according to previous estimates, in the establishment of 14 different signpost label types by as early as July 2006 – less than four months after the initial establishment of the scheme.[56] None of these were identical to the UK FSA template and no two were the same as each other. A scheme designed to create clarity was adding to the confusion. No-one was

---

[54] Regulation (EC) No 1924/2006 of the European Parliament and of the Council of 20 December 2006 on nutrition and health claims made on foods [2007] OJ L 12/3.

[55] Food Standards Agency, 'Front-of-pack traffic light signpost labelling technical guidance', Issue 2, November 2007. Available at: www.food.gov.uk.

[56] C MacMaoláin, *EU Food Law: Protecting consumers and health in a common market* (Oxford, Hart Publishing, 2007) 235.

obliged to adhere to the template, so no-one did. This would continue to be the case unless a compulsory scheme were to be introduced by EU legislation.

The second difficulty that the use of colour-coded signpost food labelling has encountered relates to the actual information that is presented. The UK Food Standards Agency Guidance provides that:

> [i]nformation given in the signpost on the levels of nutrients present in a portion of a product should not be misleading and be based on realistic portion sizes [and where] possible, generally accepted portion sizes should be used.[57]

Again, given the absence of any domestic or EU legal backing for the UK traffic-light labelling scheme, this request, which is all it can be, is often ignored. Large packets of crisps have misleadingly represented the portion as being only one-sixth of the bag and some chocolate has proudly flaunted seemingly good news to the consumer about the profile of the product based on a 'portion' that transpires to be a meagre two squares of the bar (or in one example identified, a portion of one square of a bar of chocolate)! Again, these practices can continue legitimately and lawfully until the EU decides to take action in this area by establishing its own scheme or setting harmonised provisions on those systems used in the Member States.

It was officially recognised that the scheme first introduced in the UK during 2006 did not work. This culminated in the announcement of a new, single system for nutrition labelling in October 2012.[58] The Department of Health there stated that this would involve the use of front-of-pack information that would clearly display how much fat, saturated fat, salt, sugar and calories are contained in food products, using colour coding, guideline daily amounts contained (expressed as a percentage of the GDA) and high/medium/low text. It was noted that retailers were already using variants of a hybrid system (the UK FSA template) but were displaying this information 'with different visuals, colour and content making it hard for consumers to compare food'. The new model would be developed following collaboration between Government, industry and other partners to agree on the detail. The importance of the development of such a labelling type, which was announced following a three-month UK-wide consultation on the matter, was underlined by the Department, which stated that:

> [h]aving a clear and consistent labelling system across all retailers will allow consumers to make quick, informed decisions about the food they eat and may also help consumers to make healthier choices that address some of the serious health consequences of poor diet, including obesity, cardiovascular disease, cancer and diabetes.

---

[57] UK Food Standards Agency, 'Front-of-pack traffic light signpost labelling technical guidance', n 55 above, p 8.

[58] For further discussion on the legal implications of introducing such a scheme see also M Holle, E Togni and A Vettorel, 'The compatibility of national interpretative nutrition labelling schemes with European and international law' (2014) 9 *European Food and Feed Law Review* 148.

Three problems remain. First, determining the portion sizes on which the labelling declarations are based remains at the discretion of the retailers. Previous calls to make these 'realistic' were not adhered to.

Second, there is no mention of the application of this 'new' scheme to producers, only to retailers. Of the 14 different signpost labelling methods identified in July 2006, five were developed by food manufacturers.

Third, the scheme must again remain entirely voluntary until the EU acts to introduce specific provisions that would facilitate making national or EU food labelling requirements enforceable by law. The State must therefore look elsewhere for solutions that can be adopted and implemented at national level to address this serious public health issue.

The French 'nutri-score' scheme is different. However, it also remains subject to the limitations of EU laws on food labelling and on the free movement of food. While the UK scheme awards colours for each of the nutrients assessed, Nutri-score it is based on one overall consideration of nutritional value of the food. This should make it easier for consumers to make choices within a product type. One of the main criticisms of traffic light labels has been that certain food types would always score badly. Oils and fats or products which use a lot of these as an ingredient, would always be rated as 'red', due to their very high fat content. This could, of course, include high-quality olive oils or rapeseed oils which contain essential nutrients, such as omega fatty acids. It was this that irked several other EU Member States about the UK scheme, encouraging them to bring complaints about it to the EU Commission. Nutri-score rates a product from A to E. The colours also slide from dark green (A) to lighter green (B) to yellow (C) to orange (D) to red (E). The awarded letter/colour is enlarged, to stand out. Two products, made with the same ingredients, but with different quantities of these ingredients used, could be rated differently due to an overall fat or sugar content. The comparison can be easily drawn for the consumer who has a choice between biscuits or crackers marked with a 'C', compared to those marked with a 'D'. All scores are based on the nutrient declaration per 100g of the product as sold. The overall score for a food is then determined by subtracting favourable points (awarded for the inclusion of fruits, vegetables, nuts) from the unfavourable points (sugars, salts, energy levels, fats). The calculation method is more complicated than that for the UK traffic lights,[59] and it could be argued that the French scheme is possibly more compatible with EU rules on free movement and on food labelling. However, Nutri-Score, which came into operation on 31 October 2017, is still subject to the same EU rules as the UK traffic-light scheme and may also therefore be subject to further EU Commission and possibly Court of Justice scrutiny.

---

[59] The advantages of the scheme for consumers and for the protection of public health are dealt with in more detail and with more expertise elsewhere. See, for example, C Julia and S Hercberg, 'Nutri-Score: Evidence of the effectiveness of the French front-of-pack nutrition label' (2017) 64 *Ernährungs Umschau* 181. Available at: www.ernaehrungs-umschau.de.

9.4.3. Other Policy Initiatives

It has been made clear in this chapter that regardless of any proposals introduced to use food labelling as a mechanism to tackle obesity, these will always have to remain voluntary unless and until the EU introduces a harmonised standard or allowance for this. A UK Government White Paper, published in November 2010, presented alternative methods that can be used to combat food-related health concerns. This document, entitled 'Healthy Lives, Healthy People: Our strategy for public health in England' sees the facilitation of better food choices as an essential component of the more general aim of improving the longevity and well-being of the population.[60] Given the lack of legislative control over its content and format, labelling is, unsurprisingly, not mentioned anywhere in the White Paper, except when dealing with tobacco consumption and smoking. Alternative, practical and EU-permitted, interventionist measures related to food are addressed in the document. It states that '[r]esearch has shown that social networks exert a power-ful influence on individual behaviour, affecting our weight, smoking habits and happiness'.[61] In addition to this, it further asserts that:

> [t]he quality of the environment around us also affects any community [as] pollution, air quality, noise, the availability of green and open spaces, transport, housing, access to good-quality food and social isolation all influence the health and wellbeing of the local population.

Action points set out in this White Paper that are designed to assist in enhancing the quality of food available and the environment in which it is produced and in which people live include the promotion of community ownership of green spaces and access to land, so that people can grow their own food. It is also stipulated that there must be more collaborative work with business and the voluntary sector through the UK Government's Public Health Responsibility Deal, including the establishment of networks on food, alcohol and physical activity. This would be extended to specifically target changes that were deemed necessary to reduce salt intake, provide better information to consumers about food and the promotion of more socially responsible retailing and consumption of alcohol.

Other initiatives proposed in the UK White Paper included providing support for families to assist them in making informed choices about their diet and physi-cal activity levels, while also maintaining the Department of Education standards for school food. There would also be consideration of the UK Department for

---

[60] Department of Health, 'Healthy lives, healthy people: Our strategy for public health in England', The Stationery Office, 30 November 2010, ISBN: 9780101798525.

[61] The research referred to includes J Hall and T Valente, 'Adolescent smoking networks: The effects of influence and selection on future smoking' (2007) 32 *Journal of Addictive Behaviour* 3054; H Achat and others, 'Social networks, stress and health-related quality of life' (1998) 7 *Quality of Life Research* 735; and N Christakis and J Fowler, *Connected: The surprising power of our social networks and how they shape our lives* (New York, Little, Brown, 2009).

Environment, Food and Rural Affairs (DEFRA) Fruit and Vegetable Task Force recommendation that food containing fruit or vegetables along with other types of food should be added to the '5-a-day' licensing scheme, allowing the reproduction of a '5 a day' logo on the labelling or promotional material of food.

A nutrition task force was established in the UK in October 2009, charged with increasing the consumption and production of domestic fruit and vegetables. This body was to come into existence for one year, after which a report would be published, outlining proposals designed to improve the competitiveness of national farmers and to support the ability of low-income families to increase the quantity of fruit and vegetables in their diet. The task force has since published two documents: a report in August 2010 and an action plan to deliver on the recommendations made in this report, in October of the same year.

This UK Task Force was made up of representatives of the Guild of Food Writers, the Department of Health, the School Food Trust, the National Farmers' Union, the British Dietetic Association, retailers and the UK Food Standards Agency. The report highlighted that poor nutrition was estimated to cost the National Health Service in the region of £6–7 billion annually by 2002, suggesting that this had probably risen to £8 billion by 2009.[62] Added to this was the estimation that an overall increase in the consumption of fresh produce to five portions per day could help avoid up to 42,000 premature deaths per year. It was also noted, however, that despite widespread recognition of the '5-a-day' message, overall fruit and vegetable consumption levels were actually falling. Where there was any increase, this had tended to be in relation to fruit juices and not vegetables. Demand for domestically produced fruit had remained relatively stable but, alarmingly, sales of British-grown vegetables had reduced by 23 per cent. Import levels had risen 51 per cent over the same period[63] and UK self-sufficiency in indigenous fruit and vegetables continued to fall. The importance of increased fruit and vegetable consumption clearly relates not only to health protection and the associated cost benefits to the UK's National Health Service but also to the economy as a whole, highlighted by the fact that agri-food is the largest manufacturing sector in the UK, contributing over £80 billion to the economy annually and employing over 3.6 million people.[64]

The UK Task Force Report identified several ways in which the increased consumption of fruit and vegetables can be encouraged. The first of these is to

---

[62] Data taken from M Rayner and P Scarborough, 'The burden of food related ill-health in the UK' (2005) 59 *Journal of Epidemiology and Community Health* 1054.

[63] According to DEFRA and HM Revenue and Customs figures on the Adjusted National Food Survey Data 1974–2000 and the Economic and Social Data Service Expenditure and Food Surveys. Available at www.esds.ac.uk.

[64] Council of Food Policy Advisors, *Food: A recipe for a healthy, sustainable and successful future. Second report of the Council of Food Policy Advisors* (London, DEFRA, 2010). Some estimates suggest that value of the agri-food sector to the UK economy may have risen to closer to £110 billion when assessed by adding the values of non-residential catering, food and drink retailing, food and drink manufacturing, food and drink wholesaling and agriculture. These figures are taken from www.statista. com during 2018 but calculated for 2015.

try to influence or change consumer behaviour. The report indicated that this can be achieved in two broad ways. The first is the use of government advertising and information campaigns. The second is by ensuring the reliable availability of good value and quality foods that the consumer can prepare or consume easily. Domestic growers would have to be able to compete with imports on this basis. It was suggested that behaviour change campaigns that simply tell people what they should do are usually ineffective or insufficient in achieving the desired aims. Other methods must be used to complement the original information provided. These include the reinforcement of positive decision making on an ongoing and at point-of-sale basis; providing opportunities for consumer experimentation with new foods, in particular by the use of devices which suggest healthier alternatives; preparation and/or cooking instruction; normalising behaviour by demonstrating that others have already changed or maintained the preferred position; and regulating through what is termed 'supportive choice architecture', which stipulates that certain foods have to be available to consumers, for example obliging schools to provide that fruit and vegetables form an integral part of school lunches and dinners. A programme like this, designed to promote more fruit and vegetable consumption, has been established for some Irish schools, with over 3,000 schools participating. The 'Food Dudes' programme, originally developed by the University of Wales, Bangor, is now managed by the Irish Food Board, Bord Bía, with financial support from the Department of Agriculture, Food and the Marine. The programme also receives some support from the EU School Fruit Scheme, which has now been amalgamated with the aid schemes for the supply of vegetables and milk in educational establishments.[65] This EU scheme provides this support on the basis that the agricultural products distributed in nurseries, pre-schools, primary and secondary schools[66] do not contain any added sugars, added salt, added fat, added sweeteners or specified added artificial flavor enhancers.[67] The EU Regulations on the operation of these schemes for the distribution of agricultural products leave most of the organisation and administration of this to the individual Member States. However, they do stipulate that Member States must also provide accompanying educational measures to make the schemes more effective.[68]

---

[65] As set out in Regulation (EU) 2016/719 of the European Parliament and of the Council of 11 May 2016 amending Regulations (EU) No 1308/2013 and (EU) No 1306/2013 as regards the aid scheme for the supply of fruit and vegetables, bananas and milk in educational establishments [2016] OJ L 135/1.

[66] Art 22 of Regulation (EU) No 1308/2013 of the European Parliament and of the Council of 17 December 2013 establishing a common organisation of the markets in agricultural products and repealing Council Regulations (EEC) No 922/72, (EEC) No 234/79, (EC) No 1037/2001 and (EC) No 1234/2007, as amended by Reg 2016/719, n 65 above.

[67] Art 23(6) of Reg 1308/2013, as amended by Reg 2016/719, n 65 above.

[68] Art 23(10) of Reg 1308/2013, as amended by Reg 2016/719, n 65 above. The EU Regulations set out a maximum budget of €250 million per school year in aid to support the schemes, with up to €150 million being provided for the distribution of fruit and vegetables and up to €100 million for the supply of milk.

The second recommendation that was made by the UK Task Force that would assist in increasing overall fruit and vegetable consumption levels was that there should be marketing programmes run on a collaborative basis with industry, designed to promote British fruit and vegetables when they are in season and ensuring that they are provided with adequate shelf space in retail outlets. There should also be more promotion of frozen fruits and vegetables as alternatives, in particular because of the ability of the freezing process to ensure that vital nutrient levels are maintained in the food. Freezing also helps to minimise waste and ensures that there is an availability of domestic produce all year round. It was also recommended that the Healthy Start voucher scheme, run by the Department of Health and the National Health Service, should therefore be extended to frozen produce. This has now happened, providing these products, as well as milk and infant formula, for qualifying pregnant women and children under four years of age. The '5-a-day' licensing scheme was also extended to include composite foods which contain at least one portion of fruit or vegetables that count towards reaching this target for individuals. Frozen fruit and vegetables are also included in this, as are dried fruits, juices and smoothies. Much of the promotion of healthy diet in Ireland, including the increased consumption of fruit and vegetables, is carried out by Safefood. This includes educational campaigns on 'The Food Pyramid', which recommends five to seven portions of vegetables, salad and fruit per day, down to a maximum of one or two foods or drinks that are high in fat, sugar and salt per week.[69]

Value added tax (VAT) rates should, according to the UK Task Force Report, also be changed to ensure that fruit juices and smoothies are subject to the same lower rates of tax as biscuits and cakes, which can be subject to as little as 0 per cent VAT. The former are deemed to be fruits and vegetables for '5-a-day' licensing purposes but the English courts ruled in 2010 that they are also 'luxury products' and are therefore liable to the then standard VAT rate of 17.5 per cent.[70] Having a zero per cent VAT rate for food has not been deemed incompatible with EU law.[71] It is potentially justifiable on the basis that it is used to pursue a legitimate social objective. The argument in *Innocent*, however, was that smoothies have significant nutritional value and should therefore be exempt from VAT on the basis that their consumption contributes to the achievement of the necessary 'social policy'.

---

[69] The Food Pyramid. Available at: www.safefood.eu/Healthy-Eating.

[70] *Innocent Limited v The Commissioners for Her Majesty's Revenue and Customs* [2010] UKFTT 516. Schedule 8 to the Value Added Tax Act 1994 stipulates that the sale of food should not be liable to VAT, with some exceptions set out. These include, for example, ice cream, frozen yoghurt, confectionery (but not including cakes or biscuits other than those with a chocolate coating) and, most significantly here, beverages. The question in *Innocent* was whether a smoothie was a 'beverage' for VAT purposes and whether this evaluation should take aspects of social policy into consideration.

[71] Case 416/1985, *Commission v UK* [1988] ECR 3127. The 0% VAT rate has not necessarily been deemed compatible with EU law either. The European Court of Justice merely found that the Commission had failed to establish that the UK was not in compliance with its obligations under what were the applicable provisions of EU law at the time, in particular, those set out in Directive 1977/388/EEC [1977] OJ L 145/1.

In *Kalron* it was held[72] and upheld on appeal,[73] that liquidised fruits and/or vegetables must be considered as 'beverages' for taxation purposes. In *Innocent* the same conclusion was reached about fruit smoothies. The Tribunal actually used the fact that other 'healthy' drinks, such as fruit juice and bottled water, were taxed at the standard rate as an explanation as to why it was consistent to subject smoothies to the same level of VAT.

In Ireland, many foods are subject to a zero per cent rate of VAT. This includes items that are we are encouraged to consume regularly by the Food Pyramid, such as fruit, vegetables, cheese and soup. The zero rate also applies to sugar. Food and drink that is normally liable to the zero rate becomes liable to the standard rate of VAT if it is supplied during catering or by a vending machine, unless the catering services are provided to patients in a hospital or students at their school. As in the UK, most soft drinks, including bottled drinking water, juices and smoothies are subject to the standard rate of VAT. There is significantly more VAT on bottled water or a fruit and/or vegetable smoothie than there is on sugar. In addition to this, there is a reduced rate of VAT on some foods, including some cakes, biscuits, crackers and wafers. Cakes are subject to the lower second reduced rate if supplied with a meal. Some of the anomalies in the VAT rate include the fact that a biscuit that is covered in chocolate is subject to VAT at the standard rate of 23% in 2018, while a biscuit that is not covered in chocolate is subject to a reduced VAT rate of 13.5%. Caramel spread is 0% rated. White bread carries 0% VAT. Bagels are normally subject to the 13.5% reduced VAT rate. Pub grub also benefits from the second reduced VAT rate of 9%.[74]

No state can legitimately claim that it wishes to encourage its population to eat healthily if it imposes a significantly higher tax on water, fruit smoothies and blended fruit than on biscuits and cakes.[75] Repeatedly, studies show that one of the primary considerations in purchasing determinations is price.[76] Yet little has been done to make fruit and vegetables, in what might be considered by many as

---

[72] *Kalron Foods Ltd v The Commissioners for Her Majesty's Revenue and Customs* [2007] STC 1100.
[73] [2007] EWCH 695.
[74] As set out in the Value-Added Tax Consolidation Act 2010, s 46.
[75] The distinction between different types of biscuits is complicated by the absence of proper definitions of cakes or biscuits. However, according to the Revenue Commissioners (relying on the State Chemist), the moisture content for a biscuit is no more than 12% and, once over this level, it becomes a cake. This complication was most famously addressed in the UK in the case of 'Jaffa cake' biscuits, which were originally 0% VAT-rated by Customs and Excise there as they were considered to be 'cakes', but which were later re-classified as 'biscuits partly covered in chocolate'. United Biscuits challenged this, arguing that they were, in fact, cakes. Their appeal was successful, the Tribunal finding that although 'Jaffa cakes' had the characteristics of both cakes and biscuits, they possessed enough characteristics of 'cake' to be considered as such for VAT purposes. United Biscuits (LON/91/0160).
[76] See, eg, T Andreyeva, M Long and K Brownell, 'The impact of food prices on consumption: A systematic review of research on the price elasticity of demand for food' (2010) 100 *American Journal of Public Health* 216; and S French, 'Pricing effects on food choices' (2003) 133 *Journal of Nutrition* 8415. The latter study showed how reducing the price of lower-fat foods led to significant increases in the sale of these products. Price reductions also led to a fourfold increase in the sale of fresh fruit and a doubling of sales of fresh vegetables.

their most palatable form, more affordable. What is most alarming about the decisions in both *Innocent* and *Kalron*, when applied to a similar VAT regime to that in operation in Ireland, is that the Tribunal and the English High Court respectively found that fruit and vegetables were significantly different in their pre- and post-liquidised forms. The appellants in *Kalron* argued that their products, a blend of liquidised fruits and/or vegetables, were a soft form of food, as distinct from a beverage. Beverages were subject to the higher rate of VAT. The applicants in *Innocent* claimed that fruit smoothies (provided they have retained fibre and have not ended up as a juice nor have had any sugar added) are essentially the same as a fruit salad and should therefore be treated the same for taxation purposes. In both cases the Tribunal and the Court disagreed. In the former, Warren J stated in the High Court that '[t]he blending transforms a solid, albeit soft, food into a liquid which can be drunk'. The process could, therefore, change the VAT treatment of the ingredients. In the latter it was found that:

> fruit smoothies are not merely drinkable liquids, they are drinks [and] as drinks, fruit smoothies are unusual (but not unique) in that they are quite thick and do require digestion: we do not think this is sufficient to mean that they are not a beverage if they are drunk as other beverages would be drunk.

The Tribunal also chose to overlook the fact that the majority of consumers saw smoothies as being more of a snack than a drink. This was deemed inconsequential on the grounds that they were:

> wary of putting too much weight on market research which gives different answers to similar questions from one survey to another and where answers depend so much on how the question was asked and what alternatives were given.

The taxation of fruit smoothies has not been reconsidered in the light of either overall nutrition policy or, perhaps more questionably, by the fact that they retain many of the key characteristics of and are produced entirely from food – albeit in liquidised form. The UK Fruit and Vegetables Task Force Report suggested that reducing the VAT to 0 per cent on these healthier options could lead to an increase in overall nutritional benefits derived from diet to the extent that it could save the UK National Health Service nearly 1 per cent of its overall budget. It could, in effect, be a cost-saving measure. It should certainly be considered as an option for Ireland also, possibly as a counter to the introduction of a sugar tax there in 2018.

A range of possible interventions to assist in reducing obesity rates have been considered here. A number of the initiatives put forward in the UK Task Force recommendations as to what could be done there to improve diets have been put into effect in Ireland. These include the promotion of healthy eating by bodies such as Safefood and the fruit and vegetable consumption programmes in schools. Much of the international debate thus far has tended to focus on the introduction of so-called 'fat taxes', which lead to an increase in the price of some foods and sugary drinks. This is often put forward as a potential panacea to the obesity problem. It did not, however, work in Denmark and was withdrawn soon after its introduction. It has been suggested that the use of fiscal measures to discourage the consumption of nutritionally inferior foods can only work as one of a range of related measures, operating as part of an overall strategy, based on a mix of policy tools.[77] This could include the reduction of taxes on healthier foods, as well as the introduction of additional pricing measures for some unhealthy foods. The Irish Sugar Tax, discussed in more detail below, is one example of this. It could also involve the use of a well-constructed alternative labelling scheme, which makes it clear to the consumer that the food is not just 'high' or 'low' in a particular substance. Instead, it must clearly indicate the impact that the long-term consumption of the food or drink in question will have. Simply displaying fat or sugar levels is not suitable. The consumption of many types of fats is essential for good health. Similarly, sugar content arising from fruits is different from that present in a product due its addition as an ingredient in processing.

9.5. International Policy and Recommendations

While it is recognised that most individual States or interstate organisations, such as the EU, have their own policies on nutrition and food safety, the WHO has drafted an action plan designed to assist the European region in its efforts to tackle disease associated with, in particular, obesity.[78] This plan was endorsed by the WHO Regional Committee for Europe, which called on its own Member States to develop related food and nutrition policies.

The WHO Action Plan set out four main aims. These were stated as reducing the prevalence of diet-related non-communicable disease; reversing the obesity trend in children and adolescents; reducing the prevalence of micronutrient deficiencies; and reducing the incidence of food-borne diseases. The first three of these relate directly to nutrition, both deficiency and excess. The third relates to the absence of recommended minimum quantities of certain vitamins and minerals, such as vitamin A and iron, from diets. These three nutrition-related aims would be tackled by reductions in saturated fatty acid, transfat, salt and sugar consumption, coupled with an increase in the quantities of fruit and vegetables eaten. Specific actions designed to achieve these aims were listed as including the promotion of school nutrition policies, such as the establishment of fruit and vegetable distribution schemes; improving the availability and affordability of fruit and vegetables; promoting the reformulation of mainstream food products to reduce the quantities of fats, salts and sugars used in the manufacture of food; promoting appropriate micronutrient fortification of staple food items, in particular where

---

[77] A Alemanno and I Carreño, 'Fat taxes in Europe: A legal and policy analysis under EU and WTO law' (2013) 8 *European Food and Feed Law Review* 97.

[78] WHO, 2nd European Action Plan for Food and Nutrition Policy 2007–2012 (Copenhagen, WHO, 2008).

micronutrient deficiencies have become a public health problem; improving the nutritional quality of the food supply in public institutions, such as health services, schools and workplaces; exploring the use of economic tools, such as taxes and subsidies to influence the affordability of food and drinks in line with dietary guidelines; and establishing targeted programmes for the protection of vulnerable and low socioeconomic groups.

More specifically, the WHO Action Plan sets guidelines for the provision of comprehensive information and education to consumers. It states that '[a] sound communication and information strategy … is essential for supporting the adoption of healthy lifestyles'. Specific action to assist in delivering on this was stated to include the development of dietary guidelines, aimed at both the general population and at vulnerable groups; conducting public campaigns aimed at informing consumers about food and nutrition; ensuring the employment of appropriate marketing practices for all food products in line with internationally agreed recommendations; and the promotion of adequate and suitable labelling for food products, designed to improve consumers' understanding of product characteristics and supporting healthy choices. This labelling recommendation also stipulated that regulations and guidelines should be developed that reflect best practice, such as 'front-of-pack signposting'. Whichever method is used, the Action Plan recommends that it should establish 'an efficient method for assessing the nutrient quality of food products'.

9.6. Irish Sugar Tax

A sugar sweetened drinks tax came into effect in Ireland on 1 May 2018. It applies at the point that the product enters Ireland, either from within the State or as an import. The supplier of the drink is liable for the payment of the tax.[79] Suppliers of these drinks must register or already be registered with the Revenue Commissioners.[80] There is relief available for those sugar-sweetened drinks that are either produced in Ireland or which are imported into Ireland but are then ultimately supplied to a recipient outside the State.[81] The tax, established by the Finance Act 2017,[82] applies to all water and juice-based drinks that have sugar added as an ingredient and a total sugar content of 5 grams or more per 100 millilitres.[83] 'Added sugar' includes sugar or substances containing sugar, except for juices.[84]

---

[79] As set out in the Value-Added Tax Consolidation Act 2010, s 2.
[80] Finance Act 2017, s 38.
[81] Ibid, s 40.
[82] Ibid, Part 2, Chapter 1. Notified to the EU Commission under the terms of Directive 2015/1535, [2015] OJ L 241/1.
[83] Finance Act 2017, s 36(1) provides that '[…] a duty of excise, to be known as sugar sweetened drinks tax, shall be charged, levied and paid at the rates specified in Schedule 4 on each sugar sweetened drink, with a sugar content of 5 grams or more per 100 millilitres, supplied in the State by a supplier'.
[84] Finance Act 2017, s 35.

Establishing which drinks may be subject to the tax requires cross-reference with the EU combined nomenclature, defining products.[85] In general terms, it means that fruit juices and vegetable juices with added sugar, as well as 'waters, including mineral waters and aerated waters, containing added sugar [...] and other non-alcoholic beverages' are liable to the sugar tax, provided the sugar levels exceed 5 g per 100ml. This includes flavoured waters, carbonated or 'fizzy' drinks, sports drinks or juice-based drinks that have sugar added above the threshold level. Drinks sold in concentrated form are liable to the tax if they contain added sugar at the required level. Some sweetened drinks are exempt from the tax. These include alcohol-free beers, milk, soya, nut, cereal or seed-based drinks and those products which are defined as 'food supplements'. Products that are exempt from the labelling requirements set out in the Food Information Regulation because of small-scale production levels are also exempt from the sugar tax.[86]

As with any national measure like this, approval would first have to be sought and granted by the EU Commission.[87] This was obtained in April 2018. When introduced, the rate of the tax was set at 16.26 cents per litre, or 20 cents including VAT, for those drinks with a total sugar content between 5 and 8 g per 100mls. Drinks which contain more than 8 g of sugar per 100ml would be taxed at 24.39 cents per litre, or 30 cents including VAT. Therefore, a 2-litre bottle of sugar-sweetened carbonated drink would carry an additional tax of 60 cents. The European Commission concluded that Ireland's sugar sweetened drinks tax did not involve any State aid. It found that the design of the tax was consistent with health policy objectives being pursued by Ireland, in particular tackling obesity and other sugar-related disease. This was a relatively quick process, with the State having informed the Commission of its intention to introduce the tax in February 2018. It is much easier for a State to gain this type of approval for a national measure when it is in the form of taxation. This is because the EU Member States have retained the right to determine their own taxation regimes. The only possible legal issues for a tax like this would be whether there were any outstanding competition law concerns, such as those related to state aid, or whether the tax would be discriminatory against non-national producers, as prohibited by Article 110 TFEU. The EU Commission, in its assessment, had also found that sugary drinks could be treated differently to other sugary products as the former were seen to be the main source of calories that were devoid of any nutritional value, thereby raising specific health concerns. They were also seen as products that were liable to overconsumption and therefore represented a higher risk to the prevalence of

[85] As set out in Council Regulation (EEC) No 2658/1987 of 23 July 1987 on the tariff and statistical nomenclature and on the Common Customs Tariff, [1987] OJ L 256/1.
[86] For more on this exemption from the general labelling obligations set out in the Food Information Regulation see Ch 7.
[87] For an assessment of other measures that can possibly be employed to deal with diet-related risks among young people see W Schroeder, 'Age restrictions on the sale of energy drinks from an EU law perspective' (2016) 11 *European Food and Feed Law Review* 400.

obesity when compared to solid foods. Finally, support for the Irish tax was also found in the fact that it was one of a range of measures that would be adopted and implemented as part of an overall policy designed to tackle obesity rates in Irish adults and children, accounting for World Health Organization recommendations this, which indicated that limiting the consumption of sugary drinks would be an important part of obesity-tackling strategies in Member States.

Assessing whether sugar taxes work is complicated. It is also quite subjective. The success, or otherwise, of a new charge like this can be measured in several different ways. The most obvious of these is whether it leads to reduced consumption of the targeted product. On this, the evidence from other countries that have previously introduced such a tax is mixed. It also depends on how this evidence is presented. How it is presented tends to follow who it is that is presenting it. A sugar tax could, for example, lead to significant reductions in consumption rates amongst target sections of society, like children or adolescents. However, it may also be presented as an average across the entire population of a country, including those who rarely consumed these products prior to the introduction of the tax. This dilutes the figures, suggesting that the tax has been less successful than it has been at achieving the desired outcome. The second measurement of success is reformulation. In some ways, this is the most appropriate indicator. If the introduction of a new sugar tax leads to producers reducing the quantities of added sugar in their products, then it could be argued that it is successful immediately. The UK Treasury estimated that around half of producers of soft drinks there reduced the added sugar content in advance of the introduction of the Soft Drinks Industry Levy in April 2018,[88] in some cases by between half and two-thirds.[89] Overall consumption rates of these drinks may not necessarily fall, but if the products being consumed contain significantly less added sugar then the introduction of the tax has clearly been a success. The third measurement of success is what happens to the revenue generated by the tax. If this is linked to other public health measures with measurable outcomes, then the tax can also be viewed as a success, even where the consumption of sugar does not necessarily fall by any significant amount. Fourth, from a legal perspective, the use of a sugar tax can be judged as successful to the extent that it more readily complies with EU law than some other measures that States may choose to adopt to address the issue of the over-consumption of sugar. The Court of Justice in *Scotch Whisky*,[90] made it clear that using taxation in the form of increased duties, which is how the Irish tax works, '[…] may be less restrictive of trade and competition within the European Union' than other measures, such as minimum unit pricing. However, as discussed in the context of fiscal measures designed to target the over-consumption of alcohol,

---

[88] As set out in The Soft Drinks Industry Levy Regulations 2018, SI No 41/2018.

[89] For example, the manufacturers of some well-known soft drinks reduced the sugar content from 13g per 100 ml to less than 4.5g per 100 ml. Many others cut the sugar content by similar amounts.

[90] Case C-333/2014, *Scotch Whisky Association and others v Lord Advocate, Advocate General for Scotland* ECLI:EU:C:2015:845. This case was also discussed in Ch 4.

taxes may not always have the desired effect, especially when considering that the additional charge can then be absorbed by the producer or the retailer rather than being passed on to the consumer that the charge is designed to deter.

9.7. Public Health and Alcohol

An undertaking was included in the original EU Framework Food Labelling Directive in December 1978 to introduce more specific labelling rules for alcoholic products, including ingredient listing requirements, within four years.[91] As previously stated, this directive was replaced in 2000.[92] The only significant additions to the list and format of the compulsory labelling indications that were made by this newer version of the Directive were the incorporation of quantitative ingredient declarations for those products which stated or suggested that certain foods had been included in production; the new durability category of 'use by' date for highly perishable foods; and the requirement to disclose alcohol content for beverages where this was more than 1.2% by volume.[93] There was still no inclusion of compulsory ingredient listing for alcoholic drinks, despite the original undertaking alluded to above to address this matter by the mid-1980s. No other labelling requirements for alcoholic drinks were included in the second framework directive.

Many EU Member States, including Ireland, have a problem with the over-consumption of alcohol. The Health Research Board, which is an autonomous statutory agency set up under the Health Research Board (Establishment) Order 1986,[94] reported in 2016 that '[…] alcohol is responsible for a considerable burden of death, disease and injury [in Ireland]',[95] and that this was a problem that was getting worse. More specifically, this report found that the number of wholly attributable alcohol-related discharges from Irish hospitals rose from 9,420 in 1995 to 17,120 in 2013, an increase of 82 per cent. Males accounted for 72.4 per cent of these discharges, females 27.6 per cent. In 2013, alcohol-related discharges

---

[91] Directive 1979/112, Art 6(3). Despite this, comprehensive labelling requirements for alcoholic products had still not been introduced by June 2018. Alcoholic beverages are exempt from many of the food labelling requirements set out in the harmonising legislation. For more on this see Ch 7. Also see L Vaqué, 'Listing ingredients on the labels of alcoholic beverages in the EU: A reality?' (2018) 13 *European Food and Feed Law Review* 233; and L Vaqué, 'Self-regulation of the labelling of the list of ingredients of alcoholic beverages: A long-term solution?' (2017a) 12 *European Food and Feed Law Review* 413.

[92] Directive 2000/13/EC of the European Parliament and of the Council of 20 March 2000 on the approximation of the laws of the Member States relating to the labelling, presentation and advertising of foodstuffs, [2000] OJ L 109/29.

[93] All inserted into Directive 2000/13, Art 3(1).

[94] SI No 279/1986.

[95] D Mongan and J Long, 'Overview of alcohol consumption, alcohol-related harm and alcohol policy in Ireland' (2016) Health Research Board: Dublin, ISSN: 1649-7198. Also available at: www.hrb.ie.

accounted for over 160,000 bed days in Irish hospitals (up from 56,264 in 1995), meaning that each day 439 beds were occupied by a wholly attributable alcohol-related condition. The report also analysed mortality data from the National Drug-Related Deaths Index (NDRDI) for the years 2008–2013, finding that there were nearly 6,500 alcohol-related deaths during this period, accounting for nearly 4 per cent of all deaths in Ireland, or three deaths per day. There is a considerable economic cost. According to the report's analysis of the National Alcohol Diary Survey 2013, almost 80,000 employees missed work days due to alcohol, putting the direct cost of alcohol-related absenteeism at over €41 million per annum. This figure does not account for reduced productivity costs. It was estimated that nearly 5,500 people on the unemployment register in Ireland had lost their jobs due to alcohol use. The overall economic cost of alcohol abuse to the State, excluding emergency care, general practice, psychiatric care and alcohol treatment services, was estimated to be €1.5 billion in 2012. Other studies put the cost of this even higher. A review, commissioned by the Department of Health, found that alcohol-related crime costs the State nearly €700 million per annum and a further €258 million arising out of alcohol-related road accidents, with lost economic output costing €641 million during 2013.[96] The total cost to the exchequer set out in this report was thought to be closer to €2.4 billion. Almost one in three presentations to accident and emergency departments in Irish hospitals at weekends, especially during the early hours of Sunday mornings, are alcohol-related.[97]

The prevalence of alcohol misuse in Ireland led to the introduction of the Public Health (Alcohol) Bill in December 2015. It is expected that this Bill will become an Act during 2018. It contains five main provisions. These are the introduction of minimum unit pricing; health labelling; advertising and sponsorship regulation; separating alcohol from other products in mixed retail outlets like supermarkets and convenience shops; and regulating the sale and supply of alcohol in some circumstances.

Part 2 of the Bill commences by setting out how minimum unit pricing in Ireland should work. It is similar to that which was introduced by the Alcohol (Minimum Pricing) (Scotland) Act 2012. The most significant difference is that the Irish system is to be based on a minimum price per gram of alcohol, where the Scottish system bases this on the more traditional 'units' measurement. It is proposed that the minimum price per gram of alcohol will be €0.10.[98] This is subject to change by the Minister for Health at any stage from three years after the initial introduction of the Act, or 18 months after any subsequent change,[99] taking a number of set factors into consideration in determining what this rate per gram

---

[96] A Hope, 'Alcohol Literature Review' (2014). Available at: www.health.gov.ie.

[97] B McNicholl, D Goggin, D O'Donovan, 'Alcohol-related presentations to emergency departments in Ireland: a descriptive prevalence study' (2018) 8 *BMJ Open* e021932.

[98] The Public Health (Alcohol) Bill 2015, s 10(1). In Scotland this is set at £0.50 per unit. According to www.drinkaware.co.uk, there are 8 grams of alcohol in a unit. On this calculation this makes the Irish minimum price higher than that set for Scotland (approximately €0.80 versus €0.57 per unit).

[99] Public Health (Alcohol) Bill 2015, ss 10(3) and 10(4).

should be.[100] As discussed in Chapter 4, the European Court of Justice has some issues with the use of minimum unit pricing in this way. It prefers that taxation, similar to the system which now operates for sugary soft drinks, is used instead, finding that '[…] increased excise duties […] may be less restrictive of trade and competition within the European Union'.[101] However, it did ultimately decide that '[i]t is for the referring court to determine whether that is indeed the case, having regard to a detailed analysis of all the relevant factors in the case before it'.[102] Given that retailers and/or producers could absorb any additional tax costs themselves, as is the case for the Irish sugar sweetened drinks tax, minimum unit pricing can be seen as a more appropriate charge in circumstances such as these. With minimum pricing the charge must be met directly by the purchaser.

As noted above, the three main pieces of EU framework food labelling legislation, including the current Food Information Regulation, have all refrained from introducing the same obligations for alcoholic beverages as they have for other products. It is not just that these drinks do not have to carry additional labelling requirements, they must bear fewer. The most significant exemptions for alcoholic drinks are the list of ingredients and the nutrient declaration.[103] EU Member States are, however, permitted to adopt and maintain national measures compelling the inclusion of a list of ingredients on the label, as an interim measure.[104] Many producers in States such as Ireland do now voluntarily present the ingredient information. The Public Health (Alcohol) Bill has moved to make the presentation of some of this information obligatory. It has also gone further by introducing health warnings for the labelling of these products.

Under the terms of the Bill, it would be an offence to sell an 'alcohol product' that is not labelled with a number of health warnings and disclosures.[105] These include warnings about alcohol consumption generally and alcohol consumption while pregnant, as well as information on the total quantity in grams of alcohol in the container, the energy value as kilojoules and kilocalories and details about a website, that is to be established by the Health Service Executive and which will provide public health information in relation to alcohol consumption.[106] This does not apply to alcohol products that are sold in reusable containers, but these must

---

[100] Ibid, s 10(5).

[101] Para 50 of the Judgment in Case C-333/2014, *Scotch Whisky*, n 90 above.

[102] Ibid.

[103] Reg 1169/2011, n 2 above, Art 16(4).

[104] Ibid, Art 41. These national measures can be maintained until a decision is taken at EU level on whether the compulsory indication of ingredients will be applied across the Union. The Commission is to make a decision on this following the procedure set out in Art 16(4) of the Food Information Regulation. The first part of this process has taken place, namely the production of a Commission Report on the labelling of alcoholic beverages. Discussed further in this chapter, this report from the Commission to the European Parliament and the Council is regarding the mandatory labelling of the list of ingredients and the nutrition declaration of alcoholic beverages, COM(2017) 58.

[105] 'Alcohol product' is as defined in s 73 of the Finance Act 2003, where this is deemed to be '[…] beer, wine, other fermented beverage, spirits or intermediate beverage'. These 'technical specifications' also have to be notified to the EU Commission under the terms of Directive 2015/1535, n 82 above.

[106] The Public Health (Alcohol) Bill 2015, s 11(1).

still be accompanied by a document that specifies this information.[107] Pubs, clubs and other licensed establishments that sell alcoholic drinks must also display most of this information, including the health warnings and the website details.[108] They must also make the other information on energy content and grams of alcohol available for inspection, if requested. The format for the health warnings may be prescribed by the Minister for Health.[109]

The evidence suggests that some warnings or marketing restrictions on alcoholic products can be introduced in EU Member States and elsewhere. Other EU Member States have successfully done this. France, for example, has enacted laws requiring that all alcoholic beverages carry a warning about the risk of damaging the foetus by drinking alcohol during pregnancy. The warning may be presented as a pictogram or as text. The producer and/or seller has the choice of which to use and the evidence suggests that they tend to use the pictogram more often. Germany has introduced marketing restrictions on the sale of 'alcopops'. The minimum age for purchasing these drinks is 18 under the terms of the Protection of Minors Act, whereas it is 16 for other products containing alcohol. This is to be made very clear with a statement to this effect on the front of the packaging, with the same font size as the brand name. They are also subject to additional taxation. Russia has introduced some health warnings on wines and spirits, including mandatory indications that alcohol is not suitable for minors, pregnant or nursing women or people with specified illnesses or disease.

Other countries which have introduced laws on alcohol warning labels include Argentina, where there is a requirement to include a prominent statement to the effect that consumers should 'drink in moderation' and that the products are 'not to be sold to anyone under 18 years of age'.[110] Since 1996, Brazilian retailers must include a statement that consumers should 'avoid the excessive consumption of alcohol'. Since 1994 there has been a requirement in Colombia to indicate that 'an excess of alcohol is harmful to your health'. There are similar laws in Costa Rica, Ecuador, El Salvador, Guatemala, Mexico and Taiwan. Drinking during pregnancy warnings are also prescribed in the United States of America. Perhaps the most developed laws are those in South Africa (2007), where labels must clearly carry one of seven listed health messages; and Thailand (2008), where under the terms of the Alcohol Beverage Control Act warning pictures and messages must be used. This includes warnings that 'liquor drinking may cause less consciousness and death'; 'liquor drinking is harmful to you and destroys your family'; 'drunk driving may cause disability or death'; and 'liquor drinking may cause cirrhosis and sexual impotency'.

---

[107] Ibid, s 11(2) and (3).
[108] Ibid, s 11(4).
[109] Ibid, s 11(10).
[110] Art 5 of Law No 24.788 of 5 March 1997, National Law on the Prevention of Alcoholism.

According to a Eurobarometer study in 2007,[111] 77 per cent of EU citizens favour the introduction of warnings on alcohol bottles aimed at pregnant women and drivers. In only five EU Member States were more than one-third of consumers against the introduction of these warnings (Netherlands, Denmark, Finland, Estonia and Slovenia). In Ireland, 82 per cent of respondents were found to be in favour of such labelling indications, with only 11 per cent against.

A study conducted for the EU Commission on alcoholic beverage labels found that there was relatively little use of health warnings and, where they are being used, there was wide divergence in this across the EU Member States.[112] It was therefore recommended that standardised guidelines were now necessary on the use of these forms of labelling disclosure. The findings also suggested that regulation may be more effective than voluntary agreements. The difficulty alluded to throughout this book remains, however, as to how and whether an individual Member State, such as Ireland, can unilaterally introduce new labelling requirements when considering the existing obligations that persist in EU law. The introduction of any legal requirements in this area would have to take cognisance of the fact that (i) they will be subject to EU rules on the free movement of goods; (ii) they are beyond what is specifically required and therefore are not automatically allowable, under EU labelling regulations; and (iii) for any such scheme to be justifiable, a real need for it must be identified, communicated to the Commission and acceptable to the other EU Member States – convincing all parties that it is both necessary and proportionate. This is not always an easy thing to do. It has formed the basis of arguments against the passage of the Public Health (Alcohol) Bill into Irish law.

The EU Food Information Regulation does create the possibility for Member States, such as Ireland, to introduce measures like those which are set out in the Public Health (Alcohol) Bill. As already stated above, Article 41 of the Regulation provides that '[m]ember States may […] maintain national measures as regards the listing of ingredients in the case of beverages containing more than 1.2% by volume of alcohol'. The Regulation also provides, in Article 39, that '[M]ember States may, in accordance with the procedure laid down in Article 45, adopt measures requiring additional mandatory particulars for specific types or categories of foods, justified on grounds of [inter alia] the protection of public health'.

The procedure set out in Article 45 of the Regulation works on the basis of notification. It states that:

> [the] Member State which deems it necessary to adopt new food information legislation shall notify in advance the Commission and the other Member States of the measures envisaged and give the reasons justifying them.

[111] Special Eurobarometer 272 on 'Attitudes towards alcohol', March 2007.
[112] GFK Report for the European Commission on the state of play in the use of alcoholic beverage labels to inform consumers about health aspects: Action to prevent and reduce harm from alcohol. ISBN: 9789279369834.

It further stipulates that:

> [t]he Commission shall consult the Standing Committee on [Plants, Animals, Food and Feed] if it considers such consultation to be useful or if a Member State so requests [and if] the Commission's opinion is negative [...] the Commission shall initiate the examination procedure [...] in order to determine whether the envisaged measures may be implemented subject, if necessary, to the appropriate modifications.

Member States cannot implement any measure that goes beyond the terms of the Regulation until at least three months after notification to the Commission and provided that no negative opinion has been passed on the proposal.[113]

It is clear from the legislation and from the case law discussed in Chapter 4, that Member States can introduce measures that have an effect equivalent to a quantitative restriction on trade, provided they can convince the Commission and the other Member States, that such a measure is necessary on health protection grounds. It must also be proportionate, meaning that no less trade-restricting measure could have been introduced instead, one that would still have achieved the aims being pursued by the State. However, it must also be remembered that some of the case law of the European Court of Justice indicates that even where a seemingly and accepted legitimate health concern is being addressed by a new legislative measure, this does not mean that it will be automatically compatible with EU law. For national measures designed to protect public health from the dangers posed by alcohol misuse, this was most obviously seen in the decision of the Court in *Rosengren*.[114]

Other measures put in place by the Public Health (Alcohol) Bill include restrictions on advertising and sponsorship. Alcohol products cannot be advertised, for example, unless they include a prescribed health warning, a pregnancy health warning and details of the related HSE website.[115] This does not apply to alcohol-related merchandise, fixtures or fittings in licensed premises, wholesalers' or manufacturers' premises or their vehicles.[116] Again, these warnings and limitations are to be set by the Department of Health and the Minister.[117] Alcohol products cannot be advertised, under the proposals set out in the Bill, in certain places. They cannot, for example, be advertised in local authority parks, on public service or most public transport vehicles or their stations or stops, within 200 metres of school, nursery or playground perimeters.[118] Alcohol products should not be advertised at sports arenas.[119] They are prohibited from being sponsored at events at which the majority of competitors or participants

---

[113] Reg 1169/2011, n 2 above, Art 45(3). Also, the procedure set out in Dir 2015/1535, n 82 above.
[114] Case C-170/2004, *Klas Rosengren and others v Riksaklagaren* [2007] ECR I-4071.
[115] Public Health (Alcohol) Bill 2015, s 12(2).
[116] Ibid, s 12(1).
[117] Ibid, s 12(4) and (5).
[118] Ibid, s 13(2).
[119] Ibid, s 14.

are children or at events aimed primarily at children.[120] They are also prohibited from being sponsored at vehicle racing events, such as rally car driving or motor car or motorbike racing.[121] Restrictions are also placed on the promotion or presence of alcohol products, or references to them, on children's clothing,[122] and advertising in publications,[123] or at cinemas.[124]

9.8. Conclusion

This chapter has focused on three things that can be done, from a legal perspective, to assist in addressing the prevalence of ill-health arising out of poor diet. These are: (i) labelling measures; (ii) fiscal measures; and (iii) marketing restrictions. Proper labelling measures have yet to be adopted for either foods or alcoholic beverages. The only legislative response on labelling so far for foods has been to make the nutrient declaration compulsory at a time when the vast majority of products were carrying this information anyway. As has been discussed in this chapter, the format in which this is presented is crucial to the facilitation of consumer understanding. A satisfactory EU-wide response has not been found on this latter point yet either. It is also highly unsatisfactory that alcoholic beverages remain exempt from some of the most significant labelling requirements. One of the main findings from a 2017 EU Commission Report on this matter is to allow the sector to devise its own self-regulatory proposals, rather than actually implementing the requirements that consumers clearly seek and that it was undertaken to introduce as far back as the late 1970s.[125] Until this changes, it will remain up to individual Member States, such as Ireland, to adopt their own measures to address this shortcoming. These, like those on alternative food labelling formats, will however remain subject to EU rules on free movement – meaning that their proper implementation within those States is far from guaranteed.

Fiscal measures have shown signs that they can work to address some of the concerns raised in this chapter. The use of a sugar tax, like that introduced in

---

[120] Ibid, s 15(1).

[121] Ibid, s 15(1)(c).

[122] Ibid, s 16.

[123] Ibid, s 17. These restrictions include limiting the total amount of advertising space for alcohol products to a maximum of 20% of the advertising space and prohibiting the advertising of these products in publications aimed at children or which are likely to have a readership where 20% or more are likely to be children. They can also not be advertised on the front or back cover of a publication or on any wrapper, envelope or other covering for the publication. This includes imported publications on sale in Ireland but does not include publications that are not intended for sale or distribution in the State or, where they are, they are alcohol trade publications.

[124] Ibid, s 18. Alcohol products can, however, be advertised at the screenings of films that have been certified by the Director of Film Classification as being fit for viewing by persons aged 18 and over. They can also be advertised at licensed premises in a cinema.

[125] Report from the Commission to the European Parliament and the Council regarding the mandatory labelling of the list of ingredients and the nutrition declaration of alcoholic beverages, n 104 above.

Ireland in 2018, or the use of tax-reducing measures for healthier products, as has been mooted in the UK, can influence consumer behaviour. The main impediment to the success of these incentives to opt for healthier alternatives is that additional taxes can be absorbed by producers and retailers. Unless these are passed directly to the consumer, either as a tax increase or a tax reduction, then behavioural change is unlikely to follow. This, of course, was one of the key arguments made in support of minimum unit pricing for alcohol in Scotland. So, although the Court of Justice of the EU prefers taxation to minimum pricing, the fact remains that it is only where this charge must be imposed on the consumer that the desired effect of consumption reduction will be more likely to follow.

Marketing restrictions, in particular those which limit advertising aimed at children and minors, or those which place limitations on the advertising of certain products, such as alcoholic beverages, have been successfully used by several Member States in their attempts to curb unhealthy behaviour. However, this is always subject to EU Commission approval of the aims and objectives of the restrictions, coupled with an acceptance that these are appropriate steps to be taking in the circumstances. There must be a demonstration that any marketing rules are necessary, proportionate and that they do not discriminate against non-national producers, or those from other States who are seeking to access the domestic market, in any way. Otherwise, they will remain subject to Article 34 TFEU scrutiny, requiring justification by the Member State.

It is clear, therefore, that Member States can act. There are a range of options open to them. However, all require EU approval, in one form or another, before implementation.

10

Ethical and Environmental Aspects of Food Law

10.1. Introduction

It has been demonstrated throughout this book that the preponderance of Irish food law now comes directly from EU legislative initiative and interpretation through the case law of the European Court of Justice and European Commission policy documentation. These laws do not always reflect the different priorities of consumers and industry in their provisions and application. A whole range of other considerations may need to be considered in the drafting of new EU legal requirements. This is a difficult thing to achieve when the general moral, ethical or environmental preferences themselves differ from one Member State to another. Issues such as animal welfare, climate change and the preservation of local ecosystems may need to be considered in the creation of rules which are primarily designed to promote free movement and maintain some sort of minimum quality standards. The rules are created on a European basis, but they may be at odds with more specific national or local priorities. Some of these issues are examined in more detail in this chapter.

10.2. Food Law and Climate Change

Climate change is likely to have a very significant impact on global and national food production. The Intergovernmental Panel on Climate Change (IPCC) has reported that carbon dioxide emissions need to drop to half of 1990 levels by the year 2050 to have even a 50 per cent chance of avoiding a 2 degree rise in temperatures.[1] This could lead to increased shortages of food. Higher temperatures lead to lower global production yields. It was reported in *Science* as early as 2003 that corn and soya levels could drop by 17 per cent for every degree rise in temperature.[2] This – and other estimates – suggests that billions of

---

[1] IPCC Fourth Assessment Report, 2007. Available at: www.ipcc.ch. Further contributions have since been made to the Fifth Assessment Report, such as that on 'Climate Change 2014: Impacts, Adaptation and Vulnerability', also available at www.ipcc.ch.
[2] D Lobell and G Asner, 'Climate and management contributions in US agricultural yields' (2003) 299 *Science* 1032.

lives could be put at risk from lower food production levels arising out of rises in global temperatures. Agriculture is a big part of the problem. While food production levels need to increase to feed the world's ever-rising population, the growing and production of food accounts for around 20 per cent of all greenhouse gas emissions.[3] This would suggest that the way in which food is made, transported, marketed and consumed needs to change if we are to see higher population levels fed by a sector that needs to reduce its own impact on climate change. Food law has a key role to play in this.

In 2009 a report was published in *The Lancet* which suggested that a clear message needs to be sent about the strong links between climate change and human health.[4] There are two parts to this. The first is that climate change is likely to have a significant impact on the ability to produce food. This could lead to starvation, malnutrition, disease and death. The second is that traditional messages about the need to change individual behaviour in a way that reduces the human factors, such as carbon emissions, in climate change are not having the desired effect. It would be preferable, therefore, to change these so that the message becomes a demonstration of how leading a low-carbon-emitting lifestyle is good for the individual's health. It can lead to lower rates of heart disease, obesity and diabetes. There would also be lower levels of pollution, making for cleaner air and better lung health.

Food law and policy can be used to address some of the issues raised here. These range from adopting regulations that support and promote environmentally friendly farming practices to the development of labelling schemes which indicate where the product has been made in an environmentally friendly manner. The former has been addressed, to some degree, by the EU regulations on organic foods. This is discussed in more detail below. The latter suggestion is more problematic. Individual retailers have developed their own labelling disclosures, designed to provide the consumer with information on the impact of certain products on the environment. These have, however, tended to be limited to details on 'food miles', showing whether the product has travelled a long distance to the supermarket shelf. These types of label can be misleading or meaningless. It has been highlighted, for example, that the transportation of food makes up a very small part of the sector's carbon emissions. A whole range of factors would therefore have to be considered in setting any meaningful and verifiable labelling scheme that could be used to provide more useful disclosures to concerned consumers. Some foodstuffs that have travelled relatively short distances to shops are amongst the highest of carbon emitters in their production.

---

[3] This figure varies depending on how it is calculated and on what is taken into consideration. Agriculture alone has been estimated to account for 20% of emissions in C Cole et al, 'Global estimates of potential mitigation of greenhouse gas emissions by agriculture' (1997) 49 *Nutrient Cycling in Agroecosystems* 221. However, it has also been estimated to be at the lower level of 10–12% in the IPCC Report. It was noted by S Friel et al, 'Public health benefits of strategies to reduce greenhouse-gas emissions: Food and agriculture' (2009) 374 *The Lancet* 2016, that these figures could rise by half by 2030, caused in particular by increased demand for meat.

[4] A Costello and others, 'Managing the health effects of climate change' (2009) 373 *The Lancet* 1693.

A UK Department for Environment, Food and Rural Affairs (DEFRA) report has clearly indicated that using 'food miles' alone is not a valid indicator of sustainable development of environmental friendliness.[5] This report stated that food accounted for 30 per cent of all goods transported on UK roads. Food now travels further than was the case a few decades previously. The total mileage that food has travelled has increased by 50 per cent since 1978, however the quantity was only up by 23 per cent. Air transportation of food rose 140 per cent between 1992 and 2002, accounting for just 1 per cent of the total mileage, but 11 per cent of the carbon emissions.

Air transportation of food creates 177 times the carbon output of shipping it. This also leads to associated economic and social costs. It was estimated in the DEFRA report that the transportation of food on British roads costs the economy £9 billion per annum through added traffic congestion. The pollution costs stand at around £2 billion. This is all related to a sector where agriculture adds around £6.4 billion to the UK economy.

It is clear from this data that while the air transportation of food is a contributor to the carbon output of the food sector, it is only a small part. Despite this, existing carbon labelling schemes, adopted by supermarkets in particular, have tended to base their indications on the miles flown by imported food only. The reality of impact on climate change is much more complex.

Calculating the total carbon emissions of the production, transportation and marketing of food must be based on a range of factors. Seemingly environmentally friendly foodstuffs can sometimes be the worst offenders in this regard. 'Local' products can be grown on the farm and then transported to the packer, then on to the distribution centre, then back to the shop near where it was produced in the first place. Refrigeration of both local and organic foods can result in significant carbon output. Foods grown 'out of season' can have all sorts of damaging consequences for the environment.

It has been reported, for example, that it is less harmful to bring a consignment of tomatoes by road from Spain than it is to produce and sell them 'locally', where the former has been produced using natural heat and sunlight while the latter has involved artificial versions of these in greenhouses. It can be better for the environment to ship lamb 11,000 miles from New Zealand for sale in the UK than to have it produced and sold in the UK. This is due to the decreased use of fertilisers and increased recourse to renewable energy sources in New Zealand production. The type of food and/or method of production can also have an effect on its environmental impact. Organic food, for example, tends to be made using less energy and lower quantities of fertilisers and chemicals. However, while organic food sales have started to grow again, they are still relatively low. By 2016, organic food sales in Ireland totalled €142 million following four consecutive years

---

[5] DEFRA, 'The validity of food miles as an indicator of sustainable development: Final report' (2005); Report Number: ED50254.

of growth in the market.[6] However, this was from a very low base. As at February 2013 there were just over 1,500 organic operators in Ireland using 1.2 per cent of the total agricultural land.[7]

Other aspects of production can have a significant impact on the environment and the utilisation of natural resources. Meat, for example, has a much higher water usage in production than most fruit and vegetables do. It can take 2,400 litres of water to make a hamburger. It takes around 13 litres of water to produce a tomato. Cows emit large quantities of methane gas. In fact, the mere existence of food-producing livestock produces more carbon dioxide and greenhouse gases than all food transportation combined. The production of red meats tends to lead to around one-and-a-half times the emissions of the same quantities of chicken. Overall, the figures clearly show that most of the greenhouse gas that is produced by the food sector comes from its production, not from its transportation. The former has been calculated to account for 83 per cent of the sector's emissions in the US.[8] The same study noted that delivery from the producer to the retailer was responsible for only 4 per cent of the sector's carbon output there.

It has been made clear that the transportation mode and distance travelled, refrigeration, time of year, production methods and food type all contribute to the carbon output of food, yet voluntary labelling schemes operating in Ireland that are designed to indicate the carbon emissions attached to foods have tended to focus on 'food miles' only. The law could be used to address this by the creation of a new labelling format that would provide the consumer with a more holistic assessment of the relationship between the product and its potential to impact on climate change and pollution.

There is no publicly regulated food labelling indication which clearly indicates the overall environmental impact of food. If food purchasing and consumption habits do not change, we will possibly see further shortages in the availability of food which are, at least partially and probably significantly, caused by any failure to bring about this required alteration. While there is an EU Ecolabel, it is not presently used for food or drink, instead giving an overall environmental protection assurance for products such as cosmetics, cleaning products, clothes, paints, furniture, paper products and some household appliances. It is an entirely voluntary scheme.[9]

---

[6] Figures available at: www.bordbiavantage.ie. Organic food sales in the UK during the same period were measured at around £1.23 billion annually by 2013. They have been higher than this in the past, peaking at £2.1 billion in 2008, but they did rise again during 2012–2013 after several years of successive falls in sales coincided with a recession in the economy. These figures are taken from the Soil Association's Organic Market Report 2013. Available at: www.soilassociation.org. The 2018 version of the Report suggest that sales have risen again, possibly even surpassing their previous peak at £2.2 billion per annum.

[7] Department of Agriculture, Food and the Marine, 'Organic Farming Action Plan 2013–2015'. Available at: www.agriculture.gov.ie.

[8] C Weber and H Matthews, 'Food-miles and the relative climate impacts of food choices in the United States' (2008) 42 *Environmental Science and Technology* 3508.

[9] As legislated for by Regulation (EC) No 66/2010 of the European Parliament and of the Council of 25 November 2009 on the EU Ecolabel, [2010] OJ L 27/1.

Experiences in other areas of food law could be used for guidance in the development of such a labelling indication. Disclosures such as this should be backed up by legislation and made compulsory, rather than being introduced by a voluntary scheme. For example, it has been claimed that it is only with the introduction of compulsory indication requirements for protected geographical food names that these products could become better known to and more readily identifiable by consumers.[10] The use of an environmental impact labelling indication should also be introduced by way of harmonising and effective EU legislation.

It is clear that rules on the free movement of goods would prevent a Member State like Ireland from introducing its own unilateral and compulsory scheme. Applying this to domestic producers only could also put them at a competitive disadvantage, especially where products carried a negative indication. The adoption of voluntary and complementary nationally applied schemes, while very useful in some ways, are not therefore desirable or appropriate in the long term. Fair-trade labels, which have also operated without legal support, are often self-awarded and open to abuse by those using them. With no legally-binding minimum criteria for certification, traders can set their own standards which may be little better, or possibly worse, than their non-fair-trade counterparts. It can also lead to the same indication being made but based on an entirely different set of criteria. Any labelling indication designed to indicate environmental impact must also be clear and user friendly. The discussion about the way in which nutrition information has been presented since the introduction of the Nutrition Labelling Directive in 1990 has highlighted how such disclosures can often lack usefulness, indeed possibly mislead, if the template is not set in a manner which offers the details in an accessible and understandable format.[11]

Most importantly, as has been made clear above, any carbon-labelling scheme for food must be based on the full range of appropriate criteria rather than the more blinkered approach of indicating (air) miles travelled only. This is one factor, but consideration should also be given to the transportation method, the production emissions, the food type, water usage and storage conditions. These can have a far more significant bearing on the environmental impact than the criterion on which these assessments, where they do exist, have traditionally been based. The EU Ecolabel which, as stated, is not used for food products, sets the criteria for award as being those which are based on the latest strategic objectives on environmental protection including impact on climate change, biodiversity, resource consumption, waste generation, emissions and pollution.[12] This then extends to a

---

[10] Recital 28 of Preamble to Regulation (EU) No 1151/2012 of the European Parliament and of the Council of 21 November 2012 on quality schemes for agricultural products and foodstuffs [2012] OJ L 343/1.

[11] See, eg, G Cowburn and L Stockley, 'Consumer understanding and use of nutrition labelling: A systematic review' (2005) 8 *Public Health Nutrition* 21; and A Shine, S O'Reilly and K O'Sullivan, 'Consumer attitudes to nutrition labelling' (1997) 99 *British Food Journal* 283.

[12] Art 6(3)(a) of Reg 66/2010, n 9 above.

consideration of those products which substitute hazardous substances for safer ones, reduce environmental impact due to durability and reusability, compatibility with international conventions including relevant International Labour Organisation standards and codes and, as far as possible, reducing the use of animal testing.[13] Something similar could certainly be done for food. At present, the only meaningful environmental indication regarding food products is organic certification.

10.3. Organic Food

Sales of organic food in Ireland are at significantly lower level than in many other EU Member States, standing in 2016 at 0.7 per cent of all retail sales. According to the Research Institute of Organic Agriculture (FiBL), there are far more organic products sold in Denmark (7.6%), Sweden (6%), Germany (4.4%) and the Netherlands (3%). However, the sale of organic products in some EU Member States is almost non-existent. In Poland, Portugal, Latvia and Slovakia, for example, they represent a mere 0.2 per cent of retail sales. Having said that, sales have clearly started to rise, both across the EU and internationally, increasing by 11.4 per cent in Europe during 2016, with almost all of the main markets experiencing double-digit growth rates that year.

The reasons as to why consumers buy and are usually willing to pay a premium price for organic food differ. Most think that organic food is healthier. This is often disputed.[14] Around one-third find that organic food tastes better than its conventional counterparts. Nearly half of consumers surveyed buy organic for environmental reasons. Just under one-third take animal welfare considerations into account when buying organic food.[15]

Around 2 per cent of agricultural land in Ireland is designated as being used for organic farming. This is a third lower than the percentage for the UK, about one-third of the figure for France and less than 10 per cent of the amount of land used for this type of farming in Austria. The EU average is just below 7%.[16] To summarise, organic land use and the sales of organic produce have remained relatively low in Ireland, despite increased consumer interest in these products, especially in the immediate aftermath of the horse-meat scandal of 2013,[17] which had initially led to increased sales in organic foodstuffs.

---

[13] Art 6(3)(b)–(g) of Reg 66/2010, n 9 above.

[14] See M Jensen, H Jørgensen and C Lauridsen, 'Comparison between conventional and organic agriculture in terms of nutritional quality of food – a critical review' (2013) 8 *Perspectives in Agriculture, Veterinary Science, Nutrition and Natural Resources* 1.

[15] Data all taken from the Soil Association's Organic Market Report 2013. Available at: www.soilassociation.org/marketreport.

[16] Figures are from the International Federation of Organic Agriculture Movements (IFOAM) and are available at: www.ifoam-eu.org.

[17] In early 2013, the Food Safety Authority of Ireland tested 27 frozen beef burgers and 37% of these contained equine DNA. It emerged that equine DNA was present widely in foods in other countries, including the UK. Approximately 16 countries in total appear to have been affected by the scandal.

10.3.1. European Union Regulation of Organic Produce

The first framework EU Regulation on the production and marketing of organic foodstuffs was introduced in 1991.[18] It subsequently became one of the most amended pieces of EU food legislation; by 2016, changes had been made on 41 occasions. The provisions originally contained in the Regulation had become very piecemeal. This was one of the reasons underlying the need to introduce a new Organic Food Regulation in 2007.[19] The European Commission had previously launched an Action Plan for Organic Food and Farming in 2004: this document had also called for changes to be made, in particular by simplifying the general principles contained in the Regulation and making it more transparent, improving farming standards, increasing consumer awareness and even allowing the provision of State aids for the sector.[20] It also specifically called for clarity in relation to the labelling of foods as 'organic', even where they contained genetically modified organisms. The original 1991 Regulation did not prohibit the use of genetic modification in the production of organic food, a surprising allowance which was later certified by the Court of Justice.[21] Regulation 834/2007, the new Organic Food Regulation, came into effect in 2009. Organic foods are also regulated at national level by the European Union (Organic Farming) Regulations 2016.[22]

Organic Foods Regulation 834/2007

The objectives for organic production are set out in Article 3 of Regulation 834/2007. It provides that the key objective is to establish a sustainable management system for agriculture that is natural, contributes to a high level of biological diversity, involves the responsible use of natural resources and operates on the basis of high standards of animal welfare. The 'principles' of organic production include the use of living organisms and mechanical agricultural methods, the practice of land-related crop cultivation and livestock production and excluding

---

[18] Council Regulation (EEC) No 2092/1991 of 24 June 1991 on organic production of agricultural products and indications referring thereto on agricultural products and foodstuffs [1991] OJ L 198.

[19] Council Regulation (EC) No 834/2007 of 28 June 2007 on organic production and labelling of organic products and repealing Regulation (EEC) No 2092/1991 [2007] OJ L 189/1. Recital 4 of the Preamble to this Regulation states that '[i]n its conclusions of 18 October 2004, the Council called on the Commission to review the [Union] legal framework in this field with a view to ensure simplification and overall coherence and in particular to establish principles encouraging harmonisation of standards and, where possible, to reduce the level of detail'.

[20] Communication from the Commission to the Council and the European Parliament on a European Action Plan for Organic Food and Farming, COM (2004) 415.

[21] Case C-156/1993 *European Parliament v Commission* [1995] ECR I-2019. The use of genetic modification in the production of organic food was not prohibited until amendments to Art 5(3) of Reg 2092/1991 were made by the introduction of Council Regulation (EC) No 1804/1999 of 19 July 1999 supplementing Regulation (EEC) No 2092/1991 on organic production of agricultural products and indications referring thereto on agricultural products and foodstuffs to include livestock production [1999] OJ L 222/1. Despite this, some confusion about the use of genetic modification techniques in the production of organic food remained.

[22] European Union (Organic Farming) Regulations 2016 (SI No 683/2016).

the use of GMOs.[23] All of this should be based on risk assessment and the use of the precautionary principle when appropriate. Additional and specific principles are also to be applied to the production of processed organic food. The Regulation states that these foods should be made from organic ingredients except where they are not available in organic form, the use of additives and processing aids should be kept to a minimum and processes and substances should not be used where they could mislead consumers about the nature of the final product.[24]

The Regulation makes the prohibition on the use of GMOs much more explicit than that which had originally appeared in Regulation 1804/1999.[25] Article 9 of Regulation 834/2007 provides that:

> GMOs and products produced from or by GMOs shall not be used as food, feed, processing aids, plant protection products, fertilisers, soil conditioners, seeds, vegetative propagating material, micro-organisms and animals in organic production.

This is an important provision. It underlines the fact that the only way that consumers and/or retailers can completely avoid the use of genetic modification is to choose the organic option. As is discussed below, meat or animal products from animals that have been fed a GM diet do not have to carry any indication of this on the label. The only exception to this is Article 9(1) of the Organic Foods Regulation, which explicitly prohibits the use of GM animal feed in organic production. The Regulation then further states that:

> [o]perators may assume that no GMOs or products produced from GMOs have been used in the manufacture of purchased food and feed products when the latter are not labelled, or accompanied by a document, pursuant to [the GMOs regulations].[26]

Operators using non-organic products in the production of organic foods can also oblige their ingredient suppliers to confirm that the products supplied have not been produced from or by GMOs.[27] This is all a very marked departure from that which was permitted under the original regulations in the 1990s, where genetically modified microorganisms were specifically listed as being amongst those non-organic ingredients that could be lawfully used in the manufacture of organic products. The use of ionising radiation for the treatment of organic food, feed or the ingredients of organic produce is also explicitly prohibited.[28]

For food to be lawfully labelled as 'organic', the entire agricultural holding which produces it should usually be managed in compliance with the requirements applicable to organic production.[29] There are some circumstances where

---

[23] Reg 834/2007, Art 4(a).
[24] Ibid, Art 6(a)–(c).
[25] See n 21 above.
[26] See European Union (Organic Farming) Regulations 2016, n 22 above, Art 9(2). The GMOs Regulations are discussed in more detail below.
[27] Reg 834/2007, Art 9(3).
[28] Ibid, Art 10.
[29] Ibid, Art 11.

this does not have to be the case, but this is only allowed when the holding is split into clearly separated units. There are additional rules for plant production and standards for animal production. The former includes obligations to use tillage and cultivation practices that maintain or increase soil organic matter and enhance soil biodiversity, for example. It also includes the use of multi-annual crop rotation, a ban on mineral nitrogen fertilisers and a preference for the use of natural pest, weed and disease control measures.[30] A restricted list of non-organic fertilisers, soil conditioners, plant protection products, feed materials and feed additives that can be authorised for use in organic production is drafted by the Commission, using comitology.[31] However, authorisation is only to be granted where this is necessary for ensuring sustained production. This may be the case if their use is deemed essential for the control of a harmful organism or a particular disease and alternative treatments are not available.

It is certainly arguable that the very highest of welfare standards for animals are those contained in the Organic Foods Regulation. The legislation also includes a range of requirements designed to maintain the organic purity of food-producing animals. Organic livestock, for example, must be born and raised on organic holdings.[32] Some non-organically raised animals may be brought onto a holding for breeding purposes under set conditions. However, these must go through a 'conversion period' before they, or their products, can be deemed 'organic'. The same rules apply to those animals which may have been kept on a farm before the conversion to organic production began, provided all the other requirements of the Regulation have been properly applied during this period.

Welfare of Organic Food-producing Animals

The Organic Foods Regulation sets out a range of production rules, designed to ensure that animals are raised in the most natural manner possible. One of the main outcomes of this is that welfare standards tend to be higher in the production of organic animal-derived foods than their more intensive or conventional counterparts. In particular, the Regulation stipulates that, for livestock,

> husbandry practices, including stocking densities, and housing conditions shall ensure that the developmental, physiological and ethological needs of animals are met.

This is roughly similar to the general welfare requirements applicable to all food-producing animals, which are discussed in more detail later in this chapter. However, the Regulation then further provides that,

> the livestock shall have permanent access to open air areas, preferably pasture, whenever weather conditions and the state of the ground allow this unless restrictions

---

[30] Ibid, Art 12.
[31] Ibid, Art 16.
[32] Ibid, Art 14.

and obligations related to the protection of human and animal health are imposed on the basis of [Union] legislation.[33]

This is the crucial welfare requirement for animals used to make organic produce. They have full access to the outdoors, unless there is some very good reason as to why this cannot be the case. Tethering and isolation are prohibited for organic livestock, again unless there is some significant justification for this, such as for safety, welfare or veterinary reasons.[34] The duration of the transportation of live-stock is also to be minimised. As will be seen below, this is not necessarily the case for non-organic animals.

The Organic Foods Regulation also sets clear environmental protection provi-sions attached to the rearing of livestock. It stipulates that the quantity of livestock should usually be relatively limited to minimise the potential for overgrazing, erosion and pollution. Controversial breeding methods are prohibited. While artificial insemination is allowed, cloning and embryo transfer are not.[35] There are strict requirements on feed. It must be organic. It should be locally produced, where possible. There should be permanent access to pasture or roughage. Growth promoters should never be used.[36] Significantly, the Organic Foods Regulation has loosened the rules on the use of veterinary medicines. Previously, there was an emphasis on the use of alternative veterinary treatments, which arguably reduced the overall welfare standards attached to organic production. Now the Regulation states that,

> disease shall be treated immediately to avoid suffering to the animal; chemically synthe-sised allopathic veterinary medicinal products including antibiotics may be used where necessary and under strict conditions, when the use of phytotherapeutic, homeopathic and other products is inappropriate.[37]

It could, of course, be argued that the use of these latter remedies must generally be considered inappropriate in the absence of scientific evidence to the contrary about their efficacy. Immunisation is permitted. So are treatments related to the protection of human and animal health introduced by EU laws. Adapted, but simi-lar, rules apply to organic aquaculture.[38]

Labelling Organic Foods

The Organic Foods Regulation provides that any labelling or advertising which refers to organic production methods, including the use of terms such as 'bio' or 'eco', can only legitimately appear where a product and all of its ingredients have

---

[33] Ibid, Art 14.3(b).
[34] Ibid, Art 14.
[35] Ibid, Art 14.1(c).
[36] Ibid, Art 14.1(d).
[37] Ibid, Art 14.1(e).
[38] Ibid, Art 15.

been produced according to the standards set out in the legislation.[39] Having said that, there may be reference to organic production for processed foods which are made from mostly organic ingredients. However, for this to be permitted, at least 95 per cent of the agricultural ingredients used must be organic.[40] All of the organic ingredients used in the manufacture of such products must be clearly indicated in the ingredients list. The total percentage of organic ingredients should also be clearly labelled. The Regulation further prohibits the appearance of any terms, including those used in registered trademarks or any practices used in labelling or advertising which are liable to mislead consumers into believing that the product is organic.[41] Unlike previous versions, the 2007 Regulation also makes it very clear that references to organic ingredients or production can never be used for foods that contain or have been produced from genetically modified organisms.[42]

One of the key changes made by the 2007 Organic Foods Regulation to the labelling requirements is that from now on all such foods must also carry the stipulated EU logo.[43] This has been compulsory since July 2010.[44] National and private logos may also be used, such as that introduced by the Irish Organic Association or the Organic Trust.[45] Member States are also obliged under the terms of the Regulation to designate competent authorities responsible for overseeing the application of the Regulation.[46] This, along with the other necessary national implementations, has been done in Ireland through the introduction of the European Union (Organic Farming) Regulations 2016.

10.3.2. Irish Organic Regulations

Whilst most of the focus so far in this chapter on the legal requirements related to the production and marketing of organic food has been on EU Regulation 834/2007, two other regulations contribute to the overall regulatory package here. These are Commission Regulation 889/2008,[47] which sets out more detailed rules for the implementation of the Organic Foods Regulation 834/2007 and Commission Regulation 1235/2008,[48] which provides detail on the arrangements for the

---

[39] Ibid, Art 23.1.
[40] Ibid, Art 23.4.
[41] Ibid, Art 23.2.
[42] Ibid, Art 23.3.
[43] Ibid, Art 24.
[44] Ibid, Art 97 in conjunction with Art 58 of Commission Regulation (EC) No 889/2008 of 5 September 2008 laying down detailed rules for the implementation of Council Regulation (EC) No 834/2007 on organic production and labelling of organic products with regard to organic production, labelling and control [2008] OJ L 250/1.
[45] Ibid, Art 25.
[46] Ibid, Art 27.
[47] See n 44 above.
[48] Commission Regulation (EC) No 1235/2008 of 8 December 2008 laying down detailed rules for implementation of Council Regulation (EC) No 834/2007 as regards the arrangements for imports of organic products from third countries [2008] OJ L 334/25.

sale and marketing of organic products imported from third countries. These are the product of the recourse to the comitology procedure referred to throughout the Organic Foods Regulation. The organic produce of third countries can only be imported into EU Member States like Ireland if produced in compliance with the terms of the 2007 Regulation or verifiably equivalent standards.[49] Any trade in organic produce with third countries must be properly notified to the Department of Agriculture.[50] This and all other detail on the implementation and application of the EU regulatory package under national law is provided by the 2016 Irish Regulations.[51]

The European Union (Organic Farming) Regulations 2016 make several aspects of the 2007 EU Regulation specific to its application in Irish law. It is made clear that the use of GMOs in organic production is an offence under Irish law.[52] As is the use of ionising radiation.[53] There are specific provisions on mushroom production,[54] beekeeping[55] and seaweed.[56] Primarily, the 2016 Irish Regulations make breach of the provisions of EU Regulation 834/2007 an offence under Irish law. They provide for a number of functions and related powers for authorised officers to ensure that the EU and domestic regulations are complied with,[57] including the power to issue compliance notices[58] or to take emergency measures where necessary.[59]

10.4. Genetic Modification

It is arguable that the two most significant events which have impacted upon EU food law and consequently Irish food law are the BSE crisis, which was discussed extensively in Chapter 5 and the use of genetically modified organisms (GMOs).[60] What gave rise, in particular, to debate over the inclusion of GMOs in the food chain was the initial poor regulation of this sector. Although EU directives were introduced as early as 1990,[61] they failed to properly account for the types of concern that consumers might have over the use of genetic modification techniques

---

[49] Arts 32 and 33 of Reg 834/2007, n 19 above.
[50] Reg 45 of the European Union (Organic Farming) Regulations 2016, n 22 above.
[51] Above, n 22.
[52] Ibid, reg 3.
[53] Ibid, reg 4.
[54] Ibid, reg 12.
[55] Ibid, regs 21–23.
[56] Ibid, reg 13.
[57] Ibid, regs 54–56.
[58] Ibid, regs 57–58.
[59] Ibid, reg 59.
[60] Other issues that gave rise to more temporary concerns include the horse meat controversy, dioxins in pork, which was mostly an Irish problem, E. coli (several times) and listeria in cheese.
[61] Council Directive 1990/219/EEC of 23 April 1990 on the contained use of genetically modified micro-organisms [1990] OJ L 117/1 and Council Directive 1990/220 of 23 April 1990 on the deliberate release into the environment of genetically modified organisms [1990] OJ L 117/15.

in food production. There were no proper labelling requirements indicating where foods had been made with or from a GMO.

10.4.1. Issues with Early Genetically Modified Organisms Legislation

There are really two areas where the use of GMOs has given rise to controversy and created cause for concern. The first relates to environmental law and any in-depth examination of this is really beyond the scope of this book.[62] However, it should be noted that the growing of genetically modified crops in EU Member States has raised several environmental issues, in particular the potential for there to be cross-contamination between these and their conventional counterparts. This can affect both the farmer, who either wishes to produce entirely GMO-free crops and the consumer, whose choice can become restricted where the complete absence of GM ingredients cannot be guaranteed. There is also the possibility that the growing of conventional crops could be impaired if contaminated by cross-pollination with genetically modified ones. Given the existence of wind, insects and birds, it is very difficult to control cross-contamination between farms. It has been pointed out that issues surrounding the 'co-existence' between genetically modified and conventional crops are now limited to economic ones, the most obvious of which would be the potential for the non-GM grower to have a marketing advantage amongst many consumers. This is due to the fact that other environmental and/or health issues should have now been addressed by the authorisation processes that must be completed before any GMO is released into the environment or onto the consumer market.[63]

The second controversial aspect to the use of genetic modification in food production relates to the fact that this practice has often been concealed from the consumer. The issue really came to broader public attention when it was reported in the late 1990s that feeding laboratory rats a diet containing genetically modified potatoes could have toxic effects on their intestines.[64] From a consumer protection

---

[62] Having said that, the General Court of the EU has found during 2018 that GMO labelling rules whose objective is to regulate the effect of GMOs on human or animal health also fall within the area of environmental protection and may therefore also be subject to the scrutiny of the Aarhus Regulation, Regulation (EC) No 1367/2006 of the European Parliament and of the Council of 6 September 2006 on the application of the provisions of the Aarhus Convention on Access to Information, Public Participation in Decision-Making and Access to Justice in Environmental Matters to Community Institutions and Bodies, [2006] OJ L 264/13. See Case T-33/2016, *TestBio Tech v Commission* ECLI:EU:T:2018:135. This could have significant consequences for those, such as interested non-governmental organisations, who wish to have a say in the approval and authorisation processes for genetically modified organisms.

[63] See M Lee, *EU Environmental Law: Challenges, Change and Decision-Making* (Oxford, Hart, 2005), esp 255–259.

[64] S Ewen and A Pusztai, 'Effect of diets containing genetically modified potatoes expressing Galanthus nivalis lectin on rat small intestine' (1999) 354 *The Lancet* 1353. This is discussed in more detail below.

perspective, this served to highlight that the original GMO directives did not create adequate labelling requirements for genetically modified food.[65] Avoiding these products would therefore prove difficult for those consumers who wished to make such a choice. The Novel Foods Regulation was introduced in 1997,[66] and this had created some additional and clearer labelling requirements for those foods which were different from their conventional counterparts. Novel foods were defined in this Regulation as being those 'which have not hitherto been used for human consumption to a significant degree'.[67] They specifically included 'foods and food ingredients containing or consisting of genetically modified organisms' and those 'produced from, but not containing, genetically modified organisms'.[68] The Regulation provided that:

> the following additional specific labelling requirements shall apply to foodstuffs in order to ensure that the final consumer is informed of any characteristic or food property ... which renders a novel food or food ingredient no longer equivalent to an existing food or food ingredient [and it] shall be deemed to be no longer equivalent ... if scientific assessment ... can demonstrate that the characteristics assessed are different in comparison with a conventional food or food ingredient, having regard to the accepted limits of natural variations for such characteristics.[69]

Where a food or food ingredient was accordingly deemed to be 'novel', it would have to carry labelling disclosures which clearly indicated this. This was consequently the first meaningful labelling condition set for genetically modified foods. The Regulation specifically provided that novel foods must have:

> labelling [which indicates] the characteristics or properties modified, together with the method by which that characteristic or property was obtained [including] the presence of an organism genetically modified by techniques of genetic modification, the non-exhaustive list of which is laid down in [the original Deliberate Release Directive, 1990/220].[70]

Some other additional requirements for genetically modified organisms were also set in the Novel Foods Regulation, such as those related to the granting of consent for deliberate release and the supply of technical dossiers.[71] However, these related to the treatment of the GMO before it would be placed on the market and did not affect the labelling requirements as such, other than to the extent that the food could not be sold to consumers in the first place without meeting these

---

[65] Council Directives 1990/219 and 1990/220, n 61 above.

[66] Regulation (EC) No 258/1997 of the European Parliament and of the Council of 27 January 1997 concerning novel foods and novel food ingredients [1997] OJ L 43/1.

[67] Ibid, Art 1(2).

[68] Ibid, Art 1(2)(a) and (b). These provisions were later deleted from the Novel Foods Regulation by Regulation 1829/2003, of the European Parliament and of the Council of 22 September 2003 on genetically modified food and feed [2003] OJ L 268/1, Art 38.

[69] Ibid, Art 8.1.

[70] Ibid, Art 8(1)(a) and (d).

[71] Ibid, Art 9(1).

requirements as well. Similarly, some further environmental considerations were also addressed in the Regulation.[72]

While the Novel Foods Regulation did set out additional labelling requirements for some genetically modified foods and included a safeguard clause which facilitated the suspension by Member States of trade in GMOs where they had sufficient grounds for believing that its continued use could endanger human health or the environment,[73] it did not provide regulators with a sufficiently stable legal basis for dealing with the controversies that broke in the late 1990s. It was not just the negative results of studies measuring the impact of GMO consumption on the intestines of lab rats that gave cause for concern, it was also the fact that the regulatory framework which had developed up to that point contained too many loopholes and shortcomings to ensure that all such foods should be clearly labelled to this effect. There was potential danger to human health from the consumption of foods made from or containing a GMO, but the presence of these substances would not necessarily have to be disclosed to the consumer.

Shortcomings with the GMO legislation became apparent when a regulation was introduced in 1997 to close a loophole that had allowed genetically modified soya and maize to avoid being subject to some labelling requirements.[74] Some EU Member States had taken their own action to counter this deficiency in the law, including setting labelling requirements for these products. The Commission took action in the form of this Regulation, relying on the principle that unilateral Member State action would have implications for the EU rules on the free movement of goods, consumer protection and fair competition. Despite this, another regulation had to be introduced in 1998, as the first attempt to close the loophole identified had failed to set full and adequate labelling requirements for genetically modified soya and maize.[75] This regulation provided that:

> where the food consists of more than one ingredient, the words "produced from genetically modified soya" or "produced from genetically modified maize", as appropriate, shall appear in the list of ingredients provided for by [the framework food labelling directive] in parentheses immediately after the name of the ingredient concerned [or] these words may appear in a prominently displayed footnote to the list of ingredients by means of an asterisk to the ingredient concerned.[76]

While this is quite explicit about the need to indicate the presence of a genetically modified ingredient or ingredients, the provision is unsatisfactory. The disclosure

---

[72] Such as that set out in Art 9(2), which dealt with the evaluation of GMO release authorisation applications and the environmental safety requirements set out therein.

[73] Regulation (EC) No 258/1997, Art 14.

[74] Commission Regulation (EC) No 1813/1997 of 19 September 1997 concerning the compulsory indication on the labelling of certain foodstuffs produced from genetically modified organisms of particulars other than those provided for in Directive 1979/112/EEC [1997] OJ L 257/7.

[75] Council Regulation (EC) No 1139/1998 of 26 May 1998 concerning the compulsory indication on the labelling of certain foodstuffs produced from genetically modified organisms of particulars other than those provided for in Directive 1979/112/EEC [1998] OJ L 159/4. This was later repealed by Regulation 1829/2003, above n 68, Art 37.

[76] Reg 1139/1998, n 75 above, Art 2(3).

did not need to be any more prominent on the label than an inclusion in the ingredients list, or a footnote to this. It was only where the product was not required under the terms of the Framework Food Labelling Directive to provide any list of ingredients at all that that words 'produced from genetically modified soya' or 'produced from genetically modified maize' had to be printed clearly on the labelling.[77] The original Framework Food Labelling Directive, which was in effect at the time of the introduction of this 1998 Regulation, provided that a list of ingredients was not required for fresh fruit and vegetables, carbonated water, vinegar, cheese, butter, fermented milk products or single-ingredient products.[78] Therefore, it was only this limited list of foodstuffs which had to carry the clearest indication that genetic modification had been used in production. For all other products, a note in the ingredients list would suffice.

It was not just weaknesses in the legislation that caused initial issues with the regulation of genetically modified organisms in the production of food. The European Court of Justice specifically supported the inclusion in the regulatory framework of genetically modified substances as being amongst those ingredients that could be used in the production of organic food.[79] When the European Parliament sought the annulment of a Commission Regulation,[80] on the grounds that the Commission had exceeded its powers by permitting the use of genetically modified micro-organisms in organic production, the Court held that this inclusion was not contrary to the principles and obligations set out in the original Organic Production Regulation.[81]

It had noted that the legislation did permit the use of non-organic ingredients and substances in organic products, albeit within set limits. The Commission argued – and the Court accepted – that the legislative institutions had not sought a prohibition on the use of genetic modification in organic farming. Genetically modified organisms and micro-organisms had not therefore been excluded from the lists of permitted substances of non-organic agricultural origin that could be used in organic food. The law was later changed, in 1999, to reflect the inappropriateness of allowing the inclusion of genetically modified substances in organic food.[82] The Preamble to this amending regulation stated that '[g]enetically modified organisms and products derived therefrom are not compatible with the

---

[77] Ibid, Art 2(3)(b).

[78] Article 6 of Council Directive 1979/112 of 18 December 1978 on the approximation of the laws of the Member States relating to the labelling, presentation and advertising of foodstuffs to the ultimate consumer [1979] OJ L 33/1. This exemption from having to provide a list of ingredients is now set out in Art 19 of Reg 1169/2011, [2011] OJ L 304/18.

[79] Case C-156/1993 *European Parliament v Commission* [1995] ECR I-2019.

[80] Commission Regulation (EEC) No 207/1993 of 29 January 1993 defining the content of Annex VI to Regulation (EEC) No 2092/1991 on organic production of agricultural products and indications referring thereto on agricultural products and foodstuffs and laying down detailed rules for implementing the provisions of Art 5(4) thereto [1993] OJ L 25/5.

[81] See Reg 2092/1991, n 21 above.

[82] See Council Regulation (EC) No 1804/1999 of 19 July 1999, n 21 above.

organic production method' and therefore they 'should not be used in products labelled as from organic production'.[83]

The use of genetic modification in food production received widespread negative publicity following a television programme broadcast in the UK that echoed the claims that were made in a research letter to the *Lancet*, published in 1999.[84] It was stated that the research had identified that diets containing genetically modified potatoes had negative effects on the gastrointestinal tracts of rats. Much media and public attention ensued. There was such a backlash against the use of genetic modification across the UK, Ireland and the majority of EU Member States that an unofficial moratorium on the approval of new GMO uses was introduced. This, coupled with further action taken by individual States, ultimately led to the USA, Canada and Argentina bringing complaints to the Dispute Settlement Body of the World Trade Organization.[85] There it was decided that the EU had applied a general de facto moratorium on the approval of biotech products between June 1999 and August 2003, something which the EU had previously denied.

The Dispute Panel further found that by applying this moratorium, the EU had taken action that was inconsistent with obligations set out in the Agreement on the Application of Sanitary and Phytosanitary Measures (SPS, discussed in Chapter 2), in particular Article 8 thereof which provides that WTO Members must observe the terms of the Agreement on the operation of approval procedures. More specifically, the actions of individual EU Member States, which had limited and restricted the use of GMOs, was found to be contrary to Articles 2.2 and 5.1 of the SPS Agreement as the safeguard measures adopted were not based on appropriate risk assessments. The Panel Reports were adopted in November 2006.

The first decade or so of GMO regulation in the EU was a troubled one. The absence of proper labelling requirements, shortcomings with aspects of the legislation, consumer unrest, scientific uncertainty, the taking of action by individual Member States that was contrary to EU legislative requirements and the actions of the EU that were inconsistent with its WTO obligations all combined to lead to a clear recognition that new measures were required.

An overhaul of most of the existing legislative framework thus commenced with the introduction of a new GMO directive in 2001 and two new regulations – on genetically modified food and on traceability and labelling, in 2003. The Novel Foods Regulation has mostly ceased to apply to aspects of genetic modification but, as will be discussed in more detail below, the original 1997 Regulation has now also been subject to review.[86]

---

[83] Ibid, Recital 10 of the Preamble to Reg 1804/1999.

[84] See Ewen and Pusztai, n 64 above.

[85] DS 291, 292 and 293, *Measures Affecting the Approval and Marketing of Biotech Products.*

[86] Following the introduction of Commission Proposal for a Regulation of the European Parliament and of the Council on Novel Foods, COM (2013) 894. As will also be discussed further below, this was not the first time that proposals had been brought forward on changes to the Novel Foods Regulation, a previous Commission document having been published in late 2007 (COM (2007) 872). However, progress on its introduction stalled during the legislative process, primarily due to disagreement on animal cloning. For more on the regulation of animal cloning see L Petetin, 'The revival of modern

10.4.2. Defining Genetically Modified Organisms

The legal definition provided in the legislation for genetically modified organisms is that they are:

> [any] organism, with the exception of human beings, in which the genetic material has been altered in a way that does not occur naturally by mating and/or natural recombination.[87]

Examples of genetically modified foods include golden rice. To produce this, three genes are inserted into the seed, two of which are taken from daffodils. The other is bacterial. These insertions increase the beta-carotene levels in the rice, which turns into vitamin A in the body. The hope is that the consumption of this rice can help to fight levels of blindness arising out of nutrient deficiency in developing countries. Another example of a GM food would be sweetcorn (Bt-corn) that has been modified to produce its own poison (Bacillus thuringiensis), which can then kill insects. This would reduce the need for insecticides. However, it could also result in the killing of other insects, such as butterflies, which have a vital role to play in the ecosystem. It would appear that there are both advantages and disadvantages to genetically modifying foods. Regardless, it is crucial that the sector is regulated in a manner that can ensure, as far as possible, public confidence in the use of genetic modification techniques in food production. As outlined above, early regulation failed to do this. The revised legislative package should be better equipped to deal with the controversial elements of GMO should the need arise. The first part of this package is the EU Deliberate Release Directive. This has been transposed into Irish law by the 2003 Regulations.

10.4.3. Genetically Modified Organisms (Deliberate Release) Regulations 2003

The GMO Regulations 2003 set the Environmental Protection Agency (EPA) as the national competent authority for matters related to the deliberate release of these organisms into the environment.[88] By 'deliberate release' we mean:

> [...] any intentional introduction into the environment of a genetically modified organism or a combination of genetically modified organisms for which no specific

agricultural biotechnology by the UK Government: What role for animal cloning?' (2012) 7 *European Food and Feed Law Review* 296. The new Novel Foods Regulation finally came into effect in January 2018 with the introduction of Regulation (EU) 2015/2283 of the European Parliament and of the Council of 25 November 2015 on novel foods, amending Regulation (EU) No 1169/2011 of the European Parliament and of the Council and repealing Regulation (EC) No 258/97 of the European Parliament and of the Council and Commission Regulation (EC) No 1852/2001, [2015] OJ L 327/1.

[87] Art 2(2) of Directive 2001/18 on the deliberate release of genetically modified organisms [2001] OJ L 106/1. Transposed into Irish law by s 3(1) of the Genetically Modified Organisms (Deliberate Release) Regulations 2003, SI No 500/2003.

[88] Irish GMO Regs 2003, reg 3(1).

containment measures are used to limit their contact with, and to provide a high level of safety for, the general population and the environment [...]

'Deliberate release' covers two types of situation. The first relates primarily to the environment. This is 'deliberate release for any purpose other than placing on the market'. This includes farm-scale or field trials of genetically modified crop cultivation. Applications to use GMOs for any such research and development must be made in Ireland to the Environmental Protection Agency. Under the 2003 Regulations, anyone intending to deliberately release a GMO for these purposes must first notify the EPA.[89] This notification must include a technical dossier on the proposed deliberate release, a summary of the notification, an environmental risk assessment and the conclusions arrived at by the notifier about the consequences of the deliberate release,[90] including details on any findings made about the possibility of cross-pollination and any possible impact on human or animal health.[91] The second situation covered by 'deliberate release' is placing products that contain or consist of a GMO on to the market. This includes the marketing of GM crops that have been cultivated, including as food intended for humans or feed for animals. 'Placing on the market' is defined as

[...] any transaction in which a genetically modified organism is supplied or made available to a third party, whether in return for payment or otherwise [...],[92]

while 'products', for the purposes of the Regulations, include:

[any] preparation consisting of, or containing, a genetically modified organism or a combination of genetically modified organisms, which is placed on the market.[93]

Authorisation for placing genetically modified food or feed products is not made to the EPA in Ireland but is instead made to the European Union authorities. Applications for the authorisation of non-food GM products, such as flowers, can still be made under the terms of the Deliberate Release Directive and the transposing 2003 Irish Regulations,[94] but any application to market a GM product as food or feed must instead be done by following the procedures set out in EU GM Food and Feed Regulation,[95] which is discussed in more detail below.

---

[89] Ibid, reg 14(1).
[90] Ibid, reg 14(2).
[91] The full list of possible conclusions that may be drawn here are set out in Sch 2 to the 2003 Irish Regulations.
[92] See Genetically Modified Organisms (Deliberate Release) Regulations 2003, SI No 500/2003, n 21 at reg 3(1).
[93] Ibid.
[94] The procedures and requirements for this type of notification are set out in Chapter 2 of the Irish Genetically Modified Organisms (Deliberate Release) Regulations 2003, n 87 above. As these do not relate to food or feed following the introduction of EU Regulation 1829/2003, they are not discussed in any detail here.
[95] Regulation No 1829/2003 n 68 above.

10.4.4. European Union Genetically Modified Organisms Regulations

The regulatory regime for GM foods was mostly completed by the introduction of two EU regulations in 2003. Taken together, the Deliberate Release Directive – as transposed into domestic law by the GMO Regulations 2003, the EU Regulation on Genetically Modified Food and Feed,[96] and the GMO Traceability and Labelling Regulation,[97] the latter two both being directly applicable in national law, form the initial framework for GMO regulation in Ireland. Additional implementing measures for both the GM Food and Feed Regulation and the GM Traceability and Labelling Regulation are provided for at national level by the European Union (Genetically Modified Foodstuffs) Regulations 2013,[98] and the European Communities (Feedingstuffs)(Genetically Modified Feed) Regulations 2004.[99]

Genetically Modified Food and Feed

The EU GM Food and Feed Regulation sets out that the key aim of the legislative framework provided must be to ensure, as far as possible, that genetic modification does not have adverse effects on human health, animals or the environment.[100] It must also be designed to ensure that consumers are not misled about the composition of foodstuffs, or the techniques used in their production. Article 4 of the Regulation also provides that genetically modified foods cannot:

> differ from the food which it is intended to replace to such an extent that its normal consumption would be nutritionally disadvantageous for the consumer.

The primary way of satisfying these aims is the establishment of a rigorous authorisation procedure for all GMOs.[101] Under the terms of the Regulation, applications for authorisation are first sent to the competent authority in a Member State.[102] Regulation 3 of the European Union (Genetically Modified Foodstuffs) Regulations 2013 provides that the competent authority for this purpose is the Food Safety Authority of Ireland. It is then the FSAI's responsibility to send the

---

[96] Ibid.

[97] Reg (EC) No 1830/2003 of the European Parliament and of the Council of 22 September 2003 concerning the traceability and labelling of genetically modified organisms and the traceability of food and feed products produced from genetically modified organisms and amending Directive 2001/18/EC [2003] OJ L 268/24. For further discussion on the introduction and implications of this regulation see L Andersen, 'The EU rules on labelling of genetically modified foods: mission accomplished?' (2010) 5 *European Food and Feed Law Review* 136; and C MacMaoláin, 'The new genetically modified food labelling requirements: Finally a lasting solution?' (2003b) 28 *European Law Review* 865.

[98] SI No 268/2013.

[99] SI No 424/2004.

[100] EU Reg 1829/2003, Art 4(1).

[101] Ibid, Art 4(2).

[102] Ibid, Art 5.

application for authorisation on to the European Food Safety Authority (EFSA), without delay.[103]

All applications for GM food use must include a range of details on the producer, the product and its use. This includes the name and address of the applicant; the name of the food, including the transformation event used; information needed to comply with the terms of the Cartagena Protocol on Biosafety;[104] detailed descriptions of methods used in production; copies of studies, including independent and peer-reviewed studies where these exist, which demonstrate that the food is safe; data which demonstrate that the food is not significantly different from its conventional counterpart; proposed labelling details; samples of the food; and plans for post-release monitoring.[105] Full technical dossiers, in accordance with the requirements set out in the EU Deliberate Release Directive, should also be provided for foods containing or consisting of GMOs.[106]

After the application for authorisation has been made to the Food Safety Authority of Ireland, it then turns to EFSA to make its assessment on use of the GMO.[107] Normally, EFSA should issue an opinion on the application within six months. It can ask the applicant for additional information to help it in forming its opinion. The General Food Law Regulation also obliges EFSA to make any opinion on the use of a GMO public.[108] The public can then, in turn, make comments to the Commission on the EFSA opinion. The EFSA opinion is not binding on the Commission. EFSA delivers an opinion only. The Commission makes the decision on authorisation.[109] The GM Food and Feed Regulation just prescribes that any decision taken in respect of the application will take 'into account the opinion of the Authority'.[110] The Commission makes its decision following consultation with its own Standing Committee on Plants, Animals, Food and Feed. This Committee, as discussed in Chapter 2, was also established by the General Food Law Regulation, although originally as the Standing Committee on the Food Chain and Animal Health. The Commission must explain to the Committee the reasons underlying any differences that there might be between its

---

[103] Ibid.

[104] The Cartagena Protocol on Biosafety, adopted in January 2000, is an international agreement, signed up to by 167 states, which is designed to ensure the safe handling, transport and use of modified organisms. It entered into force in September 2003. It contains 40 articles and three annexes on a range of issues related to the minimisation of risks related to GMOs. Text of the Protocol is available at: bch. cbd.int/protocol/text.

[105] Reg 1829/2003, Art 5(3).

[106] Ibid, Art 5(5).

[107] Ibid, Art 6. This has been described as being '[o]ne of the most controversial areas of EFSA's activities' in S Poli, 'Scientific Advice in the GMO area' in A Alemanno and S Gabbi (eds), *Foundations of EU Food Law and Policy* (Farnham, Ashgate, 2013).

[108] Art 38(1) of Regulation (EC) No 178/2002 of the European Parliament and of the Council of 28 January 2002 laying down the general principles and requirements of food law, establishing the European Food Safety Authority and laying down procedures in matters of food safety [2002] OJ L 31/1.

[109] Ibid, Art 7.

[110] Ibid, Art 7(1).

decision and the preceding EFSA opinion. Comitology is then employed to arrive at a final decision on authorisation.[111] All of this should happen within time limits stipulated in the Regulation.

Authorisations can be modified, suspended or revoked. EFSA is specifically entitled to issue an opinion on whether one of these three courses of action should be taken. It can do this either on its own initiative, or at the request of a Member State or the Commission.[112] Once arrived at, the EFSA opinion should then be transmitted to the Commission, the authorisation holder and the Member States. The opinion should also be made public, subject to the deletion of any information that has been identified as confidential. The public has the right to comment on the EFSA opinion to the Commission. It is then up to the Commission to examine the EFSA position and comments from the public before deciding whether the authorisation should be modified, suspended or revoked. Applications for the renewal of previously granted authorisations should be made directly to the Commission at least one year before the expiry of the original granting of consent.[113] Renewals can be for a maximum of 10 years.

Labelling requirements for foods containing or consisting of GMOs are set out in several pieces of EU legislation already referred to. As noted above, there are stipulations on labelling contained in the Deliberate Release Directive. The GM Food and Feed Regulation also provides that:

> [w]ithout prejudice to the other requirements of [Union] law concerning the labelling of foodstuffs, foods falling within the scope of this [legislation] shall be subject to the following specific labelling requirements: (a) where the food consists of more than one ingredient, the words 'genetically modified' or 'produced from genetically modified (name of the ingredient)' shall appear in the list of ingredients provided for in [the framework food labelling directive] in parentheses immediately following the ingredient concerned.[114]

This is the most common type of labelling disclosure that is required for genetically modified food.

Where a GM ingredient has been used in production, this must be stated in the ingredients list. The main exception to this relates to those products which are not obliged to produce a list of ingredients under the terms of the Food Information Regulation.[115] These products must have a clear presentation on the label

---

[111] As set out in Arts 7(3) and 35(2) of the GM Food and Feed Regulation 2003, n 68 above, in conjunction with Council Decision 1999/468/EC, as amended by Council Decision 2006/512/EC, [2006] OJ L 200/11. This procedure has since been altered by the introduction of Regulation (EU) No 182/2011 of the European Parliament and of the Council of 16 February 2011 laying down the rules and general principles concerning mechanisms for control by Member States of the Commission's exercise of implementing powers [2011] OJ L 55/13. The revised comitology procedures are discussed in more detail in ch 2.

[112] Reg 1829/2003, n 68 above, Art 10.

[113] Ibid, Art 11.

[114] Ibid, Art 13(1)(a).

[115] As set out in Art 19 of the Food Information Regulation 1169/2011, [2011] OJ L 304/18.

informing the consumer that they have been 'genetically modified' or 'contains (name of ingredient) produced from genetically modified (name of organism)'.[116] Foods which contain trace amounts of GMOs are not subject to these additional labelling requirements. The Regulation states that there does not need to be disclosure about the presence of a GMO for:

> foods containing material which contains, consists of or is produced from GMOs in a proportion no higher than 0.9% of the food ingredients ... provided that this presence is adventitious or technically unavoidable.[117]

To be able to avail of this provision for the presence of very low levels of GMOs in foodstuffs, operators must provide evidence that they have taken appropriate measures to prevent the inclusion of genetically modified material in the finished product.[118] The 0.9 per cent maximum threshold can also be reduced by comitology.[119] While the GM Food and Feed Regulation does set out that there should be clear labelling indicating the presence of GMOs where appropriate, it goes further than this for those products which are deemed to be different from their conventional counterparts. There must be a statement on the labelling where food produced from or containing a GMO varies from the original variety in relation to composition, nutritional value, usual use, health implications and/or where it may give rise to religious or ethical concerns.[120] There should be a statement like this on the label detailing the characteristics of the food even where no conventional counterpart exists.[121]

Similar requirements are set out in the Regulation for animal feed. There are general obligations to ensure, for example, that GM feed does not have adverse effects on humans, animals or the environment.[122] It should also be relatively similar to the feed that it is designed to replace and its consumption should not therefore be nutritionally disadvantageous for animals or humans in any way. GM feed must first be authorised through the national competent authority,[123] then sent on to EFSA for its opinion[124] before responsibility passes over to the Commission, which, in consultation with the Standing Committee on Plants, Animals, Food and Feed, makes a final decision on authorisation.[125] As is the case for human food, any authorisation granted can be modified, suspended or revoked at any time.[126] The Commission can also consult with the European Group on

[116] See Reg 1829/2003, n 68 above, Art 13(1)(c).
[117] Ibid, Art 12(2).
[118] Ibid, Art 12(3).
[119] Ibid, Art 12(4).
[120] Ibid, Art 13(2).
[121] Ibid, Art 13(3).
[122] Ibid, Art 16(1).
[123] The European Communities (Feedingstuffs)(Genetically Modified Feed) Regulations 2004, n 99 above, provide in Reg 3 that the national competent authority for these purposes is the Minister at the Department of Agriculture, Food and the Marine.
[124] Reg 1829/2003, n 68 above, Art 17.
[125] Ibid, Art 19.
[126] Ibid, Art 22.

Ethics in Science and New Technologies to obtain its opinion on any matter related to the genetic modification of food or feed.[127] Finally, emergency measures can be adopted where there is good reason to suspect that an authorised product constitutes a serious risk to humans, animals or the environment.[128] This should be done in accordance with the procedures set down in the General Food Law Regulation.[129] Any such emergency measures can only be adopted by EU Member States if they can properly establish, in addition to urgency, that there is a clear and serious risk to human health, animal health or the environment.[130]

Genetically Modified Food Labelling and Traceability

The GM Traceability and Labelling Regulation makes amendments to the Deliberate Release Directive and, consequently the Genetically Modified Organisms (Deliberate Release) Regulations 2003. The 2003 EU Regulation is also designed to provide a framework for the traceability of products which consist of or contain GMOs to achieve more accurate labelling and better monitoring of the effects of these products on the environment and human health.[131] Most importantly, a proper system of traceability also assists in the taking of appropriate risk management measures should any safety concerns arise. The Regulation applies to all genetically modified foods as well as feed produced from GMOs.[132]

'Traceability' is defined in the Regulation as 'the ability to trace [GMOs] at all stages of their placing on the market through the production and distribution chains'.[133] This happens in the first instance by obliging all operators to ensure that full information on the presence of a GMO is transmitted to others receiving raw materials or product from them.[134] Each GMO is also to be assigned a unique identifier code; details of this should be passed on though all stages of production and marketing as well.[135] The products should also be clearly labelled, with

---

[127] Ibid, Art 33. The European Group on Ethics in Science and New Technologies is an independent advisory body of the President of the European Commission. Established in 1991, it now gets its legal mandate from Commission Decision (EU) 2016/835 of 25 May 2016 on the renewal of the mandate of the European Group on Ethics in Science and New Technologies, [2016] OJ L 140/21.

[128] Ibid, Art 34.

[129] Arts 53 and 54 of Reg 178/2002, n 108 above. The emergency procedures themselves have been discussed in more detail in Ch 5.

[130] Case C-111/2016, *Giorgio Fidenato and Others* ECLI:EU:C:2017:676. The Court also noted here, in para 50 of its judgment, that the standard for what constitutes the necessary 'risk' type differs for provisional and emergency measures, with more and/or better evidence required in support of the ongoing emergency measure that may be adopted by a Member State. Provisional measures can be based on 'possibility', due to the precautionary principle. However, emergency measures may only be adopted under Art 34 of Reg 1829/2003 if it is 'evident' that products authorised by the reg are likely to constitute a 'serious' risk to human health, animals or the environment.

[131] See Reg 1830/2003, Art 1, n 75 above.

[132] Ibid, Art 2.

[133] Ibid, Art 3(3).

[134] Ibid, Arts 4(1) and 5.

[135] Ibid, Arts 4(1) and 8. Later developed by Commission Regulation (EC) No 65/2004 of 14 January 2004 establishing a system for the development and assignment of unique identifiers for genetically modified organisms, [2004] OJ L 10/5.

an indication on pre-packaged products that they contain genetically modified organisms.[136] Following the introduction of EU Regulation 1829/2003 on genetically modified food and feed it was made clear in Irish law that:

> where the food consists of more than one ingredient, the words "genetically modified" or "produced from genetically modified (name of the ingredient)" appear in the list of ingredients provided for in [the Food Information Regulation] in parantheses immediately following the ingredient concerned [or] where the ingredient is designated by the name of a category, the words "contains genetically modified (name of organism)" or "contains (name of ingredient) produced from genetically modified (name of organism)" appear in the list of ingredients [or] where there is no list of ingredients, the words "genetically modified" or "produced from genetically modified (name of organism)" appear clearly on the labelling.[137]

This is, of course, subject to the exception, discussed above, for 'adventitious or technically unavoidable' trace amounts.[138] Following the introduction of Regulation 1830/2003, the 2013 Irish Regulations further provide that:

> for pre-packaged products consisting of, or containing GMOs, the words "This product contains genetically modified organisms" or "This product contains genetically modified (name of organism)" [must] appear on a label, or for non-pre-packaged products consisting of, or containing GMOs, offered to the final consumer the words "This product contains genetically modified organisms" or "This product contains genetically modified (name of organism) appear on, or in connection with, the display of the product".[139]

The GM Food and Feed Regulation stipulates that all ingredients that have been subject to genetic modification must be labelled as such by highlighting this in the list of ingredients. The GM Traceability and Labelling Regulation brings this further by requiring that food business operators ensure that genetically modified foods, pre-packaged or non-pre-packaged, include a clear disclosure that the product, or at least some part of it, has been genetically modified. This disclosure must be placed on the label where there is one, or in a related display where there is no label or packaging. All, of course, subject to the exemptions, such as those for small amounts of adventitious presence.

Under the European Union (Genetically Modified Foodstuffs) Regulations 2013, it is the responsibility of the Food Safety Authority of Ireland, or an officially appointed agency acting pursuant to a service contract with the FSAI, to enforce the provisions of these two main EU Regulations on genetically modified food in Ireland.[140] A range of powers are provided in the Irish Regulations

---

[136] Ibid, Art 4(6).

[137] Reg 7(4) of the European Union (Genetically Modified Foodstuffs) Regulations 2013, n 98 above.

[138] As set out in Art 12 of EU Regulation 1829/2003, n 75 above and Art 4(7) and 4(8) of EU Regulation 1830/2003, n 97 above. Also set out in Reg 7(2) of the European Union (Genetically Modified Foodstuffs) Regulations 2013, n 98 above.

[139] See European Union (Genetically Modified Foodstuffs) Regulations 2013, n 98, reg 11.

[140] These being Regulations 1829/2003, n 95 above and 1830/2003, n 97 above. This responsibility for the FSAI is set out in Reg 15 of the 2013 Irish Regulations, n 98 above.

for authorised officers, appointed under section 49 of the FSAI Act 1998, to take food samples for analysis,[141] inspect food labels,[142] examine procedures connected with the manufacture of a food,[143] seize, remove or detain foodstuffs over which there is a suspicion that they may not comply with the Regulations, including the labelling requirements,[144] destroy or dispose of food to prevent it being used for human consumption[145] or request the personal details, such as name and address, of food business operators.[146] It is an offence under these 2013 Irish Regulations to obstruct or interfere with authorised officers in their exercise of these powers.[147]

Although primarily relating to matters of environmental law, it should be noted here that EU Member States do now have the option of restricting or prohibiting the cultivation of genetically modified crops in their territory.[148] Directive 2015/412 amends the Deliberate Release Directive 2001/18 to the extent that a Member State:

> [...] may demand that the geographical scope of the written consent or authorisation [for a GMO] be adjusted to the effect that all or part of the territory of that Member State is to be excluded from cultivation.[149]

For a Member State to avail of this allowance it must inform the Commission about this restriction or prohibition soon after the circulation of the GMO assessment report that has been submitted as part of the application for authorisation or renewal or soon after the receipt of an opinion on the use of the GMO from EFSA. After following the procedures specified in the 2015 Directive, the Member State can adopt measures restricting or prohibiting cultivation, provided that these measures are shown to be in compliance with relevant EU laws, reasoned, proportional and non-discriminatory.[150] There must also be compelling grounds for the adoption of the measure which are related to environmental policy objectives, town and country planning, land use, socio-economic impacts, avoidance of GMO presence in other products, agricultural policy objectives and/or public policy.[151]

---

[141] See 2013 Irish Regulations, Reg 16.

[142] Ibid, Reg 20(1).

[143] Ibid, Reg 20(2).

[144] Ibid, Reg 21(1).

[145] Ibid, Reg 21(2).

[146] Ibid, Reg 22.

[147] Ibid, Reg 24(3). With liability on summary conviction to a class A fine or three months' imprisonment, or both or on indictment to a fine of up to €500,000 or imprisonment for up to three years, or both.

[148] Directive (EU) 2015/412 of the European Parliament and of the Council of 11 March 2015 amending Directive 2001/18/EC as regards the possibility for the Member States to restrict or prohibit the cultivation of genetically modified organisms (GMOs) in their territory, [2015] OJ L 68/1.

[149] See Art 1(2) of Directive 2015/412, n 148 above.

[150] For more on this passing of some decision-making on GMOs from the EU to the Member States see L Salvi, 'The EU regulatory framework on GMOs and the shift of powers towards Member States: An easy way out of the regulatory impasse?' (2016) 11 *European Food and Feed Law Review* 201.

[151] It should be noted that these grounds can be invoked individually or in a combination, with the exception of 'public policy', which must form part of a justification in combination with one of the other objectives listed.

Novel Foods, Cloning and Nanotechnology

It was recognised for some time that the original Novel Foods Regulation was in need of updating, before this finally happened with the introduction of a new regulation in 2015,[152] that came into effect in 2018.[153] Both the White Paper on Food Safety[154] and the initial proposal for new novel foods legislation identified that there was a broad consensus on the need for change.[155] One of the key changes that had already been made to the original 1997 Novel Foods Regulation was the removal of foods and ingredients containing or consisting of GMOs and food and ingredients produced from, but not containing GMOs, from the scope of its provisions.[156] The Preamble to the GM Food and Feed Regulation states that this was done 'to ensure clarity, transparency and a harmonised framework for authorisation of genetically modified food'.[157] The first proposal to have a significant overhaul of the Novel Foods Regulation, published in January 2008, was later abandoned. The Regulation was to be introduced via the ordinary legislative procedure and much of the debate on it during this process surrounded the provisions on nanotechnology, animal cloning and risk analysis. The discussions reached an impasse, however, particularly on the animal cloning issues. Having reached the conciliation stage of the legislative process, the Committee failed to reach any agreement by its final meeting on the matter in March 2011. As a result, a second proposal for a new regulation on novel foods did not deal with the cloning issue. This is to be dealt with in separate proposals instead. The European Commission has presented two proposals for directives on this matter, but neither had become legislation in the five years following their initial introduction.[158] However, the use of cloning as a farming practice has effectively been suspended for the time being.[159]

---

[152] See Regulation (EU) 2015/2283 of the European Parliament above n 86.

[153] See also P Coppens, 'The revision of the novel foods regulation' (2013) 8 *European Food and Feed Law Review* 238 and C Jones, 'The novel food regulation: revision required?' (2012) 7 *European Food and Feed Law Review* 81.

[154] White Paper on Food Safety, COM (1999) 719.

[155] The Explanatory Memorandum to the Proposal for a Regulation of the European Parliament and of the Council on novel foods, COM (2007) 872, noted how a stakeholder consultation undertaken following a Commission discussion paper in 2002 highlighted the need to develop and update Reg 258/1997.

[156] Art 38(1) of Reg 1829/2003, above n 75, deleted Art 1(2)(a) and (b) from Reg 258/1997.

[157] Recital 6 thereof.

[158] Proposal for a Directive of the European Parliament and of the Council on the cloning of animals of the bovine, porcine, ovine, caprine and equine species kept and reproduced for farming purposes, COM (2013) 892 and Proposal for a Council Directive on the placing on the market of food from animal clones, COM (2013) 893. The former proposal identified food from clones as involving new techniques and therefore being considered as a 'novel food'. However, it could not be included in the streamlined procedures for novel food approvals due to the failure to reach agreement on this over ethical and welfare concerns. EFSA has previously stated that it views animal cloning as an 'animal welfare hazard' due to the low efficiency of the technique, confirming that 'surrogate dams used in cloning suffer in particular from placenta dysfunctions contributing to increased levels of miscarriages'. In addition, 'clone abnormalities and unusually large offspring result in difficult births and neonatal deaths'. Scientific Opinion of the Scientific Committee on Food Safety, Animal Health and Welfare and Environmental Impact of Animals derived from Cloning by Somatic Cell Nucleus Transfer (SCNT) and their Offspring and Products Obtained from those Animals, available at www.efsa.europa.eu.

[159] Art 3 of Proposal for a Directive of the European Parliament and of the Council on the cloning of animals of the bovine, porcine, ovine, caprine and equine species kept and reproduced for farming

Some of the more significant recent legislative developments on food at EU level including, for example, the Food Information Regulation, have tended to be designed in a manner that corresponds with the broader aims of policy direction documentation, such as the Strategy for Better Regulation.[160] The proposal for a new novel foods regulation was more specifically aimed at pursuing the objectives of the Communication on Smart Regulation in the EU[161] and the Europe 2020 Strategy.[162] The hope is that the new Novel Food Regulation will help to simplify and streamline the regulatory process for novel foods, at a time when there is an increase in its use and aid the development of new technologies in food production. Overall, new regulations, such as this, are being designed in a manner that should reduce regulatory burdens. This will, it is hoped, consequently increase the competitiveness of the European food industry. Also, it will ensure the maintenance of food safety standards and public health protection, as well as providing that the EU and the Member States, comply with their international obligations. As was discussed above, this has not always been the case when regulating for new technological processes being used in the food sector, most significantly when poor regulation led to findings of non-compliance with WTO obligations in relation to the application of the legislation on GMOs.

The new Novel Food Regulation 2015/2283 is designed to achieve most of the same outcomes at the original version, Regulation 258/1997. However, the new version accounts for those developments that have been made in the intervening period in the science and technology of food production. The Regulation provides for the simplification of the legislation and related administrative burdens for both public authorities and private parties by creating only one centralised procedure for the assessment and authorisation of novel foods. Applications are to be made directly to the European Commission,[163] who may then request a scientific opinion on the risk assessment from EFSA.[164] The Commission will also continue to be assisted in its decision making by what is now the Standing Committee on Plants, Animals, Food and Feed.[165] This should remove some of the national administrative procedures and duplication. The resulting authorisation procedure has become

---

purposes, n 158 above, permits EU Member States to provisionally prohibit both the cloning of animals and the placing on the market of animal clones and embryo clones. Article 5 provides that the Commission should report back on the use of these techniques in agriculture, taking account of reports on this submitted by the Member States, scientific and technical progress in particular relating to the animal welfare aspects of cloning and international developments.

[160] As now set out in the Communication from the Commission to the European Parliament, the Council, the European Economic and Social Committee and the Committee of the Regions on Regulatory Fitness, COM (2012) 746.

[161] See the Communication from the Commission to the European Parliament, the Council, the European Economic and Social Committee and the Committee of the Regions on 'Smart Regulation in the European Union', COM (2010) 543.

[162] COM (2010) 2020.

[163] Regulation 2015/2283, n 152 above, Art 10(1).

[164] Ibid, Art 10(3).

[165] Ibid, Art 30.

more streamlined, which also reduces the administrative burden and related costs for private parties. It should also become a quicker process, with authorisation being automatically granted if it can be shown that there is no danger to human health or potential to deceive the consumer and that the 'novel' food is substantially equivalent to its conventional counterpart. This will also significantly reduce the volume and consequent costs of applications.

Significantly, the need to be granted authorisations for individual foods is replaced in some cases with generic authorisation for a food type.[166] The EU Commission can include novel foods on an EU list where the food can be shown to pose no safety risk to human health and where its intended use does not mislead the consumer such as where there is a significant alteration, usually detrimental, to its expected nutritional value. Previously authorised novel foods should be automatically included on this list.[167] The list itself can be amended at any stage by the Commission.[168]

'Novel food' is defined in the Regulation as 'all food that was not used for human consumption to a significant degree … before 15 May 1997'. This includes food with a new or intentionally modified molecular structure; food consisting of, isolated from or produced from micro-organisms, fungi or algae; food consisting of, isolated from or produced from material of mineral origin; food consisting of, isolated from or produced from plants or their parts, except when the food has a history of safe food use within the EU and is consisting of, isolated from or produced from a plant or variety of the same species obtained by traditional propagating practices or by non-traditional practices where these practices do not give rise to significant changes in the composition or structure of the food affecting its nutritional value, metabolism or level of undesirable substances; food consisting of, isolated from or produced from animals or their parts obtained by traditional breeding practices and the food from those animals has a history of safe food use within the EU; food resulting from a production process which gives rise to significant changes in the composition or structure of a food, affecting its nutritional value, metabolism or level of undesirable substances; food consisting of engineered nanomaterials; vitamins, minerals or other substances considered as 'novel'; food used exclusively in food supplements.[169] This broad definition expands the scope of the new Novel Foods Regulation to account for new technologies, such as nanotechnology and new uses for other edible substances, such as fortification materials. 'Engineered nanomaterials' are those which are 'intentionally produced' and which have 'one or more dimensions of the order of 100 nm or less'.[170] Food business operators are obliged to verify whether the

[166] Ibid, Art 7.
[167] Ibid, Art 8.
[168] Ibid, Art 9.
[169] Ibid, Art 3(2).
[170] Ibid, Art 3(2)(f).

food that they intend to place on the market is a 'novel food' by first consulting with the relevant authorities in the EU Member State where they first intend to place the product on the market. These authorities can then consult with the other Member States and with the Commission to determine whether the product is a 'novel food'.[171] The FSAI is the competent authority for novel foods in Ireland.

While novel foods are subject to all of the relevant requirements of the EU Food Information Regulation and the Nutrition and Health Claims Regulation where relevant;[172] they must also include additional labelling disclosures that inform the consumer about any specific characteristic or property of the novel food, such as the composition, nutritional value or nutritional effects and intended use of the food where this renders the novel food no longer equivalent to an existing food or where this has implications for the health of specific groups of people.[173]

10.5. Protecting the Welfare of Food-producing Animals

Irish law and standards on the protection of farm animals are based on a range of domestic and EU policy documents, codes of practice and legislation. Minimum welfare requirements have traditionally been wide and varied across EU Member States. Many of the EU provisions are now set at a level which is either below that often applied in Ireland or which have been introduced at a time when Irish farmers were already meeting the requirements set by EU directives and regulations. But this has not always been the case.

There are two main types of legislation applicable to the welfare of food-producing animals. The first are the general requirements. These apply horizontally across all types of animals and methods or stages of production, including transportation and slaughter. The second type, which often links into the former, is animal specific. We here focus on three food-producing animals: poultry, pigs and cattle, to provide examples of the level and type of requirement that has been set. All these animal-specific requirements come directly from EU directives which have been transposed into Irish law.[174]

---

[171] Ibid, Art 4. Examples of novel foods listed in the EU Commission Novel Food Catalogue include spirulina, creatine, lutein, palm sugar, ethyl esters from concentrated fish oils and young tissue extract from incubated hen eggs.

[172] Regulation (EC) No 1924/2006 of the European Parliament and of the Council of 20 December 2006 on nutrition and health claims made on foods, [2006] OJ L 404/9.

[173] Art 9(3)(b) of EU Reg 2015/2283.

[174] The importance of this animal welfare legislation has been recognised by Humphreys J in the Irish High Court in *Sfar v Minister for Agriculture, Food and the Marine* [2016] 4 JIC 505, where it was stated that '[a]nimals are powerless to protect themselves against neglect or cruelty [and therefore] upholding their welfare is an urgent matter and must not be put on hold'.

10.5.1. European Union Animal Welfare Strategy

The general principles of EU policy on the protection of food-producing animals are set out in the Strategy for the Protection and Welfare of Animals 2012–2015.[175] This document, which followed on from the Community Action Plan on the Protection and Welfare of Animals 2006–2010,[176] is designed to set out a range of ways of both introducing and applying mechanisms to enforce the protection of the billions of animals which are kept for economic purposes in the EU. The Animal Welfare Strategy estimates that livestock farming is worth around €150 billion annually to the economies of the Member States. The Central Statistics Office has calculated that cattle output alone in Ireland was worth nearly €2.5 billion by 2017. The output value of pigs for the same year was found to be over half a billion euros. Ireland is the fifth largest beef exporter in the world and the largest in Europe. Ireland is also the highest consumer of poultry meat per person in the EU.

It is recognised in the EU Strategy Communication that although the animal welfare agenda has been advanced through the introduction of specific pieces of legislation, such as those which are discussed in more detail below, there are still areas which are not covered by any legislative requirements. The more general welfare requirements, which are also discussed below, can also be difficult to apply in some sectors. It is therefore proposed that a process of simplification of these broad stipulations could be undertaken to address common issues related to the welfare of animals. An evaluation of EU animal welfare policy has previously concluded that the imposition of standards has led to additional costs of around 2 per cent on the overall value of the livestock sector. It also found that at this level, this does not threaten economic sustainability in any way. The additional costs should also be lower in those States, like Ireland, where higher welfare standards were already being applied. There is also recognition in the strategy document that while the costs of improved welfare have tended to be low, the economic value added of this policy should be continually monitored to ensure that the competitiveness of the agricultural sector is maintained.

The Strategy for the Protection of the Welfare of Animals has recognised four key issues that affect the well-being of animals across the EU and these will be used as the basis for any changes that are to be made to related legislation in the coming years. The first is that there remains a lack of enforcement by Member States across several areas. Second, studies show that consumer interest in welfare issues is significant, if not that high, but they also demonstrate that it is only one

---

[175] Communication from the Commission to the European Parliament, the Council and the European Economic and Social Committee on the European Union Strategy for the Protection and Welfare of Animals 2012–2015, COM (2012) 6.

[176] Communication from the Commission to the European Parliament and the Council on a Community Action Plan on the protection and Welfare of Animals 2006–2010, COM (2006) 13.

of a range of factors which affects consumer choice.[177] Poor understanding about production methods and the impact of these on animals also leads to purchasing decisions that do not necessarily relate to levels of concern about welfare. The report suggested that the use of 'reserved terms' was a good way of informing purchasers and consumers about product characteristics and farming methods. Perhaps the best example of 'reserved terms' is the way in which they have been used in the marketing standards for eggs. Legislation has prescribed that eggs are labelled according to production method, be they 'eggs from unenriched caged hens' (since banned), 'barn eggs', 'free-range eggs' or, those which employ the highest welfare standards, 'organic eggs'.[178]

The report notes that since this labelling system was introduced, the quantity of non-caged egg production increased significantly in nearly all EU Member States. Similar 'reserved terms' are already also employed in the marketing of poultry. This is discussed in more detail below. The report also stated that 'in addition to price, consumers' purchasing decisions are influenced by a number of "interpersonal" (culture, societal norms, social status, group and family influences) and "intrapersonal" (involvement, emotions, motives, attitudes, norms, personality) determinants'. While it was accepted that, in principle, more information provided by labels should facilitate consumers in making more informed choices, it was also recognised that they would need to have reliable knowledge about the value added of animal welfare-friendly products if expected to pay a higher price for these.

Labelling would therefore only have the desired effect if consumers are: (i) adequately informed on the meaning of the label; (ii) the information provided is readily understandable; and (iii) consumers, or their relevant sub-groups, are interested in having this information made available to them before making their purchasing decisions. It would not, therefore, be just about welfare labelling. Any efforts to encourage more ethical and considered purchasing would also require proper information and education campaigns.

The results presented in the report also show that animal welfare labelling could itself be used to raise consumer awareness and 'accelerate market penetration of animal welfare-friendly products that go beyond the minimum standards foreseen in EU legislation'. As a consequence, the development of new animal welfare practices would be more motivated by market demand. Additional specific communication and education initiatives could also contribute to further raising awareness amongst consumers on welfare issues, provided this is based on reputable scientific data.

---

[177] A report was presented by the European Commission in 2009 entitled 'Options for animal welfare labelling and the establishment of a European Network of Reference Centres for the protection and welfare of animals', COM (2009) 584. Available at: ec.europa.eu/food/animal/welfare. The surveys undertaken indicated that animal welfare was a significant issue for 64% of consumers across the EU.

[178] As mostly set out in the European Communities (Marketing Standards for Eggs) Regulations 2009, SI No 140/2009. The welfare standards for laying hens are set out in the European Communities (Welfare of Farmed Animals) Regulations 2010, SI No 311/2010.

A lack of understanding about the detriment that some production systems can have on animal welfare can itself be an impediment to calls for change, or the increased employment of more welfare-friendly practices. Any such information and/or education campaigns could also be used to address aspects of the third of the four key issues raised in the Strategy for the Protection of the Welfare of Animals: many of the stakeholders in the sector lack sufficient knowledge about animal welfare. According to the report, a common lack of awareness about alternative practices in food-production systems often leads to resistance to changes that could be brought in to improve welfare standards. Finally, the report recognised that there is a real need to develop clearer principles on animal welfare.

The framework directive on the protection of farm animals,[179] now transposed into Irish law by the European Communities (Welfare of Farmed Animals) Regulations 2010,[180] was identified as containing provisions that are too general to have meaningful practical effects. An example was given of the provision contained in the Annex to the directive which states that '[a]ll animals must have access to feed at intervals appropriate to their physiological needs'.

The Strategy is to be based on two complementary approaches. The first is to move away from the use of specific legislation designed to tackle specific problems. Instead, there should be a set of general principles established in a consolidated and revised EU legislative framework. This would also, it is hoped, facilitate better enforcement of animal welfare provisions. The second is the reinforcement or better use of actions which the Commission was already performing. Therefore, in addition to the envisaged simplified legislative framework, it is also to develop tools to strengthen Member States' compliance; increase its support for more international co-operation in the field; provide consumers and the public with more appropriate information; optimise synergistic effects from the current Common Agricultural Policy; and carry out investigations into the welfare of farmed fish. However, all of this is to be done with regard for any impact that measures could have on fundamental rights, including those contained in Article 10 of the Charter of Fundamental Rights of the European Union and Article 9 of the European Convention on Human Rights, on freedom of religion.[181]

Taking all of this into consideration, it should also be noted at this stage that the issues related to the welfare of food-producing animals have taken on increased significance at EU level since relevant insertions on the matter were

---

[179] Council Directive 1998/58/EC of 20 July 1998 concerning the protection of animals kept for farming purposes [1998] OJ L 221/23.

[180] SI No 311/2010, n 178 above.

[181] The Court of Justice has confirmed that 'ritual slaughter' comes within the definition of 'religious rite' and therefore falls within the scope of the freedom of religion guaranteed by the Charter of Fundamental Rights of the EU. See Case C-426/2016, *Liga van Moskeeën en Islamitsche Organisaties Provincie Antwerpen VZW and Others v Vlaams Gewest* ECLI:EU:C:2018:335.

introduced into the Treaty on the Functioning of the European Union (TFEU), which came into effect in December 2009. Most significantly, Article 13 TFEU states that:

> [i]n formulating and implementing the Union's agriculture, fisheries, transport, internal market, research and technological development and space policies, the Union and the Member States, since animals are sentient beings, pay full regard to the welfare requirements of animals, while respecting the legislative or administrative provisions and customs of the Member States relating in particular to religious rites, cultural traditions and regional heritage.

This is contained in Title II of the TFEU, which lists the key principles that should underpin Union activities, including policy, decision-making and legislative initiatives. Its inclusion here puts the protection of animal interests on a par with other such principles, including the promotion of gender equality, social protection, human health, eliminating discrimination, sustainable development, the protection of consumers and the protection of personal data.

New Legislative Initiatives on Animal Health

The Strategy for the Protection and Welfare of Animals suggests ways in which EU law could be modified and reorganised in a manner that would offer better protection, increase consumer and other stakeholder awareness and maximise compliance within the Member States. Coupled with other, more general, strategies developed by the EU,[182] a proposal for a new regulation on animal health was developed in 2013.[183] The Explanatory Memorandum to this proposal noted that there were almost 50 basic directives and regulations and around 400 pieces of secondary legislation within the EU animal health framework. Some of these dated back to 1964. A number of problems were identified. These included the overly complex existing animal health policy, a lack of overall strategy, an insufficient focus on disease prevention and issues related to intra-Union trade in live animals. The resulting Animal Health Law was to be designed to address these concerns by providing a legal framework for the priority issues identified in the Animal Health Strategy, published in 2007.[184] These issues included ensuring a high level of public health and food safety protection by minimising the incidence of biological and chemical risks to humans; promoting animal health by preventing or reducing the

---

[182] See the Communication from the Commission to the European Parliament, the Council, the European Economic and Social Committee and the Committee of the Regions on 'Smart Regulation in the European Union', above n 161; and the Communication from the Commission, 'Europe 2020: A strategy for smart, sustainable and inclusive growth', COM (2010) 2020.

[183] Proposal for a Regulation of the European Parliament and of the Council on Animal Health, COM (2013) 260.

[184] Communication from the Commission to the Council, the European Parliament, the European Economic and Social Committee and the Committee of the Regions on 'A new animal health strategy for the European Union (2007–2013) where prevention is better than cure', COM (2007) 539.

incidence of animal diseases; improving economic growth and competitiveness by the promotion of the free movement of goods and the proportionate movement of animals; and promoting farming practices and animal welfare standards which prevent animal health related threats and minimise environmental impacts in support of the EU Sustainable Development Strategy.[185] All of this is to be achieved by revising the legal framework in a manner which establishes

> a single, simplified, transparent and clear regulatory framework that sets out systematically the objectives, scope and principles of regulatory intervention; based on good governance and compliant with international (eg the World Organisation for Animal Health (OIE)) standards; focusing on long-term preventative measures and working together with all relevant stakeholders.

With a clear link to the way in which previous animal health issues have been mismanaged in the past, most notably in the case of BSE, the proposal included as specific objectives of this new Animal Health Law a commitment:

> to introduce overarching general principles allowing a simplified legal framework in order to be prepared for the new challenges, to enable quick reaction in case of emerging diseases; whilst ensuring the same quality of reaction as provided for in current legislation [and] to reduce the impact of animal diseases on animal and public health, animal welfare, economy and society as far as possible by enhancing disease awareness, preparedness, surveillance and emergency response systems at national and EU level.

To address all of this, a new regulation was introduced in March 2016 setting out this revised, updated and streamlined 'Animal Health Law'.[186] The Regulation, which will come into effect in April 2021, recognises the obvious impact that the spread of disease amongst food-producing animals can have on the animals themselves, their keepers, the economy, public health and food safety. However, it also recognises a relationship between animal health and biodiversity, climate change and other environmental aspects.[187]

The Animal Health Law Regulation runs to over 200 pages. Its primary focus reflects that of the preparatory documents, ultimately being:

> [...] to promote animal health by placing greater emphasis on preventive measures, disease surveillance, disease control and research, in order to reduce the incidence of animal diseases and minimise the impact of outbreaks when they do occur.[188]

The Regulation sets a series of disease-specific rules for a number of established diseases, including foot and mouth disease, swine fever and avian influenza, as well as a number of other diseases listed in Annex II, including rabies, Newcastle

---

[185] As revised by the Council of the European Union, 'Review of the EU Sustainable Development Strategy', 15–16 June 2006.

[186] Regulation (EU) 2016/429 of the European Parliament and of the Council of 9 March 2016 on transmissible animal diseases and amending and repealing certain acts in the area of animal health, [2016] OJ L 59/1.

[187] Preamble to Reg 2016/429, recitals 1–3.

[188] Preamble to Reg 2016/429, recital 8. Further reflected in Art 1 of the Regulation.

disease, anthrax and bovine tuberculosis.[189] New diseases can be added to this list where there is evidence to show that it is transmissible, has negative effects on animal health and that animal species that are susceptible to it exist within the EU, amongst other reasons.[190]

The first set of measures that must be taken to maintain animal health are a series of responsibilities that are placed on operators and those involved in the rearing and health protection of animals. They must maintain the health of kept animals, use veterinary medicines responsibly, minimise the risk of disease spreading and engage in good animal husbandry.[191] They must also take appropriate biosecurity measures, regarding both kept and wild animals, including physical prevention measures such as using proper fencing and roofing as well as cleaning and disinfecting housing, controlling insects and rodents and taking management measures related to the use of equipment, entering animal establishments, quarantine use and the safe disposal of dead animals.[192] Animal professionals are responsible for taking appropriate actions to minimise the risk of the spread of disease.[193] Further stipulations specifically aimed at veterinarians are also set out in the Regulation.[194] All operators and animal professionals must also have adequate knowledge of animal diseases, biosecurity principles and welfare standards.[195]

The second set of responsibilities set out in the Regulation are those aimed at the EU Member States. The first thing that Member States must do is to ensure that they have qualified personnel and adequate facilities, equipment and financial resources in place to meet the needs of the Regulation.[196] There is a strong emphasis on public information, including obligations to inform the public about any possible risks posed by products or animals and the measures taken to address these possible or real risks.[197] Food business operators must notify the national authorities where they suspect any listed disease may be present in animals as part of this process,[198] following proper and ongoing surveillance of animals in their care.[199] The Member State must then notify the Commission and the other Member States where there is any outbreak of one of these listed diseases.[200] A series of appropriate control measures must then be applied by the national

---

[189] Ibid, Art 5(1).
[190] Ibid, Art 5(3).
[191] Ibid, Art 10(1).
[192] Ibid, Art 10(4).
[193] Ibid, Art 10(2).
[194] Ibid, Art 12.
[195] Ibid, Art 11(1).
[196] Ibid, Art 13.
[197] Ibid, Art 15.
[198] Ibid, Art 18. Arts 26 and 27 further provide that national authorities are also obliged to maintain surveillance of animals to identify whether they may be carrying a listed disease. Under Art 28 the Member States must report on these surveillance measures to the EU Commission.
[199] Ibid, Art 24.
[200] Ibid, Arts 19–23.

competent authorities, normally the Department of Agriculture, Food and the Marine.[201]

The Animal Health Law Regulation does not contain provisions that specifically regulate animal welfare. It is primarily designed to help control and, where possible, eradicate animal disease. It contains many provisions in this regard that are similar to those already in operation under existing EU law. Some of these were identified in the food safety context in Chapter 5. The Animal Health Law brings many of these provisions together into a substantial consolidated regulation. While the Animal Health Law does not really address the treatment of food-producing animals in the welfare context, it does recognise that animal health and welfare are linked: 'better animal health promotes better animal welfare, and vice versa'.[202] The welfare of food-producing animals is addressed in other EU secondary and transposing Irish legislation.

10.5.2. Animal Welfare Requirements

While there are a series of general strategies and some new general laws on animal welfare and health, most of the legal requirements in this area come from specific provisions which detail how different animals are to be treated and also how all animals are to be treated in different situations. There are, for example, specific provisions on the care of food-producing poultry, pigs and cattle. There are also general provisions applicable to all food-producing animals about their transportation and slaughter. These are all discussed in more detail below.

Welfare of Farmed Animals Legislation

The main framework legislation on the protection of animals in Ireland is the Animal Health and Welfare Act 2013. However, when it comes to food-producing animals, the key legislation is the European Communities (Welfare of Farmed Animals) Regulations 2010.[203] These Irish Regulations also give effect to the main provisions of EU law in this area, first introduced through a series of directives in the 1990s.[204] In the most general of senses, the welfare of farm animals is also guided by what are known as 'the five freedoms of animal welfare'. These provide

---

[201] Arts 55 and 56 set out what sorts of preliminary measures should be applied in these circumstances, pending confirmation of the disease. Arts 60–69 set out what should be done where the suspected disease is confirmed.

[202] Preamble to Reg 2016/429, recital 7. Art 1(2)(b) of the Regulation provides that animal health rules must 'take into account the relationship between animal health and [...] animal welfare, including the sparing of any avoidable pain, distress or suffering'.

[203] SI No 311/2010, n 178 above.

[204] Most significantly, Directive 1998/58 on the protection of animals kept for farming purposes, n 179 above. The 2010 Irish Regulations also now transpose the EU directives on chicken welfare, laying hens, calf welfare and pig welfare, all of which are discussed later in this chapter.

that animal keepers must, at all times, ensure that the animals are (i) free from hunger and thirst – animals must have access to fresh water and a healthy diet; (ii) free from discomfort – an appropriate environment should be provided, including shelter and a comfortable resting area; (iii) free from pain, injury or disease – to include rapid diagnosis and treatment of illness; (iv) free to express normal behaviour – by ensuring that they have sufficient space, proper facilities and the company of animals of their own kind; and (v) free from fear and distress – by providing conditions and treatment which avoid mental suffering.[205]

The 2010 Regulations enable the Minister for Agriculture to publish and amend codes of practice related to the welfare of farm animals.[206] Codes that currently exist include the Animal Welfare Guidelines for Beef Farmers, produced by the Farm Animal Welfare Advisory Council, as well as those on the Emergency Killing of Pigs on Farms, the Transport of Cattle, Sheep, Horses, Pigs and Poultry, the Welfare of Laying Hens and the Welfare of Pigs, amongst others.[207] These codes must be adhered to and they can be admitted in evidence in court proceedings.[208]

Different parts of the Regulations set out the welfare requirements for different species of food-producing animals, as well as different parts of the food-production process. These transpose the original and amended key provisions of secondary EU law in this area into the domestic legal system. This includes, for example, the transposition of Directive 1999/74 on the protection of egg-laying hens,[209] Directive 2007/43 on meat-producing chickens,[210] Directive 2008/119 on the protection of calves,[211] and Directive 2008/120 on the protection of pigs,[212] as well as the horizontal directive protecting all animals at their time of slaughter.[213]

Schedule 1 to the 2010 Regulations deals sets out the general conditions under which all farmed animals should be kept. This includes requirements on staffing (sufficient numbers and competence), inspection systems (accessible and regular), record keeping (on health matters), freedom of movement (relatively unrestricted), accommodation (clean, safe and comfortable), protection from adverse weather, soundness of mechanical equipment, breeding procedures, feed and water

---

[205] As now set out in Farm Animal Welfare Advisory Council Guidelines. Available at: www.agriculture.gov.ie/fawac.

[206] SI No 311/2010, n 178 above, Reg 3(1).

[207] All available at: www.fawac.ie/publications/animalwelfareguidelines/.

[208] Farm Animal Welfare Advisory Council Guidelines, n 205 above, Reg 3(4).

[209] Council Directive 1999/74/EC of 19 July 1999 laying down minimum standards for the protection of laying hens [1999] OJ L 203/53.

[210] Council Directive 2007/43/EC of 28 June 2007 laying down minimum rules for the protection of chickens kept for meat production, [2007] OJ L 182/19.

[211] Council Directive 2008/119/EC of 18 December 2008 laying down minimum standards for the protection of calves, [2008] OJ L 10/7.

[212] Council Directive 2008/120/EC of 18 December 2008 laying down minimum standards for the protection of pigs, [2009] OJ L 47/5.

[213] Council Directive 1993/119/EC of 22 December 1993 on the protection of animals at the time of slaughter or killing, [1993] OJ L 340/21. This has since been replaced by Council Regulation (EC) No 1099/2009 of 24 September 2009 on the protection of animals at the time of killing [2009] OJ L 303/1.

(wholesome, appropriate, free from contamination) and a prohibition on the use of electrical currents for the immobilisation of animals. The requirements reflect those set out in the framework EU Directive 1998/58. This also contains provision for the recognition of the European Convention for the Protection of Animals, which is discussed in more detail below.

Welfare of Egg-laying and Meat-producing Poultry

Part 3 of the 2010 Regulations deals with more specific requirements which are applicable to the keeping of egg-laying hens. It applies to any premises where there are 350 or more laying hens.[214] This now also deals with hens that are kept in unenriched cage systems. First flagged as a possibility in the EU Action Plan on Welfare,[215] the keeping of hens in unenriched cages has been banned since January 2012. This prohibition, initially introduced by EU Directive 1999/74,[216] was later confirmed in Part 3 of the 2010 Irish Regulations.[217] It represents one of the most significant advances made by EU intervention into unethical farming practices. Prior to the ban, which several EU Member States lobbied against for many years, egg-laying hens were categorised as being held in either enriched cages,[218] unenriched cages[219] or, for the luckier ones, 'alternative' systems.[220] Those accommodated in the latter are provided with perching and nesting opportunities, as well as access to open runs. Enriched cages do include nests and perches, as well as a minimum requirement of 750 cm^2 of space per hen, although only 600 cm^2 of this must be 'usable'. This was reduced to 550 cm^2 for those held in unenriched cages, with no nesting or perch requirements. The requirements for meat-producing chickens are different. They are set out in EU Regulation 543/2008,[221] combined with the European Communities (Marketing Standards for Poultry-meat) Regulations 2010.[222] More general welfare standards for meat-producing poultry are set out in Part 4 of the European Communities (Welfare of Farmed Animals) Regulations 2010. Authorised officers, who oversee compliance with the Poultrymeat Regulations, are appointed by the Department of Agriculture, Food and the Marine, as set out in the European Communities (Agriculture, Fisheries and Food) (Compliance) Regulations 2009.[223]

---

[214] SI No 311/2010, n 178 above, Reg 6(1).
[215] See n 176 above.
[216] See n 209 above.
[217] SI No 311/2010, n 178 above, Reg 9(3).
[218] See Art 6 of Directive 1999/74, n 209 above.
[219] Ibid, Art 5.
[220] Ibid, Art 4.
[221] Commission Regulation (EC) No 543/2008 of 16 June 2008 Laying down detailed rules for the application of Council Regulation (EC) No 1234/2007 as regards the marketing standards for poultrymeat, [2008] OJ L 543/2008.
[222] SI No 328/2010.
[223] SI No 424/2009, Reg 4 thereof.

The 2008 EU Regulation covers a range of aspects related to the production and marketing of poultrymeat, including welfare standards. It defines the different types of poultry (chickens, turkeys, ducks, geese, guinea fowl), the cuts of meat that can be taken from poultry (half, quarter, breast, leg, thigh, drumstick, wing) and there is special provision for the definition of 'foie gras'.[224] The Regulation sets out a range of definitions for the different kinds of farming methods that are employed in the production of poultry meat. This includes the setting of requirements that must be met before a producer can use descriptions such as 'free range', 'traditional free range', 'extensive indoor' (barn reared).[225] The highest welfare standards, which are those related to organic production methods, are not covered by this Regulation but are dealt with in Regulation 834/2007, as was discussed above. Annex V to the EU Regulation provides that the term 'free range' can only be used for poultry where the following conditions are satisfied:

> [t]he stocking rate in the house and the age of slaughter are in accordance with the limits fixed [for barn reared but] the birds have had during at least half their lifetime continuous daytime access to open-air runs comprising an area mainly covered by vegetation of not less than 1 m² per chicken or guinea fowl, 2 m² per duck or per capon, 4 m² per turkey or goose [and] the feed formula used in the fattening stage contains at least 70% of cereals [and] the poultryhouse is provided with popholes of a combined length at least equal to 4 m per 100 m squared surface of the house.[226]

The requirements for use of the term 'traditional free range' are slightly higher. So, for example, the open-air run size increases to 2 m² per chicken, 6 m² for turkeys and 10 m² for geese. Minimum slaughter ages are also increased for some poultry in this category, such as that for chickens which rises to a minimum life of 81 days, from 56 days, if the bird is to be labelled as 'traditional free range', or between 126 and 140 days for turkeys depending on whether they are intended for cutting up or for roasting whole. Finally, a description of 'free range – total freedom' can be used where the poultry have had continuous day-time access to open-air runs of an unlimited area. The 2008 EU Regulation includes a requirement that producers who use free-range systems must also keep records of the dates when birds were first given access to open-air runs.[227]

The standards for free-range are different for eggs. As noted above, one of the most significant legal developments related to the welfare of food-producing animals to have taken place at EU level has been the banning of egg production from hens housed in unenriched cages. Several different standards of welfare in egg production remain. These are now set out in EU Regulation 589/2008,[228]

---

[224] Art 1 of Reg 543/2008, n 221 above. 'Foie gras' is specified as being 'the livers of geese, or of ducks of [specified species] which have been fed in such a way as to produce hepatic fatty cellular hypertrophy'. 'Hypertrophy' is an abnormally large growth, in this case in the liver.

[225] Ibid, Art 11 in conjunction with Annex IV.

[226] Ibid, Annex V.

[227] Ibid, Art 12 thereof.

[228] Commission Regulation (EC) No 589/2008 of 23 June 2008 laying down detailed rules for implementing Council Regulation (EC) No 1234/2007 as regards marketing standards for eggs [2008] OJ L 163/6.

which is given further effect at national level by European Communities (Marketing Standards for Eggs) Regulations 2009.[229]

The 2008 EU Eggs Regulation provides a set of minimum requirements for the various egg farming methods. Annex II to the Regulation states that 'free range eggs':

> must be produced in systems of production which satisfy ... the following conditions: (a) hens must have continuous daytime access to open-air runs. However, this requirement does not prevent a producer from restricting access for a limited period of time in the morning hours in accordance with usual good farming practice, including good animal husbandry practice. In case of other restrictions, including veterinary restrictions, adopted under [EU] law to protect public and animal health, having the effect of restricting access of hens to open-air runs, eggs may continue to be marketed as "free-range eggs" for the duration of the restriction, but under no circumstances for more than 12 weeks.

In a similar provision to that made for free-range poultrymeat, the Regulation further stipulates that the open-air runs referred to:

> must be mainly covered with vegetation and not be used for other purposes except for orchards, woodland and livestock grazing if the latter is authorised by the competent authorities; [they must also have a] maximum stocking density [not] greater than 2,500 hens per hectare of ground available to the hens or one hen per 4 m² at all times [and the] open-air runs must not extend beyond a radius of 150 m from the nearest pophole of the building.

The Regulation affords protection to both the poultry covered by its provisions and consumers who are willing to pay extra for food produced according to higher welfare standards. It protects these purchasers by setting the minimum requirements that must be met before the stated sales descriptions can be used on the labelling of poultrymeat and eggs. The legislation also establishes a coding system, which must be used on all commercially produced eggs, which assists in the identification of the process used in production. The code includes details about the farming method, the Member State of production and the identification of the establishment where it was produced. Where a code starts with the number '0', this shows that the egg has been organically produced. The numbers '1', '2' and '3' are used to represent free-range, barn and caged production respectively. Thereafter there should be a country code, such as 'IE', followed by a unique number attached to the producing establishment. This is set out in the Annex to EU Directive 2002/4.[230] The coding scheme is now directly applicable in Irish law since the introduction of EU Regulation 589/2008.[231]

---

[229] SI No 140/2009.

[230] Commission Directive 2002/4/EC of 30 January 2002 on the registration of establishments keeping laying hens, covered by Council Directive 1999/74/EC [2002] OJ L 30/44.

[231] Art 9 of Reg 589/2008, n 228 above. Directive 2002/4, n 230 above, is also given further effect in Irish law by the European Communities (Welfare of Farmed Animals) Regulations 2010, n 178 above.

Welfare of Calves

Part 5 of the 2010 Irish Welfare of Farmed Animals Regulations sets out additional conditions for meat-producing calves. The production of calf meat, or veal, has been controversial in some EU Member States, including Ireland, for some time.[232] This has often been due to the conditions in which it has been reported that the calves are being kept, rather than concerns over the young age of the animal at slaughter. However, the Irish Regulations clearly prohibit several of the practices to which there have been objections in the past. For example, calves cannot be confined in an individual stall or pen after the age of eight weeks, unless a veterinary surgeon has certified that this is necessary for its health or due to some behavioural issue.[233] Where the use of a stall or pen is permitted, they must meet a range of minimum size requirements. They must also have perforated walls that allow the animal to have visual and tactile contact.[234]

Calves must have sufficient room to stand up, lie down, turn around, rest and groom without hindrance.[235] They must also be able to see at least one other calf where they are kept on a holding of more than one animal. They should be inspected at least twice a day, reducing to once where they are kept outdoors.[236] Schedule 4 to the 2010 Regulations also prohibits the use of tethering, with the exception of up to one hour for the purposes of feeding. A series of requirements are also set for the animals' housing, including stipulations related to the use of artificial light, sanitation, flooring and bedding. They should be fed at least twice per day. They should have sufficient quantities of fresh drinking water, according to their needs and/or to the weather conditions.

Welfare of Pigs

In addition to veal calves and caged egg-producing hens, the conditions in which many pigs are kept have given rise to most concern amongst welfare-conscious consumers. Minimum standards for the protection of pigs were initially set out in Directive 1991/630[237] since replaced by Directive 2008/120[238] and now transposed

---

[232] In the UK this included the bringing of an action by the Royal Society for the Prevention of Cruelty to Animals (RSPCA) and Compassion in World Farming (CIWF) against the UK Minister of Agriculture, Fisheries and Food, challenging a refusal to restrict the export of veal calves to other EU Member States where they would be kept in veal crates. Case C-1/1996 *The Queen v Minister of Agriculture, Fisheries and Food, ex parte Compassion in World Farming Ltd* [1998] ECR I-1251. The Court held that the Art 36 TFEU exception to the Art 34 TFEU rule on the free movement of goods could not be used to justify such a restriction on exportation on the basis of the protection of public order or public morality. For further discussion on this see R Muñoz, 'Case C-1/96, *The Queen v Minister of Agriculture, Fisheries and Food, ex parte Compassion in World Farming Limited*' (1999) 36 *Common Market Law Review* 831.
[233] SI No 311/2010, n 178 above, Reg 17(1).
[234] Ibid, Reg 17(2).
[235] Ibid, Sch 4, Part 2.
[236] Ibid, Sch 4, Part 1.
[237] Council Directive 1991/630/EEC, [1990] OJ L 340/33.
[238] n 212 above.

into Irish law by Part 5 of the 2010 Regulations, with additional detail specific to pigs set out in Schedule 4 thereto. All of this provides that pigs must be inspected daily, that they may not be tethered,[239] that they should be separated from aggressive or fighting pigs and that they are given access to adequate amounts of food and water daily. Pigs must be free to turn around in their accommodation, without difficulty and at all times.[240] Slatted floors can be used, but maximum widths for the openings between the slats are set depending on the degree to which the pig has matured and developed.[241]

Farrowing crates are also permitted,[242] but sow stalls are not. The two systems are quite different. Stalls have been banned across the EU since 2013.[243] The use of stalls and farrowing crates are amongst the more controversial elements of pig meat production. To look first at the provisions on farrowing, the Regulations provides that pens used for this purpose must incorporate some means of protecting the piglets from being smothered should the sow roll over on top of them. This is the key purpose behind the use of farrowing crates. It is designed to keep piglet mortality rates down. However, the design of some of the crates employed for this purpose has given rise to some controversy. Many are deemed to be both uncomfortable and overly restrictive for the sow and her ability to move freely. Stalls are different. They are often used to restrict the movement of the sow and to keep her separated from other animals during her gestation period. Some EU Member States had already prohibited the use of stalls, before the introduction of the EU ban in 2013. The UK introduced a ban on their use in 1999, primarily due to welfare concerns.[244] Sweden acted prior to this, introducing its own ban in 1988.[245] Luxembourg also prohibited the use of stalls before the introduction of the EU-wide ban.

The 'Report of the European Commission's Scientific Veterinary Committee on the Welfare of Intensively Kept Pigs', published in September 1997, carried the results of a comparative analysis of the figures for pig mortality in Sweden – where stalls were banned – and Denmark, where they were not. Despite the arguments that have been made in favour of continuing with the use of sow stalls, the data here showed that there was little difference between the mortality rates on those farms where stalls were used (Denmark, average mortality 11.7 per cent) and many of those farms where they were not being used (Sweden, average mortality among

---

[239] The ban on tethering sows and gilts was introduced on 1 January 2006, initially by Art 3(3) of Dir 2008/120, n 212 above.

[240] Reg 18 and Schedule 4 to the 2010 Irish Regs, n 178 above.

[241] Reg 20.

[242] Schedule 4, Part 3, Chapter III to the 2010 Irish Regs, n 178 above.

[243] Introduced by Art 3(9) of EU Dir 2008/120, n 212 above.

[244] UK Welfare of Pigs Regulations 1991, SI No 1477/1991.

[245] It should be noted, however, that it has been argued elsewhere that a ban on the use of crates can actually be detrimental to the health of sows. See, for example, J McGlone, 'Comparison of sow welfare in the Swedish deep-bedded system and the US crated-sow-system' (2006) 229 *Journal of the American Veterinary Medicine Association* 1327.

best herds 12.9 per cent). The average overall was slightly higher for Sweden, but not significantly so. It also appeared from the studies examined that most of the threat to piglet mortality from the sow over-lying on and crushing them was in the few days immediately after birth.

As stated, the EU has now acted on the use of these stalls from four weeks after gestation, introducing a prohibition on their use in the vast majority of Member States where this was not already the case. Directive 2008/120 states that:

> [m]ember states shall ensure that sows and gilts are kept in groups during a period starting from four weeks after [gestation commences] to one week before the expected time of farrowing. The pen where the group is kept must have sides greater than 2.8 m in length. When fewer than six individuals are kept in a group the pen where the group is kept must have sides greater than 2.4 m in length. By way of derogation [from this] sows and gilts raised on holdings with fewer than 10 sows may be kept individually during the period mentioned [above] provided that they can turn around easily in their boxes.[246]

EU Member States were given 12 years to bring about this change, with the decision to ban the use of individual sow stalls originally being taken in 2001.[247]

Despite the provision of this lengthy transitional period, nine Member States had to be served with a formal notice in February 2013 due to their failure to properly implement this significant welfare provision. The list of non-conforming Member States included Ireland, as well as France, Germany, Denmark, Belgium, Cyprus, Greece, Poland and Portugal. Failure to comply after this could lead to further enforcement action being taken, including the issuing of a reasoned opinion and ultimately action before the Court of Justice. Those Member States that had complied with EU obligations like this would have an obvious grievance here, as would those holdings based in countries where the prohibition on stalls had yet to become fully operational. There is a clear competitive advantage for those operators who do not invest in higher welfare systems, both from a set-up cost and possibly from an ongoing operating cost perspective.

Transportation of Live Animals Provisions

The introduction of a new EU regulation in 2005 on the transportation of live animals marked a significant tightening-up of existing requirements on live animal transportation,[248] including the adoption of more stringent measures

---

[246] Art 3(4) of Council Directive 2008/120/EC 2008, n 212 above. There is one possible derogation from this prohibition on the use of stalls and that is where the sows and gilts are being reared on holdings with fewer than 10 sows. These may be kept individually after gestation, provided that they are able to turn around freely in their crates.

[247] See Council Directive 2001/88/EC of 23 October 2001 amending Directive 1991/630/EEC laying down minimum standards for the protection of pigs [2001] OJ L 316/1.

[248] As established by Council Directive 1991/628/EC of 19 November 1991 on the protection of animals during transport and amending Directives 1990/425/EEC and 1991/496/EEC [1991] OJ L 340/17.

designed to prevent pain and suffering, as well as others designed to minimise the occurrence and spread of infectious diseases.[249] The European Parliament had previously called upon the Commission to draft proposals amending these existing EU rules on the transportation of livestock. The use of a Regulation for this legislative initiative was specifically chosen after a series of difficulties were identified in the application of the earlier directives due to differences in transposition at national level. One of the key proposals put forward was to make transporters more accountable and their activities more transparent. The Preamble to the 2005 Regulation noted that the welfare conditions of animals during transport results mainly from the daily conduct of the transporters. They would share the burden of the new regulations, along with the other relevant operators, such as farmers, traders and slaughterhouses. Although the provisions of this Regulation are directly applicable in Irish law, further detail on how these provisions are to be administered in Ireland is set out in the European Communities (Protection of Animals During Transport) Regulations 2006.[250]

The Regulation sets out several general conditions for the transportation of live animals. The most general of these is that there is a prohibition on transporting in a way that is likely 'to cause injury or undue suffering'.[251] There are also a set of more specific conditions. These include ensuring that all necessary arrangements have been made in advance to minimise the length of journeys and to meet the animals' needs while these take place.[252] The animals must be fit for the journey.[253] The means of transport and loading must be designed, constructed, maintained and operated so as to avoid injury and suffering, providing sufficient floor area and height for the animals appropriate to their size and journey.[254] Personnel should be properly trained and/or competent and must check the animals regularly, providing water, feed and rest at appropriate intervals.[255]

As stated above, the Regulation places a lot of responsibility on the transporters for the operation of the legislative requirements set out. More specifically,

---

The two directives referred to here in the title of Directive 1991/628 were not transportation directives as such, but instead dealt more specifically with veterinary checks on animals entering the EU from third countries.

[249] Council Regulation (EC) No 1/2005 of 22 December 2004 on the protection of animals during transport and related operations and amending Directives 1964/432/EEC and 1993/119/EC and Regulation (EC) No 1255/1997 [2005] OJ L 3/1. The Regulation applied from January 2005, but most of its provisions came into effect during 2007 and 2008.

[250] SI No 267/2006.

[251] EU Reg 1/2005, Art 3.

[252] Ibid, Art 3(a).

[253] Ibid, Art 3(b).

[254] Ibid, Art 3(c), (d) and (g). Reg 6(2)(a) and (b) of the 2006 Irish Regs, n 250 above, provides that '[a] person shall not load [or unload] an animal into [or out of] a means of transport, or cause or permit an animal to be loaded [or unloaded], in a way as is likely to cause injury or unnecessary suffering to the animal'.

[255] Ibid, Art 3(e), (f) and (h). The CJEU has held that these provisions on watering, feeding and resting during the transportation of live animals extend beyond the borders of the European Union where the animals' journey has started in an EU Member State. See Case C-424/2013 *Zuchtvieh-Export GmbH v Stadt Kempten* ECLI:EU:C:2015:259.

this includes carrying the appropriate documentation,[256] planning journeys properly,[257] being in possession of authorisation from the national competent authority[258] and ensuring that the means of transportation has been inspected and approved.[259]

As is the case for many of the welfare regulations, the real detail is set out in the Annex. This provides the more specific and practical requirements on how animals are to be treated before, during and after transportation. Annex I to Regulation 1/2005 sets out the technical rules about this, including a prohibition on the transportation of animals which are deemed unfit for their intended journey. More specifically, if an animal is unable to move or walk unassisted, has a severe open wound, is nearing the end of pregnancy or is a new-born mammal – including all journeys in excess of 100 km for pigs under three weeks, lambs under one week and calves under 10 days – it should not be transported. There are some exceptions to this, such as the transportation of an injured animal under veterinary supervision. Lactating females who are not accompanied by their offspring should be milked at least every 12 hours. Piglets, lambs and calves under a certain weight or age must be provided with appropriate bedding material.

One of the most significant progressions that has taken place in relation to welfare issues during animal transportation is the setting of more stringent requirements on watering, feeding and resting periods. Animals should be offered water, feed and the opportunity to rest, as appropriate to their species and age, at suitable intervals. Mammals and birds should be fed at least every 24 hours and watered at least every 12 hours, unless specified otherwise. Clear requirements are set for different types of animals which are being transported by road. Unweaned calves, lambs and piglets must all be given a rest period of at least one hour after nine hours of travel. Pigs can only be transported for a maximum period of 24 hours. They must be given continuous access to water for the duration of their journey. Most other animals must be given a rest of at least one hour after 14 hours of travel. They may then be transported for a further 14 hours after this. There are, of course, exceptions to these rules, depending on the type of animal, the mode of transportation and the geographical location of the points of departure and arrival, especially for journeys by sea.

Some of the other stipulations contained in the Regulation include those related to the temperature and ventilation during transportation. The general rule is that it should not get hotter than 30 degrees Celsius, nor cooler than 5 degrees Celsius. Means of transportation should be fitted with alarms which indicate to the driver that maximum or minimum temperatures have been exceeded. All the data

---

[256] Ibid, Art 4.

[257] Ibid, Art 5.

[258] Art 6 of Reg 1/2005, n 249 above. Authorisations to act as animal transporters beyond the territory of the State are granted in Ireland by the Department of Agriculture, Food and the Marine, as set out in Reg 12 of the European Communities (Protection of Animals During Transport) Regulations 2006, n 250 above. Under Reg 11, those transporting animals domestically must register with the department.

[259] Ibid, Art 7.

related to this should be recorded. Similarly, road vehicles used for the transportation of animals should be fitted with navigation devices which record relevant information about journeys undertaken. Finally, all journeys involving animal transportation should be properly logged. Annex II to the Regulation provides that this should include verifiable set details on the route plan, which should be made available to the competent authorities in the Member State of departure.[260]

Welfare at Time of Slaughter

In addition to the introduction of the ban on the use of unenriched cages in egg production, the EU Action Plan on Welfare also called for proposals to be brought forward on new legislation regulating the slaughtering process. This ultimately resulted in a new regulation being introduced on this matter in 2009.[261] This Regulation sets a series of both general and specific requirements for abattoirs, designed to make the slaughter process as free of stress and pain as possible for the animals. Whether it achieves this is open to debate. Amongst the general requirements and adhering to the 'five freedoms of animal welfare' is the provision that animals should, in general terms, be spared any avoidable pain or distress during slaughter.[262] This includes handling and housing the animals in a manner that has regard for their normal behaviour, as they await their fate at the abattoir. They should also be provided with feed and water if necessary and they should be provided with physical comfort and protection, in particular by being kept clean in adequate thermal conditions and prevented from falling or slipping.[263] The stunning of animals before slaughter is required under the legislation, subject to some exceptions, which are discussed below.

Animals can only be killed after stunning in a manner that is in accordance with the methods and specific requirements related to the application of those methods set out in Annex I to the Regulation. The loss of consciousness and sensibility of the animals must be maintained until they are dead. The methods referred to in Annex I which do not result in an instantaneous death must be followed as quickly as possible by a procedure that does ensure death, such as bleeding, pithing, electrocution or prolonged exposure to anoxia.

The methods used in stunning can adapt over time, particularly where there are technological developments in this area. The Regulation can and should,

---

[260] The details to be completed in the route plan are set out as a template in Sch 2 to the 2006 Regulations, n 250 above. Under Reg 10(1)(i), these plans must be submitted to an inspector 'not less than 24 hours prior to the proposed first time of departure of the animal indicated in that route plan, on which must be indicated the number or numbers of the health certificates if any and the authorisation number allocated to him or her in accordance with Regulation 12 and which shall then be stamped and signed by an inspector where the inspector is satisfied that the route plan complies with these regulations'.

[261] Council Regulation (EC) No 1099/2009 of 24 September 2009 on the protection of animals at the time of killing [2009] OJ L 303/1.

[262] Ibid, Art 3.

[263] Ibid, Art 3(a) and (e).

therefore, be amended to take account of any such scientific and technical progress following an opinion of EFSA on the matter. Any such amendments must consider maintaining a level of animal welfare that is at least equivalent to that which was ensured by the already existing methods.

Animals which are subjected to methods of slaughter that are prescribed by religious rites are not subject to these stunning requirements.[264] Similarly, stunning is not required for the private killing of poultry.[265] This is the first in a list of slaughter requirements which, although applying to most animals, are not required for poultry. This includes the suspending or hoisting of live animals and the tying of legs or feet or clamping.[266] Certificates of competence are required for all animal killing operations.[267] Welfare officers should be appointed for all slaughterhouses over a certain minimum size.[268] Finally, imports of meat into Ireland or any other part of the EU from third countries must be certified as having been slaughtered to equivalent welfare standards to those set out in the 2009 Regulation.[269] The Regulation, which replaces EU Directive 1993/119 and the transposing European Communities (Protection of Animals at Time of Slaughter) Regulations 1995,[270] came into effect in January 2013.

The slaughter of animals without stunning was permitted in some limited circumstances by the 1995 Irish Regulations. Regulation 3(3) provided that the welfare provisions set out in either the domestic legislation or the 1993 EU Directive did not apply to, amongst others, 'animals which are killed in cultural ... events', while Regulation 5(2) more specifically stated that '[i]n the case of animals subject to particular methods of slaughter required by certain religious rites, the requirements [on stunning] shall not apply', echoing precisely what was provided for in Article 5(2) of Directive 1993/119. The Preamble to the present legislation on the matter, Regulation 1099/2009, states that:

> [d]erogation from stunning in case of religious slaughter taking place in slaughterhouses was [originally] granted by Directive 93/119/EC. Since [Union] provisions applicable to religious slaughter have been transposed differently depending on national contexts and considering that national rules take into account dimensions that go beyond the purpose of this Regulation, it is important that derogation from stunning animals prior to slaughter should be maintained, leaving, however, a certain level of subsidiarity to each Member State. As a consequence, this Regulation respects the freedom of religion and the right to manifest religion or belief in worship, teaching, practice and observance, as enshrined in Article 10 of the Charter of Fundamental Rights of the European Union.[271]

---

[264] Ibid, Art 4.
[265] Ibid, Art 10.
[266] Ibid, Art 15.
[267] Ibid, Art 7.
[268] Ibid, Art 17.
[269] Ibid, Art 12.
[270] SI No 114/1995. These Regulations also set general requirements for the operations of slaughterhouses in Ireland. The primary source for the rules applicable to Irish slaughterhouse now are those contained in Chapter III and Annex III of EU Reg 1099/2009, n 261 above.
[271] Recital 18 of the Preamble to Reg 1099/2009, n 261 above.

Regulation 1099/2009 specifically provides for this, stating:

> [i]n the case of animals subject to particular methods of slaughter prescribed by religious rites, the requirements [on stunning] shall not apply provided that the slaughter takes place in a slaughterhouse.[272]

Some stunning before slaughter is permitted under the Muslim rules for Halal meat production and the evidence shows that the majority of animals killed in this way are usually stunned first. However, a European Parliament report in 2010 noted that although only 1 per cent of consumers in Ireland were Muslim, around 6 per cent of cattle and 34 per cent of sheep were being killed without stunning, primarily due to the fact that Ireland exports large quantities of non-stunned meat to other States.[273] Shechita, the Jewish method of slaughtering animals and poultry for food, does not permit any pre-killing stunning. The Slaughter of Animals Act 1935 had traditionally provided an exemption for shechita in Ireland.[274] Article 17 of the European Convention for the Protection of Animals for Slaughter also provides that Contracting Parties can authorise derogations from the provisions concerning prior stunning where the slaughter is to be done in accordance with religious rituals, such as halal and shechita. However, this is subject to the requirement that States ensure that at the time of such slaughter or killing the animals are spared any avoidable pain or suffering.

European Convention for the Protection of Farmed Animals

Another significant influence on domestic animal welfare law has been the Council of Europe's Convention for the Protection of Animals Kept for Farming Purposes. Originally drafted in 1976 and amended in 1992 the Convention lays down a range

---

[272] Ibid, Art 4(4). The Court of Justice has since confirmed, in 2018, that this provision of the Regulation is valid and that all slaughter without stunning must take place in an approved slaughterhouse, even during religious festivals; this is in no way affected by other EU guarantees on freedom of religion. See Case C-426/2016, *Liga van Moskeeën en Islamitsche Organisaties Provincie Antwerpen VZW and Others v Vlaams Gewest*, n 181 above.

[273] Library of the European Parliament Briefing on 'Religious Slaughter of Animals in the EU' (2012). Available at: europarl.europa.eu. A UK Food Standards Agency report, published in 2012 and based on a survey of slaughterhouses taken in September 2011, found that around 3% of cattle there were slaughtered by the Shechita method at four establishments, with 10% of these stunned immediately after bleeding. Approximately 4% of cattle were slaughtered by the Halal method at 16 establishments. Of these, 84% were stunned before slaughter and less than 1% were stunned after bleeding. For sheep and goats, less than 1% were slaughtered by the Jewish method, none of which were stunned. Around 50% were slaughtered by the Muslim method, of which 81% were stunned before slaughter. Again, around 1% of all poultry slaughtered in the UK were by Shechita without stunning and around 30% were slaughtered by the Halal method, almost all of which were stunned before slaughter. According to the UK Food Standards Agency, the results indicate that the number of animals not stunned prior to slaughter is relatively low, accounting for 3% of cattle, 10% of sheep and goats and 4% of poultry. They also show that the majority of animals destined for the Halal trade in both the red and white meat sectors are stunned before slaughter. See Food Standards Agency, 'Results of the 2011 FSA Animal Welfare Survey in Great Britain', 22 May 2012. Available at: http://multimedia.food.gov.uk/.

[274] Section 15(2) thereof.

of minimum standards to apply in the national laws across all Contracting Parties, including Ireland. It is applicable to all animals kept for farming purposes, including food production, wool, skin or fur and it also covers those animals which have been produced from genetic modification techniques. It is particularly concerned with animals reared and kept in intensive farming systems. Compliance with the Convention is deemed to demonstrate the implementation of an acceptable level of animal welfare protection.[275]

The main aims of the Convention are reflected in the key provisions of the framework EU and national legislation, most notably the objective of protecting farm animals from unnecessary injury or suffering. Article 1 broadly provides that:

> [t]his Convention shall apply to the keeping, care and housing of animals, and in particular to animals in modern intensive stock-farming systems [including] animals bred or kept for the production of food.

The key provisions, which should be given legal effect by each of the Contracting Parties to the Convention, are contained in Articles 3–7. This includes the requirement that:

> [a]nimals shall be housed and provided with food, water and care in a manner which, having regard to their species and to their degree of development ... is appropriate to their physiological and ethological needs in accordance with established experience and scientific knowledge.[276]

The Convention identified at an earlier stage than the EU and many of its Member States that freedom of movement for animals was crucial to their welfare. This was later reflected in initiatives such as those introduced on the use of farrowing crates and stalls and unenriched caged systems for egg-laying hens. Article 4 of the Convention states that:

> [t]he freedom of movement appropriate to an animal, having regard to its species and in accordance with established experience and scientific knowledge, shall not be restricted in such a manner as to cause it unnecessary suffering or injury.

Other provisions of the Convention include the condition that animals should not be provided with food or liquid, or provided with those substances in a way, that can cause unnecessary suffering or injury.[277] There are also requirements on the daily inspection of animals and farming equipment, especially in intensive stick-farming systems.[278] The relevance of – and the similarities between – the Convention and the content of EU and national law are obvious. The Convention has had a significant persuasive effect in shaping both European and domestic law in this area. The implementation and application of the Convention is overseen

---

[275] See Case C-1/1996, at para 69, n 232 above.
[276] Art 3 of the Convention.
[277] Ibid, Art 6.
[278] Ibid, Art 7.

by a Standing Committee, which is made up of representatives of each of the Contracting Parties and observers.[279]

10.6. Future Challenges for Food Law

The way in which the food sector is regulated has the most significant impact on the well-being of society. It has obvious health, economic, environmental and ethical consequences. Being informed about and protected from risks to health has been recognised as an important human right. Its incorporation into policy making and law enforcement must be an integral part of all public-health decision making.[280] The application of this right must also be guaranteed through the corporate activities of food business operators.[281] Food law has long needed to be rebalanced to give increased consideration to the promotion of consumer concerns. This process has now begun in many areas.

It has been made clear throughout this book that there is a public health crisis. It is largely related to a combination of the consumption of low-quality food and drink and low levels of physical activity, along with other medical factors. Levels of overweight, obesity and related illness and disease are at record highs. Food law has not been properly used to play a part in dealing with this crisis. The economic, physical, mental and societal consequences of this have all been outlined. The limits within which individuals should continue to be permitted to self-administer toxic and harmful substances without regard to the social and economic costs to society generally may need to be re-examined. It is the most pressing concern for those responsible for the introduction and enforcement of food laws. But it must be balanced against the extent to which it is really the responsibility of the State to promote health by the encouragement of specific measures or possibly by the imposition of sanctions – complicated by the fact that this is often an imposition that may not be possible due to EU obligations. This latter point also raises questions about whether it is helpful to have both EU laws and Irish laws that set the limits on what can be done to change behaviour and to promote good health (a point that has repeatedly been made by Brexiteers in the UK as one of their reasons for wanting to leave the EU). In some cases, the disparities between Ireland and other EU Member States may be too great to comprehend dealing with these important issues in one over-arching legal system.

New technologies also give us cause for concern, as do other food safety matters, be they real or anticipated. Nanotechnology, cloning, agricultural

---

[279] Ibid, Arts 8–13.
[280] D Feldman, 'The contribution of human rights to improving public health' (2006) 120 *Public Health* 61.
[281] For further discussion on the way in which human rights impact on companies as well as on states and individuals see A Dignam and D Allen, *Company Law and the Human Rights Act 1998* (London, Butterworths, 2000).

intensification and the importance of water regulation are all issues that must be properly addressed by the law, designed to ensure that increasing demand for food is satisfied in a way that does not compromise safety standards or ethical considerations. Campaigns for food autonomy have emphasised some of the positive consequences of altering production and marketing processes, including the crucial issues related to food waste,[282] and plastic packaging waste.[283] These issues must be addressed to ensure that the present generation is not allowed to postpone the costs of maintaining a safe environment for food production at a cost to future generations. The introduction of higher welfare standards for both egg-laying hens and pigs used for meat production have provided us with examples of the types of positive change that can be made by the laws that govern how food is produced and consumed, provided people are sufficiently motivated to ensure that this change happens.

[282] For more on the efforts that are being made in some EU Member States to reduce food waste see L Vaqué, 'French and Italian food waste legislation: An example for other EU Member States to follow?' (2017b) 12 *European Food and Feed Law Review* 224.

[283] Approximately 100,000 tonnes of plastic waste from EU countries ends up in the sea every year, from coastal land areas alone. See JR Jambeck, R Geyer, C Wilcox, TR Siegler, M Perryman, A Andrady, R Narayan and KL Law, 'Plastic waste inputs from land into the ocean' (2015) 347 *Science* 768. A study published in April 2018 found that plastic food packaging, despite claims to the contrary, was actually fuelling rather than combatting the EU's food waste problem. It also showed that both food packaging and food waste had doubled in the EU between the years 2004 and 2014. See JP Schweitzer, S Gionfra, M Pantzar, D Mottershead, E Watkins, F Petsinaris, P ten Brink, E Ptak, C Lacey and C Janssens 'Unwrapped: How throwaway plastic is failing to solve Europe's food waste problem' (2018) Institute for European Environmental Policy (IEEP), Brussels. Available at: foeeurope.org.

BIBLIOGRAPHY

Books

Alemanno, A *Trade in food: Regulatory and judicial approaches in the EC and the WTO* (London, Cameron May, 2007).

Byrne, D 'The genesis of EFSA and the first 10 years of EU food law' in A Alemanno and S Gabbi (eds), *Foundations of EU Food Law and Policy* (Farnham, Ashgate, 2013).

Friant-Perrot, M and A Garde, 'From BSE to obesity: EFSA's growing role in the EU's nutrition policy' in A Alemanno and S Gabbi (eds), *Foundations of EU food law and policy* (Farnham, Ashgate, 2013).

Gabbi, S 'The scientific governance of the European Food Safety Authority: *Status quo* and perspectives' in A Alemanno and S Gabbi (eds), *Foundations of EU food law and policy* (Farnham, Ashgate, 2013).

Poli, S 'Scientific Advice in the GMO area' in A Alemanno and S Gabbi (eds), *Foundations of EU food law and policy* (Farnham, Ashgate, 2013).

Barnard, C *The substantive law of the EU*, 5th edn (Oxford, OUP, 2016).

Chalmers, D, G Davies and G Monti, *European Union Law*, 3rd edn (Cambridge, CUP, 2014).

Christakis, N and J Fowler, *Connected: The surprising power of our social networks and how they shape our lives* (New York, Little, Brown, 2009).

Craig, P and G de Búrca, *EU law: Text, cases and materials*, 6th edn (OUP: Oxford, 2015).

Dignam, A and D Allen, *Company law and the Human Rights Act 1998* (London, Butterworths, 2000).

Doyle, O *The Constitution of Ireland: A contextual analysis*, (Hart: Bloomsbury, 2018).

Garde, A *EU law and obesity prevention* (Alphen aan den Rijn, Kluwer Law International, 2010).

Kelly, F *A guide to early Irish law* (Dublin, Dublin Institute for Advanced Studies, 1988).

Lee, M *EU Environmental Law: Challenges, change and decision-making* (Oxford, Hart, 2005), esp 255–259.

MacMaoláin, C *EU Food Law: Protecting consumers and health in a common market* (Oxford, Hart Publishing, 2007).

Oliver, P *Free movement of goods in the European Union*, 5th edn (Oxford, Hart, 2010).

Pennington, H *When food kills: BSE, E. coli and disaster science* (Oxford, OUP, 2003).

Weatherill, S *EU consumer law and policy* (Cheltenham, Edward Elgar, 2005).

Journal Articles

Achat, H, I Kawachi, S Levine, C Berkey, E Coakley, G Colditz, 'Social networks, stress and health-related quality of life' (1998) 7 *Quality of Life Research* 735.

Alemanno, A 'The European Food Safety Authority before European Courts: Some reflections on the judicial review of EFSA scientific opinions and administrative acts' (2008) 5 *European Food and Feed Law Review* 320.

Alemanno, A and I Carreño, 'Fat taxes in Europe: A legal and policy analysis under EU and WTO law' (2013) 8 *European Food and Feed Law Review* 97.

Amat, E and L Rihouey-Robini, 'A scientific report rekindles the controversy over energy drinks in France' (2013) 8 *European Food and Feed Law Review* 414.

Andersen, L 'The EU rules on labelling of genetically modified foods: mission accomplished?' (2010) 5 *European Food and Feed Law Review* 136.

Andreyeva, T, M Long and K Brownell, 'The impact of food prices on consumption: a systematic review of research on the price elasticity of demand for food' (2010) 100 *American Journal of Public Health* 216.

Anon. 'Food adulteration in Ireland' (1903) 162 *Lancet* 1519.

Arnull, A 'Private applicants and the action for annulment since *Codorniu*' (2001) 38 *Common Market Law Review* 7.

Bartlett, O and A Garde, 'Time to seize the (red) bull by the horns: The European Union's failure to protect children from alcohol and unhealthy food marketing' (2013) 38 *European Law Review* 498.

Bast, A, WM Briggs, EJ Calabrese, MF Fenech, C Jaap, 'Scientism, legalism and precaution: Contending with regulating nutrition and health claims in Europe' (2013) 8 *European Food and Feed Law Review* 401.

Benyon, P 'Community mutual recognition agreements, technical barriers to trade and the WTO's most favoured nation principle' (2003) 28 *European Law Review* 231.

Berends, G and I Carreno, 'Safeguards in food: Ensuring food scares are scarce' (2005) 30 *European Law Review* 386.

Bonsmann S, LF Celemín, A Larrañaga, S Egger, JM Wills, C Hodgkins, and MM Raats, 'Penetration of nutrition information on food labels across the EU-27 plus Turkey' (2010) 64 *Journal of Clinical Nutrition* 1379.

Borgmeier, I and J Westenhoefer, 'Impact of different food label formats on healthiness evaluation and food choice of consumers: a randomised-controlled study' (2009) 9 *BMC Public Health* 184.

Brouwer, O 'Free movement of foodstuffs and quality requirements: Has the Commission got it wrong?' (1988) 25 *Common Market Law Review* 237.

Capelli, F and B Klaus, 'Chocolate can also be made from pure cocoa but one should be careful how to communicate this on the label' (2011) 6 *European Food and Feed Law Review* 88.

Carreño, I 'Developments on front-of-pack nutrition declarations in the EU' (2017) 12 *European Food and Feed Law Review* 321.

Chalmers, D 'Food for thought: Reconciling European risks and traditional ways of life' (2003) 66 *Modern Law Review* 532.

Charleton, P and A Cox, "Accepting the judgments of the Court of Justice of the EU as authoritative" (2016) 23 *Maastricht Journal of European and Comparative Law* 204.

Cole, C, J Duxbury, J Freney, O Heinemeyer, K Minami, A Mosier, K Paustian, N Rosenberg, N Sampson, D Sauerbeck, Q Zhao 'Global estimates of potential mitigation of greenhouse gas emissions by agriculture' (1997) 49 *Nutrient Cycling in Agroecosystems* 221.

Coppens, P 'Regulation (EU) No 432/2012 establishing a list of permitted health claims' (2012) 7 *European Food and Feed Law Review* 162.

Coppens, P 'The revision of the novel foods regulation' (2013) 8 *European Food and Feed Law Review* 238.

Costello, A, M Abbas, A Allen, S Ball, S Bell, R Bellamy, S Friel, N Groce, A Johnson, M Kett, M Lee, C Levy, M Maslin, D McCoy, B McGuire, H Montgomery, D Napier, C Pagel, J Patel, JA de Oliveira, N Redclift, H Rees, D Rogger, J Scott, J Stephenson, J Twigg, J Wolff, C Patterson, 'Managing the health effects of climate change' (2009) 373 *The Lancet* 1693.

Cowburn, G and L Stockley, 'Consumer understanding and use of nutrition labelling: A systematic review' (2005) 8 *Public Health Nutrition* 21.

Dévényi, P 'The new regulation on the provision of food information to consumers: is new always better?' (2011) 6 *European Food and Feed Law Review* 210.

Dietz, W 'Health consequences of obesity in youth: Childhood predictors of adult disease' (1998) 101 *Pediatrics* 518.

Downes, C 'Only a footnote? The curious Codex battle for control of additive regulations' (2012) 7 *European Food and Feed Law Review* 232.

Ewen, S and A Pusztai, 'Effect of diets containing genetically modified potatoes expressing Galanthus nivalis lectin on rat small intestine' (1999) 354 *The Lancet* 1353.

Feldman, D 'The contribution of human rights to improving public health' (2006) 120 *Public Health* 61.

French, S 'Pricing effects on food choices' (2003) 133 *Journal of Nutrition* 8415.

Friel S, AD Dangour, T Garnett, K Lock, Z Chalabi, I Roberts, A Butler, CD Butler, J, AJ McMichael, A Haines 'Public health benefits of strategies to reduce greenhouse-gas emissions: Food and agriculture' (2009) 374 *The Lancet* 2016.

Fuentes, V 'The rapid alert system for food and feed: A critical approach' (2017) 12 *European Food and Feed Law Review* 121.

Gakidou E, A Afshin, AA Abajobir, KH Abate, C Abbafati, KM Abbas, F Abd-Allah, AM Abdulle, SF Abera, V Aboyans and LJ Abu-Raddad 'Global, regional and national comparative risk assessment of 84 behavioural, environmental and occupational, and metabolic risks or clusters of risks, 1990–2016: A systematic analysis for the Global Burden of Disease Study 2016' (2016) 390 *The Lancet* 1345.

Gragnani, M 'The EU Regulation 1151/2012 on quality schemes for agricultural products and foodstuffs' (2013) 8 *European Food and Feed Law Review* 376.

Grunert KG, L Fernández-Celemín, JM Wills, S Storcksdieck Genannt Bonsmann and L Nureeva 'Use and understanding of nutrition information on food labels in six European countries' (2010) 18 *Journal of Public Health* 261.

Haber, H and A Meisterernst, 'Proposals for a revision of Regulation (EC) 1924/2006' (2011) 6 *European Food and Feed Law Review.*

Jensen, M H Jørgensen and C Lauridsen, 'Comparison between conventional and organic agriculture in terms of nutritional quality of food – a critical review' (2013) 8 *Perspectives in Agriculture, Veterinary Science, Nutrition and Natural Resources* 1.

Hagenmeyer, M and A Hahn, 'EFSA's secret health claims' (2013) 8 *European Food and Feed Law Review* 10.

Hall, J and T Valente, 'Adolescent smoking networks: The effects of influence and selection on future smoking' (2007) 32 *Journal of Addictive Behaviour* 3054.

Handler, M 'The WTO Geographical Indications Dispute' (2006) 69 *Modern Law Review* 70.

Holle, M, E Togni and A Vettorel, 'The compatibility of national interpretative nutrition labelling schemes with European and international law' (2014) 9 *European Food and Feed Law Review* 148.

Jambeck, J R, R Geyer, C Wilcox, T R Siegler, M Perryman, A Andrady, R Narayan and K L Law, 'Plastic waste inputs from land into the ocean' (2015) 347 *Science* 768.

Jones, C 'The novel food regulation: revision required?' (2012) 7 *European Food and Feed Law Review* 81.

Julia, C and S Hercberg, 'Nutri-Score: Evidence of the effectiveness of the French front-of-pack nutrition label' (2017) 64 *Ernahrungs Umschau* 181.

Kanska, K 'Wolves in the clothing of sheep? The case of the European Food Safety Authority' (2004) 29 *European Law Review* 711.

Klaus, B 'Restriction of use for health claims in regard to water: Interpretation in conformity with the EU law' (2012) 7 *European Food and Feed Law Review* 251.

Lawless, J 'The complexity of flexibility in EU food hygiene regulation' (2012) 7 *European Food and Feed Law Review* 220.

Lawless, J and K Wiedemann, 'European meat inspection: Continuity and change in building a (more) risk-based system of regulation' (2011) 6 *European Food and Feed Law Review* 96.

Lobell, D and G Asner, 'Climate and management contributions in US agricultural yields' (2003) 299 *Science* 1032.

Mahy, A and F d'Ath, 'The case of the Champagner sorbet: Unlawful exploitation or legitimate use of the protected name Champagne?' (2017) 12 *European Food and Feed Law Review* 43.

MacMaoláin, C 'Reforming European Community Food Law: Putting quality back on the agenda' (2003a) 58 *Food and Drug Law Journal* 549.

MacMaoláin, C 'The new genetically modified food labelling requirements: Finally a lasting solution?' (2003b) 28 *European Law Review* 865.

MacMaoláin, C 'Using the precautionary principle to protect human health' (2003c) 28 *European Law Review* 723.

Mayor, S 'Regulation has not reduced food poisoning in Britain' (1997) 315 *British Medical Journal* 1111.

McCann D, A Barrett, A Cooper, D Crumpler, L Dalen, K Grimshaw 'Food additives and hyperactive behaviour in 3-year-old and 8/9-year-old children in the community: a randomised, double-blinded, placebo-controlled trial' (2007) 370 *The Lancet* 1560.

McGlone, J 'Comparison of sow welfare in the Swedish deep-bedded system and the US crated-sow-system' (2006) 229 *Journal of the American Veterinary Medicine Association* 1327.

McNicholl, B, D Goggin, D O'Donovan, 'Alcohol-related presentations to emergency departments in Ireland: A descriptive prevalence study' (2018) 8 *BMJ Open* 21932.

Meloni, G and J Swinnen, 'L'Histoire se répète: Why the liberalisation of the EU vineyard planting rights regime may require another French Revolution' (2015) LICOS Discussion Paper Series, No. 367. Available at: www.econstor.eu.

Meneton, P, X Jeunemaitre, H de Wardener and G Macgregor, 'Links between dietary salt intake, renal salt handling, blood pressure, and cardiovascular diseases' (2005) 85 *Physiological Reviews* 679.

O'Connor, B 'A note on the need for more clarity in the World Trade Organization Agreement on Agriculture' (2003) 37 *Journal of World Trade* 839.

O'Neill, S 'The Implication of the BSE Crisis on the Demand for Beef in Ireland: An Econometric Investigation' (1997) 11 *Student Economic Review* 222.

Parsons, T, C Power, S Logan and C Summerbell, 'Childhood predictors of adult obesity: A systematic review' (1999) *International Journal of Obesity* 23.

Pauwelyn, J 'The WTO Agreement on Sanitary and Phytosanitary Measures as Applied in the First Three SPS Disputes: EC – Hormones, Australia – Salmon and Japan – Varietals' (1999) 2 *Journal of International Economic Law* 641.

Petetin, L 'The revival of modern agricultural biotechnology by the UK Government: What role for animal cloning?' (2012) 7 *European Food and Feed Law Review* 296.

J Phillips and M French, 'Adulteration and Food Law, 1899–1939' (1998) 9 *Twentieth Century British History* 350.

Quick, R and A Blüthner, 'Has the Appellate Body erred? An appraisal and criticism of the ruling in the WTO *Hormones Case*' (1999) 2 *Journal of International Economic Law* 603.

Rayner, M and P Scarborough, 'The burden of food related ill-health in the UK' (2005) 59 *Journal of Epidemiology and Community Health* 1054.

Ricci, A, A Bolton, D Chemaly, M Speybroeck, R Niko, G Ru 'Bovine Spongiform Encephalopathy (BSE) cases born after the total feed ban' (2017) 15 *EFSA Journal* 4885.

Rubino, V 'From Cambozola to Toscoro' (2017) 12 *European Food and Feed Law Review* 326.

Sacks, G M Rayner and B Swinburn, 'Impact of front-of-pack traffic-light nutrition labelling on consumer food purchases in the UK' (2009) 24 *Health Promotion International* 344.

Salmon, N 'A European perspective on the precautionary principle: Food safety and the free trade imperative of the WTO' (2002) 27 *European Law Review* 138.

Salvi, N 'The EU regulatory framework on GMOs and the shift of powers towards Member States: An easy way out of the regulatory impasse?' (2016) 11 *European Food and Feed Law Review* 201.

Schroeder, W 'Age restrictions on the sale of energy drinks from an EU law perspective' (2016) 11 *European Food and Feed Law Review* 400.

Shine, A, S O'Reilly and K O'Sullivan, 'Consumer attitudes to nutrition labelling' (1997) 99 *British Food Journal* 283.

Smith, A, S Terry and D Detken, '10 years of the European Food Safety Authority' (2012) 7 *European Food and Feed Law Review* 111.

Szajkowska, A 'The impact of the definition of the precautionary principle in EU food law' (2010) 47 *Common Market Law Review* 173.

van der Meulen, B 'The function of food law: on the objectives of food law, legitimate factors and interests taken into account' (2010) 5 *European Food and Feed Law Review* 83.

van Der Meulen, B 'The concept of unsafe food: A critical reflection on the tenet of EU food law' (2012a) 9 *Zeitschrift für Stoffrecht* 195.

van der Meulen, B 'The core of food law' (2012b) 7 *European Food and Feed Law Review* 117.

Vaqué, L 'The European Commission proposal to simplify, rationalise and standardise food controls' (2013a) 8 *European Food and Feed Law Review* 308.

Vaqué, L 'The new European regulation on food labelling: are we ready for the "D" day on 13 December 2014?' (2013b) 8 *European Food and Feed Law Review* 158.

Vaqué, L 'French and Italian food waste legislation: An example for other EU Member States to follow?' (2017a) 12 *European Food and Feed Law Review* 224.

Vaqué, L 'Self-regulation of the labelling of the list of ingredients of alcoholic beverages: A long-term solution?' (2017b) 12 *European Food and Feed Law Review* 413.

Vaqué, L 'Listing ingredients on the labels of alcoholic beverages in the EU: A reality?' (2018) 13 *European Food and Feed Law Review* 233.

Vaqué, L and I Roda, 'The impact of international agreements on European Union food law' (2016) 11 *European Food and Feed Law Review* 130.

von Heydebrand, H 'Free Movement of Foodstuffs, Consumer Protection and Food Standards in the European Community: Has the Court of Justice Got it Wrong?' (1991) 16 *European Law Review* 391.

Weber, C and H Matthews, 'Food-miles and the relative climate impacts of food choices in the United States' (2008) 42 *Environmental Science and Technology* 3508.

Zboralska, M 'Trap of stereotypes: the EU model of a consumer' (2011) 6 *European Food and Feed Law Review* 283.

Reports and Other Works Consulted

26th Annual Report on Monitoring the Application of Community Law (2008), COM (2009) 675.

Adjusted National Food Survey Data 1974–2000 and the Economic and Social Data Service Expenditure and Food Surveys. Available at www.esds.ac.uk.

AND-International report for the European Commission, 'Value of production of agricultural products and foodstuffs, wines, aromatised wines and spirits protected by a geographical indication'. Available at: www.ec.europa.eu/agriculture/external-studies.

ASAI Code of Standards for Advertising and Marketing Communications in Ireland, 7th edition, which came into effect on 1 March 2016. Available at: www.asai.ie.

Atkinson, N 'The impact of BSE on the UK economy' (1999). Available at: www.veterinaria.org/revistas/vetenfinf/bse/14Atkinson.html.

BAI Children's Commercial Communications Code, August 2013. Available at: www.bai.ie.

Bel-Serrat, B, MM Heinen, CM Murrin, L Daly, J Mehegan, M Concannon, C Flood, D Farrell, S O'Brien, N Eldin, CC Kelleher [2017]. 'The Childhood Obesity Surveillance Initiative (COSI) in the Republic of Ireland: Findings from 2008, 2010, 2012 and 2015'. (Dublin, Health Service Executive). Available at: www.hse.ie.

BSE Inquiry: The Report, The Inquiry into BSE and variant CJD in the United Kingdom (London, Phillips Report, 2000).

Codex Alimentarius Commission, 'Procedural manual', 25th edition, Rome, 2016. ISBN: 9789251093627.

Commission Communication on the free movement of foodstuffs within the Community [1989] OJ C 271/3.

Commission Evaluation of (a) Regulation (EC) No 1924/2006 on nutrition and health claims made on food with regard to nutrient profiles and health claims made on plants and their preparations and of (b) the general regulatory framework for their use in foods. Available at: http://ec.europa.eu/smart-regulation/roadmaps/docs/2015_sante_595_evaluation_health_claims_en.pdf.

Commission Green Paper on the General Principles of Food Law, COM (1997) 176.

Commission Green Paper on promoting healthy diets and physical activity: A dimension for the prevention of overweight, obesity and chronic diseases, COM (2005) 637.

Commission interpretative communication on the names under which food products are sold [1991] OJ C 270/2.

Commission of the EU, 'Options for animal welfare labelling and the establishment of a European Network of Reference Centres for the protection and welfare of animals', COM (2009) 584.

Commission Report on the Working of the Committees During 2014, COM (2015) 165.

Commission Report to the European Parliament and to the Council regarding the mandatory indication of the country of origin or place of provenance for milk, milk used as an ingredient in dairy products and types of meat other than beef, swine, sheep, goat and poultry meat. COM (2015) 205.

Commission Report No 2132/2012 on the Implementation of the Audiovisual Media Services Directive, 28/02/2013.

Commission Report to the European Parliament and the Council regarding the mandatory labelling of the list of ingredients and the nutrition declaration of alcoholic beverages, COM (2017) 58.

Commission White Paper on Food Safety, COM (1999) 719.

Commission White Paper on a strategy for Europe on nutrition, overweight and obesity related health issues, COM (2007) 279.

Communication from the Commission on the precautionary principle, COM (2000) 1.

Communication from the Commission to the Council and the European Parliament on a European Action Plan for Organic Food and Farming, COM (2004) 415.

Communication from the Commission to the European Parliament and the Council on a Community Action Plan on the protection and Welfare of Animals 2006–2010, COM (2006) 13.

Communication from the Commission to the Council, the European Parliament and the European Economic and Social Committee; EU Consumer Policy strategy 2007–2013; Empowering consumers, enhancing their welfare, effectively protecting them, COM (2007) 99.

Communication from the Commission to the Council, the European Parliament, the European Economic and Social Committee and the Committee of the Regions on 'A new animal health strategy for the European Union (2007–2013) where prevention is better than cure', COM (2007) 539.

Communication from the Commission to the European Parliament, the Council, the European Economic and Social Committee and the Committee of the Regions on 'Smart Regulation in the European Union', COM (2010) 543.

Communication from the Commission, 'Europe 2020: A strategy for smart, sustainable and inclusive growth', COM (2010) 2020.

Communication from the Commission to the European Parliament, the Council and the European Economic and Social Committee on the European Union Strategy for the Protection and Welfare of Animals 2012–2015, COM (2012) 6.

Communication from the Commission to the European Parliament, the Council, the European Economic and Social Committee and the Committee of the Regions on Regulatory Fitness, COM (2012) 746.

Council Conclusions of 2 December 2002 on Obesity [2002] OJ C 11/3.

Council of the European Union, 'Review of the EU Sustainable Development Strategy', 15–16 June 2006.

Council of Food Policy Advisors, *Food: a recipe for a healthy, sustainable and successful future. Second report of the Council of Food Policy Advisors* (London, DEFRA, 2010).

DEFRA, 'The validity of food miles as an indicator of sustainable development: Final report' (2005); Report Number: ED50254.

Department of Agriculture, Food and the Marine, 'Organic Farming Action Plan 2013–2015'. Available at: www.agriculture.gov.ie.

Department of the Environment, 'National Climate Change Strategy 2007–2012'. Available at: www.housing.gov.ie.

Department of Health, 'A Healthy Weight for Ireland: Obesity Policy and Action Plan 2016–2025', ISBN 9781406429268.

Department of Health, 'Healthy Ireland: A Framework for Improved Health and Wellbeing 2013–2025'. ISBN: 9780957579903.

Department of Health, 'Healthy lives, healthy people: Our strategy for public health in England' (London, The Stationery Office, 30 November 2010). ISBN: 9780101798525.

Department of Health, 'Non-broadcast media advertising and marketing of food and non-alcoholic beverages, including sponsorship and retail product placement: Voluntary codes of practice', December 2017. Available at: www.health.gov.ie.

DG SANCO Report on Self-Regulation in the EU Advertising Sector, July 2006. Available at: www.ec.europa.eu/dgs/health_consumer/self_regulation/docs/report_advertising_en.pdf.

DG SANCO, 'Labelling: Competitiveness, consumer information and better regulation for the EU' Consultative Document, February 2006. Available at: https//:ec.europa.eu/food.

EPA Report on Private Water Supplies, March 2017, ISBN: 9781840957082.

European Parliament Report on alleged contraventions or maladministration in the implementation of Community law in relation to BSE, without prejudice to the jurisdiction of the Community and national courts, as established by EP Decision of 17 July 1996, OJ C 239/1.

FAO and WHO, 'Origins of the Codex Alimentarius' in *Understanding the Codex Alimentarius* (1999), ISBN 92-5-104248-9.

Farm Animal Welfare Advisory Council Guidelines. Available at: www.agriculture.gov.ie/fawac.

FSAI (2003) 'Industry Attitudes to Food Safety in Ireland'. Available at: www.fsai.ie.

FSAI Strategy 2016–2018. Available at: www.fsai.ie.

GFK Report for the European Commission on the state of play in the use of alcoholic beverage labels to inform consumers about health aspects: Action to prevent and reduce harm from alcohol. ISBN: 9789279369834.

A Hope, 'Alcohol Literature Review' (2014). Available at: www.health.gov.ie.

IPCC Fourth Assessment Report, 2007. Available at: www.ipcc.ch. Further contributions have since been made to the Fifth Assessment Report, such as that on 'Climate Change 2014: Impacts, Adaptation and Vulnerability'.

Library of the European Parliament Briefing on 'Religious Slaughter of Animals in the EU' (2012). Available at: https//europarl.europa.eu.

D Mongan and J Long, 'Overview of alcohol consumption, alcohol-related harm and alcohol policy in Ireland' (2016) Health Research Board: Dublin, ISSN: 1649-7198. Available at: www.hrb.ie.

NICE, 'Prevention of cardiovascular disease' 25 June 2012. Available at: www.nice.org.

OECD, Obesity Update 2017. Available at: www.oecd.org.

Perry, I 'The cost of overweight and obesity on the island of Ireland' (Safefood, 2012), ISBN: 978-1-905767-335.

Report of the Working Party on Bovine Spongiform Encephalopathy (Southwood Report) (London, Department of Health/MAFF, 1989).

Safefood, Weight Status of the Population in the Republic of Ireland, National Adult Nutrition Survey 2010–2011. Available at: www.safefood.eu.

Schweitzer, JP, S Gionfra, M Pantzar, D Mottershead, E Watkins, F Petsinaris, P ten Brink, E Ptak, C Lacey and C Janssens *Unwrapped: How throwaway plastic is failing to solve Europe's food waste problem* (2018) Institute for European Environmental Policy (IEEP), Brussels. Available at: www. foeeurope.org.

Scientific Opinion of the Scientific Committee on Food Safety, Animal Health and Welfare and Environmental Impact of Animals derived from Cloning by Somatic Cell Nucleus Transfer (SCNT) and their Offspring and Products Obtained from those Animals. Available at: www.efsa.europa.eu.

Soil Association Organic Market Report 2013. Available at: www.soilassociation.org/marketreport.

Special Eurobarometer 272 'Attitudes towards alcohol', March 2007. Available at: http://ec.europa.eu/ health/ph_determinants/life_style/alcohol/documents/ebs272_en.pdf.

Special Eurobarometer 410 on Europeans, Agriculture the Common Agricultural Policy, March 2014. Available at: ec.europa.eu/public_opinion.

UK Food Standards Agency, 'Results of the 2011 FSA Animal Welfare Survey in Great Britain', 22 May 2012. Available at: http://multimedia.food.gov.uk/.

UK Food Standards Agency, 'Front-of-pack traffic light signpost labelling technical guidance', Issue 2, November 2007. Available at: www.food.gov.uk.

UK White Paper on Public Health, 'Choosing health: Making health choices easier' (London, Department of Health, 2004).

WHO Progress Monitor 2017. Available at: www.who.int.

WHO Global Status Reports on Non-Communicable Diseases 2010 and 2014. Available at www.who.int.

WHO, 2nd European Action Plan for Food and Nutrition Policy 2007–2012 (Copenhagen, WHO, 2008).

INDEX

Note: Alphabetical arrangement is word-by-word, where a group of letters followed by a space is filed before the same group of letters followed by a letter, eg 'legal protection' will appear before 'legality'. In determining alphabetical arrangement, initial articles and prepositions are ignored.

Page numbers followed by the letter 'n' refer to footnotes on the quoted pages.

authorisation procedures, 107, 108–10
BSE status of, 140
Court actions brought by, 32, 34
genetically modified crops cultivation,
     restriction or prohibition, 314
geographical food names, 233, 234–35
health protection action, 261
imported products from, 15
limits on legislative activities, 102
materials in contact with foodstuffs:
     national competent authorities, 168
national food rules, 175–76
national nutrition policy in, *see* nutrition
negotiations with, 30
obesity rates reduction, 264, 265
organic foods sales, 294
origin labelling, 194
overweight issues, 265
pesticides, 164
     draft assessment reports to European
          Commission, 165–66
precautionary principle; action based on,
     106–107
Rapid Alert System, 158–59
recognition of laws of other Member
     States, 81
suspension of trade in GMOs, 303
trade between, customs duties prohibited,
     117, 118
traditional speciality guaranteed
     applications to, 242
TSE monitoring system, 141
White Paper on Food Safety
     comments, 146
wine classifying with traditional terms
     in, 249
wine traditional terms classifying in, 249
national procedural autonomy, 66n
organic foods logo, 299
Parliament, *see* European Parliament
regulations, *see* regulations, EU
Strategy for the Protection and Welfare of
     Animals, 2012–2015, *see* animal
     welfare
supremacy of food law, 13–15
White Paper on Food Safety, 144–46, 315
see also Treaty on the Functioning of the
     European Union
European Union (Drinking Water)
     Regulations 2014, 73–74
European Union (Food Additives)
     Regulations 2015, 116

European Union (Genetically Modified
     Foodstuffs) Regulations 2013,
     308, 313
European Union (Marketing of Fruit Juices
     and Certain Similar Products)
     Regulations 2013, 216–17
European Union (Nutrition and Health
     Claims Made on Foods)
     Regulations 2014, 204
European Union (Organic Farming)
     Regulations 2016, 295, 299, 300
European Union (Origin Labelling of Meat)
     Regulations 2015, 192
European Union (Plastics and other
     Materials)(Contact with Food)
     Regulations 2017, 168
European Union (Provision of Food
     Information to Consumers)
     Regulations 2014, 178–79
European Union (Transmissible Spongiform
     Encephalopathies) Regulations
     2015, 143
Eurostat, 264
evaluation of risks, 151
events for children:
     alcohol advertising and sponsorship banned
          at, 286–87
evidence:
     precautionary principle, 150
     scientific, *see* scientific evidence
evocation:
     designation of origin, wine, protection
          from, 248
     geographical food names protection,
          235–37
     geographical indication, wine, protection
          from, 248
examination procedure:
     European Commission, 27
exception, consumer protection, 100
excessive consumption of wrong
     food, 262
Executive Council, Saorstát Eireann, 12
exemptions:
     labelling, 194–96
expectations:
     consumers, 89–90
expert groups:
     European Commission, 28–29
exports:
     charges of equivalent effect to customs
          duties, 120–21